THE MEINERTZHAGEN MYSTERY

THE MEINERTZHAGEN MYSTERY
THE LIFE AND LEGEND OF A COLOSSAL FRAUD

BRIAN GARFIELD

Potomac Books, Inc.
Washington, D.C.

Library of Congress Cataloging-in-Publication Data

Garfield, Brian, 1939–
The Meinertzhagen mystery : the life and legend of a colossal fraud / Brian
   Garfield. — 1st ed.
      p. cm.
   Includes bibliographical references and index.
   ISBN-13: 978-1-59797-041-9 (hardcover : acid-free paper)
   ISBN-10: 1-59797-041-7 (hardcover : acid-free paper)
      1. Meinertzhagen, Richard, 1878–1967. 2. Great Britain—History,
Military—20th century. 3. Great Britain. Army—Biography. 4. Soldiers—Great
Britain—Biography. 5. Spies—Great Britain—Biography. 6. Ornithologists—
Great Britain—Biography. I. Title.
   DA69.3.M4G37 2006
   355.0092—dc22
   [B]
                                                          2006024131

Printed in the United States of America on acid-free paper that meets the
American National Standards Institute Z39-48 Standard.

Potomac Books, Inc.
22841 Quicksilver Drive
Dulles, Virginia 20166

First Edition

10   9   8   7   6   5   4   3   2   1

CONTENTS

PREFACE

He used to be one of my heroes.

He was a warrior who decried the folly of war; a hunter who promoted environmental protection long before it became fashionable; a scientist who discovered many new species and who refused to accept the conventional wisdom; a spy who rescued innocents; a diplomat who decried his own government's policies when they sacrificed honor to expediency; a subordinate who did not hesitate to rip a strip off superiors (including Winston Churchill) when he knew they were wrong; a self-described anti-Semite who learned to recognize his own foolishness and then became a champion of Zionism and Israel (a square in Jerusalem is named after him[1]); a killer-soldier of Victoria's colonialism who, half a century later, helped African nations achieve their independence peacefully; a despised son who became a loving father.

Several biographies of him have been published since his death in 1967, his ninetieth year. He had been a great star of British military intelligence. He became an iconic movie hero (*The Lighthorsemen*[2]) and the subject of histories, novels, docu-dramas, and documentary films. He appears in enough books and articles to fill long shelves. There's even an internal textbook, published by and for the CIA[3], devoted to his most spectacular military-intelligence ruse.

During his colorful military and scientific careers he won decorations and hearts, married twice, sired three children, explored unknown lands, discovered new species, fought wars, survived shipwrecks and ambushes, became one of the grand elder-statesmen of espionage and ornithology, and had a room named after him in the British Museum (Natural History).

According to legend, he was "licensed to kill" by authority of the British Crown; he is widely believed to have perpetrated murders and massacres, some of which to this day are cited by politicians and social scientists in support of theories about colonialism or African tribes or anti-Communist hysteria or human behavior. He owned up to such incidents long afterward and stated that at the time of their occurrence several of his slaughters had been brushed under the rug by military courts and government offices.

His life was one of high adventure. He became a model for his friend Ian Fleming's fictional spy James Bond and allegedly for John Buchan's fictional hero Sandy Arbuthnot.[4]

He represented Zionism's interests at the 1919 Paris Peace Congress, and later in negotiations throughout the 1930s with Hitler. He wasn't Jewish, but he made himself important to Chaim Weizmann and David Ben Gurion. He'd been at Harrow with Churchill, he was a member of Britain's aristocracy-of-money (he came from an international merchant-banking family that had been second in importance to the Rothschilds), and the future state of Israel needed gentile friends in positions of social influence.

Richard Meinertzhagen assisted generations of historians who welcomed his sardonic observations and relied on his firsthand recollections. After World War II he published several volumes of selections from his diaries. He was anointed a hero by students of the battlefields and scientific regions he inhabited. His diaries, now at Oxford, are regarded as primary sources on key events in Britain, Europe, Africa, and the Middle East.

At the very least, he had dreams of glory.

In September 2005, *Nature* Magazine published the article "Ornithologists Stunned by Bird Collector's Deceit," by Rex Dalton. It was followed in January 2006 by publication of Pamela Rasmussen's mammoth guide to the birds of South Asia, and in May 2006 by John Seabrook's *New Yorker* article "Ruffled Feathers: Uncovering the Biggest Scandal in the Bird World."[5]

Dalton's piece showed how Meinertzhagen's half-century career of bird fakery, exposed only recently, has been not only embarrassing but costly to natural science. Ornithologists have had to re-draw their maps of bird distribution and behavior, and they've had to re-write their charts of endangered and extinct species.

The weird story of Meinertzhagen and the birds is one facet of a crazily flawed stone. He perpetrated potent frauds in military, political, intelligence, and social respects. He changed history, and his self-serving versions of events have become the accepted "truths."

ACKNOWLEDGMENTS

My good and patient wife Bina has accompanied and assisted me on the quest, has examined the various drafts with infinite good humor, and with her keen editorial eye has improved the book greatly.

Several members of the Meinertzhagen family have contributed to this project. Without exception, they all have been unhesitatingly helpful and open-minded. For his extremely generous assistance I'm especially indebted to Ran Meinertzhagen, Richard's son, who provided vital access to the typescripts at Oxford, and permissions to quote from them. I'm also indebted to the late Sir Peter Meinertzhagen, who provided introductions and contributed a number of inherited photographs for our use in this publication, and to Hermione Hobhouse, whose recollections are both informative and amusing. And I'm most thankful for the friendship, candor, hospitality and generosity of Nicholas Meinertzhagen, who has provided lengthy recollections and great insights.

Two dear friends gave me *sine qua non* assistance and companionship throughout the long quest. Robert W. O'Hara has been the project's steadfast ferret in the labyrinths of the Public Records Office at Kew and in other British archives. Time and again, Bob went prowling on his own and discovered great troves of previously hidden information. And Gerald Rilling, with his great experience of Africa, his encyclopedic knowledge of sources, and his huge library of rare Africana, has been the investigation's principal guide through Meinertzhagen's military and ornithological wanderings in that great continent. Both gentlemen have found reams of fascinating material. I hope they are not too disappointed by the amount of it that had to be left out, in order to keep the book down to a manageable size.

My late long-time friend James P. Pierce contributed hugely to this book with his explorations in German archives, with his English translations of passages from Lettow's memoir and Kress von Kressenstein's books and other German sources, and with his long dialectic discussions with Jerry Rilling and me during several years of inquiry. We sorely miss Jim.

Mark Cocker—author of *Richard Meinertzhagen: Soldier, Scientist, Spy* (1989)—has become a good friend during the long trek. He has provided the hospitality of his home and family, has opened a fund of materials that were sent to him after his book was published, and has been magnanimous in sharing his wisdom and critical sensibility. I'm sure there are mistakes in this book, but there would have been far more had it not been for Mark's sharp editorial eye—and had it not been for the equally sharp eye, and generosity far "above and beyond," of the eminent bird experts Nigel J. Collar and Robert Prys-Jones. Robert, Nigel, and Mark have "vetted" versions of this manuscript, and while they probably haven't cured me (that's beyond hope), I'm sure that without them, the book would have suffered from even more faults than it now has.

Our friend Dustin Weir has helped beyond measure with both the research and the preparation of the book. Without his keen-eyed assistance it might have been another year or more in the making.

Many experts have assisted in these investigations—some for academic reasons and others who, like me, seem to have been driven by astonished curiosity. There is no adequate way to express my admiration and gratitude toward each of them. We may have enjoyed the quest, as fellow investigator-teammates running clues to ground, but most of them also slogged through a great deal of very hard work.

Pawanjit Singh Ahluwalia, head of Premier Investigations in New Delhi, prowled tirelessly in military records held in both Pakistan and India, in search of the truth about RM and the Syce.

The late and remarkable (Henry) St. John Armitage (1924–2004) helped steer me through thickets of the various calendars in use in the Middle East in 1917; he knew RM, and in occasional letters St. John Armitage provided, from the vast store of recollection in his databank mind, corrections of some of my errors, and fascinating opinions on an array of RM-related topics.

Hatice Babavatan of Ankara labored to bring forth translations from the Turkish.

Several Baldwins—Ian, Margo and Michael—great and generous friends all, were instrumental in steering the manuscript toward publication.

Roger Barrington provided excellent geneological information as well as access to (and information from) files of the Hartley Library and the India Office Library.

Frank Contey provided detailed and very helpful information about the East Africa Campaigns and the failed effort by Zeppelin L-59 to resupply German forces there.

Donald M. Cregier, Ph.D., Prof. of History (Ret.), University of Prince Edward Island, who has been writing a biography of Freddie Guest, has shared his knowledge freely, and has been most helpful in clarifying what otherwise might have been lingering doubts about Hermann Le Roy-Lewis.

Ann Crichton-Harris helped considerably with information and sources about the battle of Tanga.

Robert Dalgleish, Smithsonian Research Associate and researcher in the Department of Entomology of the San Diego Natural History Museum, expert in *mallophaga*, has shared most generously not only of his recent inquiries into the Meinertzhagen-Clay tag frauds but also of his longtime interest in and curiosity about Theresa and Richard.

Jack Duckworth, historian and keen observer, has provided facts, sources, and pithy commentaries when they were most needed.

Ed Erickson provided key information about Turkish records and sources regarding the Beersheba haversack incident.

Our dear friend J. Dennis Evans, of the University of Arizona, was inexhaustibly generous in providing leads to, and sometimes copies of, elusive academic documents.

Old acquaintance Ronald Florence, who is completing a book about the Aaronsohns and T. E. Lawrence, kindly and good-humoredly shared shards from his excavations—items about RM from Aaron Aaronsohn's full-length unpublished diary at Zichron Ya'aqov.

M. R. D. Foot (author of the entry on Richard Meinertzhagen in *The Dictionary of National Biography*) kindly directed me toward works by Sir Peter Wilkinson and others who had recorded firsthand recollections of their service with British intelligence organizations.

As long ago as 1964 Brian Gardner (author of *German East* and *Allenby*) encouraged my then-beginning pursuit of the story of Lettow and Meinertzhagen.

Sir Martin Gilbert, official biographer of Winston Churchill, very kindly provided confirmation of "negative" evidence.

Derek Goodwin knew, and went birding with, RM; his recollections (some of them provided via Mark Cocker) have been enlightening and very useful.

The late John Gunther encouraged my quest for more information about the East Africa campaigns that he had summarized in his *Inside Africa*.

Katharina Josephine "Karin" Hall with utmost kindness provided information and allowed us to photocopy vital diary entries by her stepfather, the late Arthur C. B. Neate—entries which, along with Neate's letters that RM incredibly preserved in his diaries, demolish RM's claims about his role in dropping the Beersheba haversack.

John Harlow kindly shared discoveries he made while writing a piece about Richard Meinertzhagen that appeared in August 2006 in a weekend edition of the *Times* (London).

Nancy Poss Hatchl, ace private eye and dear friend, provided not only encouragement but also vital introductions to investigators in various parts of the world, while Nancy's irrepressible husband Sidney Hatchl provided a hilarious sidebar re-enactment of a Victorian frontier battle.

John Hatt—founder of the respected publishing house Eland Books— in 1983 published a trade paperback reprint of RM's *Kenya Diary* with a new preface by Elspeth Huxley. The book became the best-selling title Eland had printed up to that time. Nevertheless Hatt abruptly withdrew the book distribution. He told me he couldn't explain precisely why he stopped the sales of the fastest-selling book on his list, but he had suddenly come to believe it was full of lies. It was entirely an instinctual decision. John Hatt's courage helped propel me into these investigations.

Jay Jakub, nephew-in-law and longtime friend, generously provided introductions to some of his contacts at Oxford (where he earned his doctorate) and in the British intelligence services.

Gordon Johnson of Caithness, Scotland (no relation to RM's aide Gordon Saffery Johnson), put his police-detective experience to work in a lengthy and dogged search for evidence about the death of Annie Meinertzhagen in 1928. He found the death certificate and other public-record documents that, according to (unfounded) rumor, had been said to be "sealed" for years to come.

Alan Knox, a pioneer scientist in studying the Meinertzhagen bird frauds, has encouraged and supported this project from the outset.

Andrew Lycett, author of the biography *Ian Fleming: The Man Behind James Bond* (1996), assisted and corrected by e-mail.

Ross Mallett, in Australia, went far out of his way to dig up relevant documents including letters and an unpublished memoir by Harry Chauvel.

Michael Margerison contributed information and a key question regarding Meinertzhagen in East Africa, and material about the Loyal North Lancashire soldiers.

Ernst Mayr, the great late centenarian scientist, openly shared recollections of—and his correspondence of thirty years with—RM.

Denis McDonnell, bookseller and publisher, helped greatly in locating obscure publications, particularly on the "African front."

Mary Meiners, psychologist and research partner of Robert Dalgleish, is pursuing the Meinertzhagen-Clay frauds from a psychiatric examiner's point of view; we have had cheerful (and sometimes baffled) discussions about that.

Derek O'Connor wrote letters to Mark Cocker after Mark's *Richard Meinertzhagen* was published in 1989; O'Connor's piece-by-piece demolition of RM's claims has been very useful in allaying misgivings that might otherwise have caused us to hesitate in dismissing RM's purported adventures in Soviet Russia.

Michael Occleshaw, author of two books about RM, has been the soul of gentlemanly courtesy in disagreeing with me, and I applaud the steadfastness of his faith in RM's integrity.

John Parker, like Derek O'Connor, responded at length to the publication of Mark Cocker's book; he has been very helpful in pointing out absurdities in RM's Soviet-adventure claims, and in defining RM's character. ("Many of his boastings suggest the mentality of a boy of 12 or so.")

Ken Pierce, editor and friend, helped steer the book toward publication.

Oliver Prys-Jones, brother of the ornithologist and a doctor who practices in Ruthin (Wales), very kindly went in search of information about Richard Meinertzhagen's 1929 self-commitment in the sanitorium at Ruthin Castle.

Robert Prys-Jones, head of the Birds Division of the Natural History Museum, continues to carry forward the scientific investigations into RM's birds (the real as well as the fake), and has helped and encouraged this work all along the way.

Julian Putkowski amiably provided guidance toward unusual sources of information (like a BBC Radio Four interview of New Year's Eve 2000 about RM, featuring Nigel Collar, Pamela Rasmussen, Ran Meinertzhagen, Mark Cocker, and Nick Meinertzhagen); Putkowski was not shy about offering his frank opinion that "Meinertzhagen was a congenital liar and fantasist."

Ursula Gräfin zu Rantzau, daughter of Gen. Paul von Lettow-Vorbeck, was most helpful with information about her father's contacts with RM, and in clarifying entries in her father's autobiography *Mein Leben*.

Pamela Rasmussen of Michigan State University, and long affiliated with the Smithsonian Institution, continues to investigate and clarify the Meinertzhagen bird frauds; her two-volume 2006 study, *A Guide to the Birds of South Asia: The Ripley Guide*, discusses RM's hoaxes. Dr. Rasmussen has been an excellent guide and a valued contributor, especially in the unraveling of RM's confused travel records and birding expeditions.

Harold E. Raugh, Jr., contributed excellent judgments and guidance based on knowledge he gathered while writing his biography of Wavell; he also cheerfully reconsidered some of the material he had written about RM's haversack claims.

Colin Rickards, ace journalist and a good acquaintance from long ago, was more than kind in sharing his recollections of his, the last face-to-face, interview with the aging RM.

Unhappily the marvelous Dame Miriam Rothschild died in January 2005. Her recollections of both RM and Theresa Clay were invaluable to this study. (RM wrote in the 1930s: "Miriam Rothschild dined here tonight. . . . She is a great talker and kept us all amused. Her conversation is on a high level and she does not talk trash nor bore people about herself. . . . I am delighted she has taken such a fancy to Tess [Clay] for she is the right sort and a loyal companion. She typifies to me the character of Scarlett O'Hara in Gone With the Wind." [Source: RMD, Vol. 45, p. 118.])

John Seabrook, author of the *New Yorker* article "Ruffled Feathers: Uncovering the Biggest Scandal in the Bird World" (May 29, 2006), has cheerfully exchanged information with me so that both his article and my book could be more accurate.

Jay Shapiro, valiant resident of Israel and author of *The Colonel's Team* (2002), has been an ongoing lively correspondent, especially with regard to the continuing reputation RM enjoys in Israel.

Yigal Sheffy, Israeli historian and author, has been extremely generous in providing facts from the mundane (the location of Meinertzhagen Square) to the fabulous (the truth about the mythical Fritz Frank).

David Snow knew Meinertzhagen and Theresa Clay from 1949 on and has contributed significant recollections, especially concerning Meinertzhagen's final overseas trip (to Trinidad in 1961).

Prof. David Soren provided useful guidance to our explorations of the role of British society ("the old boy network") in the continuing concealment of some of RM's more egregious and obvious transgressions.

James O'Shea Wade, my longtime friend and frequent editor, slashed patiently through early drafts of the manuscript in order to make the later ones more crisp and readable.

Ralfe Whistler has been extraordinarily candid and generous in providing recollections of his parents' run-ins with RM.

The late Sir Peter Wilkinson, famed SOE veteran, provided fascinatingly cagey hints about where we might look for information about Meinertzhagen's service (or lack thereof) in the 1940s.

Jeremy Wilson, official biographer of T. E. Lawrence, has provided invaluable wisdom and guidance.

Nicholas Wollaston (RM's nephew), has expressed great skepticism about this project; nevertheless he has been candid and forthcoming with information.

Archivists and librarians have been of great help throughout the research. Some who made "finds" and contributions to this study are: John Pinfold and Allan Lodge of Rhodes House (The Bodleian Library, Oxford); John Jackson and Roy Vickery of the Natural History Museum; William Cox and ornithologist Storrs Olson of the Smithsonian; Margaret Ferre of Her Majesty's Stationery Office; Kate Cummins of the Australian War Memorial; the Imperial War Museum's Christopher Hunt, Anthony Richards, Simon Robbins, and Mary Wilkinson; Deborah Hayward Eaton, librarian of the Emden Collection of intelligence materials in St. Edmund Hall, Oxford; Dr. Lesley Gordon of the Robinson Library, University of Newcastle Upon Tyne, who kindly granted permission to reprint selections from Gertrude Bell's writings; librarians of the National Army Museum in Chelsea (London) who found the Pope-Hennessy records of the 1905–1906 Fort Nandi and Ket Parak Hill episodes; and David Blake of the India Office Library, who kindly granted permissions to print excerpts from the "Hatter" Bailey correspondence.

Great thanks to them all.

CHAPTER 1
LEGEND

When Richard Meinertzhagen arrives late for a dinner party he carries a revolver in his hand. The party is in a posh British country estate. The hosts and dinner guests wear evening attire. For this company Meinertzhagen wears a hunter's jacket and a pair of rumpled military slacks over scuffed boots. He can dress properly when he chooses to, but among his friends and their friends he seems to enjoy the disapproval he arouses, especially among the women.

His stride has the indolent menace of the very tall and very well-born. He makes his belated entrance without apology and offers the revolver to his host. The weapon is warm to the touch and smells of cordite: it has been fired—it is literally a smoking gun. Meinertzhagen asks in a not-quite stage whisper whether his host would mind putting it out of sight and holding onto it for a few minutes.

Then he takes his seat as if nothing out of the ordinary had happened.

The guests around him are by turns startled, puzzled, awed, and amused. After a bit someone asks Meinertzhagen a question—something neutral, nothing about the revolver, of course. The innocuous question is enough to launch Meinertzhagen into an off-the-cuff speech.

He is a valued dinner companion, lionized for his monologues. So high and wide that he is conspicuous in any company, Richard Meinertzhagen in maturity is like a great striking sculpture, with a falcon's sharp-edged face and hazel-brown eyes that swing from one guest's face to another with the gaze of a raptor: alert, hungry, ready for prey.

He possesses a big voice—he can be heard by neighbors, through walls—and a magnificent presence, if a daunting one. Few who meet him ever forget him.

Depending on the occasion and his mood he delivers a scathing—and often hilarious—appraisal of the current policies of His Majesty's government or of some foreign power, or the antics of ornithological bureaucrats,

1

or the offenses visited upon him by Soviet border guards or Arab princes or Himalayan soldiers. He is viciously and wittily contemptuous of the French, whom he claims to despise as the lowest race on the planet. When in a rare mood he can be cajoled to expound on the subject of the food he was expected to eat by a Bedouin host—his descriptions of such banquets can soar to hilariously nauseating heights.

He usually can be coaxed into relating one of his keystone high adventures: the celebrated haversack stunt in Palestine in 1917; the massacres on (and the mapping of) the Serengeti; the terrible stalkings and counter-stalkings of his years-long conflict with German master spy Fritz Frank, whose wife Meinertzhagen admits he shot to death by mistake (she having been disguised as a man); his righteous battles with the stupid bureaucrats of various scientific societies and museums, who think they can tell him how to manage the huge collection of birds he has studied, shot, and stuffed; his vigorous firefight against Arab snipers on the beaches of Haifa where he saved a group of Israeli soldiers when he was seventy years old; or his several meetings with Hitler in Berlin, to one of which (in the Chancellory in 1939) he took a revolver in his pocket. He has wondered, ever since, whether he ought to have used it—whether he ought to have killed Hitler on the spot.

Melodramatic and witty by turns, the iconoclastic colonel is a cherished asset for any upper-class dinner party.

Not far into the evening, having caused a few men to applaud in awe and a few women to fall in love with him while others do not conceal their displeasure, Meinertzhagen rises to leave; he is an early-to-bed gentleman. Inasmuch as no police have arrived to inquire about murder, he murmurs a request to his host for the return of the handgun. The host gives him the weapon without comment, but perhaps with the sober wink of a co-conspirator. Meinertzhagen slides the revolver into his coat pocket and departs.

He never mentions the matter again, and of course the host is much too polite ever to inquire.

Making his dinner-party entrance with a smoking gun seems to have been so effective a curtain-raiser that Richard Meinertzhagen pulled it off several times over the years. Apparently he never repeated it among members of the same crowd because none of the several witnesses who report this intriguing gambit (each describing a different place and often a different decade) seems aware that it was not a unique event. In one version of the story, as author Ian Fleming told it to friends, Meinertzhagen asked one of the women guests to hide the revolver among the folds of her skirt for him. In yet another he asked a butler to hold the pistol. He did this in full view and hearing of other guests.[1]

More than a decade before he died, Col. Richard Meinertzhagen, D.S.O., C.B.E.—revered dean of British ornithology, author of definitive texts on the birds of various regions—gave about twenty thousand taxidermically prepared "skins" (i.e., taxonomically stuffed birds) to the British Museum (Natural History), where he'd been a leading light for fifty years. It was a spectacular collection, in size and importance nearly comparable to the gift that had been made by his mentor, the late Lord Walter Rothschild, whose brother had been Meinertzhagen's classmate at Harrow.

A full thirty years after Meinertzhagen's extraordinary gift to the British Museum, and a generation after his death, two stunning articles appeared in the journals. These were to be the initial axe-whacks into the Bunyanesque tree of Meinertzhagen mythology. The two pieces, by natural scientist Alan Knox and science journalist Gail Vines,[2] showed how zoologists, in their long struggle to catalogue the gift, determined that Meinertzhagen had faked the origins of some of his rare specimens and had stolen many of his birds from other collectors and museums—even from the British Museum itself.

Sometimes these bold acts of vanity are dismissed as benign eccentricities. Meinertzhagen pulled them off like a clever criminal in a caper novel. In that sense they can be very amusing, but they were not harmless. It has taken researchers many years and vast expenditures of labor—and they still haven't finished the job—to redraw maps of bird distributions in order to undo Meinertzhagen's misinformation. In a science that devotes much of its energy to trying to prevent extinction by preserving endangered species, his fakes have misled naturalists about the locales and scarcity of animals and insects.

Discovery of these deceptions is forcing them now, at huge cost, to rewrite whole chapters of natural history. According to many ornithologists, including Nigel Collar of Birdlife International and Robert Prys-Jones of the Natural History Museum, the damage he caused was catastrophic.[3]

Pamela Rasmussen, formerly of the Smithsonian Institution and now at Michigan State University, reported in August 2005 at a meeting of the American Ornithologists' Union in Santa Barbara, California, that by 1920, Meinertzhagen was already stealing specimens from individual collectors and from institutions like the British Museum. For the next forty years he amassed creatures and re-tagged them, fabricating information. He was good at hiding his inventions. Some of the hoaxes were proved only after the skeletons of stuffed birds were X-rayed.

Robert Prys-Jones described Meinertzhagen's lifelong fakery as "the most egregious example of fraud that I'm aware of."[4]

His fabulous success as a con man can be measured by the fact that many of his frauds are still believed by a minority of scientists (and perhaps a majority of lay observers) to be truths, forty years after he died.

He was a great scientist; he was a scientific fraud.

He was a military hero; he was an incompetent officer.

He was beloved; he was scorned.

He was a killer. But he was not the mass murderer he pretended to be. It is possible that only one of the storied massacres occurred. He was undoubtedly there—but he may not have shot anyone. Conversely, the shooting death of his wife Annie was ruled an accident by Scottish authorities in 1928 but many, then and now, believed it was murder.

The real Richard Meinertzhagen is elusive. He can be glimpsed but rarely seen. He reflects hall-of-mirrors images—in shards: no two are the same, and none is complete.

Over several years our pursuit of the real Richard Meinertzhagen became a cold-case investigation that involved some of the key figures of his time: Churchill, Lawrence, Hitler, and various field marshals, generals, and scientists.

The more we probed, the more our team discovered astounding gaps between the accepted myths and the realities.[5]

Some elements of the Meinertzhagen legend are true. He was chief of British Military Intelligence in the East Africa theater of war in 1915–1916. In 1917 he served in a minor capacity on Allenby's intelligence staff in Gaza. In 1918, during the horrible trench war, he served as one of Gen. Sir Douglas Haig's headquarters intelligence officers in France. To this day one of military intelligence's most useful texts is the handbook on wartime intelligence tactics and procedures that Temporary Lt. Col. Richard Meinertzhagen wrote during the late summer of 1918 while serving at Western Front Headquarters.[6]

He did his genuine best to defend Zionism's interests in the Paris Peace Congress of 1919—the conference that led to the signing of the Versailles Treaty. In that Congress, both his efforts on behalf of the Jews and his friend T. E. Lawrence's efforts on behalf of the Arabs were betrayed by politicians for political reasons. Both Lawrence and Meinertzhagen were dismayed by the outcome. The two men continued to work together, if often at cross-purposes; after the treaty was signed, Meinertzhagen was appointed—first under Allenby, then under Churchill (by Churchill's express request)—to be Britain's political officer for Palestine, while Lawrence was his Arab-connected co-worker in the same section of Churchill's department of the Colonial Office.

When not making war or gathering intelligence he studied wildlife and explored jungles and mountains that no European had ever seen. He fought a three-decades-long battle with several governments to have the vital nesting island of Heligoland designated an international wildlife sanctuary. He accumulated major collections of birds and insects—acquiring some of these specimens with great difficulty and hardship.

He was an irascible but valued mentor to young natural scientists, some of whom were to become world-famous, like India's treasured Sálim Ali. They, and many other contemporaries, cherished him as a wonderful being—irregular but splendid. (As we shall see, Sálim Ali often was ill-treated by the imperious Englishman, but nonetheless continued to regard Meinertzhagen with good-humored affection, both as a scientist and as a friend.)

He became a noted figure in science, war, and espionage. In all three, a few of his accomplishments were unique and splendid. He was a man of talent and courage, with a personality that often seemed majestic.

But in all three fields he also was a fantasist who perpetrated colossal deceptions.

When we allow ourselves to be duped by events that did not occur but are part of the "common knowledge," we do ourselves a radical disservice. Where history is concerned, our first duty is to know the facts. Only after the facts are identified can we approach interpretation and understanding.

History is a reflection of events. Our understanding of it is a reflection *on* those events.

The few who saw through Richard Meinertzhagen during his lifetime and said as much were iconoclasts—Lawrence of Arabia, Malcolm Muggeridge, rival ornithologists, soldiers who performed feats for which Meinertzhagen took credit, perceptive scientists in out-of-the-way corners of the world.

Their objections were dismissed as radical and perhaps irresponsible. Some were accused of having axes to grind. But it turns out they were right.

He was not Jewish. He described himself as a reformed anti-Semite, and he became a valued friend of Dr. Chaim Weizmann, the Jewish émigré chemist who headed the Zionist organization in England. Meinertzhagen was admired by David Ben Gurion. For years he did his best to serve and protect the interests of Zionism in the Middle East.

His loyalty to Zionism had not existed at all until 1917, when it seems to have exploded into being the way Minerva sprang from the brow of Jupiter, but it was sincere. His dedication was passionate from the beginning. His efforts often failed or backfired, and afterward he lied about them, and then he went out of his way to draw attention to his fabrications until they became accepted truths—but the original impulses seem to have been genuine.

Right through World War II he convinced friends, family, and quite a few high-ranking officials that he was engaged at the highest level in hush-hush espionage work. During that war he dressed up in his colonel's uniform and prowled the halls of Whitehall.

Ian Fleming believed, and apologists declare to this day, that the furtive intelligence agencies MI-5 and MI-6 maintained a conspiratorial silence about the clandestine missions he carried out for them. Serious historians have published entire books about some of these alleged operations.[7] Virtually none of them happened. The agencies failed to mention Meinertzhagen for one excellent reason: he didn't work for them.

Much of the time Meinertzhagen was a wild eccentric and, to some, a lovable rogue. His early frauds may have been more mischievous than malicious. He was an irrepressible yarn-spinner and at first he may have been surprised when people took his narratives seriously. But he matured into a full-blown narcissist. Solipsistically he invented his life as he went along. He became a grand hybrid of heroics and hoaxes.

His lies metastasized. They became malignant until in the end it became clear that none of his statements could be taken at face value if they could not be traced back to, and confirmed by, primary sources that were independent of him and his influence.

When we approach the record from that premise, history changes.

🐦 🐦 🐦

Some of the detective work was not possible until recently. Only lately have some of the most revealing diaries and letters been given to public and academic archives by prominent people (or their estates) whose paths intersected with Meinertzhagen's. In the late 1990s the British government began to release files that had been kept secret for decades—sometimes a century.

The more one exposes the lies by which Meinertzhagen made himself look like a hero, the more unsympathetic he becomes in light of his actions.

Yet he was generous, often likeable, widely admired, loved by some, and—at times—authentic.

Great villains can make fascinating characters. Meinertzhagen was a fascinating character but he was not a conventional villain. He was more, and he was less. His complexities were Shakespearean.

He liked to entertain. (His annual Derby Day parties were famous, and invitations to them were coveted.) He spoke and wrote in torrents. He pretended his vast "diaries" were records of events as they were occurring, but in fact they are memoirs, created and then re-created long after the events, with the author's retrospective (and often fictional) "spin."[8]

He may or may not have understood the harm he was causing. Certainly he did not understand some of the impulses that drove him.

He and his circle managed to be not only puzzling but also appealing. Their actions seem to provoke more interest than rage—more curiosity than contempt. Attempting to understand them seems much more rewarding than attempting to dismiss or diminish them.

He was an Englishman who claimed Danish ancestry. In fact he'd fabricated the Danish family tree;[9] his father was the scion of a German merchant banking dynasty. In the early nineteenth century Richard's grandparents had emigrated from Bremen and Cologne where they had been financiers, burghers, and mayors for centuries. His grandfather became a British subject. His father was born in England.

Richard was at Harrow with Churchill and was related by blood or marriage to an amazing number of aristocrats, industrialists, financiers, opinion-makers, and government leaders. Although possessed of a German name, he was like the Windsors and the Battenburg/Mountbattens: entirely English—"one of us" in Victorian and Edwardian society.

His father, his brother Louis, and several nephews and grand-nephews distinguished themselves in industry, international affairs, and finance. Some became directors of the Bank of England, the London Stock Exchange, and/or the Commonwealth Fund. A number of his close relations by blood or marriage served in Parliament.

Still he felt compelled to equip himself with the fiction of Danish ancestry. It may have begun during World War I to deter fellow officers from associating him with the hated enemy. But why did he persist in maintaining the fiction all the way into the 1960s?[10] And why did so many distinguished members of his circle—some of whom read his books and must have recognized the falsehoods of this and other inventions—fail to come forward and object?

In some cases they were bamboozled. Britain's former prime minister, David Lloyd George, wrote that Meinertzhagen "struck me as being one of the ablest and most successful brains I had met in any army. That was quite sufficient to make him suspect and to hinder his promotion to the highest ranks of his profession."[11] Quite a few admirers, including the historians, seem to have felt the same way—as if Meinertzhagen could have been one of the top generals of the army if only he'd been a bit stupider and a bit more willing to play by the book. The fact is, however, that Lloyd George met Meinertzhagen just once or twice, and his description of Meinertzhagen clearly is based on what Meinertzhagen himself told the Prime Minister.[12]

Meinertzhagen called one of his books *Diary of a Black Sheep*, and in a way he was just that—he gave up the family bank in order to explore the world as a soldier-scientist. But his family remained at London's financial center, and Richard was no outcast. Despite the huffy disapproval of some relations he remained accepted amongst the landed-estate set as a war hero, a great scientist, a boisterous crank, a master spy, a clever observer of the world scene (or a boorish unsophisticate, depending on one's mood), and a fabulous raconteur.

Some men revered him; others detested him. Some women found him powerfully attractive; others feared him—they believed he was a conscienceless killer who had murdered his wife.

His relationships with women seem to have defined his character in several ways. He was married twice but found his most comfortable long-term relationship in his cousin Theresa Clay, who, when she was still a teenager, came to look after him and his three small children after his second wife was shot to death. He helped mold Theresa Clay's life, tutored her to an Edinburgh doctorate, and shepherded her into a successful career as a mallophaga (chewing bird lice) expert in entomology. They never married, but cousin Tess, thirty-three years younger than Meinertzhagen, stayed with him through the last four decades of his life and remained his ferocious defender until her own death in 1995.

Meinertzhagen was part real hero, part pathological destroyer; part genius, part bluffer. That's why he's captivating, but it also is why his story is so difficult to parse and to understand.

The contrast between the accepted legends and Richard Meinertzhagen's actual life is a stark reminder that our beliefs about events can depend too easily on credulous historians' willingness to accept outrageous adventures (like Meinertzhagen's) as truths because they make good stories or because previous historians accepted them.

There is, for example, Meinertzhagen's assertion that in 1939 he had a loaded revolver in his pocket when he went to meet with Hitler in Berlin in order to beg, not for the first time, for the lives of Jews in the Nazi regions. He was there as a spokesman for his friend Chaim Weizmann, head of the Zionist movement in Britain. One of Meinertzhagen's missions throughout the 1930s was to negotiate with the Nazis to allow Jews to emigrate from Germany with their families and with at least a bit of their personal property. Later, Weizmann and David Ben Gurion praised him for his earnest efforts in behalf of the Zionist cause.

At his final meeting with Hitler at 11:00 A.M. on June 28, 1939, in the Berlin Chancellory, Meinertzhagen had a loaded revolver in his coat pocket. He later wrote, "I had ample opportunity to kill both Hitler and Ribbentrop and am seriously troubled about it. If this war breaks out, as I feel sure it will, then I shall feel very much to blame for not killing these two; on the other hand I am quite sure that if I killed them both there would be no war and I should be written off as a madman. But I did satisfy myself that I had the opportunity to kill them both."[13]

Did it happen that way?

Such avowals can be proved or disproved, given an inquisitive will and a stubborn imperviousness to the dust and clutter of old archives. The result of such investigation, in this case, will come as a stunning surprise both to those who believe Meinertzhagen's story and to those who feel he may have embellished it with a fictitious revolver.

Two specific actions, more than most others, defined his public persona: the "Meinertzhagen Haversack Ruse," which allegedly enabled British armies to capture and liberate Palestine from the Turks in 1917, and the death of Meinertzhagen's wife Annie in 1928—a shooting that was ruled "accidental" but was believed by some to have been murder.

Truth, in those as in other matters, has been difficult to find. Distinguishing the real from the false requires close examination of contemporary records that were not contaminated by Meinertzhagen's creative influence. That can be hard to do, because he talked a lot and wrote prolifically—letters to historians, endless neatly typed "diaries." (He saved his verbosity for the diaries and his books and articles; his letters tended to be short and on point—often just a sentence or two.)

He had a compulsive drive to amass collections. In addition to some twenty thousand stuffed birds, some of which recently have been exposed as frauds and/or thefts, he gave more than six hundred thousand insects (mainly bird lice, many of which he and his cousin Theresa Clay had catalogued meticulously and perhaps sometimes speciously) to the British Museum, and at various times he collected stamps, rifles, books, bird pictures, photos, military souvenirs, dried plants, and so forth. He published about a dozen books, including the huge, definitive (despite allegations of plagiarism) *Birds of Arabia*, and hundreds of scientific papers, some of which provoked very funny comments from those who didn't agree with him. His book *Pirates and Predators*, about bird behavior, makes for engaging reading. It gets too anthropomorphic at times, but parts of it are quite lyrical. He was not always scientifically precise; like other eccentrics in the world of binoculars and birds he often stretched facts to fit his romantic illusions. When others challenged his articles for their inaccuracies, his retaliatory temper was quick to rise: he said his critics were misinformed, carping, disturbed, impertinent, and libelous.[14]

He and his works had an impact of one kind or another on the awareness of thousands of people. People's views of him seldom coincide, but one mystery that connects the dots even while it obscures them is this: How and why did such a large number of diverse people of prominence share knowledge of his fakery, or at least suspect it—and choose not to disclose it?

The answer to that question is in part an illustration of our general laziness, but it also is an indictment of the class to which he belonged. The Empire waned but the dominant class still tried to persist in its full glory. This could be seen by a head count of those who attended the memorial service for Richard Meinertzhagen's funeral in 1967 at London's Church of the Holy Sepulchre. He was seen off by scores of eminent scientists, top government officials, generals and admirals, bankers, spymasters, birdwatchers, and Meinertzhagens. (It was and is a very large family.)

They collaborated in concealing his transgressions. The cover-ups seem to have been spawned by class habit—old boys and old girls looking out for their interests. They had reasons to want to believe him, but in the end his fabrications seem to have succeeded because he managed to fool nearly everyone on his own, without the aid of conspiracies or cabals.

He could do that. The cover-up, to a large degree, is testimony to three of his characteristics: magnetic charm, earnest plausibility, and the intimidating power of his huge presence and personality. He was articulate, he thought fast on his feet, he projected an air of utter self-assurance, and when he was "on" it seemed unthinkable to dispute him.

In part it was this quality of larger-than-life manliness that encouraged mess-mates, superior officers, and prime ministers to believe what he told them, whether it was an intelligence report about enemy movements and strength or a yarn about one of his glorious adventures.

In contrast, his diaries expose a man who reveals weakness and uncertainty without intending to—a man prowling the shadows between truth and lies with the sinuous stealth of an agent roaming cautiously behind enemy lines in unfamiliar country, not knowing what cover story he may be called upon to provide: confused, unsure of what is expected of him or what he ought to expect of himself.

One reads those long diaries with their perfect typing and their pasted-in testimonials and their contradictory statements and their ideas that curl back upon themselves, with their thousands of photos and postcards and currency notes and telegrams and dried leaves—and one sees that the diarist is talking not only to Posterity but to himself. With the instincts of a novelist, he is trying to contrive a character whose life the author would like to have lived.

This book began as the accidental result of detective work on another case. I first encountered Meinertzhagen as a source of chronicles of the 1914–1918 war for Kilimanjaro. That war in East Africa was a succession of slapstick calamities, masterminded by scores of British generals whose failures provided a humiliating contrast with the victories of their German opponent, the inventive and good-humored Lt. Col. Paul von Lettow-Vorbeck, who won the four-year campaign even though he was blockaded and even though he and his soldiers (most of them black Africans) were outnumbered twenty-to-one.

From 1914 until early 1917 Meinertzhagen was a key figure in the British force there. His diaries and books, laced with withering castigation, became highly entertaining guides through that African *veldt*.

Dozens of stories of that campaign, including quite a few novels (e.g., C. S. Forester's *The African Queen*), have been published. In many of them the picture of the experiences of both British and German forces in the theater (including even that in Lettow's own autobiography[15]) is based in part on the caustic recollections of Richard Meinertzhagen.

In looking at those accounts, my colleagues and I began to perceive that we, and so many others, had been bamboozled. In East Africa the Allies had overwhelming advantages over their German opponents. Yet the Allies (including more than 180 generals and a quarter of a million troops) lost their war to a German force that never numbered more than fifteen thousand men. The British lost because they could not find the enemy and they could not anticipate his moves. Time and again they closed their trap and the German wasn't there. Miles away in some unexpected quarter he would pop up like the Roadrunner in one of Chuck Jones's cartoon films. Lettow would thumb his nose at the British Wile E. Coyote; he would attack, win, and disappear.

To find the German and his little army was, by definition, the duty of British Intelligence.

Britain's Chief of Intelligence in the theater was Capt. Richard Meinertzhagen.

We felt obliged to complete that syllogism.

As the quest began, we saw many testimonials on his behalf from the mighty. Only a few had questioned the veracity of his swaggering boasts. We began to find isolated evidences of a long record of suspicion and disbelief.

The rap sheet is long and appalling. I seem not to be the originator of any of its charges but, until now, questions and disclosures have been compartmentalized within separate circles: family, science, the military, friends, the reticent people of espionage, "history." The precision and energy that scientists invested in re-examining his zoological cons were not replicated in other circles. There was no effort to verify and collate his separate parallel paths.

We felt challenged to make that effort.

Our investigation of the Meinertzhagen mystery was greeted at first with scoffing and dismissals. Of course Meinertzhagen's haversack ploy won Jerusalem for the Allies in 1917; how can we question that when everyone from Lord Allenby to Prime Minister Lloyd George to Lawrence of Arabia himself attests to it? The man was a decorated hero, after all. We can't very well pretend he wasn't there—of *course* he was there!

Yes, he was there. But what did he *do* there?

Then it became another sort of thing. We ourselves became the accused. We who examined the records were astonished to be charged with abetting a conspiracy of hatchet-men whose sole purpose was to destroy the record of a great hero's outstanding achievements.

If my accusers felt that I was setting out to launch a book-length attack on Meinertzhagen out of pure hostility, they might have been right in assuming it to be either a malicious vendetta or a silly exercise in petty excess. After all, the fact that a man made up stories in which he himself played the role of hero is not unique or newsworthy. Why not just let him have his fun?

Unfortunately Meinertzhagen's fun wasn't harmless. Too many books and articles about Israel, about various wars, about science, and about the European presence in the Middle East, Africa, and India during the first half of the twentieth century, have used his diaries as primary source materials. They are not.

This dossier examines the evidence and tries to arrive at fair-minded verdicts, beyond a reasonable doubt. The book is not a work of revisionist history; what it attempts to revise is not our interpretation of the past but our knowledge of it.

Forty years after he died, the English superspy-scientist (1878–1967) is still a subject of spirited controversy.

I've had Meinertzhagen in the corner of my eye for more than forty years, and have pursued the facts of his life for nearly a decade. This book attempts to understand him rather than attack him, but it does attack a great many myths. The supporting proofs are clearly documented. The result is complex (he wasn't a simple man), but I hope it is enticing and exciting.

First, let's sort out what he did and did not do. Then let's try to determine why he created an epic of lies, and how he got away with it.

He led several lives. To enter his world is to enter a kind of madness. His story is less a continuum than a mosaic—a maze turned inside out.

To solve the puzzle we must begin at its middle.

CHAPTER 2

HAVERSACK

During World War II, whenever Richard Meinertzhagen was introduced to a high-ranking stranger in Whitehall, the stranger was likely to reply something like, "Meinertzhagen, oh yes—the haversack ploy."

The stranger's reaction might be admiring or wary, depending on how much he had heard about the lean, tall colonel with the piercing eyes. By then Richard Meinertzhagen was known for his storybook heroics in the previous war, when the greatest glory of his achievements had been the success of his brilliant 1917 satchel-trick in winning Palestine and liberating Jerusalem for General Allenby.

In recent years his triumphant "haversack ruse" has become a frequent feature in books and newspapers. It was the cornerstone on which rested his reputation as a military-intelligence hero.

Here is the haversack history as it has been accepted, and as Richard Meinertzhagen—hereafter usually called "RM" in this book—wished us to remember it:

October 10, 1917: In the desert the tent-camp at Khan Yunis stands north of Rafah, on the road that ribbons ahead through Gaza into Palestine.

Major Meinertzhagen strides from his tent, carrying a haversack and a Lee-Enfield rifle. He slides the rifle into the horse's saddle scabbard and secures the straps of his full water canteen and of the haversack. It contains his field-ration lunch, his wallet, his field glasses, a few odds and ends that constitute a rudimentary survival kit, and a sheaf of papers some of which are stamped *"secret."*

At thirty-nine, the major is a tall man with the raptor eyes, wide, flat shoulders, and narrow hips of an outdoorsman. His hat brim is pulled low across his face to shield him from the blast of sun because too much brightness still provokes blurring, the result of a gunshot that nearly blew away his right eye four years ago in India. The brightness also intensifies a headache, legacy of concussion suffered three years ago in East Africa when one of his own ships' British naval shells slammed him against a tree, while he was under white flag in a German camp to negotiate an exchange of prisoners.

His sight was saved in India by determined doctors. Headaches from the East Africa shell and other explosions are still with him but there is hardly a visible scar to mark the injuries. Maj. Richard Meinertzhagen is handsome, lithe, confident, steady. He also is very likeable. (Miriam Rothschild, niece of Lord Walter, recalled, "He had a graceful carriage & considerable charm & an interesting way of talking. Never dull. He also had an agreeable manner if he respected anyone—for example my aged grand-mother, who was rather a formidable old woman.")[1]

RM's haversack contains a £20 Bank of England note—a small for-tune on a soldier's pay—and a variety of official and unofficial documents. One letter is handwritten, from a young Englishwoman, proffering love to her far-away husband and chatting with brave cheeriness about the new baby he has never seen. That young woman's face is clear in RM's mind when he straps the haversack and the canteen to his saddle and climbs onto the horse.

In the painful brightness he takes the salute of the waiting groom, wheels the horse, and trots away from Headquarters Row. His seat on the fast-gaited horse is easy; in his time RM has ridden to the hounds in Scot-land, has rounded up thousands of native cattle in East Africa, has traveled horseback across half of Asia, and has survived a good many vigorous games both in the colonies and in England where, on more than one occasion, he played polo with Winston Churchill.

The horse carries him past company-rows of tents. There are pegged-down camels and parked open-top armored cars. Platoons of men work on their equipment or curry their horses or drill sweating in the heat. In the desert the waiting for war is malodorous, gritty, itchy, anxious, hot, tense, and so tedious that a man can begin to find comfort in the anticipation of battle in spite of all its terrors.

He lifts his mount to a canter and rides toward the enemy's guns, pleased to be in motion even though he is pained by bruises from a crash-landing four days ago, and even though he knows there is a good chance he will not return alive from this one.

By this time—three years into the war—RM has acquired dazzling skills in analyzing terrain and topography. He has become the British Expe-ditionary Force's chief mapmaking source for information about water, roads, railways, towns, and the characteristics of local resident populations. Allenby has come to rely on RM to tell him where he can take his armies. RM can predict with great accuracy whether or not motor convoys can proceed by a specific route from point "A" to point "B" without getting bogged down in loose sand or being forced to turn back because of gullies or low cliffs. Both in East Africa and in the Gaza desert he has drawn fastidious maps. Any intelligence officer could take justifiable pride in such accomplishments.[2]

Riding east and north by intervals, he accompanies an Australian Light Horse patrol for a few miles before he cuts away on his own into the afternoon. He trots down the rutted floors of *wadis*, tacking with their switchbacks as long as they tend northward. The flood-cut banks are high enough to hide him for a while from enemy machine-gunners on the towers of the Turkish line.

His mission is crucial. Many will judge it to have been a significant factor in the outcome of the World War.

Alone on his horse, with rifle and canteen and haversack, RM is riding into history.

British and ANZAC (Australia-New Zealand Army Corps) troops have been stalled all spring and summer. They made two attempts in force to blast their way into fortress Gaza, but against well-armed German-Turkish forces both frontal assaults collapsed in carnage.

Now Gen. Archibald Murray, who led the two failed British attacks, is gone. His replacement is rugged cavalry commander Gen. Sir Edmund Allenby, who has become one of RM's heroes. Allenby, fifty-six, addicted to fast movement and sharp-edged tactics, is a tough and seasoned commander known to his men (with both fear and affection) as "The Bull." Allenby is under fretful orders from Prime Minister David Lloyd George to buy time for Britain in the Great War that seems ready to devour the nation and perhaps Western civilization as well. In Europe the best the exhausted Allies can do is hold their ground and hope the Germans are as dog-tired as they themselves are. Morale has dropped. The British War Cabinet is close to desperation.

By mid-1917 Lloyd George believes he knows what is needed, and where it is. He puts it to Edmund Allenby in the form of an imperial demand:

"Jerusalem. By Christmas."[3]

RM has passed the new commander's weeding-out examination. One can picture Allenby demanding, "What's he good at?" and an aide responding, "The lie of the land and the birds." Perhaps RM is accepted in part because he's a recent arrival who isn't identified with the Murray regime, or perhaps it has something to do with the Freddie Guest connection: Frederick Guest, RM's friend and recent second-in-command as Chief of Intelligence in East Africa, is a first cousin of Winston Churchill and a close friend of Allenby's secretary, Lord Dalmeny.

RM and the rough-and-ready general are comfortable with each other. They share a keenness for adventure, a ruthless impatience with incompetence, and an enchantment with ornithology. Along the Gaza coast, RM has found bits of time to tutor a small coterie of noted amateur birdmen that includes Allenby,[4] Maurice Portal, and Lord William Percy.[5] (RM and "Willy" Percy's will become a lifelong friendship.)

The challenge of liberating Jerusalem as a Christmas present to the Allied powers is one Allenby does not appear likely to meet. The Turkish army, modernized and equipped by the Germans, is as tough as any in the world. It is fresh from two heroic victories at Gaza and from its repudiation of Allied forces the previous year, when it drove them from their suicidal footholds on Turkey's Gallipoli peninsula.

Allenby cannot invade Palestine without first dislodging the Turk from Gaza, one of the world's oldest fortified cities. Its forbidding walls and towers stand astride the coastal path north from the Suez Canal into Palestine. Twice in the past few months it has proved impervious to British attack. But Allenby must drive the Turk from Gaza and then must chase him back all the way up the rugged length of Palestine. Gaza cannot be bypassed. Its defense forces are formidable and can be moved quickly along interior rail lines.

On paper Allenby is defeated before he can begin. Britain's greatest strength is her navy but that asset has dubious utility in a desert war. On land it is axiomatic that in order to succeed, an attacking force against a fortified position has to be more powerful than the defenders. That is an advantage Allenby does not have: he is outnumbered.

Gaza's west shoulder stands against the sea; its east shoulder stands against the waterless Judean desert and the Negev beyond—a thousand miles of crumbling clay, loose sands, and mountain rocks too jagged for tires, hoofs, or booted human feet. Even on drivable terrain armies cannot move without enormous amounts of water, and there is no significant supply of water in the desert east of Gaza except for an oasis-grouping of ancient wells about thirty miles inland at Beersheba—deep artesian wells that Allenby knows have been mined by the Germans.

Beersheba is an ancient village on the dry-caked banks of the Wadi Saba, in a valley rimmed by stark limestone Judean hills. It is not much to look at: a few scrubby trees, ancient houses scattered as if by a storm, raw new barracks thrown up to shade Turkey's soldiers, a sun-blasted railway platform, a squat white mosque. There are the precious wells, and from the aerial photographs RM has assembled, one can see a handful of motor lorries and automobiles, and several corrals with rudimentary stables for horses and camels.

The village itself is not defensible. It sprawls in the open, dominated by higher ground in several directions, and its patternless layout hardly allows for fortification.

The German-trained Turks have built their lines of defense three miles out—on heights that provide long visibility and wide fields of fire toward any potential attack.

Those high Turkish positions are entrenched, bermed with sandbags, armed with machine guns, and heavy with rifle positions. They are supported by field guns on rocky outcrops. No army can attack Beersheba without first coming under the guns of these defenses.

The Turks' garrison on semicircular defenses above the town numbers three divisions—mixed cavalry and infantry—and a number of artillery batteries. Thousands of soldiers, plenty of guns; the Turks know the value of their wells.

Facing them are two under-strength British divisions (one of infantry and the other of Light Horse, or mounted infantry[6]) spread at intervals on a line that staggers among wadis and hills a dozen miles south and east of Beersheba.

The Turks need merely to hold onto their wells—and their forces here are more than sufficient to defend the water against any attack by two (or even four or five) British divisions.

As long as his forces remain within hauling distance of the coastal railway from Suez, Allenby has enough water. His men can survive in decent health and rudimentary comfort although none of them can be blamed for failing to regard this desert as a summer holiday resort.

But they don't have transport for the amounts of water his men and animals and machines need. As soon as they strike forward they will run dry.

Jerusalem seems unlikely at best; Jerusalem by Christmas looks impossible.

Allenby and Richard Meinertzhagen have seen one sliver of possibility. If they were able to seize the wells of Beersheba intact, their armies could base themselves on its water and use Beersheba as a hinge on which to swing inland behind Gaza.

If the troops could move swiftly enough they might split the Turkish army in two, isolating or scattering the Gaza garrison. Then it would be the Turks, not the British, who must scramble for each drop of water.

But if Allenby fails to capture Beersheba—or if the Germans implode the wells—his machines will stop, his men and horses will be dehydrated, easy targets for enemy attack, and Britain will lose yet another hundred thousand troops who do not deserve to die.

The wells are tempting and there is hope in one fact: they are as vital to the enemy as they are to the British. The enemy will destroy the precious water supply only as a last resort. Allenby knows all this and of course the enemy knows it too. Major Meinertzhagen's bold idea may solve the dilemma. Allenby knows it is a long shot but it seems to be the only shot he has.

So on October 10, 1917, the lone horseman rides into the desert intending deliberately to draw the enemy's fire. Today's daring gallop is the culmination of his ingenious, desperate, and perhaps lunatic effort to give Allenby the wells of Beersheba.

His line of travel does not take him within sight of Beersheba but he knows the town and its defenses because it is his job to know every knob and ditch and redoubt of the front. In the past weeks, he writes, he has flown over every square mile of the front. His plane crashed just four days ago—he walked away from that one but his companion in the two-seater, Sandy Machintosh, is still in hospital. RM, who later will profess to have been the top man among hundreds who contribute information to Allenby's intelligence section, has collated his own daily reports with those from every artillery-spotter, every hilltop lookout, every Royal Flying Corps pilot, and every reconnaissance patrol in the Sinai-Gaza theater. He has compiled wireless intercepts from Turkish and German transmissions, some of them deciphered by the crossword-solving mathematical geniuses who hunch over drab tables in London's top-secret Room 40. He has talked with Englishmen and Arabs and Jews who have interrogated captured enemy soldiers; he has interrogated some of them himself (he does not speak Turkish and his Arabic is rudimentary, but his German is fluent). He has gathered constant updates from espionage conducted by his own agents and by his friends the Jewish spies of the super-efficient NILI Ring, who operate at great risk behind enemy lines in Turkish-ruled Palestine. (Within a few more months, nearly all the heroic men and women of Aaron and Sarah Aaronsohn's NILI organization will have been identified and slaughtered by the Turks.)

RM is the author of the daily overlay chart of enemy positions, a copy of which goes to every field commander, showing his detailed pinpointing of enemy positions and numbers. These include details right down to the names and particulars of commanders of current outposts. They show supply dumps, fuel and ammunition stores, number and location of serviceable aircraft, routes used by cavalry patrols, probable movements of every enemy military section, and the current conditions of roads and bridges on both sides of the front lines.

In military terms such knowledge is what defines intelligence. That is RM's job, and he is good at it. Even the brilliant and romantic T. E. Lawrence, whose seldom occupied desk has been next to RM's, is impressed by his fellow officer's skills if not always by his etiquette: "Meinertzhagen [was] a student of migrating birds [who] drifted into soldiering, whose hot immortal hatred of the enemy expressed itself as readily in trickery as in violence. He persuaded Dawnay: Allenby reluctantly agreed: Bols assented, and the work began."[7]

This work consists of devising and making forgeries—an exercise in which RM has become expert by now, having flooded German East Africa with his own hand-designed counterfeit German rupee money.

He writes:

> Our actual plan was to assume the offensive at the end of October by capturing Beersheba and then enveloping the enemy's eastern flank.
>
> It was therefore the object of camouflage to make the enemy believe that we could not assume an offensive before the middle of November or later, [and] that the blow would fall on their western flank at Gaza. Also that all movement towards Beersheba was done with the object of inducing them to detach the bulk of their forces in that direction.
>
> It was therefore decided to drop a notebook which purported to belong to a G.H.Q. officer who was on reconnaissance towards Beersheba. It contained . . . :
>
> A. £20 in notes to gain the impression that the loss of the notebook was not intentional.
>
> B. Copy of a letter purporting to come from the wife of the Staff Officer announcing the birth of a son. Such a letter would be of great value to the husband who would not willingly lose it. (It was actually written by my sister Mary who had never had a baby. . . .)

He describes several papers designed to fool the enemy into expecting a feint against Beersheba and then an attack in force against Gaza.

And finally, RM writes, the haversack contains "[a] few rough notes on a cipher which would enable enemy to decipher any camouflage messages we might send later on."[8]

The trick now is to deliver the papers into the enemy's hands in a way that will convince him of their genuineness.

RM's horse takes him on a northwesterly curve and somewhere in the vicinity of Girheir village his movement draws the glance of a Turkish cavalryman whose patrol swings around to come toward him at the charge. The Englishman, startled, wheels his horse and sinks his spurs. He flees at a dead run.

He spares them an occasional over-the-shoulder glimpse. After about a mile the Turks grow bored with the pursuit. They rein in. They make a tempting stationary target, so RM dismounts, levels his rifle across the saddle, and aims high to compensate for the third of a mile distance between. He squeezes off a shot. It is too far to see if he's hit anyone but the provocation is enough to bring the Turks after him again and this time the galloping enemy cavalrymen shoot from their saddles.

The Turks can see that RM has been hit. He lurches—nearly falls. He has trouble getting on his horse; he loses his grip, drops his rifle, grabs for the saddle, and drops his canteen as he scrambles up by one stirrup. The haversack, stained with blood, falls to the sand. RM sways and slumps forward, clearly injured, and gigs his horse into a shoddy, panic-driven gallop toward the distant refuge of British lines.

Behind him one of the Turks stops and dismounts. RM sees the cavalryman pick up the fallen Lee-Enfield rifle and the haversack—and then there is no time left for eyeing the enemy; there is nothing left but to run for it, full out.

RM distances the pursuit, walks his horse a while to cool it, and returns to his base quite satisfied. When he steps down from the no longer lathered horse he shows no sign of the severe injury he appeared to have suffered from a Turkish bullet a few hours ago.

Headquarters immediately puts up a display of alarmed dismay. Orders are dispatched to all headquarters: "URGENT. While on reconnaissance patrol in No Man's Land this afternoon, about x 21 d 4. 3, a Staff officer lost a haversack. If found, the haversack is to be returned forthwith to General Headquarters without being opened or its contents examined in any way."

At the same time a wireless message is broadcast in a cipher the enemy is known to have broken: "Determined efforts are to be made to-night by troops in the sector involved to recover the lost haversack mentioned in G.R.O. No. 102."[9]

Too late for that: the prize is in enemy hands. It makes its way up the line until it is upended finally on the desk of Maj. Gen. Baron Friedrich Kress von Kressenstein.[10] After the war Kressenstein will describe the bag's contents:

> During one fight between an English and a Turkish cavalry patrol the Chief of Intelligence at the English Headquarter[s], Major Meinertz-hagen, lost a bag containing his maps. The bag contained not only a considerable amount of money and a number of private letters but also a lot of interesting papers.
>
> Those papers contained the following information:
>
> The English had postponed the attack till the end of the year or the beginning of next year; the main attack was to be directed against the south-western front at Gaza; a mixed brigade was to land to the north of Gaza; simultaneously to the attack of the English the French would attempt a landing at the Syrian coast.
>
> The English considered the grounds at the left side of German-Turkish lines as not suitable for bigger cavalry units. Therefore they did not plan to attack Beersheba. The only reason for actions against Beersheba was to induce the Germans to concentrate their forces there and therefore to weaken other areas.[11]

The enemy has swallowed the deception: he prepares to defend against attacks from his rear and for a frontal assault against Gaza.

Now Allenby posts his orders of attack.[12] There are no forces to attack the enemy's rear. On his front, XXI Corps is to hold the front against Gaza, making a great noise but risking as few lives as possible.

Meanwhile a surprise attack against the Turkish left at Beersheba is to be led by Australia's Gen. Harry Chauvel and his Desert Mounted Corps.

On the night of October 30, in the brain-rattling din of a British artillery and naval barrage, the enemy hides his ears and eyes under his pillows while Chauvel's Corps—more than forty thousand British troops and guns—steals a full thirty miles to the east, to positions from which by daylight they can launch a mounted attack on Beersheba.

Their achievement must be measured by an appreciation of how difficult it is for mounted troops to move quietly. The racket of the Gaza bombardments over the horizon thirty miles to the west cannot have been significant as the troopers approached Beersheba. They must muffle the thud of hoofbeats, the creak of leather, the snorts of horses, and the bang of metal gear. And there is the risk, in any nighttime movement, of accidents, obstacles, and equine traffic jams. Multiply these hazards by tens of thousands of men and horses and the challenge becomes apparent.

Horrendous bombardments hold the enemy's attention and keep his head down at Gaza. At Beersheba the Desert Mounted Corps throws itself against the outer entrenchments in a tentative sort of attack that the Turks think is a diversionary hoax.

RM's ruse has worked: the enemy has committed no reinforcements to Beersheba because he believes the attack is a feint.

The "diversion" is capped by an exploit of heroic magnitude. In mid-afternoon the New Zealand Mounted Rifle Brigade takes the last Turkish-occupied hill overlooking the town from the southeast. The Turks still have no idea of the size of the force in front of them, and the German commander in Beersheba can see with his own eyes that no British infantry troops are within anything like striking distance. So there is no hurry about defending the wells.

What the Turks fail to take into account is that both Allenby and Chauvel are not infantry officers. They are cavalrymen.

Australia's Brig. Gen. William Grant, urged forward by Chauvel, leads eight hundred horsemen in a bold charge across three miles of open ground.

The Light Horse sweeps toward the eastern end of the town. Nearly out of water and exhausted from hard riding, the ANZAC troopers throw themselves against the Turks' last line while Chauvel's artillery brings its aim down to wire-cutting precision and crumples one German machine-gun position after another.

The artillery breaks up enemy resistance and allows the charge of the Fourth Light Horse Brigade to reach the enemy line without ever breaking stride. The Australians leap their mounts over the trenches, wheel to fire into the Turks from behind, and harpoon enemy troops on the tips of their bayonets.

It is a spectacular action, ghastly and sudden and horrible and archaically glorious and, well, cinematic.[13]

The wheeling attack from their rear is so sudden it prevents the Turks from withdrawing toward the wells.

The Light Horse men gallop through Beersheba at a dead run. They capture the vital water supply before the handful of flustered Turkish and German officers realize they no longer have time or soldiers to detonate the charges.

The wells are Allenby's.

The Light Horse Brigade stamps its imprint on history in what some will describe as the last great cavalry charge.[14] The Australians and the New Zealanders capture intact not only the vital wells but also reservoirs containing ninety thousand gallons of fresh water. These make it possible for Allenby to refresh his armies and move them north even faster and farther than he anticipated.

At Gaza, the main Turkish force, pounded by howitzers and naval guns in front and Chauvel's horse at the rear, collapses. Kressenstein's army is shaken and demoralized. Half his men seem to evaporate into the desert; those who remain are trembling with shell shock. Allenby's soldiers scale the walls of Gaza against minimal opposition, taking few casualties. In less than a day of soldier-to-soldier fighting, Allenby takes the fortified city.

By November 6, the enemy is in full retreat. The Turks have abandoned Gaza, and Chauvel's Mounted Corps widens its spearhead into a big wedge between the two halves of the fleeing Turkish force.

Having divided, Allenby conquers: he scatters the remaining enemy forces as if he were an axe turning logs to kindling.[15]

Chauvel's Light Horse takes and keeps the point. The Brigade rides into Jerusalem on December 10, 1917. The Holy City is free—liberated with two weeks to spare.

History will record it as Meinertzhagen's victory as much as Chauvel's, Grant's, or Allenby's.

The success of the haversack ruse in fooling the Germans and the Turks will become the foundation of RM's fame. Britain's official war historian states: "[Turkish General] Hussein Husni's summing up of Kress's action in the battle is contained in the sentence: 'He relied on _____'s pocket book.'" (The blanked-out name is RM's, of course.)[16]

RM wrote: "To illustrate the complete deception of the enemy by this notebook, see . . . Turkish documents cited below."

Copy of Turkish Army Corps Order.

1. On 10 October, 1917, One of our N.C.O. patrols sent out to Abu Sahiban Tepe came back with some very important maps and documents left by a high-rank General Staff Officer of the British Army. . . . The information contained in these documents is of such great value to us that we have been able to ascertain the date of the enemy's offensive and it will enable us to forestall him in that all our reinforcements will now be near Gaza in time for us to crush the arrogant English. . . .

(Signed)

Col. Ali Fuad

O.C. 20th Army Corps.

In *Army Diary* RM cites several other German and Turkish documents, and concludes:

> In the Turkish *Yilderim* by Hussein Husni Amir, pp. 112–114, it is clear that von Kress was completely taken in by my notebook, insisting on its authenticity whilst the Turkish General Staff were suspicious and wished to put their main reserve behind the centre of their position so as to deal with an attack either on Gaza or through Beersheba. But von Kress had his way and reinforced Gaza, much to our advantage.[17]

That—the key episode of the Meinertzhagen legend—is largely a lie.

The ruse was devised, but not by RM. The bag was dropped, but not by RM. It had no effect on the enemy's plans or decisions—and its failure was largely RM's fault.

Those facts can be demonstrated. The more intriguing question, and the hardest to answer, is why those facts were not exposed long ago—why the hoax became the history.[18]

The haversack was part of a wide web of deceptions inspired by Brig. Gen. Sir Philip Chetwode,[19] Allenby's commander of field troops and tactics. Chetwode had proposed a structure of crafty deceptions that were endorsed by Allenby months before the action, when RM knew little or nothing about them.[20]

As part of the deceptions, Allenby made demands on the War Office for enormous numbers of guns, planes, and divisions of troops. An excited RM wrote—unsuspectingly—that these calls for reinforcement showed how determined Allenby was to jump into action.[21]

RM was unaware that these requests could not and would not be met; their purpose was not to bring help (London had no troops to spare) but to fool the enemy.[22] RM was not entrusted with strategic matters. Perhaps that had to do with the way he seemed to prefer the fictions of his own imaginary ploys (like dropping opium-laced cigarettes from an airplane over Turkish trenches[23]) to the realities of the elaborate and sometimes effective stratagems that did take place.

Superficially, Major Meinertzhagen played the part of the good old chap in the Officers' Club, but privately he was the antithesis of the organization man. Give him a job and he could do it; give him his head and he could do havoc. So his knowledge was limited to what he needed to know.

What did he need to know, and why did he need to know it? At this point a search for his precise assignment becomes more than an idle question.

RM is routinely discussed as the chief intelligence officer of General Allenby's army in 1917, but he was nothing of the kind. A major in a head-quarters full of colonels and generals, he was a minor staff officer, so low on the ladder of command that he does not appear on Allenby's staff rosters. He was technically seconded to an Intelligence unit, but it was not Allenby's Intelligence unit—it was MI-7, a London-based organization responsible for censorship and propaganda.

RM's commission was in the City of London Regiment of the Royal Fusiliers. From that organization he had been assigned temporarily to various frontier units during much of his previous seventeen years' service. At the end of 1916 he had been invalided from East Africa back to London, where he did office work while he recovered from tropical ailments. The office was that of Director of Military Intelligence (DMI) Maj. Gen. George Macdonough.[24] RM and the DMI established a relationship that would last until Macdonough's death nearly thirty years later. It was Macdonough who introduced RM to Zionist leader Chaim Weizmann, in whose international efforts RM was to become an important and trusted associate.[25]

RM dismisses his London work during the early months of 1917 as an annoying and boring desk job, but it seems to have taught him some intricacies of army politics. Big and emphatic and often clever—and an ingratiating if impolitic presence—RM clearly impressed Macdonough, who would keep securing prominent postings for him during the rest of the war.

Macdonough dispatched RM to Cairo in advance of Allenby's arrival. RM was not sent out there to be Macdonough's spy (that was Wavell's job). Nor was he sent out to hunt German spies, to install a clandestine wireless broadcasting tower on top of the Great Pyramid at Giza, to make an emergency landing in a shot-up plane (its pilot unconscious), or to concoct a scheme—allegedly abetted by several generals—to drop a haversack full of forgeries under the noses of the Turks. He would claim all these enterprises for himself, but as we shall see, the claims are false.

The MI-7 section of Military Intelligence was one of Macdonough's subsidiaries. MI-7 was assigned the separate duties of overseeing propaganda and censoring news dispatches.[26] By the DMI's authority Maj. Richard Meinertzhagen[27] served under that directorate during his service as a staff officer during the last twenty months of the Great War. (He again served in the same section when it was revived more than twenty years later for a brief period at the beginning of World War II.)[28]

RM's duties in Allenby's theater went beyond MI-7's strict limitations,

but not nearly as far beyond them as he later remembered. He drew maps—
that was the principal job. In order to draw them accurately, he needed to
have a range of information. It came in reports from front-line observers,
from mounted patrols, from overflights by Royal Flying Corps aviators, from
interviews with enemy prisoners, and from newspapers, magazines, letters,
and other documents captured from the enemy.

He also prepared documents for propaganda purposes (i.e., to fool the
enemy) and he censored outgoing information. His propaganda efforts included leaflets that were dropped on the enemy by biplane pilots. Notices
were posted in "friendly" areas, ostensibly directed toward locals but also
meant for the eyes of enemy spies; a good example of this sort of dual-
purpose document is the seemingly panic-stricken broadsides that were
nailed up after the "loss" of the haversack.

We do not know whether RM knew the real architect of the ruses; he
never mentions James D. Belgrave[29], the young officer behind the Chetwode-
Allenby stratagems, and actual author of the Haversack Ruse.

James Dacres Belgrave took his commission at age seventeen and
fought a full year in Europe before he was gassed on the Western Front. He
recuperated painfully, and—assigned to limited duty—was promoted to lieutenant colonel and posted out in July 1917 as GSOI (General Staff Officer,
Intelligence) to Allenby's Egyptian Expeditionary Force.

By then Major Meinertzhagen was pushing forty, with eighteen years'
Army service behind him. He had come to Cairo with an impressive reputation as Jan Christiaan Smuts's recent chief of intelligence in the East Africa
campaign. Young Belgrave was just turning twenty, had no reputation in
Intelligence, and did not come to the theater until sixty days after RM. It
may have galled RM if he saw how, within days, Belgrave achieved the
inside track with Allenby and Chetwode; but Meinertzhagen may not have
been aware of Belgrave at all, because the young man served most of his
duty on Cyprus.

Belgrave outlined his proposals at length, in a typed seven-page
SECRET memo to Allenby. It suggested that a parcel of GHQ documents be
"dropped" where the enemy would find it. He proposed its contents. With a
few modifications, Belgrave's proposed collection of documents is what ended
up in the haversack.[30]

History tells us that the haversack fooled the enemy into reinforcing
the wrong defenses. This history seems based largely on RM's statements
about "the effect of the notebook." Evidently he believed no one would check
his accuracy, and evidently he was correct in that belief even though he makes
several obvious mistakes in his own stories. (Take for example his slip with

dates—he alleges enemy plans and activities starting September 26 were influenced by the dropped haversack. If the haversack wasn't dropped until October 10—two weeks later—how can it have had an influence on the foe?)

RM cites the book *Yildirim*, by Turkish officer Hussein Husni Emir, as the source for his assertion that German commandant Kressenstein "was completely taken in by my notebook."

That's not what *Yildirim* says at all. And RM's statements do not reflect what Kressenstein said or did; quite the reverse.

Yildirim[31] was published two years after the war. It is in Turkish, and has not been published in an English-language edition. RM had access to a copy, because in the 1920s he makes reference to it in his letters to Cyril Falls, Britain's official war historian. *Yildirim* reports the pick-up of the dropped haversack on October 10, 1917. But the rest of RM's version of what the book says—as seen in the "translation" he kindly provided to Cyril Falls—is less than accurate. One discovers this when one tries to backtrack his reference to Gen. Kress von Kressenstein's reliance on "___'s pocket book."

There is no reference to Kressenstein's reliance or to anyone's pocketbook or notebook anywhere in *Yildirim*.[32] What it says is that the satchel contained documents signed by an officer named Weinertshagen [*sic*]—documents that describe British plans to attack Gaza. *Yildirim* describes a bit of confusion at Turkish Army HQ amongst the Turkish and German staffs, caused by everyone's suspicion that "Weinertshagen" did not seem to be an English sort of name. It states that everybody—the Turks as well as German generals Kressenstein and Falkenhayn—suspected the documents might be fakes. Because they couldn't be sure, the Turks and the Germans agreed they had little choice but to ignore the haversack.[33]

Kressenstein later explained:

> The bag contained not only a considerable amount of money and a number of private letters but also a number of interesting papers. Those papers concerned the following matters:
> — The English were postponing their attack until the end of 1917 or the beginning of the next year.
> — The main attack would be directed against the south-western part of Gaza.
> — A combined brigade would land to the north of Gaza.
> — Simultaneously with the attack of the English, the French would land troops on the coast of Syria.
> — The English considered the ground at the German-Turkish left flank [i.e., Beersheba] to be unsuitable for bigger cavalry units. An

action against Beersheba, therefore, would be limited to a feint to induce the Germans to concentrate our forces there, and thus weaken
the Gaza defenses. . . .

The question—whether the loss of the satchel was an attempted
deception by the English or if it was just good luck for the Turks—
caused a great deal of discussion. At the beginning there were many
different opinions. But finally we all agreed that it must be treated as
an attempted deception.

There is an opinion to be found in English and Turkish war literature that I [Kressenstein] was deceived by the satchel of Herr
Meinertzhagen to move my only reserve (the 7th division) behind our
right wing just before the 3rd Battle of Gaza instead of sending it to
Beersheba. This is false. [The English knew they could not begin a
large campaign after the beginning of the rainy season, but]
Meinertzhagen committed the mistake of mentioning in his papers [in
the haversack] that the attack was to be postponed until the end of this
year or the beginning of next year. . . . There could be no doubt that the
attack on Beersheba and Gaza was to begin very soon. Therefore I was
sure the information of the satchel must be dismissed as fake.[34]

The season of cloudbursts and flash floods usually began in mid-to-
late November and made parts of the desert into impassable mud-flats. German Intelligence knew Allenby had to incorporate that fact into his timetable.
It just wouldn't make sense, while German reinforcements continued to
arrive from the north, for the British to sit idly by and consume huge quan-
tities of supplies.

A desert veteran would have known about the impending monsoon
season. RM, the newcomer, apparently did not know about it, and did not
think to ask. So the enemy's decision to ignore the haversack was provoked
by the very documents that were supposed to inspire the opposite decision.

It was just RM's good luck, and that of the Allied armies, that
Kressenstein did not follow his own reasoning to its logical conclusion and
defend Beersheba. Neither the Germans nor the Turks believed Allenby could
move a large force toward Beersheba without being seen in plenty of time to
allow the Turks to send reinforcements down the railway.

No big changes took place in the positioning of German-Turkish forces
during the weeks that led up to Chauvel's attack on Beersheba. A few units
underwent normal rotations, but no significant reinforcements were sent to
Beersheba.[35]

It was an ingenious and heroic effort whether it succeeded or not. Therefore its creator—Belgrave, not Meinertzhagen—deserved recognition.

So did the horseman who actually made the drop.

This portion of the forensic inquiry begins with what appears to be a red herring—the letter allegedly written by RM's sister Mary.

An unsigned copy of the letter is pasted into RM's typescript diaries. Where did this copy come from? RM never explains how he managed to involve his sister (who was in England) in the scheme. Even if she had the highest security clearance (she didn't), how could he have requested such a letter from her, explained precisely what he needed and why he needed it, and then got the letter delivered to him in time for the caper? Letters followed the same route RM himself had followed in getting to Rafah—trains across Europe, ships (RM's own transport ship, the *Transylvania*, was torpedoed and sunk off Italy; he was lucky to survive to cross the Mediterranean into Egypt), horse-wagons in Cairo, motor lorries on hard rubber tires with radiators boiling over at quarter-hour intervals, more trains, even camels. Nothing moved very fast except for telegraph and wireless signals. There was no air mail because—except for German Zeppelins—no aircraft of the time had a range of more than two or three hundred miles.

The scheme itself was not approved until a few weeks before the haversack drop. When it comes to the letter allegedly written by Mary Meinertzhagen, are we left to speculate about such possibilities as jet-powered carrier pigeons?

Another version of the wifely letter, more believable if editorially overblown, can be found in Ferdinand Tuohy's *The Secret Corps*, which became a bestseller in 1920. Tuohy served in Allenby's HQ contemporaneously with RM. Like many journalists he was as much entertainer as reporter, but aside from its tinted prose, what he wrote about the haversack makes more sense than what RM later gave us. Tuohy wrote: "And the letter concerning the first-born—the letter that saved hundreds, possibly thousands, of British lives and went far to giving us Jerusalem, and ultimately a whole country—? Has the little hospital nurse at El Arish, with the girlish handwriting, forgotten all about it?"[36]

A local nurse seems more plausible than a sister thousands of miles away.[37]

But such suppositions prove little. Our search continued.

All extant accounts of the haversack drop place it on October 10,

1917. However, one fragment of an early RM typescript places it on September 12, 1917. We know about this early draft only because he sent a copy to Cyril Falls, who in a 1927 letter quotes the passage back at RM. Then Falls asks about the discrepancies in dates between RM's diary (September) and *Yildirim* (October).

In the pages RM had sent to Cyril Falls, under the September 12 date RM had written:

> A staff officer from G.H.Q. went on patrol towards El Gerheir with a small escort and induced a Turkish patrol to fire on him. . . .
>
> On the 21st September a notice was put up in Desert Mounted Corps Orders stating that a note-book had been lost.[38]

This is the earliest known of RM's written versions of the story. It is altogether different from what appears in his diary typescripts. It relates the haversack ruse matter-of-factly and briefly as an example of the work in which RM and his office-mates were asked to participate. In this surviving early fragment, he does not claim to have invented the ruse, or to have been the horseman who carried the bag.

Sometimes we had to approach the investigation as an exercise in paleontology. Few fragments of the early versions of the RM diaries survive. Where they can be found, each must be examined like a single bone from which an entire fossil skeleton can be rediscovered. In this case, however, we needed not only to extrapolate from the single bone, but actually to use its clues to help us find the rest of the skeleton.

At around the time when RM supplied the fragment of diary to Cyril Falls in 1927, an article appeared in the *Times* to commemorate the tenth anniversary of Allenby's attack on Beersheba. The *Times* article contained a long paragraph that presented in full the haversack story, much as it was to appear in RM's later publications. It appears a principal source for the *Times* article was Richard Meinertzhagen; significantly, the editor of the *Times* was his friend Geoffrey Dawson, who had attended Aysgarth (as had RM) and who turns up on the guest lists of RM's parties.

The hero-worshipful *Times* article goaded a man named Arthur Neate into composing a polite demurral, challenging RM's version of events. It was sent not to the *Times* but to RM himself.

RM preserved Neate's letter by pasting it into his diaries. Tipped in immediately after Cyril Falls's letter questioning the discrepancy in dates, the four-page letter signed "A. C. B. Neate" is hand-written on hotel stationery

(Thierry's Imperial Hotel, Tenby, Wales). Undated, but obviously written within a few days after publication of the *Times* piece, it makes interesting reading:

> Dear Colonel,
>
> You probably don't remember me for the moment, but when I mention Des Corps & Beersheba, you will remember!
>
> You may have seen in the Times of Nov. 1 (or Oct. 31?) the account of the Beersheba operations, & towards the end a mention of the famous satchel; & the operation of dropping it was graphically described but was attributed to you.
>
> Now as you and I—but probably scarcely anyone else knows—I dropped the satchel, & I thought of writing a line to the Times to correct it, but Howard Eyre (sp?) & Bartholomew both were under the impression that it was you who did it. So I am venturing to bother you to tell me what the exact situation was? Were TWO bags dropped one by you & one by me? I see the Times mentions Oct. 10 whereas I dropped the thing on Sept. 12. If there was only one bag dropped, it would be interesting to know how the error crept in.
>
> I am afraid you will think me very small minded for bothering about this, but I have during the last years seen one or two references to this incident, & as nothing I did in the war (or out of it) seems to have been worth recording I should like to be remembered in connexion with this! (Very petty, no doubt.)!
>
> Wombat advised me not to correct the thing in the paper without consulting you as he always was under the impression you performed the operation & it might give rise to an argument. But if I was really the person referred to in this account, perhaps you would not mind correcting the Times account by a line?
>
> Sorry to trouble you with all this.
>
> Yours sincerely,
>
> A.C.B. Neate.[39]

At this point there was obvious disagreement between the two men. Either of them could have been correct.

We looked for Neate, and discovered that he had died in 1976. Then we found Neate's stepdaughter, Katharina Josephine "Karin" Hall, who lives in a village in Kent. The custodian of Arthur Neate's handwritten diary, she allowed us to photocopy the pertinent pages.

Arthur Neate's handwritten understatements explain everything except the identity of the faceless "Wombat":

11th September [1917]

I went over with car to Yeomanry Div with the precious bag for Major Meinertzhagen. Had dinner at Yeoman. & turned in with Robertson.[40]

12th September

Left early with a horse lent me by Robertson & joined myself to a Yeomanry regt. of the 9th Mounted Brigade commanded by a Col. Salt, brother of H. F. Salt. We hacked laboriously over the dry sandy burning country till El Girheir. Saw many Turks moving about but none came near. Dropped the bag near Pt. 730 & returned, trusting all will be well. Returned quite tired.

6th October [1917]

In office in the morning. In the afternoon I went over to GHQ seeing Whitten, Meinertzhagen &c.[41]

That final laconic bit appears unimportant until we notice that the afternoon of October 6 is the time when, RM writes elsewhere, he was busy crash-landing a crippled airplane and rescuing its wounded pilot.[42]

His reply to Neate's letter provoked a second letter from Neate, very proper and respectful, but unmistakably a challenge. It too is bound into the typescript diaries, right after the first. Again hand-written and undated, and on the same hotel letterhead, it reads in part, "Many thanks for your letter, which makes the situation quite clear (except the remarkable credulity of the Turk—how many bags would he have found before smelling a rat?)."

Apparently RM missed its sarcasm.

It seems a key to Neate's modest sense of self-importance that, even though he was breveted Major when he became Chauvel's G.S.O.2 for Intelligence, he persisted in signing his official reports "A. Neate, Capt."[43] Popular with fellow officers, he served postwar assignments with embassies, consulates, and military missions in the Balkans and in the Far East. He worked for the Military Intelligence branch of the diplomatic service. The Army List describes his assignment as "Special Employment"—a euphemism for security and espionage. (A sample job-description from Neate's record is "Military Attaché, Bulgaria, 1922.") He was one of those servants who kept his ear to the wind and his nose to the ground while he "ran" agents in the countries to which he was assigned. He remained observant: in 1930 with C. G. Hancock he co-wrote a book for the Royal Institute of

International Affairs, *The Situation in the Balkans*.[44]

The nature of his work seems to explain his reticence and his long reluctance to pursue the dispute with RM. He occupied a position in which "making a fuss"—the sort that drew attention to oneself—not only was "simply not done" but also could be counterproductive. Neate, unlike Meinertzhagen, was still a serving Intelligence officer in 1927 and if he had published his complaints, he could have counted on his superiors' displeasure. The poor man might have been given the sack. So he wrote privately to RM in 1927 but did not "go public" until nearly thirty years later.

Neate retired from the Army at age fifty-two in 1937, in Singapore, having been mentioned in dispatches (November 28, 1917, for his courage at Beersheba) and having earned the Military Cross, the French War Cross, the Victoria Medal, and the Order of the White Eagle Fifth Class with Swords.[45]

His letter to the editor—his first public statement—appeared in the *Spectator* (London) in 1956, in response to another reader's awed letter about Colonel Meinertzhagen's self-alleged heroics. In the bemused delicacy of Neate's contempt, the painless accuracy with which he punctures the sacred cow, and his quiet reminder of RM's actual rank, he displays a subtlety that probably went over RM's head:

THE HAVERSACK

The story of Major Meinertzhagen's haversack has been told in the popular weeklies (with varying inaccuracy) over the last thirty-five years. . . . Meinertzhagen's was one of two such bags of misleading information which were passed to the Turks in what may seem suspiciously similar circumstances, before the attack on Beersheba on October 31, 1917. The other bag contained a summons to the owner to a C.-in-C.'s conference, minutes of the conference with a map showing movements to the coastal area, a memorandum from Captain Lloyd, MP (later Lord Lloyd), reporting that the country around Beersheba was unsuitable for mounted troops, and a chatty letter from a naval friend who had seen the Turkish right flank from his ship and wished the Army luck in their attack on it. Lastly, some personal correspondence, including a letter from the wife in England complaining of the air-raids on London.

It was dropped in no-man's land, was picked up by a Turkish patrol, who [sic] received a reward, and passed to the German intelligence officer at Beersheba, one Lieutenant Schilling, who thought it was too good to be true; but the Turkish Commander believed it.

How much these two tricks contributed to the final result is anybody's guess, but when the attack was launched at daybreak on October 31 the garrison of the little doll's house town among the sandhills was taken completely by surprise. I can vouch for the above facts, for the bag in question was dropped on September 12, 1917, by —

Yours faithfully,

A. C. B. Neate

late G.S. Intelligence, Desert Mounted Corps

Woolpit, Suffolk.[46]

In 1927 when he found Neate's first quiet confrontation in his post-box, RM might have settled the issue by dropping a line to the *Times*. A moment of generosity, in setting the record straight, might have done him no harm. Now in 1956 he had another opportunity to set things right. Neate was tossing him an olive branch by playing along with RM's silly proposition that there had been more than one satchel-drop. But RM refused the offer. Instead he used the opportunity to enlarge his own mythology.

In his diaries, he typed this annotation beneath one of Neate's pasted-in letters:

"'N' said Sept 12, Notebook Oct. 1, — — 10. See my Army Diary."[47]

This typed notation appears on a page supposedly created in 1927. It refers us to *Army Diary*—which didn't exist until 1960.

It was RM's habit not only to rewrite pages of the diaries but to destroy previous versions of those pages at the same time.[48] In this instance, undaunted by Neate's questions, he rewrote history again:

> In all, three notebooks were dropped, the first on 12 September by Captain A.C.B. Neale [*sic*], but the Turks failed to recover it, the second on 1 October by an Australian officer; this also failed as the Turks never pursued; and my attempt was the third. . . .
>
> In addition to the notebook, several wireless messages were sent daily from 24 September to 31 October, 1917, which hinted at our attack on Beersheba being but another and more comprehensive reconnaissance in that direction, and at General Allenby being absent at Suez from 29 October to 4 November, 1917, during which dates it was natural to presume that no offensive would be commenced. . . .
>
> Many accounts of this episode have been published, most of them inaccurate, claiming that I shot my horse, etc. The utmost secrecy was

maintained at G.H.Q.; Allenby, Dalmeny, Bols, and Guy Dawnay being the only persons besides myself who knew. But, unfortunately, a War Office man visited us soon afterwards and Bols told him of the whole episode, which this War Office man subsequently published in a book.[49] He should have been court-martialed.[50]

Neate recognized the fact that if the enemy doesn't pick up a bag after it is dropped in plain sight of him, one cannot be sure he didn't see it fall. Maybe he saw, and suspected it was booby-trapped. So: how many of these fumbles could the Turks be expected to believe? As Neate pointed out, the Turks and Germans would have had to be utter idiots to accept more than one accidental satchel drop.

By coincidence the first exchanges between Neate and RM occurred in the midst of the 1927 correspondence between Cyril Falls and RM about *Yildirim*. Neate's letter, asking if there had been a second satchel, helped RM solve the problem of the discrepancy in dates about which Falls had inquired. He may have found it hard to believe his luck. He leaped into the loophole.

October 10 was the date when the Turks picked up the haversack. September 12 was the date when Neate dropped the haversack. Therefore— two haversacks, *n'est-ce pas*? (We may speculate why RM added yet a third haversack to his house of cards, along with a notation about October 1, but in the absence of facts this kind of speculation doesn't seem to lead toward a useful destination.)

In fact, however, and in logic, there was only one haversack. How, then, can there be such a discrepancy in dates?

Turkey, in one of the final gasping policy changes by which the dying Ottoman dictatorship tried to drag itself into the modern era, began a process of conversion from the Islamic to the Gregorian calendar in—as it happens—the year 1917. The change-over wasn't completed until a decade later, and at times it led to confusion that was far worse than, say, converting to the euro.

In 1917 the Turks assigned only 306 days to the Islamic year 1330 so as to bring its final day into line with the Gregorian calendar's December 31, 1917.

It requires much patience and luck for any student to look at the date on a Turkish document and decide when (in European calendar terms) it may have been written.[51] There is uncertainty because of the number of leap years counted over the centuries and other abstruse factors. But the Ottoman date of October 10, 1917, coincides more or less with the Gregorian (i.e., British) calendar's September 12, 1917.

Once having stumbled upon this fact, one can confirm it easily enough. For example in *Yildirim*—where the satchel drop takes place on October 12—the Turkish chief of operations then writes this: "In the second half of November the indicators of an imminent British attack had increased. Enemy movements around Gaza increased. The command . . . estimates that the enemy will attack in the direction of Gaza with a great number of its forces."[52]

By "the second half of November" on the British calendar, Allenby's attack was not "imminent." It had already taken place several weeks earlier.

Arthur Neate died in 1976 at the age of ninety-one, having outlived Meinertzhagen by nearly a decade.

We can understand his bashfulness, but why did J. D. Belgrave—author of the haversack scheme and so many other ingenious deceptions—fail to challenge RM's concoctions?

Six months after the fall of Jerusalem, on June 13, 1918, Lt. Col. James Dacres Belgrave was killed in action. He was just twenty-one years of age.[53]

CHAPTER 3
NANDI

Richard's father, Daniel Meinertzhagen, known within the family as "Dee," had been born in London; his great-grandfather, Daniel Meinertzhagen IV, had died in England in 1809; his grandfather, also named Daniel, had been born in 1801 in Bremen, Germany, but had spent most of his life in England. Richard never knew that grandfather, who died nine years before Richard's birth. Daniel Meinertzhagen V had come to London to work with his father in the British offices of the German international merchant banking firm Frederick Huth & Co. In 1833 Daniel V married the boss's daughter Amelia (Manuela Felipa) Huth (1810–1887); in some quarters this may have been looked upon as a marriage of convenience for the two families, but by all accounts the union and their mutual affection were genuine.

RM's émigré grandfather so distinguished himself in the British merchant banking community that by special Act of Parliament in 1837 he was naturalized a British subject.[1]

His first son—Daniel VI, or "Dee," who was to be Richard's father—was born in 1842. Dee went up to Oxford (Oriel College) and in due course succeeded to the senior partnership in Frederick Huth & Co., which his father had helped build into one of the era's two major Anglo-German merchant banking firms, the other being Rothschild's. The Meinertzhagens, unlike the Rothschilds, were not Jewish. This fact gave them a social advantage in Victorian England.

Dee was a good-looking man who, as if in a Galsworthy novel, was injured in a horse-riding accident while visiting the Potter family at their grand estate, and was nursed back toward health by the young Georgina Potter. As his health recovered, a romance grew between them and the two were married on September 11, 1873, shortly after Dee had been made a full partner in the family-owned Frederick Huth bank.[2]

Georgina Potter was the granddaughter of Sir Richard Potter and his wife the former Mary Seddon, who was a Hebrew scholar and noted eccentric. Georgina was one of nine Potter sisters, nearly all of whom were to achieve exceptional distinction; they were the nieces of *Peter Rabbit* author Beatrix Potter.[3]

It is confirmed by several observers that Georgina's marriage to Dee seems to have been impulsive and ill-considered. From the beginning they were united by tensions and disagreements.

Richard was their third child and second son. His elder brother Dan (Daniel Meinertzhagen VII) was two and a half years Richard's senior. Their sister Barbara ("Bardie") was born between the two boys. Dee spent most of his time up in London amid club companions and unattached ladies. On the occasions when Dee came out to the country he seems to have stayed just long enough to impregnate Georgie again. The first three children were succeeded by seven more—five girls and two boys, in mixed order of birth. The last of the ten children, Betty (Georgina Elisabeth), was born in 1892.

The parental couple would prove socially successful, but Dee was more of a womanizer than a businessman: he kept the bank afloat but barely managed to steer a moderate course because he preferred devoting himself to sporting pursuits. He spent most of his time in London, but moved Georgina and the first of her children to a country estate where she felt isolated and abandoned. The marriage came to be characterized by long absences punctuated by tense quarrels.

Dee was capable and socially impressive but he also was distant and conventional. Georgie, already sharp-tongued, impatient, and adroit, became sardonic and bitter. The production of ten children in rapid succession did not draw her closer to her husband. Out of irritation she smoked incessantly. She did not like infants—they bored her—and the nursery upbringing of all ten children took place mainly under the direction of Sarah Peacock, who had been Georgie's nanny in the Potter household and had become as much a friend as a servant. RM seems to have liked her but does not mention her very much.

For children of wealth and position in Victoria's England, formal education was a process filled with contradictions. Either the children were schooled in the isolated comfort of their own homes by tutors and governesses, or they were sent away into the stark (sometimes terrifying) imprisonment of feudally organized boarding schools. For the boys, the latter were expected to provide sufficient grounding in classics and literacy to fulfill the strict entrance requirements of Eton, Harrow, and the other prestigious public schools, which trained new generations to assume the mantles of leadership in upper-class society and government. For the girls, early schooling was a preparation for brief confinement in finishing schools, which were expected to polish their charms and prepare them for the March-to-July social season of parties, dinners, and dances, for being presented at court, for "coming out" with their debuts, for marriage, for motherhood, and for proper behavior as high-ranking wives, hostesses, and genteel piano-tickling entertainers. For women of the upper middle class there were very few options: they dressed up, they went riding, they danced, they distributed their calling cards, they traveled, they flirted, they sought suitable husbands in a conscribed world where romantic love was a wonderful thing so long as its object was a person of the right sort, the right class, and the right wealth.[4]

As the Meinertzhagen girls grew into their articulate childhoods, Georgie took more interest in them—later the older girls were to become her best friends—but she had little time or attention to spare for any of her four sons other than Dan, the eldest. To her, Richard and his two younger brothers were untrustworthy ruffians, and their budding masculinity probably reminded her of what she saw as her husband's outstanding traits—indifference and irresponsibility.

Richard was born on Sunday, March 3, 1878, at N[o.] 10 Rutland Gate in London's borough of Kensington.[5] Victoria reigned, Benjamin Disraeli was prime minister, and it was said the sun never set on the British empire.

The boy's mother initially named him Oliver (it is the name on his birth certificate) but his father had not been consulted about this and became livid because he believed his wife had chosen the name to honor Oliver Cromwell, whom Dee disdained as a traitor. Dee wanted to name the boy Harry (Henry)—but Georgina, in turn, didn't like the royalist ring of that. In the end they compromised on Richard, naming him after Georgina's father Richard Potter.[6]

Several family members—including Georgina's sister, the noted Socialist leader Beatrice Webb (a prolific diarist)—later attested to Georgina's chronic unhappiness with her marriage to Dee. Richard himself wrote, many years later: "My father and mother spent their honeymoon partly in Paris and partly in the Black Forest. It was not altogether a happy one, for mother, in her puritan chastity, could not respond to father's exuberance. In Paris my father insisted on buying for my mother most unsuitable hats."[7]

Richard's brother Dan, the eldest son, held the position of greatest esteem in the eyes of his parents and of society. Many thought him an outstanding lad who possessed an abundance of excellences. Dee and Georgie doted on him. Richard, the second son, suffered by comparison. His father thought him tolerable but truant, and inadequate. His mother—he was convinced—hated him.

When Richard was seven his parents moved the growing family into a twelfth-century abbey at Mottisfont in Hampshire's Test Valley. The huge, handsome pile of a house (today preserved as part of Britain's National Trust) is the sort of mansion often used as a movie or television set to impress audiences for historical dramas and BBC mini-series. During Richard's youth, Mottisfont was the manor of a two thousand–acre estate that was tended by three hundred servants and tenants, all of them supported by Dee for a dozen years. The park was a wonderland for a young boy. The three square miles of property included lavish meadows and a wood large enough for good shooting. Several miles of the River Test, noted for the excellence of its trout-fishing, meandered through the property. Wildlife was abundant in the varied landscape. The Meinertzhagens employed several gamekeepers and wardens.

The house, only partly remodeled, was devoid of modern conveniences. It was unheated. Some of its plumbing had been updated a bit but the luxuries of life at Mottisfont Abbey in the 1880s and 1890s were more than offset by the primitive discomforts. These did not matter to the boys, who thrived on them, but they seem to have driven Georgina into a quagmire of resentment. She felt imprisoned in the abbey, where she was obliged to look after the huge property and her growing brood.

Dan and Richard learned to hunt at Mottisfont. They became keen bird-watchers as well, and would go on long country strolls with the famed philosopher Herbert Spencer, their mother's friend, who taught them to "observe, record and explain."[8]

Or so Richard later maintained. It may be true, but he writes of having met so many famous people during his childhood that one's capacity for belief becomes a bit strained. He wrote, for example, that both Thomas Huxley and Charles Darwin were quite fond of him, and that Darwin dandled Richard on his knee. Darwin was a first cousin to Georgie's friend Herbert Spencer, but nonetheless Richard's declarations seem open to question, since he was barely four years old when Darwin died on April 19, 1882, of a heart attack that was not his first. For several years failing health had limited his excursions; it prevented him from accepting the honorary degree that Oxford University wished to confer on him in 1877—several months prior to Richard's birth—and one wonders whether he would have traveled around England to visit acquaintances who'd never so much as exchanged a letter with him. (The list of correspondents in the voluminous Darwin Papers includes no Meinertzhagens, Huths or Potters.)

A darker shadow over Richard's statements about Darwin is cast by the evidence of a mahogany pipe that RM gave, with some ceremony, to the prestigious Linnean Society in 1958. He said it was Darwin's pipe, and still reeked of Darwin's tobacco. He said its stem was made of the tibia of an albatross. Thus labeled, it stood on display at the foot of the Linnean's staircase for five decades before Society member Pat Morris noticed something suspicious about the pipe. The proportions of the stem, Morris felt, made it "an improbable ratio for a tibia. It also implies an albatross that once stood about two meters high (on rather spindly legs!). This has prompted closer inspection."

After closer examination, Morris concluded: "The silver hallmarks on the stem of the bowl indicate manufacture in Birmingham in 1928."

The astute observer wondered how it was that Darwin's pipe had been manufactured forty-six years after Darwin's death. "Thus it appears that Darwin's pipe can be added to the rapidly lengthening list of bogus specimens associated with the former doyen of British ornithology and Master Spy. . . . It seems incredible that Richard Meinertzhagen's enormous assortment of fakes and frauds should have been flaunted so blatantly before his peers, and that they should have escaped notice for so long. He must be laughing in his grave."[9]

Darwin, Huxley, Cecil Rhodes, Kaiser Wilhelm, Princess Beatrice, future generals French, Haig, and Allenby, H. G. Wells, and several other celebrities of the era are among those RM professes to have met in the years before he was commissioned in his army regiment in 1899. It is possible he met them all; it is possible he met very few of them. Our chief obstacle to an understanding of his childhood is that what we know of it comes largely from his own later writings. Written records regarding nineteenth century children tend to be scarce—it was an era when they were expected to be seen but not heard—but it is true that Herbert Spencer and Thomas Huxley did drop in on Georgie now and then. She hosted soirees and dinner parties, to escape the crushing loneliness of her social isolation; her sisters often came. But the rules of the day would have kept small children at a distance from visitors.

The celebrities who probably saw young Dick more often than any others, and whose attitudes he later decried, were the noted suffrage-socialists Sidney and Beatrice Webb—but that was because Beatrice was Georgie's sister (RM's aunt). In her diaries of the 1930s Beatrice gives us several telling analyses of the grown-up Richard Meinertzhagen, but during his childhood she mentions him only once or twice, in passages that refer not specifically to him, but rather to Georgina's attitudes toward her children.

In the 1880s the very young Richard was sent as a boarding student to Aysgarth in the north of England. Clearly he enjoyed the school, and not just because it gave him an escape from the sour disapprovals he says he suffered in his mother's bailiwick. Aysgarth was a rough-and-tumble academy with endless wild acres in which he was able to hunt birds, learn self-reliance, and improve his hunting skills. In later years he kept returning to its acres and became a friend to its headmaster George Brooksbank—in the 1920s they would go fishing together.

When brother Dan completed his studies at Aysgarth and entered school at Harrow, the parents decided Richard was too young and too wild to be allowed to remain by himself (without supervision by his brother) in the rough hinterlands of the north. They enrolled him in an institute closer to home—Fonthill, a boarding school in Sussex run by two brothers who, Richard later alleged, were sadistic brutes. He said he was beaten and sexually molested by the schoolmasters when he was a boy of nine and ten.

He sought the protection of his mother but she responded with typical disapproval: if the masters had beaten Richard he must have done something to deserve a beating.[10]

All this may have happened. Being flogged, bashed about, and sexually assaulted by schoolmasters or by fellow pupils were experiences that occurred with frightening frequency in single-sex Victorian boarding schools—but they were not the sort of matters that azure-blooded English gentlemen confided to their diaries. We must note that RM's allegations of molestation did not appear until three-quarters of a century later, with the publication in 1964 of his *Diary of a Black Sheep*. By that time child-abuse had become a hot topic, spurred by the bestselling armchair psychiatrics of Havelock Ellis and the popular primers for child-rearing parents that were written by Dr. Benjamin Spock.[11]

Theorizing about his probable exposure to the popular literature of the 1950s cannot authenticate or disprove RM's declarations that he was abused by schoolmasters in the 1890s. Until the 1950s, however, he was private and secretive most of the time. He wrote about events he observed, and about matters theoretical, superficial, public, or imaginary, but he rarely expressed intimate feelings. He readily expressed admiration, indignation, dislike, amusement or anger, and occasionally a polite sort of affection, but he hardly ever revealed a hint of a sexual or intimate thought. There is the occasional exception, in what he describes as his dreams. These often seem to concern infants or young children. In one case it is not quite clear whether he is describing a dream or an alleged real event when he writes that in Africa he fell hopelessly in love with a gorgeous, young, white-robed French nun named Cecilia who happened to ride by on a white donkey while RM was bathing naked in Africa's Voi River.[12] Such outlandish fantasies aside, he seems characterized by a reticence typical of one groomed to be a gentleman in Victorian England.

It gives us pause, then, when we are confronted by his abrupt willingness in the 1960s to confide in us about childhood battery and molestation that he may or may not have endured seventy years earlier.

There are obvious competitive parallels between RM's fantasies and some of the published writings about T. E. Lawrence. Late in life RM liked to tell a story about "allowing himself to be captured by the Turks in World War I"[13]—an adventure that does not turn up in his diaries, perhaps because it's so similar to Lawrence's actual experience at Deraa. Controversy about the significance of the latter episode (in which Lawrence claimed to have been beaten, and perhaps enjoyed being beaten, by sadistic Turkish officers) erupted after the publication of Richard Aldington's bestselling 1955 exposé *Lawrence of Arabia*—a book RM read[14] prior to composing his own "diary" passages about an unrecognizably effeminate T. E. Lawrence.[15]

All this could provide us with an entryway to the psyche of a boy who may have been doubly traumatized, first by abuse and molestation at Fonthill and then by his mother's alleged reaction when he sought her protection. But did any of it happen? We don't know.

In 1891 Richard went up to the prestigious halls of Harrow, where his brother Dan was an upperclassman.

Education of boys in the eminent public schools of England emphasized a traditional ethos based on Greek, Latin, and Christian classics. These gave tone to the *fin de siècle* mood, as did the glamorizing of heroic manliness in stirring tales of adventure written by Sir Walter Scott, H. Rider Haggard, G. A. Henty, and Rudyard Kipling. Young Dick was exposed to these and other popular storytellers but he seldom expressed great fondness for greater books. He seems to have shunned any temptation to win prizes for scholarship. He does admit, though, that he "awakened to the glorious magnificence of the British Empire"[16] while at Harrow, and writes that in December 1894 he attended a dinner where the honored guest, visiting from Africa, was Cecil Rhodes, founder of Rhodesia and of the De Beers diamond empire and sometime governor of the Cape Colony (and soon to be the instigator of the final and most ferocious Boer War). RM reported that he was enthralled by the meeting, during which Rhodes allegedly gave the boy generous dollops of worldly and imperial advice.

It may or may not be true that he was taken under the wing of Cecil

Rhodes. It is unquestionable, however, that he did meet Lord Walter Rothschild when the latter came to Harrow to give a lecture on the subject of ornithology. Lord Walter's brother Charles —another naturalist in train- ing—was at Harrow during the four years of RM's term there.

Lord Rothschild was probably the best-known bird expert of his time. He endowed and built the bird museum at Tring, which still draws scien- tists from all over the world; he gave it, along with a large portion of his collections, to the British Museum, and there is no doubt that the two young Meinertzhagens became his proud protégés. This is true not only because RM says so but also because documents from Tring and from the British Museum attest to it. RM was to become an in-law of the Rothschilds, and years later it was Lord Walter who interceded with the directors to have RM reinstated after the Museum barred him for stealing.

Aside from encounters with the famous or infamous, RM's interests lay out of doors. He seized every chance to trek into untamed country. He was fascinated by the variety and behavior of wildlife of all sorts, and through- out his long life remained far more interested in the wing structure of Cooper's hawk[17] than in Caesar's *Gallic Wars* or Chaucer's *Canterbury Tales*.

Still, despite his admitted indifference toward academic work, he ap- plied supreme concentration and completed six years' worth of studies at Harrow in four years' time. By 1895 he had shot up to his full height of six feet four inches, was sharing a room with Dan, and had caught up with his brother's form.

His accomplishment in having completed six years' studies at Harrow in a span of four years (not three, as some would have it) seems to have been given little shrift by students of his life, but the achievement was ex- traordinary and would have been so even for an outstanding scholar. What lingers from this smidgen of the record is a recognition of the single- mindedness and hard work with which he was able to devote himself to a goal, especially when the goal was self-appointed. He set out to telescope six years into four and he did it. He was not ordered to do it, nor asked to do it, nor were any wheels greased by his elders. Both parents seem to have paid scant attention to their second son's unique accomplishment at Har- row. Dan was the heir; Dick was the spare. In these pursuits Richard seems to have been driven more ruthlessly by his own inner compulsions than by any sense of what others might expect of him.

The two boys' terms in Harrow overlapped that of the wild, red-headed, and eccentric Winston S. Churchill. RM subsequently recalled Churchill as an ill-mannered, bumptious youth who once shouldered young Dick off a curb for some later-forgotten effrontery. Other than that the two boys had little contact; Churchill was an upperclassman when Richard first arrived, and just a year later Churchill moved on.[18] But nearly thirty years later Churchill would place RM in a key position on his staff.

Richard was a powerful athlete. Aside from polo, however, his temperament prevented him from participating in team sports. Always a loner, he boxed, swam, and hunted.

He enjoyed his seasons at Harrow; he was more repressed at home, during holidays, when his mother criticized him while his father remained undemonstrative and usually absent, although occasionally he could be distantly thoughtful: when Dick was fourteen he received from his father the gift of a lifetime subscription to the *Times*.

In 1895, with reluctance, he obeyed his father and set to work as a clerk in the family bank. After a bit less than a year of what he regarded as punitive confinement, he was sent (or persuaded his father to allow him to go) to the Continent in 1896. He was eighteen years old. The assignment took him far from parental disapproval.

During nine or ten months in Cologne and Bremen he missed the company of his brother Dan but enjoyed visiting his cousins and their high-spirited young friends. He set about learning the German language and the trade secrets of international banking. He was moderately successful with his linguistic pursuits but hopelessly uninterested in anything that had to do with finance. He spent much of his time hunting in the famous German forests and carousing with young cousins and friends.

He returned to England in the spring of 1897—back to work in the hated office. But he soon managed to secure his father's dubious approval to join a territorial militia called the Hampshire Yeomanry. This was a reserve-guard organization whose colonel lived near the family home at Mottisfont. One of the officer-neighbors, with whom Richard reinforced an already established family friendship, was Maj. Hermann Le Roy-Lewis. The friendship between Le Roy-Lewis and Dee may have tipped the latter toward allowing his second son to join, but by this time Dee was becoming resigned to his second son's vast lack of interest in the family business.

Richard does not seem to have written about Major Le Roy-Lewis's daughter Armorel until a few years later, but she was to become his wife in 1911 and their personal relationship may have begun to develop in the 1890s.

The Hampshire Yeomanry trained weekend soldiers. Some saw it as a stepping stone to a commission in the army proper; others used it to improve their social and business contacts. For the latter reason Richard felt his father would not object, but it was the former goal that attracted his own motivations. In an era of empire and exploration he felt the army could be as good a ticket to discoveries in the natural sciences as any university degree—and he would much rather be in the field studying nature than in a university reading about it.

By 1897 his brother Dan was a brilliant and spirited young man. Both parents knew Dan would carry the Meinertzhagen-Huth bank, and the family, into the new century with distinction and honor. No doubt in due course he would be knighted; he might even be made a peer.

Records of this period are sparse, and Richard's own accounts come into fierce conflict with each other. In the 1940s he wrote, intending this for publication, that in June 1897 he went trekking into Lapland on a camping-birding expedition.[19] In the same document he wrote that his brother Dan had gone into Lapland a year later, in 1898. Perhaps we are meant to infer that brother Dan was copying Richard's trail-blazing pioneer work. In fact, it was Dan who went north through Scandinavia into Lapland in 1897. Richard did not go there until many years later; in 1897 he was at work in the bank in London.

Georgina arranged for the publication of Dan's journal of the trip and the birds observed in Scandinavia; that book came out in 1899.[20] Richard is not mentioned in it.

Toward the end of 1897 Dan went across to Germany to refresh his European languages and cement the banking relationship with the Continental branch of the family. Abruptly, he became ill with appendicitis. A telegram about Dan's illness reached his father's office and the elder Meinertzhagen boarded the first boat-train to join his son in Germany, but by the time Dee reached Bremen on Sunday, February 13, 1898, young Dan— suddenly, shockingly—had died of septic infection.

Dan was just twenty-two. The tragedy of his death was an extreme blow to the family. They all adored him—none more than Richard, who had relied on Dan to be not only brother but helmsman, compass, and anchor. Even at the worst of times, when Dick's rebelliousness had turned all the rest of them against him, Dan had been there to mediate for him, to speak up in his behalf, to soothe parental tempers.

(Throughout his life RM expressed close affection and high regard toward the memory of his older brother. His clumsy later attempt to purloin credit for the Lapland expedition suggests this relationship may have been shaded by envy. Richard was to become an oft-published authority on birds but Dan had got there ahead of him—first to publish—and may have been the brighter birdman. The celebrated ornithologist Richard Bowdler Sharpe wrote, "Of all the young naturalists whom I have known, Dan Meinertzhagen was certainly one of the most promising, and his early death was a real misfortune for ornithological science."[21] Thus, as with many other aspects of RM's life, we see a bond that seems to have been genuine but that may demand reexamination if more information surfaces.)

Suddenly Richard, at nineteen, was the eldest son.

He knew two things about himself, and all who knew him seem to agree on these points. One was that he could not see himself falling into line as a banker (and he certainly would have made a dreadful one). The other was that young Dick could face the wild things of the world much more easily than he could face up to his mother and father.

In an attempt to prepare the lad, his father apprenticed him to the brokerage house Milbank and Company in Threadneedle Street. His father saw to it that influential friends' trades—and their lucrative commissions— were passed Richard's way.[22] But none of this ignited the young man's fires. He went through the motions of filial obedience but applied his energy to the horse-riding drills and saber tactics that came with his weekend subaltern's commission in the Yeomanry.

To the extent she offered any share of herself, Georgina Potter Meinertzhagen gave it to her sisters and her eldest son (the deceased Dan), and on occasion to her daughters. None of the remaining three sons—Richard, Fritz, Louis—seems to have felt close to her. Of those three, only Louis, the youngest (1887–1941), was to end up with anything like a normal family life, with a lifelong marriage to the former Gwynedd Llewellyn and four children, all of whom grew up to compete successfully in life, including Luke the banker and Sir Peter the financier.

Fritz (George Frederick Meinertzhagen, 1881–1962), the third of the four sons, studied medicine and flunked out, went off to South Africa to get rich in the mines, failed at that too, returned to London and lived from hand to mouth, espousing communism.

Great-nephew Nick adds, "It was an age when one was expected to be 'different,' and everyone expected and tolerated the most amazing eccentricities."[23] He refers, one may assume, to people of a certain class. One doubts the local constable or greengrocer would have been tolerated very long if he had behaved like a Meinertzhagen.

If it sometimes seems RM was related, by blood or marriage, to nearly everyone of high station in England, it is to a surprising extent true. Wealthy couples who could afford to raise large broods tended to give birth to them, and—as high society was still relatively small in numbers—these offspring tended to marry within the tribe, or sometimes even within the clan. It is possible to trace multiple intermarriages between the Meinertzhagens and the Crippses, the Rothschilds, and others. One contributor to the research for this book, Hermione Hobhouse, is related to the Meinertzhagens both through her father (a descendant of the Potters) and through her mother (the Huths). Richard Meinertzhagen's grandparents may have been immigrants from Germany but his mother was one of nine wealthy British sisters who among them gave birth to more than fifty children; Richard's father was one of eleven English-born children—three boys, eight girls[24]—who in turn became parents to scores of children. In all, Richard had nearly a hundred first cousins. Add in uncles, aunts, nieces, nephews, and second cousins, and the extended-family list of those who were directly related to RM and alive during his lifetime approaches a thousand names.

If one expands the field to include in-laws, business partners, and military-professional alliances, it encompasses cross-connections among virtually all members of the burgeoning upper class in Britain's post-Industrial Revolution period of mercantile empire. Some of RM's Tory cronies might have been the last to admit it, but the Age of Empire had brought with it a severe leveling-up of social rankings, so that wealthy and accomplished commoners no longer were kept at arm's length from members of the titled aristocracy. Those lines blurred as an unprecedented flood of baronetcies and life peerages flowed forth from Buckingham Palace, and the great landed estates of impoverished aristocrats were bought by fast-rising entrepreneurs, some of whom were given lordly titles of their own.

Richard's uncle Ernest became a stamp-collecting chum of King George V; Richard's nephew Peter was to become Sir Peter Meinertzhagen, director of the Bank of England and founding CEO of the Commonwealth Fund; Richard's cousin Teresa Mayor became Lady Rothschild (wife of Lord Victor Rothschild, who was the son of RM's schoolmate Charles Rothschild). The number of members of the House of Lords who were related to or socially acquainted with "Dick" Meinertzhagen is startling.

Young Dan's death had cowed both parents. It depressed and distracted Georgina so much that she insisted on giving up the lease on Mottisfont Abbey; the vast estate reminded her of Dan. Her husband objected, but he too was subdued by grief—he hadn't the will to fight her—and it wasn't his home so much as hers.

Richard, who adored the place, begged them not to give it up, but they turned a deaf ear to him (typically, or so he felt).

For the rest of his life he continued to think of Mottisfont as his home. He made friends with its subsequent occupants and managed to get himself invited back to stay, frequently and sometimes at length.

While the family packed to move out, Richard obtained permission from his distracted father to take the examinations for a commission in the British Army's celebrated City of London regiment, the Royal Fusiliers— favored for their sons by bankers, brokers, and businessmen.

After officers' training at Aldershot, young RM was gazetted second lieutenant in the Royal Fusiliers on January 18, 1899.[25]

Just four days earlier, he said, he had gone down to Southampton to see Cecil Rhodes off on a ship to South Africa. Shaking his hand, Rhodes invited him—not for the first time—to come out to Africa.[26] RM's recollection here is incorrect, since Rhodes was not departing for Africa; Rhodes in fact was arriving in Southhampton, from Africa, on January 14, 1899.[27] It seems odd that he should have asked the youth to accompany him on a voyage he was not making. What seems more likely is that RM's recollection of the event may have been befogged by the many years that elapsed before he wrote about it.

RM was twenty-one. It was in that year, 1899, when he began regularly to keep a diary.

It also was the year in which officialdom began regularly to keep records of his activities as a serving officer and as a citizen.

These two sets of documents are in frequent disagreement.

On February 23, 1899, he embarks from England, a green subaltern, to join a battalion of his regiment in India. It is his first assignment and the beginning of a twenty-five-year military career.

Six weeks elapse, for reasons probably attributable to a miniaturized version of the traditional Grand Tour,[28] before he lands at Port Said and prepares to thread the Suez Canal. Stepping ashore in his smartly pressed uniform, every inch the proper Englishman of his well-born class, he pronounces the city disgusting, immoral, and debauched.

One may picture him plunging ahead with his colonial officer's stride, a tall man with one arm swinging high, the other crook'd stiffly over a tube-rolled map clamped under the bicep.

He will claim, later, that in a crowded street he encounters a little English girl, perhaps twelve years old and clearly afraid. She has been enslaved by an Egyptian harridan, the foul-tempered owner of a brothel. RM resolves to rescue the child: she is innocent and English. He enlists the aid of a pair of policemen—reluctant locals—and using them for distraction he dodges furious crowds of ruffians, scoops up the child, and makes a hair's-breadth escape through mobs and alleys, with savage murderers in hot pursuit.

He makes sure the little girl is safe in the custody of the British consul and the consul's wife before he writes an indignant letter reporting the incident to British Viceroy Lord Cromer in Cairo. Only then does he embark for his next port of call.[29]

That story, like many other little adventures, might be true, given the era and his personality. No historian seems to have taken the trouble to investigate it. That may be because it can be so difficult (when it is possible at all) to prove a negative, especially when it concerns an event that appears to be of no historical significance. In this instance, however, there is abundant evidence to show what did not happen, for the consul and his child-care problems are a conspicuous part of the public record. The consular correspondence for April and May 1899 is notable for the scrupulous detail in which it records each case. The conscientious consul, D. A. Cameron, even takes down in detail the complaints of an unfortunate Maltese who has run out of funds—a case that wouldn't merit a mention in the files of most consulates at all, since the problems of British subjects "of colonial birth" were not matters of high priority.

Another case of Cameron's is that of a Scotsman whose friend in Airdrie offers to send money if the consul will be so good as to redeem his friend's gold watch from a Port Said pawn shop for sixteen pounds sterling. Cameron dutifully agrees to help, provided the Scotsman will pay an additional pound to cover postal costs.

Those two instances are typical of Cameron's scrupulous record-keeping for the period when RM was ashore in Port Said.

In the same records, and in Cameron's contemporaneous letter to Lord Cromer, he makes no mention of a British lieutenant or of a rescued English girl. He reveals that his wife is ill and asks for help because it's difficult for him to carry on with his consular duties and at the same time handle the full-time job of looking after his three children while deprived of his wife's help.

Cameron clearly is a man to whom children are important.

The correspondence for the year 1899 to and from the consulate in Port Said, and to and from the Viceroy, has been preserved in London's Public Records Office.[30] No mention of Meinertzhagen appears in the consul's files or in those of the Viceroy from 1899. No newspaper of the time saw fit to print the heroic human-interest item, and none of RM's fellow soldiers in the course of the ensuing twenty-five years seems to have been aware of it.

If a brave British officer rescued an English child in a mêlée that involved police officers and pursuit in the streets, and if he then entrusted her to the protection of consul Cameron and his ailing wife and their over-crowded nursery—if all this occurred and then was *not* recorded in any of the correspondence or files or news releases, then of course RM's tale may well be true.

If it is not true, it becomes an instructive early example of what was to become a fabulous pattern of retrospective creativity.

In May 1899 Lieutenant Meinertzhagen lands in Bombay and makes his way to Nasirabad where he reports to the temporary headquarters of his assigned unit: First Battalion, Royal Fusiliers (City of London Regiment). It is a bleak garrison on a hill in Rajputana in the west of India—an arid dusty elevation on the edge of the Thar Desert.

According to RM, his disappointment is immediate. He meets his fellow junior officers and finds them wanting. They're boors, cads, bullies, and idiots.[31]

He seeks distractions and finds one when his uncle and godfather Ernest,[32] the most indulgent of his relatives, sends Richard a gift of money to buy whatever he should like to acquire. His choice is an elephant—a female named Archibald. On board the misnamed elephant, Richard and his mahout hunt birds around Nasirabad. From this elevated position, the diarist describes how he bags braces of *chinkara* and sand grouse; he stuffs them and adds them to his growing collection of exotic birds.

One day he loses track of time. He is exercising the elephant when he realizes he's late for daily parade. Anxious, he points Archibald toward the distant parade ground and urges the elephant to make all possible speed.

(One of many pursuits that will occupy RM for years is the measuring of speeds attained by various creatures. He later will publish an improbable treatise on how he measured the speed of an attacking black mamba snake by inducing it to strike at an African tribesman, whose opinion of the experiment remains unrecorded.[33] As it happens, RM's mamba seems to be in a dead heat with his elephant—both, according to the noted naturalist, can make a smart seven miles per hour when goaded. Unfortunately for RM's repute, after his death scientifically controlled tests will demonstrate that a healthy elephant can make twenty-five miles per hour and that the black mamba can slither and strike at about twenty miles per hour.[34])

As Archibald thunders toward the parade ground, a sample of RM's writing illustrates the flavor with which he will charm so many readers:

> Off we went at an amble which nearly shook me off [the elephant], with my sword and everything swinging round my legs; the nearer we got to the parade ground the faster went Archibald.
>
> I had intended dismounting near the guardroom where I should not be seen, but nothing would stop Archibald and she took me right on to the Parade Ground where to my horror I saw the battalion falling in.
>
> The mahout shouted, but it only made Archibald go faster. By the time I was in the centre of the parade ground the battalion was fallen in, in line. Capt. Johnson, the adjutant, who was mounted, came galloping towards us trying to head us off but his horse shied at Archibald and off came the adjutant and was almost trampled on.
>
> Archibald headed straight for the centre of the battalion, which broke ranks in confusion, with the sergeant-major shouting to them to keep steady as though an enemy was charging them.
>
> We crashed right through and then fortunately Archibald was prevailed on to stop, having done as much damage as she could.
>
> I felt like disappearing somewhere and hiding, but Herbert, second-in-command, rode up to me, ordered me back to my bungalow and to attend Orderly Room at 9 A.M.
>
> So I walked home followed by a penitent Archibald; I did not dare appear at breakfast.[35]

Lieutenant Meinertzhagen is given a loud dressing-down and is forbidden to ride the elephant while in uniform. (Cf. Groucho Marx—what *was* the elephant doing in his uniform?)

Soon after, he reports having ridden his pony out on a fox hunt behind a pack of dogs. He writes that he just happened to jump his horse over a wall with the pack in full cry, and—not realizing quite where he was— speared the fox only to realize that both he and the dead fox were right on the colonel's lawn. His kill had taken place in front of the colonel. He adds, "What fussy old things colonels are."[36]

In the same pages he declares that he used a cocked revolver to threaten a senior officer who made fun of him, and then writes how he kicked the colonel's camel driver.

Any of these could have been a court-martial offense, but none of the incidents is mentioned in official records.

These stories, with their narrator poking fun at himself, are typical of RM's capacity to captivate—a quality that endeared him to historians and biographers.

In a book of a few hundred pages it is not possible to examine every statement in the long diaries, and few readers would have the patience to follow such an examination. Neither the wild ride aboard Archibald nor the rescue or non-rescue in Port Said of a little English girl is an episode of historic importance; the two have a place in this account because they typify the amusing, heroic, and/or unlikely tales that pepper the RM version of the RM life. But from here on we must confine this report to a summary of the provable life and of those incidents that show new facets of his character, or are of consequence beyond the anecdotal.

The legend made for a wild ride. The truth makes for an even wilder ride.

In India at the turn of the century RM mastered the traditional test of manhood—big-game hunting. It was an era when one way to prove machismo was a with a photograph of oneself, rifle in hand, standing with one boot on the neck of a vanquished tiger. In that context RM would seem to be among the manliest of all Victorians. His bag—daily, weekly, monthly—is tallied in detailed catalogues in the typescripts at Oxford. He describes some of his hunts in gruesome detail, with well-drafted maps and drawings.

In 1900 he came down with acute enteric fever and was sent home to England on sick leave. He visited his family, renewed friendships, and regained his health by year's end. Outward bound again, he passed through Aden on January 24, 1901. There he learned about the recent death of Queen Victoria.

His battalion had been transferred to Burma. He rejoined it in February at Mandalay—a spot deemed something of a sybaritic playground for young British officers. RM regarded the transfer as good for him (lots of new animals and birds) but not for the battalion, which he viewed as next to incompetent in its out-of-date condition under senior officers who hadn't learned a thing since Agincourt.[37] This appraisal might have been useful if he had mentioned it to his superiors but there is no record outside his diaries of his having uttered it at the time.

After his return from England he soon was ordered to an individual posting in Madras, again for convalescent purposes—his fevers had recurred. He set sail from Rangoon on March 22, 1901 and arrived at Wellington in the Nilgiri Hills of southern India in April, where the Durham Light Infantry station provided him with quarters, and during his recovery he had a good deal of time on his hands.

Despite his illnesses, much of his first tour of service in India was eventful because his adventurous spirit was easily bored. Before long he took to recording mock prayers in which he asked the Heavenly Father to grant him a nice little war.[38] His prayers were not answered—he never engaged in warfare in India—but he seems to have done quite a bit of hunting and birdwatching. It was at Wellington that RM first met Hatter Bailey, a soon-to-be-famous spy who at the time had just begun his service (in one of the Sikh regiments of the Indian Army[39]). Like Harry St. John Philby, Bailey was to become an important figure in RM's life, although he rarely appears in the journals.

Frederick Marshman "Hatter" Bailey (1882–1967) was to become well known as a natural scientist. (Various insects and flowering plants are named after him.) He earned a reputation for sometimes wild behavior. He was to be one of the first Englishmen to explore Tibet (1903), partly for scientific reasons but also to spy on spies—specifically to make contact with, and report back on, the activities of Russian agents who had made their way into Tibet at the time. When Bailey returned to England he recorded his adventures as a secret agent in his book *Mission to Tashkent*, publication of which then was held back under authority of the Official Secrets Act. When it finally reached the bookshops—at a time when he had a full new generation's adventures under his belt—it became a bestseller.

RM and Bailey struck up an immediate friendship at the Durham Station in 1901, when Bailey was just eighteen years old. The friendship lasted several decades. From some of the correspondence one may infer that RM envied the younger man and sometimes sought to emulate him.

Bailey had just been commissioned in 1901 and Wellington was his first posting. The two junior officers immediately undertook what must have been raucous hunting forays; in a letter to Bailey thirty years later, RM reminiscences on how "we two irresponsible subalterns were masquerading as big-game hunters and entomologists in the Nil Giris [sic] whilst pretending all the while to take a passing interest in soldiering."[40] The casual remark seems accurate. Both youths were fanatical game-stalkers and exuberant colonialists. The world was their oyster and they partook of it hungrily.

In December 1901 Lieutenant Meinertzhagen was judged well enough to part company with the Wellington convalescent home. He rejoined his battalion in Mandalay, where he writes that he was placed in command of a company of Mounted Infantry.[41] No evidence supports this avowal of command. In his diaries RM frequently attests he was the officer "in charge" of this or that unit, but during his checkered army career one fails to find any instances of his having been entrusted with full-time command of any organization of line troops. (He was indeed the Chief Intelligence Officer of the East Africa Force during 1915 and 1916, but that office was a position on the General Staff; it was not a field command.)

He served in Mandalay until March 1902 when he received orders to ship out for the Dark Continent, where he was seconded to the King's African Rifles.

Nearly two years had elapsed since he had begun a zealous campaign to obtain a transfer to Africa. Like so many young officers he exhibited a fiery desire to go where the action was, and in the late 1890s the action was in the Boer War. The belatedness of the army's response to RM's pleas might have been routine, or it may have reflected a certain disapproval on the part of his commanding officers. Given his admitted predilections for prankish disobedience, they may have felt he wasn't ready for combat leadership.

Whatever its cause, the sluggishness of his transfer proved unfortunate for his ambitions. By the time he set forth for Africa, the main beneficiary of the Anglo-Boer War—his putative friend Cecil Rhodes—had just died of heart failure and the war was closing down. In May 1902, just as the last of the Boers surrendered, RM was delivered to a post a thousand miles north of all that, on the coast of British East Africa.

He steamed in under the guns of Fort Jesus in a driving rainstorm. He noted the beauty of the harbor and the old island city of Mombasa.

A train took him almost immediately from Mombasa west through humid coastal-plain jungles from which it climbed to the open mile-high veldt, lavish with game, on which sat a raw new town.

The railway camp at Nairobi had been founded just three years earlier beside a cold-water swamp. At the time of RM's arrival it was a scattering of tin-roofed wood shanties with a single street. Its future was in its climate: although it stood near the equator, it was located on a high plateau and enjoyed a mainly dry weather cycle of mild temperatures. The young hunter found the plain irresistible with its elegant flat-topped acacia trees and its wild animals in the millions. Surrounded by a necklace of clouds, the flat white crest of the volcano Kilimanjaro stood more than nineteen thousand feet high, undiminished by any surrounding mountain range.

Until shortly before RM's arrival, BEA (British East Africa—later Kenya) had been regarded as a corridor of access to Uganda. But now it had come to the owners' attention that the railway line could not pay its way out of debt with traffic to and from Uganda. As a result, in one of those ironies that can escape attention because they're so commonplace, the railway that was intended to feed the territory now needed to be fed by the territory.

Uganda Rail needed more fares. To attract fare-paying passengers, the line required an end to attacks by tribal warriors, hence the need for British soldiers, hence the arrival of Richard Meinertzhagen.

The legendary King's African Rifles—the "KAR"—turned out to be not quite as heroic as Lieutenant Meinertzhagen had been led to expect. In fact, to hear him tell it, they were as debauched and disreputable as the soldiers about whom he had complained in India. He was shocked and offended to learn that many of his fellow officers in Nairobi were homosexuals, or drunks who were in the habit of hauling giggling native girls into the mess tent.[42]

If one believes his accounts, RM wasted no time in cleaning up the mess before he set forth to study the region's abundance of game animals and to improve his marksmanship.

On June 1, 1902, he writes, he was ordered to escort a dozen replacement soldiers to a beleaguered outpost to the north. With this squad he set forth toward the distant site of his exile. Like many Europeans he found the African landscape magnificent, filled with wonders, and sometimes hostile. They marched over long sweeps of grass punctuated by *kopjes* (rock outcrops), acacias, and thorn trees. Marabou storks circled above in curiosity. In the pure air the soft horizon rose sixty miles away, hardly blurred. Pools of game stirred and broke into torrents as the soldiers approached: zebra, tommies (Thomson's gazelles), grants (Grant's gazelles), wildebeest, impala. RM was enthralled.

His destination, Fort Hall, was in Kikuyu country. The outpost squatted in the shadow of Mount Kenya.[43] Getting there took several days' march through grassland and bush. He was escorted by three NCOs, nine *askari* (soldiers), and two dozen porters. At some length he provides us with travelogue-style descriptions of tribal garb and customs, along with lengthy lists of wildlife seen and wildlife shot. His tallies are carefully recorded. He does not reveal the method he employed to count 4,006 zebra, 845 Coke's hartebeest or 546 Thomson's gazelle, as well as 1,467 head of Maasai cattle.[44]

His game-census notations and other such data were acquired at some cost in time and effort, little of which was authorized by his commanders. From the outset it is clear he was seen as a problem child by the KAR, as he had been earlier in India, because he was not a team player. He sometimes undertook to interpret his orders in ways unanticipated by those who had given them. An early example:

INTELLIGENCE DIVISION, WINCHESTER HOUSE, 6th June, 1903
ST. JAMES'S SQUARE, S.W.

Dear Sir Clement,

Last month we received from you several East African sketch maps, among which was one of the country to the north and west of Fort Hall, by Lieut. Meinertzhagen. This will be of great use to us as we are now embodying it in our new map of this country. The part along the Chania River is apparently quite new work and I should much like to know if the map is the result of actual journeys by Lieut. Meinertzhagen, or if not, how he got the information. The only routes shewn on the map do not traverse this region.

Could you enquire about this the next time you are writing and let me know result?

Yours sincerely,
Clement Hill, KCMG, CB.[45]

RM had neither been ordered into the country "to the north and west of Fort Hall" nor had he asked permission to go there. Without the knowledge or authority of his superior officers, he regarded himself as scientist-explorer first, and only incidentally as a soldier. He thought the unknown region should be mapped, so he went into the wild country and charted it in casual disregard of the fact that he and his porters might get lost or come down with diseases or be ambushed at any moment.

His maps, scaled to exacting accuracy, are among the least ballyhooed of his many accomplishments; apparently he didn't think they were worth flaunting. He produced them through several decades. Some were of military or ornithological value, but others may be considered separately as accurate charts of the lands and as iconic works of art. Especially in his wildlife drawings and paintings he proved to be an artist of exceptional talent, but it was a talent he apparently took for granted.

At Fort Hall, according to his diaries, he learned about African habits of humiliation (urination in prisoners' mouths), dismemberments of people while still alive, and other varieties of torture and murder. Veterans explained sanctimoniously to the newcomer how it was necessary to deal sternly and promptly with the perpetrators of such outrages.[46]

For centuries, invaders from the north had committed atrocities upon native populations with savage brutality equaling or exceeding that of the most belligerent tribes. In suppressing "risings" and "rebellions," Islamic and European powers industriously annihilated thousands of people. RM was a cartridge among many in their ammunition belt. His own account makes him out to have been a particularly lethal one—but was he?

When "native risings" occurred, colonial forces retaliated "punitively." Whether RM led, took part in, observed, or simply heard about various punitive actions is open to question. Firefights happened occasionally; sometimes one or two people were injured or even killed. But by 1902 and 1903, the KAR's retaliatory ventures were likely to focus on the confiscation of livestock rather than on the decimation of tribes. The KAR had become accomplished cattle-rustlers because the stripping of offenders' livestock was highly effective punishment. Colonial officials knew that cattle, sheep, and goats were currency to the highland tribes and that a man's wealth and importance were measured by the number and quality of his animals. (A young man could acquire a bride only by paying her father a steep price in cattle.) To confiscate a village's livestock humiliated offenders and could bankrupt the village. Murder as a policy, on the other hand, had become not only immoral but impractical—the mass depravities of troops in the Congo under orders of Belgium's sadistic King Leopold had become notorious, and as a result Europe had begun to teem with highly vocal human-rights organizations like the ones in which several of RM's aunts were active.

During his first tour in Africa RM later claimed to have been the commander of this company or that fort. Actually he served as a staff officer, third- or fourth-in-command under KAR officers who were seasoned in the bush and had experience in managing troops. At Fort Hall, for example, he served under Capt. F. A. Dickinson and Lieutenant Barlow.[47]

The diaries, and the books he derived from them, are filled with accounts of battles and bloodletting. He celebrated the civilizing mission of British imperialism. He saw himself as an instrument of virtuous policy. According to RM, he and his KAR soldiers brought order and punishment to rebellious East African tribes time after time by shooting and clubbing Africans to death in large numbers. In *Kenya Diary* he writes of one such incident: "I gave orders that every living thing except children should be killed without mercy."[48] He describes how, with bullet and bayonet, he and his *askari* annihilated entire villages. From a reading of his diaries one can estimate his body count at 1,500 Africans. No prisoners. No survivors.[49]

But also no record of any such incidents. No hints anywhere outside his diaries to indicate they may have occurred at all.

The only bloodbath in which RM provably participated was an ambush that did not involve the slaughter of an entire community—it involved a party of about twenty-five armed Nandi warriors. At some level this may be regarded as a lesser crime than the annihilation of an unsuspecting village, but even so, as we'll see, the slaying of about twenty-five people was so unusual and bloody that it became a matter of intercontinental scandal. Although the army did its best to put its "spin" on the massacre, it resulted in three successive Courts of Inquiry, and finally in RM's being relieved of his duties in Africa.

The rest of RM's self-alleged mass murders may have gone unremarked and unreported because they didn't happen. But his stories were perpetuated, and to this day they are seized upon—as factual illustrations to support one theory or another (for or against governments; for or against philosophies; for or against whites; for or against blacks)—by sociologists, historians, politicians, and educators. Elspeth Huxley wrote in her preface to the 1983 reprint edition of *Kenya Diary*: "Richard Meinertzhagen was a killer. He killed abundantly and he killed for pleasure."[50] The "record" is still reviled. Sometimes it is used to inflame political passions. Some accounts discuss RM by name, as if he'd been the architect of colonial oppression rather than a junior lieutenant without a command.[51] However, this misplacement of blame is no one's fault but RM's own.

🐦 🐦 🐦

In 1903 the lieutenant conducted a wild animal census (this one authorized, for a change) on the Serengeti and Athi Plains. He also served another tour at Fort Hall, and later professed[52] to have explored Uganda and German East Africa as well as Kenya.

He first achieved a sliver of international fame when he discovered, killed, stuffed, and shipped back to London the first known (to Europeans) Giant African Forest Hog, soon dubbed *Hylochoerus Meinertzhageni* and attributed to "Capt. Richard Meinertzhagen." (He said he had received his Army promotion to Captain on October 22, 1903.[53] His actual promotion did not occur until nearly two years later.[54])

At this same time he is fearlessly exploring and mapping areas no European had seen before.

In 1904 he visits French Somaliland and rustles more cattle.

Then, back in British East, RM goes out for a stroll on the East African plain accompanied by his pet dog Baby. The plain is freckled with wild animals by the thousands. Unusually and unaccountably, Meinertzhagen is unarmed. He espies a troop of baboon by the river. Frivolously he encourages the dog to stalk them. He aims to "give them a good fright"—so with a sudden shout he jumps up and runs toward the baboons.

Sure enough the baboons flee into the river.

Then the dog runs out ahead of her master and is set upon by the baboons.

When he sees the baboons dismember the little dog, Meinertzhagen feels horrified, then enraged. Usually more tolerant of animals' "natural" behavior than he is of humans', he now makes precise plans for a massive retaliatory strike to teach the miscreants a lesson. According to his diary he rousts out his troops and before dawn returns to the site of Baby's unfortunate demise. He marches at the head of a military column: a sergeant major and thirty soldiers armed with rifles, bayonets, and three thousand cartridges.

The British army deploys into a skirmish line and sets fire to the bush in order to drive the troop back against the base of a cliff. Now, having trapped the apes, RM and his *askari* rain fire on them.

Meinertzhagen's revenge shatters the troop of apes.

When the shooting stops, he and his army have killed every last male, and not a few females.

Inevitably one wonders what opinion of Meinertzhagen the incident may have left in the minds of his African soldiers. In any case, this incident, as bizarre as it is, forms part of a clear pattern.

Kenya Diary contains an appendix of nine fine-print pages listing the animals Meinertzhagen killed in his four years' East African duty in 1902–1906. There is little reason to doubt his count. It includes more than five hundred game animals that he killed, weighed, and measured for the record. It doesn't include the troop of baboons.

He did ship home not only animal skins but also vast numbers of insects and pressed leaves and plants. In *Kenya Diary* he describes pair by pair the taking of scores of birds. In the unabridged (typed) diaries he lists thousands, and the collections of bugs and insects that he donated to museums later in life numbered in the hundreds of thousands.[55]

He returned in August to England for several months' medical leave; he had surgery in London, for an undisclosed condition. His illnesses and injuries were frequent and sometimes serious but he seldom complained about them and he triumphed over most of them, suffering few apparent long-term physical disabilities (except for the impaired sight in one eye) until the 1940s and after.

To complete his recuperation he holidayed on the Riviera (Nice and Monte Carlo) with his mother and two of his sisters. They ventured on to Venice before returning home. Then he set forth to rejoin the KAR in East Africa.

The Nandi Massacre took place in the Kenya Highlands in 1905. The Nandi, a proud tribe with warlike traditions similar to those of its kin the Maasai, had resisted British incursion into its territory. The tribe especially resented being invaded by the Uganda Railway, many miles of whose glittering new roadbed cut straight through Nandi country. The railway was subjected to frequent raids and sabotage by the tribe. The Europeans' telegraph poles had to be twenty-four feet high so giraffes wouldn't knock the wires down or strangle on them, but that height did not discourage Nandi men from swarming up the poles to pull down the copper wires of Britain's telegraph line to Uganda: the Nandi, who used very little clothing and had no pockets, found the copper to be very handy both as currency and as adornment, since it could be coiled and carried around one's neck.

The Crown ordered the King's African Rifles—to which RM was attached—to put down what it regarded as the unacceptable Nandi revolt.

The African knew that when trouble came, it would be wearing a uniform. He watched the British columns that stood dark and weary under bright hot sunlight. He knew, when he saw them take up their lines of march over long sweeps of grass that flowed toward watery heat mirages, that they brought danger with them.

For the date March 18, 1905, at Mombasa, the diarist wrote that he had been assigned to the garrison at Nandi Fort, where he was to relieve Captain Cary and take over as company commander.[56] Again he promotes himself fictitiously: he never was in charge of Nandi Fort. The four European adults in residence there in the summer of 1905 were post commander Capt. Thomas Carey (often spelled Cary, by RM) of the Grenadier Guards, Carey's wife, RM, and civilian officer Walter Mayes. Carey was in command of a detachment of African troops. RM was subordinate to Carey, who remained in place for months to come; later in the year Carey's replacement as post commander arrived—not RM, but Capt. Donald McLeod of the First KAR.[57]

For most of the next year, RM served at Nandi Fort—never as its commander but as adjutant, without command.

The post squatted in the geographic center of the dispute—not really a fort but a collection of huts surrounded, by African habit, with a wooden *boma* stockade fence that was designed to keep livestock in and predators out.

RM had his look around the dusty neighborhood and wrote later that he made it his business to learn about the Nandi people and their customs and behavior in order to divine their weaknesses, if they had any. He watched them; they watched him. He found that although the tribe was matriarchaly structured around loosely allied clans, there were no "chiefs" as such, and only on rare occasions did groups of any size gather together in one place. Usually such gatherings were for religious and ritualistic purposes. For purposes of war, however—and the Nandi were perpetually at war with one enemy or another; it was their normal state of existence—Nandi men tended to fight individually or in small teams rather than in large bodies. RM saw that ordinary military attacks would not goad them into any organized sort of action where superior British discipline and weaponry could destroy the tribe's effectiveness, as had been accomplished so often in India and on other frontiers. The Nandi were warriors but they followed no generals, they had no army. They were a loose alliance of individual guerrilla fighters.

Their war leader was a spiritual one—a shaman or witch-doctor named Koitalel and known to whites as the Laibon (a Maasai, not a Nandi, word).[58]

The Laibon—himself a renegade Maasai—was a powerful and charismatic leader. He told his spiritual followers that the water he sprinkled upon them would protect them from British bullets. They believed him. With other misfortune-tellers they scattered back into the forest to continue making war against the invader.

RM reported these facts to his superiors in Nairobi. Then—he says—he proposed a plan to deal with the problem.

He was well aware that a large Expeditionary Force—all the troops the KAR could spare from its many African outposts—was already on the march: four infantry columns driving northwest toward Nandi Fort, scattering great herds of wildebeest and zebra ahead of them. But the Force was still some days away and its European commanders and African soldiers did not relish the thought of losing men every night to the stealthy tactics of silent bush-fighters.

RM says he proposed to the KAR that they send him out to shed some blood. His plan was ruthless and risky, but if it worked it could save a great many British and *askari* lives.

That is his version.[59] Documents written by Nandi Force commander Lt. Col. Edgar G. Harrison, DSO, and the Force's adjutant, Maj. Ladislaus Herbert Richard Pope-Hennessy (Oxford Light Infantry, seconded to KAR), show that the scheme was devised by Pope-Hennessy and that Colonel

Harrison refined and approved it. When things backfired, Pope-Hennessy, with a highly developed instinct for covering his own rear echelon, allowed RM to take credit for the idea.

Today there are Nandi tribes-people who insist that amid the aromas of Africa—the tickling red dust, the fetid stink of slack eddy water, the reek of dung—they still can smell the bitter evidence of RM's massacre of a hundred years ago, seeping up through the soil and leaking from stems and leaves.

Through native intermediaries RM sent a message to the Nandi leadership: if the Nandi would agree to peace, the British would discuss paying reparations and returning to the Nandi thousands of cattle and goats that they had confiscated.

With that bait, he arranged to meet the Laibon and his interpreters and a small group of tribal religious leaders for purposes of discussing a mutually beneficial long-term peace agreement.

RM embellishes the melodrama by telling us the Laibon's initial reply was to order two successive attempts on RM's life, one of them on the part of a native girl who was to distract the British captain with her seductive wiles while poisoning his food. RM claims to have seen through the tricks and says he sent the unfortunate (and mostly naked) girl back to the Nandi with instructions to give RM's message to the Laibon that RM still wanted a peace parley.

The Laibon finally acceded to the requested meeting, on condition it take place in an open stretch of ground at the foot of Ket Parak Hill where the British captain was to arrive with no more than a token bodyguard of four or five KAR *askari*. These were to be armed with nothing but their sidearms.

RM says he knew without doubt that the Laibon's consent to such a meeting was in itself an indication that he was up to no good because up to now he had refused to meet with any Europeans. (RM shrugs off suggestions by Carey and others that perhaps the Laibon wanted the meeting for practical reasons—he may have been aware of the strength and weaponry of the advancing British army, and may have wanted to head off a battle that could annihilate the Nandi.)

RM writes that he agreed to the Laibon's terms, even though his spies had informed him the Laibon intended to ambush him. The Laibon's plan was to shake his hand in order to pull him off balance so that a companion could skewer RM with a spear while the Laibon's companions would slaughter the members of RM's escort. He writes that the Laibon may have felt that if he eliminated the most important English chief in the area (i.e., RM) he would throw the rest of the Europeans into leaderless disorder. Such a victory would add to the Laibon's already considerable prestige.

These Meinertzhagenian speculations presuppose that the Laibon had no knowledge of the heavy-footed clattering approach of Harrison's columns, and that the Laibon believed RM was the chief of all the local Europeans; neither supposition is correct.

RM clearly hoped he appeared more naive than he really was. He had prepared his men. They knew what to expect and were not going to be surprised.

The official version: with an interpreter and just four or five lightly armed *askari* bodyguards, RM approached the meeting with an innocent face and his hands open and empty. Ket Parak Hill stood a half day's march from Nandi Fort. RM reached the landmark on the morning of October 19, 1905—two days ahead of the scheduled arrival of the big KAR Force.

RM observed that the Laibon had brought with him not just a handful but two dozen healthy young warriors armed with razor-point war spears. Still, RM strode right up to the Africans, or so he insisted afterward. He pretended to be eager to shake hands.

The ensuing action has inspired variant accounts. Each side accused the other of treachery and ambush. When the smoke cleared, one fact not in dispute was that the Laibon and his "peace party" of twenty-three to twenty-six warriors had been shot dead to the last man while RM and his five-trooper escort were still standing, virtually unscratched.

With one blow the action at Ket Parak Hill brought an end to serious Nandi opposition to British rule. Even though the tribe was not organized in the European sense, nevertheless the loss of many of its most powerful warriors along with the reputedly bulletproof Laibon was enough to subdue the people. KAR troopers put down the remaining pockets of stubborn resistance (shooting a few Nandi in the process), and forced martial law on the tribes of western Kenya.

Canny colonial administrators soon were able to impose a new "tame" Laibon on the tribe, and no further large episodes of open black vs. white warfare occurred until the Mau Mau risings of the 1950s.

RM's earliest report of the incident survives. It has been the basis for nearly all subsequent historical accounts, including those written by observers who disapproved of him and his brutal enthusiasm. He sent it to Pope-Hennessy by heliograph relay just a few hours after the action:

As soon as I came in full view of him [the Laibon] I realized that he was assembled with 12 warriors round him and about 20 behind the bush and at once his intention dawned on me, but considering the advantage his death would be to the forthcoming operation I proceeded with my five men. Just before I was about to shake hands with him, my interpreter, who is the Laibon's spy, wheeled round and was about to spear one of my men when I shot him dead; spears and arrows flew at a range of only 4 yards, but the only ones which hit were one arrow in my helmet and one spear through my sleeve. I at once seized the Laibon who was promptly shot by Mabruk Effendi. Several of his followers fell to our rifles and the remainder fled . . . .

"The enemy lost 23 killed.

"Our casualties were nil...

"I trust my actions meet with your approval. . . ."[60]

The report was accepted by his commanders without question.

It might have rested there without further investigation, but a few of his fellow officers were suspicious. How could one European and five *askari* have slaughtered such a large number of seasoned warriors at point-blank distance without suffering so much as a scratch? They believed RM and his men must have opened fire from a distance at which the Laibon's spears would have been ineffectual.

The same skepticism fueled questions that darted between Nairobi and London along cable and telegraph lines. Europeans in the early twentieth century were far from monolithic in their views toward colonial policy. What some regarded as a heroic stand by an outnumbered British officer was regarded by others as the Army's murderous treachery—this on the basis of the lopsided numbers involved and a growing public sympathy toward the innocent native who was being crushed under the steel spikes of the imperialist boot. Religious and humanist reformers, whose numbers were growing throughout Europe, heard of the incident at Ket Parak Hill and decided there must have been a cover-up: it had to have been deliberate mass murder—an ambush staged by the KAR.

RM was treated as a hero by most of his brother officers, but public sympathy supported the civilians who had misgivings, and this was enough to persuade the Army to investigate the episode.

Three Courts of Inquiry were held between the end of 1905 and the spring of 1906. RM maintains that he not only welcomed the hearings but urged the army to conduct them. Officially he was simply a witness but as a practical matter he was the defendant, even though in going out to meet the enemy (and in being prepared and well rehearsed for "treachery") he had been acting under orders from his superiors.

The three courts solemnly examined the evidence before them, including the testimony of a few Nandi hearsay witnesses (none of whom had seen the action) and that of all five African soldiers who had served alongside Captain Meinertzhagen, and at the end the officers of the court pronounced—three successive times—their unqualified acceptance of RM's report and their pride in the honor with which he had upheld the dignity of the King's African Rifles.[61]

What actually happened there?

The full story is complicated. Records survive—many volumes of them, but there was much conflicting testimony. One can trace along miles of distracting subplots involving officers and civilians of several colors and nationalities.[62] (RM himself complained that he was not allowed to see some of those records until near the end of his life.)

He played a central role in the deadly affair; that is not in dispute. But, ironically, it seems likely that he didn't actually shoot anyone that day.

The only explanation that makes complete sense is one that was offered many years after the events by RM himself—in 1957, more than a half-century after the fact.

Stephen Seymour "Sammy" Butler was a lieutenant of the Royal Warwickshire Regiment in 1905, two and a half years RM's junior. Butler lived in Hambledon, Hampshire, not far from RM's sentimental "home" at Mottisfont Abbey. In 1899 they sat together for officership examinations. He was commissioned Second Lieutenant and fought in numerous actions of the Boer War in 1900–1901.[63]

They renewed their friendship in Kenya in 1905 when Butler was seconded to the KAR.

Before the Courts of Inquiry in 1905 and 1906, Lieutenant Butler offered affidavits to the effect that he had escorted RM's little group to the site of the meeting and then had waited back in the trees as ordered, and watched Captain Meinertzhagen and his five men walk to meet the Laibon's party. Butler said that because of a rise in the land he lost sight of everything but the top of the captain's helmet; he said he was told later that the Laibon refused to come out of the shade because it was too hot, so the KAR mini-delegation had to come to him. RM then descended below Butler's range of vision.

Then, Butler said, he'd heard a lot of shooting and he immediately ran out of the trees and rushed forward with his men, but they didn't get a clear view of the action until they raced over a hump of land and saw RM and the five *askari* on their feet swathed in gun smoke and surrounded by corpses on the ground.

After the Courts of Inquiry were concluded, Butler submitted a strong recommendation that Meinertzhagen be awarded the Victoria Cross.

A hundred years later it seems clear that a substantial part of Butler's testimony[64] was balderdash, but at the time of the trials no one in the courtroom was motivated to contradict him, and in later years he was to become a major general, a prime figure in British military intelligence, and the sort of champion whose word was not questioned.

What really happened at Ket Parak Hill was simple and stark. RM posted Lieutenant Butler with a half-company of men in hiding above the appointed meeting place. RM took his five-man escort down to the meeting.

Sammy Butler was an excellent shot with his new Maxim machine gun.[65]

The lie of the land at Ket Parak Hill—the placement of the trees and the distance to the hollow—shows that the machine gun must have been set up about seventy-five yards from the site where the warriors died. Machine guns are not precision weapons. The Maxim had an effective range much greater than seventy-five yards,[66] but the gun could not be relied upon for pinpoint accuracy. It would lay down a pattern of fire—a lot of bullets in a very short time (eight per second). In terms of inflicting damage it would be deadliest when fired into a tight group of people. It easily could kill them all in a few seconds. But some bullets inevitably would miss the targets, perhaps go wide or perhaps ricochet off in unintended directions. Therefore RM and his five men must have been some distance short of their meeting with the Nandi. Otherwise RM's party would have been at risk of being hit by stray bullets.

That's why it is likely that RM did not actually shoot anybody that day. He carried only a sidearm, and most likely was too far away for effective shooting. (This makes him no less a party to the killings; it is of interest more for its irony than for its legalities.)

The careful reader may reasonably chide me: if I am skeptical of so many other claims made by RM, why should I be so willing to accept this one? I admit I am vulnerable here, and can claim only that I have attempted to sift evidence and reach the most plausible conclusion. It fits all the facts.

CHAPTER 4
SYCE

Giving in to pressure from reformers, the Colonial Department of the Foreign Office insisted that Captain Meinertzhagen be relieved of his duties and sent home. He had become a negative symbol around whom Africans and their European sympathizers could cluster. So long as he remained on duty in Africa, a lasting peace with the warrior tribes of the highlands would be at best an uncertain prospect. By showing good faith in removing the brute Meinertzhagen from the scene, His Majesty's government would have an easier time pacifying the heathen.

The Army resisted the Colonial Department's attempt to usurp its authority, but the soldier in question was a mere captain, and captains were expendable. The War Office bowed reluctantly to the Foreign Office and on May 28, 1906, feeling (with great indignation) that he personally and single-handedly had solved the generals' thorniest East African problem for them, RM found himself aboard ship being trundled back to England in disgrace and in disgust, convinced he would have to abandon the military career that he so thoroughly enjoyed.

🐦 🐦 🐦

From the moment of his return to England he felt out of step. He had no patience for fashion or comfort. He played polo with friends and puttered in museums but his restless spirit was discontent with frivolity and resentful of work that required him to sit still.

Defining British East Africa now as the place from which the Colonial desk of the Foreign Office had evicted and exiled him, Captain Meinertzhagen spent the last half of 1906 in dreary administrative War Office desk jobs pushing papers while he endeavored to rehabilitate his reputation and career. He did this partly by making a nuisance of himself and partly by making full use, for the first time, of his wide network of contacts in high places.

His father was still at the helm of Huth's. By now it had been eclipsed by J. P. Morgan's banking empire in New York and by the Bank of England, but Huth's was still a force on the world financial scene. Richard's younger brother Louis was being groomed to take their father's place in the firm. Richard felt his mother's continuing disapproval but he enjoyed the company of his sisters and brothers and some of the aunts and uncles.

Among these relations and in-laws were—in astounding numbers— many of Britain's titled, rich, and influential personages. Although he himself seems to have been doubtful of the information, Richard was in fact descended from Philip III of Spain—there was royal blood in the family line. Richard's brother-in-law, contemporary (they were born less than a year apart), and good friend was George Macaulay Booth (1877–1971), managing director of the Bank of England. Among his uncles, aunts, and cousins were prominent Labor MP and sometime cabinet officer Sir Stafford Cripps (1889–1952), who was to become Churchill's chief wartime Parliamentary rival (and of whom Churchill remarked, "There, but for the grace of God, goes God"), Socialist leaders Beatrice and Sidney Webb (Sidney became Baron Passfield), and later on, the literary-*wallah* Malcolm Muggeridge (a first cousin by marriage) and quite a few others including high military officers and academic leaders.[1]

Richard was a maverick but he shared several of these people's traits, like a compulsive dedication to the completion of goals (or, to put it another way, an unwillingness to quit in the face of discouragement). His friends describe him as resolute; his opponents as stubborn. Both adjectives were applied to RM—frequently.

He and his friends and relations badgered the government until in November the War Office consented to his request for overseas duty. He was to report to his regiment's Third Battalion in South Africa. He arrived in Cape Town on February 3, 1907, and marked time drilling and disciplining troops of the Royal Fusiliers while he studied the battlefields of the Boer War and, in his letters and diaries, passed curt judgments on its generals. He and his fellow soldiers prowled the veldt in the hot South African summer; no one was sure whether they were to be sent to put down a Kaffir revolt in one direction or a Zulu rising in another. Eventually the battalion was ordered to go marching to Pretoria. It arrived just before Christmas, clanking with gear but still peaceful.[2]

In 1908 his diary indicates that after passing a series of eligibility examinations with highest marks he is promoted major, then given command of a company of mounted infantry in South Africa. This company he describes as hopelessly slack: 121 "unserviceable" troopers and only twenty fit for duty. He is given two months to whip it into shape. He instills discipline, causes due resentment, and ultimately gets the men's attention by riding out alone in December to bring back two dangerous deserters. He hunts them down, dismounts, walks toward the two villains, and demands their surrender. They threaten to shoot him but iron will and an officer's sense of duty compel him to continue walking toward them without drawing a weapon. In the end the two deserters meekly put their guns down and return obediently with him to Standerton, where he appoints one of the men his horse-holder and the other his groom.

No record of any such steely-brave episode has survived anywhere other than in RM's diaries.[3] In reality his promotion to major did not occur for another seven years (in September 1915), and in 1908–1909 he served not as a commander but as a battalion staff officer.

In late 1909 when his battalion was transferred to Mauritius, he took six months' leave and sailed home to England.

Now—the RM version again—he takes a fresh idea to the Foreign Office (a place where, we may recall, he was none too popular after Ket Parak Hill) and explains that he's always wanted to visit the Crimea to study the fields of battle of the previous century's war. As long as he's there, might he be of use in spying on Russian installations for the Foreign Office?

His offer is refused. So he sets out to prove his mettle to the skeptics. He assigns himself a rigorous test: he infiltrates British coastal fortifications—crosses moats, rappels up stone walls—and makes accurate scale drawings of the defenses. He escapes with the drawings in hand, never having been noticed by anyone in the garrisons.

Nor is he noticed by the FO, which fails to record his insubordinate exploit in the customary daybooks or anywhere else. According to RM, however, the FO is so impressed by his daring success that it immediately authorizes him to become a spy. He is to report on a new fort the Russians are building north of Sebastopol where British naval attachés have failed to learn any details of its construction.

By the time of this alleged undercover penetration of the Crimea in 1910 by RM, British Intelligence services had for a considerable time been obtaining detailed information—including blueprints—about forts, ships, zeppelins, installations, movements, and plans throughout Europe and especially in the Balkans. For years, Intelligence director "C"—Mansfield Cumming—had been running his officers and expert agents regularly into and out of Eastern Europe. He had the region thoroughly covered, and his abundant information was at the disposal of the Foreign Office. It does seem a bit odd, therefore, that the FO should entrust a sensitive information-gathering mission to an officer with no diplomatic or intelligence ties and whose reputation among FO directors was probably that of a bull in a china shop, if not that of a ruthless butcher.[4]

RM writes that when studying the new Russian fort he notices the approach of Russian soldiers so he drops his pants and, by the time they come in sight, is pretending to be squatting in the shrubbery for defecation purposes. He shows them his bird- and plant-sketchbooks and after a few sharp moments they let him go as yet another dotty English tourist.

On his next visit he arrives in uniform and talks his way inside the fort. There the young commanding officer—an engineer charged with completing construction of the fortress—just happens to share RM's fascination with bird and plant life. The Russian officer invites him to dine and then gives his visitor a full tour of the fortifications.

As soon as he leaves, RM makes detailed drawings while his memory is fresh.

When he returns to his hotel room he notices that the strand of hair he'd left across the clasp of his valise has been disturbed. Thus he knows his belongings have been searched.

Somewhere in this stretch of days he finds himself in the riot-torn streets of Odessa during one of its anti-Semitic fits of fury. With a good deal of violence and a good deal of deadly danger to his person, he rescues a young Jewish girl from persecution by a Russian mob at the height of its pogrom.[5]

One may feel inclined to compare this adventure with the story of the rescue of the young English girl in Port Said[6] and the rescue of the cliffhanging teen-age girl in the train-wreck episode that follows this present one. Significantly, the incident of the Odessa pogrom, described in *Middle East Diary*, does not appear where one would expect it to turn up chronologically in *Army Diary*, in the section where he describes his Crimean espionage. Why don't the two tales of rescuing damsels from mobs appear in the same published volume? Does the diarist, after all, have some awareness of the concept of overkill?

There follow further melodramas: a sinister stranger with a revolver in his coat pocket, a nervous voyage on the Black Sea, furtive surveillance by shady types. After bluffing his way out of Russian interrogations, and executing a getaway from yet another narrow scrape, he triumphantly delivers his reports to the British Embassy in Constantinople[7]—reports that appear, once again, nowhere except in RM's writings.

He has not yet completed the season's heroics. On March 8, 1910, he describes a wild pitching ride in the mountains of Greece, amid shrieking passengers in a derailed train that begins to slide off the rim of a curving cliff until a railway carriage hangs half over the precipice. Hearing a girl screaming, he sees a teenager clinging to an outboard handrail, legs dangling over the abyss while the carriage continues to tip outward and begins to slide off the roadbed. RM crawls out and drags the girl to safety just before the whole train falls into the gorge with an earsplitting noise.[8]

The survivors somehow get aboard another train—his account does not specify where it came from or how it happened to arrive so opportunely.[9] A crisis soon arises in the crowded carriage: a traumatized young woman begins to give birth prematurely to a baby and RM is forced to take charge, commandeer a nearby woman and a helpful German gentleman, shoo all the other men out of the compartment, assist in the birth, see that the child is not breathing, cut the umbilical cord with his own pocket-knife, spank the baby smartly until it begins to breathe, and wash the child in the lavatory.

One may feel obliged to inquire how a whole train filled with adult Greeks couldn't help a woman who had gone into labor—why did it take a solitary Englishman, with no experience of fatherhood or assistance in childbirth, to save the day?

When RM delivers the young woman and her newborn infant to her husband on the platform at Patras, the husband is overcome with gratitude, and the German gentleman—who alone had been helpful on the train— now insists that RM come stay with him in his private resort on Corfu. This grateful gentleman, we learn, is the King of Saxony.

One's instinct may be to dismiss these yarns as outrageous but harmless self-aggrandizing fantasies—if it were not for the fact that they appear in the same "nonfiction" books that have been used for half a century as serious source works for historical texts. And while RM's wild adventures may seem ludicrous, some of them—at face value—are not impossible. Unless they can actually be disproved, may they not have happened?

The matter seems to call for a bit of detective work.

There was an actual king of Saxony—Friedrich August III, who reigned from 1904 to 1918 and had a Hapsburg wife and two children. At the time of the alleged incident there is no record of his (or any other Germanic royalty's) traveling in Greece.

Of course one may surmise that a man who tells a stranger he is the King of Saxony may, in fact, be lying, and that RM could be telling the truth about meeting a man who professed to be the King of Saxony. That certainly is possible. What is not possible is the train wreck. No train wreck in the mountains of Greece caught the attention of anyone at all (especially not the local, national or international press) at any time in 1910.

Just days after the Greek adventures he was back in England where on March 27, 1910, an engagement was published: Maj. Hermann Le Roy-Lewis announced the forthcoming marriage of his daughter Armorel to Capt. Richard Meinertzhagen.

Hermann Le Roy-Lewis, of Westbury House, was a Hampshire neighbor of the Meinertzhagens. He had served actively in South Africa during the Second South African War. Le Roy-Lewis was a close friend of both David Lloyd George and Lord Kitchener.[10] Before Lloyd George became prime minister during World War I he was Minister of Munitions, and Major Le Roy-Lewis served as his advisor.

Little seems to be known about Armorel's early life or about RM's relationship with her. If theirs was a traditional courtship it must have been conducted "on the fly," because RM's visits to England during the past ten years had been infrequent. According to his own accounts, if we accept them, he had the occasional infatuation and the occasional girlfriend. He had tarried with a few girlfriends (planters' daughters, an American tourist girl) in the Colonies. He wrote admiringly of several of those girls but nearly nothing survives of what he may have written about Armorel.

No evidence suggests that a pregnancy was involved, nor was theirs a merger of financial convenience, but they seem to have hated each other from their very first wedded moment. Richard later snapped that Armorel was the granddaughter of an American-accented Parisian prostitute whose two illegitimate sons by a Jewish pimp grew up to be (1) a Paris racing tout and (2) Armorel's father.[11] These harsh pictures of Armorel's lineage appear to be false. Her father was eminently respectable. In those young years Armorel herself was a bright, free-spirited, and perhaps fast-living girl, but she does not seem to have done anything that shocked or offended anyone (other than RM) in such a way as to cause other parties to record nasty remarks about her.

RM called her by the nickname "Tow,"[12] possibly because of the color of her hair. Beyond that, his revelations about his first marriage are obscured in a haze of anger and silence; he seems determined that we know next to nothing about Armorel Le Roy-Lewis Meinertzhagen. Evidently he preserved no photographs of her. He remarked that Armorel made no secret of her faithlessness, her belief in "free love," or her compulsive promiscuity.

One may speculate that perhaps he was intrigued and excited by Armorel's overt sexuality until he realized she had no intention of restricting her favors to him alone. One may also speculate about his own sexuality—impotence has been suggested by a few acquaintances—but guesswork is especially unreliable in a case like RM's, and all we can say for certain is that he himself summed up the relationship with economy: "I marry my first wife and am disillusioned."[13]

He rarely dwells, in his writings, on his relations with the opposite sex (although he is happy to share his extremist attitudes toward it and its members). He could be huffy but evidently he was not a prude: he claimed to admire the self-respect implicit in African nudity, and seemed to have nothing against the sort of erotic art work that some of his fellow Victorians disdained. When looking at his accounts of such girls as his three giggling, nubile, topless house-servants at Nandi Fort (of whom he took a splendid photo) one can't help being tempted to read between the lines.

By his own account he was not homosexual, and while he expressed little sympathy for those who were, he seems to have got along as well with friends who were openly homosexual as he did with those who were avowedly heterosexual. (We must take this in the context that in person he got along quite well with many people, while in his diaries he frequently waxed hypercritical as well as hypocritical toward even his closest friends.)

Aside from his Victorian romanticism he does not seem to have understood very much about the real-life intimacy that sustains a relationship. Only much later, in his fifties, after two marriages, a furious divorce, and a violent death, would he manage to settle into an attachment that would appear affectionate and mutually supportive, but about which serious questions have been raised.

Hermann Le Roy-Lewis and RM may have been distantly related and would keep crossing paths during the coming decades, but their contacts were seldom recorded by RM, who—when he mentions his onetime father-in-law at all—makes only passing reference, as if they were near-strangers.[14]

In 1910 the banns were posted, the father of the mysterious Armorel prepared for a wedding next year, and—shortly after his own father fell ill and lapsed into a coma—RM went south to rejoin his battalion, which was garrisoned offshore from South Africa on the island of Mauritius. His mother, aunts, and many of his siblings were furious with him for not obtaining permission to delay his departure at the moment of his father's crisis, but he went anyway.

By the time his ship made port in Mauritius on July 1, 1910 his father had died. He seems to have had few clues as to how he should feel about this. His father had been an aloof, sometimes forbidding figure in his life. RM seldom chose to argue with his father head-on, but the evidence is so fragmentary that one is hard-pressed to attempt any sort of definition of the relationship between the two. "Distant but cordial" seems accurate enough but explains very little.

During his tour of duty on Mauritius he wrote his first published ornithological paper.[15] Here again he pretends to have been in command of a company; he also says he put down a Creole riot and refused bribes from corrupt French businessmen. Then RM returned to England in June 1911 for another six months' leave, much of which he devoted to study so that in October he could pass the entrance examinations for the Staff College at Quetta, India.[16] He also got married to Armorel—an event he concedes with obvious reluctance.

He fails to mention that he only applied (in 1912) to the college at Quetta after he was rejected in 1911 by the infinitely more prestigious Sandhurst. In *Army Diary* he also fails to note that on September 28, 1911, he and Armorel journeyed together out to India and inland to the deep-snow country at Quetta.[17]

The combination of a regrettable marriage and his exclusion from Sandhurst seems to have put him in a bad mood, from which he fled on long hunting expeditions around Chakrata, Bodiya, and Musscorie, the latter in company with his old friend Hatter Bailey. He went from the Himalayas to the Ganges, and to Delhi on maneuvers.

After having been married just over a year, claiming but not specifying evidence that his wife was having affairs, RM wrote that he sent her packing in December 1912. According to the divorce papers she filed several years later, Armorel declared that in December 1912 her husband had deserted her. The difference seems to be a matter of interpretation and legalities. In the event, Armorel moved out of his quarters but remained in India for much of the next year, and in spite of RM's rigorous assertions to the contrary, she did see him—and even come to his aid in time of need—before she returned to England a year or so later.

Early in 1913 his right eye was injured by a shotgun-pellet in a shooting accident. Typically he played down the seriousness of the wound, but this one caused him to remain in hospital for months and he nearly lost the eye altogether. Specialists were consulted; he was referred to a surgeon in Amritsar. Still hospitalized, he wrote in May 1913, "My wife insists on accompanying me," and complained that he expected to end up having to take care of Armorel rather than the other way around.

The eye finally was repaired—very painfully—by the surgeon in Amritsar, but RM's sight in that eye was uncertain for life; he took to wearing spectacles and sometimes was forced to find relief from sharp headaches by retreating to darkened shelters.

The injury also impaired his shooting skills. The evidence is contradictory, but it sometimes apparently caused him to take up left-handed shooting, which to a right-handed man can be awkward and sometimes erratic. He had to wear eyeglasses thereafter, but when in adequate light he continued to shoot right-handed.

The threat of physical challenge seldom daunted him. He was still recovering from the eye surgery toward the end of 1913 when (he writes) he and an officer friend, Capt. Tod Maitland, obtained permission to travel during the Christmas holiday to what he calls "Mesopotamia (now Iraq)." The parentheses are his;[18] this seems a slip of unusual carelessness, even for him. The sentence is part of a passage that purports to have been written within a few weeks of the events described—that is, in 1913—but Mesopotamia was not to become the Republic of Iraq until 1932, and even though its own residents often called it "Irak" the name would have been meaningless to most Europeans in 1913 and would make no sense in the syntax ("*now* Iraq") that contains it. In the time to which RM's passage refers, British officers and colonial servants called the Mesopotamia theater "Mespot," not "Irak" or "Iraq."[19]

Why he decided to go there is a bit of a mystery since the only things he seems to have to say for it—before, during, and after the trip—are that it was a rancid, verminous hell-hole, and that no self-respecting human being should tolerate the conditions found in those unholy deserts.

The two officers spent part of January 1914 in Baghdad, lunching with British citizens and officials who lived there (and thus giving the lie to his insistence that he went there on an intelligence mission to investigate a region of which the British were ignorant). RM takes the opportunity to pontificate in his diary on the errors he sees being committed by the Crown in its lackadaisical indifference to the inroads Germany is making.[20] He is certain Germany and the Kaiser have nothing except warlike intentions toward Britain. Since these remarks, like many other "prescient" observations in his diaries, actually were written many years later, his apparent foresight is less mysterious than it may have seemed to earlier readers.

RM and Maitland (who in photos appears to have been a pudgy, good-humored sort)-visited Nineveh, Babylon, and other biblical sites. RM has little to say about Maitland and nothing particularly good to say about any of the places or people they saw. Conditions were primitive even by his rugged standards. (He had a diminishing tolerance for roughing it; in later years his safaris were noted for their lavish luxury, but until 1915 he usually traveled in the spartan fashion of a soldier).

Embarking by boat onto the Tigris, the two travelers—RM complains—were set upon by their own boatmen. Naturally the two British officers prevailed over the dozen or so armed mutineers.[21] No Mesopotamians seem to have filed any complaints, and no reports linger in British or Indian army files; no one except the diarist made note of the alleged violence.

At the end of February 1914 the officer-explorers returned to Quetta, having survived a series of alleged scrapes, escapades, and near-death experiences. He later claimed the trip was made for purposes of gathering intelligence, but he brought back no information the Army didn't already have. He did, however, bring back a number of bird skins.

Early in March 1914, just weeks after his return from Mesopotamia, RM and a new traveling companion proposed to the commandant that the two would set out disguised as Afghan tribesmen, on camels, to attempt to scale the border mountains and find a route into Afghanistan.

Afghanistan in 1914 was not much less barbaric than it was in 2005, and RM informs us that their commandant at Quetta, General Braithwaite,[22] advised the two officers not to get caught because that could cost them at least their commissions and probably their lives.[23]

If two not-so-young officers (RM was thirty-six) were to come up with such a wild-haired scheme as this and present it to the commandant of Quetta Staff College, it would seem that his sensible course would have been to order them not to go. According to RM, however, the Afghan journey was cut short not by a general's cooler head, but by the loss of a runaway camel. He writes in some disgust that he and his comrade were jumped by Afghan bandits with very long rifles and were forced to flee in a running gunfight extending into half an hour after dark.

His personal reaction to the experience is limited mainly to an observation that it is difficult to aim and shoot from the back of a camel in motion.

It was during his tenure at Quetta that one of the more infamous episodes of RM's career did or did not take place.

On Monday morning, May 26, 1913 (when according to his unpublished writings he's still hospitalized with an eye injury), he visits his two polo ponies in their stable and finds that his syce (servant-groom) has tied the horses down, splayed, and beaten them because they disturbed the syce's sleep.

In a rage RM batters the servant to the ground with his polo mallet and crouches to comfort the mistreated ponies.

Belatedly he notices that he has beaten the syce to death.

RM feels irritation and mild regret, but his general reaction is that the syce deserved what he got. He sees that he may be in a spot of difficulty, however. So he goes to his friend, District Police Superintendent F. M. A. Baily and tells his story.

Baily has a practical solution. He instructs a doctor to seal the scene and post an announcement that the syce's death is the result of bubonic plague. The horses are turned loose and the stable is burned down around the corpse, ostensibly to prevent the infection from spreading and to honor Hindi ritual.

This seems an inventive way to cover up a crime. Visible symptoms of plague include bruises and subcutaneous discoloration (the word "bubonic" means, in the colloquial, black-and-blue, and at any distance a man who's been beaten to death can be mistaken for one who died of plague—even the suspicious would be unwilling to approach the corpse).

RM and the police superintendent then request an audience with Brig. Gen. Sir Walter Braithwaite, and when it is granted, they tell the general the whole story. The gruff Braithwaite, who has seen everything and is surprised by nothing, considers the issue from all sides and responds by reprimanding RM with great severity.

The poor syce died of bubonic plague, General Braithwaite declares— *and just make bloody sure you never do that again!*[24]

We went so far as to launch an investigation in which a firm of private investigators with offices in both India and Pakistan searched for any evidence of this occurrence. Baily and Braithwaite were real people; to the extent their papers can be found, neither of them ever mentioned anything about the death of a syce, or about RM's having punished (let alone killed) one of his grooms. The searches have turned up no clue to suggest that such an event ever occurred.[25]

The absence of such documentation is not proof. (If the story were true, they would hardly implicate themselves by writing about it.) But no such incident is mentioned even, for example, in such thorough and quasigossipy documents as the 54-volume set of handwritten diaries (given in 1983 to the Liddell Hart Military Archive at King's College London) written by the late Maj. Gen. Hubert Isacke (1872–1943), who served at Quetta as a lieutenant colonel contemporaneously with RM and Braithwaite.

The mallet-murder of the polo groom in India has become a standard element in the RM mythology. It is cited frequently to illustrate his reputation for outsize violence and to support various analyses of the dreadful decay that can infect European officers when they are turned loose on colonial victims.

Was an actual murder covered up? Or are we simply being entertained by the crackle of a great punch line?

Did RM make up the whole story of how he beat his own servant to death—merely for the sake of a gruesome line that wasn't even original?[26]

CHAPTER 5
TANGA

W hen the Great War breaks out in the summer of 1914, Quetta HQ in the mountains of India buzzes with speculation. Its officers have no clear notion of the Big Picture back in Europe—they're just eager to do their bit.

In the pandemonium, Richard Meinertzhagen seems to be the only one without doubts. With typical prescience he understands even before the war begins that Europe is bound for disaster so dire that he cannot in good conscience share the elation of his fellow officers in the staff college because he sees that the fuse is lit and he fears too many of them will be killed or maimed before the year is out.

Soon enough, he is summoned to action. He writes:

18th August 1914. In the train between Quetta and Bombay.

Last night, just before going to bed, I got a note from the Commandant informing me I had been selected[1] as a Special Service Officer for an overseas expedition and that I must report myself as soon as possible to General Aitken in Bombay, so here I am, having packed up in record time. I do not know where we are going or when we sail, but I suspect it is to German East Africa. . . .

I reached Bombay on 24th August and at once reported to General Aitken, from whom I learned that our destination is German East Africa and that I am in charge of his Intelligence Section.[2]

His projection of movements will turn out to have been both accurate (except that in reality he is not "in charge of" Aitken's intelligence section) and impossible. In August 1914 he cannot know where he is bound because even High Command doesn't know where they will send Aitken's force. Three separate expeditionary forces in India are being cobbled together with frantic haste to be rushed to the battlefields of

France and/or Mesopotamia and/or East Africa and/or Egypt. Some of the generals, including Aitken, won't learn their targets until weeks later. Some will be well out to sea before they receive final orders.

This vagueness is caused not by secrecy or a lack of planning but by an excess of the latter: the various headquarters in England, France, Egypt, and India keep changing their minds about the destinations of their armies.

Expeditionary Force "B," to which RM is attached, is an assortment of leftovers being gathered in haste from every corner of India. The India Office has placed the Force's two brigades under command of newly minted Maj. Gen. Arthur Edward Aitken. Although their destination—Suez? Ypres? Mombasa? Kut?—remains undetermined, RM will turn out to have been right. His is the army that will be ordered to conquer German East Africa.[3]

Aitken is described by RM as a Blimpish blockhead. Most others agree. Aitken's incompetence will not be a product of RM's imagination; unfortunately it is all too genuine. Until just before the war, Aitken was an undistinguished colonel on backwater posts in India. Burly and mustached, the son of a Presbyterian minister in New Brunswick, Canada, he has served with the Indian Army for nearly thirty-five years. Recently he has been promoted past many officers of far greater quality.

One of the force's junior officers, Gordon S. Johnson, later wrote: "Aitken had nobody's confidence . . . . He was said to have been pushed into this job because he was not wanted as a District Commander in India. . . . In Sept. 1914 every soldier in India wanted to go to France . . . ; East Africa was an unpopular sideshow—hence 'Aitken's Menagerie' as the GEA Expeditionary Force was called, and the rather odd collection of senior officers who ran it."[4]

Aitken's advancement may have something to do with the fact that his brother Max Aitken (soon to be better known as Lord Beaverbrook) is a newspaper baron and a Member of Parliament. Lord Beaverbrook exercises enormous influence in British society and government.[5]

Powerful brother or not, East Africa will prove the wrong place to send Arthur Aitken. When he takes the field against Germany's Paul von Lettow-Vorbeck there will be no concealing the full glory of his inadequacy.

An episode in RM's typescripts is related under the title "I catch a spy in Bombay 1914." He says he found a German spy stockpiling maps and charts, and immediately went to the police to tell them to arrest the spy. Naturally the police accepted this mission without question or hesitation.[6]

No hint of such an incident survives either in British military records or in Indian police records. By this time the war had been on for two and a half months and all German offices in India had long since been shut down, their personnel deported or interned. RM decided not to publish the passage, but as happened quite often, he neglected to remove it from the diaries. (Whether or not these lapses are forgivable, they are understandable as soon as one recalls the sheer length of the typescripts. No one, not even RM, could have re-read the thousands of pages frequently enough to notice and correct all their inconsistencies.)

German rule over its colony in East Africa had been as brutal and harsh as all the other Europeans' until about 1906, but then under public pressure Berlin had sent in a new hierarchy of enlightened reformers. By 1914 German East Africa had in place an improbably advanced and humane administration. The colonial economy was thriving. Hundreds of thousands of African children were in school. DOA's hospitals, medical research facilities, agricultural development, roads, railways, shipping, and telegraph communications were up to the minute. Doctors had vaccinated more than three million Africans against smallpox. Subsequent historians would commend German colonialism in those years as "an engine of modernization with far-reaching effects for the future."[7]

The Africans themselves had not been consulted regarding the imposition of European hegemony; GEA, no matter how nicely it treated the indigenous population, was still an arm of a colonial empire. But the German "engine of moderation" had led to peace, and as a result, Germany's colonial armed force—the *schutztruppe*—had dwindled until it was one of the smallest in the world. In 1914 its strength in GEA amounted to about two thousand officers and men. Most of those were African policemen. The force contained only sixty-eight German enforcement officers.[8] The rest of the European officers were medical personnel and administrative officials whose job was to serve DOA's seven million Africans.[9]

The colony's governor, Dr. Heinrich Schnee, had discussed matters with officials from the neighboring British colony—officials who, with their wives, often dined and imbibed and played cards together in the German capital city Dar es Salaam, the very name of which could be translated as "Haven of Peace." They were friends. They lacked an urgent desire to start shooting at one another. And the Congo Act of 1885 called for colonies to remain neutral in the event of war among their European "parents." That principle was endorsed by the local British and German contingents. To emphasize their cooperation, they executed a gentlemen's covenant that prohibited naval bombardment of either colony's port cities. Because its signatories knew a bit about the trustworthiness of promises made by distant governments, they made a point in their treaty to specify that in the event any higher command overrode the Congo Act or the local agreement, any bombardment or attack from the sea must be preceded by a warning of at least twenty-four hours in order to allow for evacuation.

London chose not to listen to these people, who seemed to be acting like responsible grown-ups. On August 5, 1914, just as the war began, British Prime Minister Herbert Asquith's government announced its resolution to attack German overseas possessions wherever and whenever it could. Britain rationalized this violation of treaties by citing the need to deny safe harbors to German warships.[10] In Africa, the specific excuse was that Germany's colonies were providing shelter to naval raiding cruisers *Emden* and *Königsberg*. There was a morsel of truth in this assertion, but the underlying motive was a bit more primitive. It was a simple land-grab, in a continuation of what Joseph Conrad had termed "the scramble for Africa."

In fact, on all the high seas there were barely a half dozen German warships in play. Nevertheless, with this ringing excuse, Britannia waived the rules.

In East Africa the Congo Pact was first broken by the British. On August 4, 1914, their troops from Uganda attacked German river outposts near Lake Victoria.[11] And on August 8 came a direct naval attack on the colony's capital: British warship HMS *Astraea* bombarded Dar es Salaam from a few miles offshore, trying to destroy its wireless communications tower so the Germans could no longer communicate with raiding warship *Königsberg*.

Astraea's captain was not one of the parties who had partaken of the local agreement that prohibited such things. His orders had come from a distant admiral, and in his mind the attack was justified by the fact that Dar es Salaam for several months had been home port to surface raider *Königsberg*.[12] He was aware that the raiding cruiser had left Dar before the war started but he cannot have known that *Königsberg* would never return.

His broadsides were fired off with abysmal inaccuracy. None of them hit the target. Most of them didn't even come near it. Governor Schnee guessed, from the wide pattern of missed shots, that *Astraea*'s guns were trying to hit the wireless tower. He feared half the city would be destroyed before the mast was hit. So he ordered his own policemen to blow it up.

(The British effort was naive. The tower was of little strategic value—it contained only an antenna. It held no operational radio gear. The tower was easy to rebuild, and the Germans had it back in service in just a few days.[13])

As soon as the tower went down, Schnee raised a big white flag over Government House. The shelling stopped. The bombardment did achieve one unintended purpose: it enraged the residents.

🐦 🐦 🐦

Lt. Col. Paul Emil von Lettow-Vorbeck had arrived in East Africa half a year earlier, in January 1914, with Monte Carlo winnings in his pocket and the good wishes of his shipboard fellow passenger, Kenya resident Karen Blixen (the Danish writer better known as Isak Dinesen).

He called himself "Lettow." Many historians refer to him with the honorific "von"—"von Lettow"—and no disrespect is meant by its having been dropped in this book's references. "Lettow" is the way he signed letters and other documents. He was a proud man but not a vain one.

He was as tall as RM, and tended to walk straight up, as if on wheels—the bearing of his heritage: he came from a line of generals. At forty-four he was a balding bachelor; he'd marry his sweetheart as soon as he returned to Germany after the war. His face in photos sometimes looks more mischievous than heroic. He enjoyed a good joke, and his mind was sharp and decisive. He was a quick study with a near-photographic memory, great curiosity, and a heuristic imagination. He arrived in Dar with a fluency in Swahili that earned the surprised respect of the *askaris*. (He had served previously in Southern Africa.) From the outset just about everyone liked him—Africans, Germans, even the English; especially the English.

Lettow's eyes were large, intense, observant, and with a twinkle. He spoke with a high German accent. He was fond of tactics and wise about strategy, but war did not delight him.[14] All the same, he would prove to be the outstanding guerrilla leader of the twentieth century—a feat he accomplished in part by leaving quite a few prejudices behind: he appointed Africans as officers, sometimes over white subordinates; he said—and believed—"We all are Africans here." Without fuss and without seeming to notice it he created the first racially integrated army to serve in modern warfare.

He also created what turned into a contradiction in terms: a relatively humane form of warfare. He was politically conservative, even reactionary, and would have been shocked if anyone had called him a bleeding-heart, but the pragmatic humanism of his methods made a point then and it resonates now. If you killed an enemy soldier his army would continue to fight; if you injured him, or drew him into disease-infested regions, his army would need to look after him—an effort that would be exhaustively costly to them.

The Allies were to pour in about a million troops and support personnel in their effort to defeat Lettow, whose army never numbered more than fifteen thousand and usually was smaller than that. At the end of the war in November 1918 he and his troops would still be running circles around the British.

A key reason why the British couldn't defeat Lettow was that they couldn't find him.

In September the mob of Force "B" went to sea from Bombay to effect the invasion of German East Africa.[15] RM went on to maintain in his diaries, and later to tell every historian he could find, that he was "in charge of" the Force's Intelligence section, having been selected because (a) he was the best qualified for the job and (b) he was the only officer who knew the interior of German East Africa.

Actually—no. The Intelligence Chief of Force "B" was Lt. Col. J. D. Mackay of the Middlesex Regiment, a veteran up from the ranks who had been Adjutant of the King's African Rifles in Nairobi when RM first came to Africa in 1902; the two officers had gone on game safaris together. Now, in 1914, Mackay had served for fourteen years with the KAR and knew the interior far better than did RM, who had made only two or three visits to the German colony nearly ten years ago, mainly to hunt game and always to the west (inland) of Kilimanjaro.

Mackay previously had been a friend but now, suddenly, he became another dunce in the RM script:

> 28th October 1914—At sea off Mombasa.
>
> HMS *Fox* met us this morning, bringing Colonel Mackay and Commander Headlam with her. They were able to give us the latest information, which amounts to nothing. Mackay is quite the wrong type of man to have been sent out to collect information. I know him well, for he was with me in the King's African Rifles from 1901 to 1905. He lacks imagination, has no experience or knowledge of staff work, and still less of the type of information required by an invading force.[16]

The battle for Tanga would become the most closely studied event of the war in East Africa. It provoked numerous publications in the coming decades.[17] An exercise in tragicomic excess, it produced unanimous agreement on two things: first, it was a fiasco; second, the debacle was caused by bad generalship.

It was the result of bad intelligence as well. RM manages somehow to blame it on others, and simultaneously to claim (falsely) that he was in charge of the very intelligence that failed.[18]

By the time the convoy reached the African coast on October 30, 1914, some of the eight thousand troops of "Aitken's Menagerie" had been below decks without a break for three months. Most of them were poorly trained and ill-equipped, had never seen or been fired upon by machine guns, and had just exchanged their obsolete rifles for the new Lee-Enfields, whose mechanism and sightings were quite strange to them. They were unacquainted with war—and with their newly posted officers, many of whom did not even know each other. The men had not worked together before. A large number of soldiers were "sepoys"—drafts hastily shipped in from the Indian hinterlands to bring units up to strength.

They were short not only on training and experience but on motivation as well: they had nothing against German East Africa; most of them didn't even know where it was.

In the rancid holds of the wallowing, overcrowded transports (maximum convoy speed: eight knots) many of the troops had spent the voyage helpless with seasickness. There was no room for physical exercise and hardly enough space to sleep; men had to lie down in shifts. The stench was indescribable.[19] Quite a few soldiers who came from varied sectors of India were not provided with anything like their customary food. Their religious practices were offended and their digestive tracts erupted. The generals and their staffs—including Captain Meinertzhagen—aboard luxury liner SS *Karmala* were oblivious to the appalling misery below the decks of the accompanying transports.[20]

A conference ashore at Mombasa on the morning of October 31 included all the major British players—Maj. Gen. Aitken and his staff, the commanding generals of his two brigades, British East Africa's governor, the commanders of several ground-force contingents already in East Africa, Lt. Cdr. Caulfield of the Royal Navy's cruiser *Fox* (standing in for Admiral King-Hall, who was away chasing *Königsberg*), and two intelligence officers whose ranks and positions were superior to Captain Meinertzhagen's—Lieutenant Colonel Mackay and Major Norman King.

RM was there, but the others do not seem to have felt his presence was worth remarking.

General Aitken's target of decision was the port city of Tanga, about 120 miles down-coast from Mombasa. He announced that he would attack in thirty-six hours.

Aitken's staff kept minutes of the meeting,[21] but RM's caustic account has become the accepted version. He wrote:

Caulfield then announced that the Navy had contracted a truce with both Tanga and Dar-es-salaam, agreeing not to attack either town provided the harbours were not used for naval or military purposes. I asked if the Admiralty had agreed. He said the Admiralty had not been informed. Caulfield went on to say that if we attacked Tanga he would have to give previous warning to the Germans. Both [sic] Aitken, Sheppard, and I said that would destroy the element of surprise, but Caulfield was adamant and Aitken gave in.[22]

Much of this is not true. Back in August the Admiralty had been informed of the informal truce with its terms requiring twenty-four hours' advance warning of any attack. There had been spirited debates about whether it should be repudiated or ratified. In the end London's cynical decision was that British honor required that the truce must be repudiated prior to any attack on the enemy. But the canny Churchill, then serving as First Lord of the Admiralty, left it up to local commanders in their discretion to decide just when (by implication, the later the better) to inform the Germans that Britain no longer felt obliged to honor the agreement.[23]

In August—more than two months before—that instruction had been cabled from the Admiralty to Aitken, and to the East African naval command, with copies to the War, India, and Foreign Offices.

The instruction from London was cagily couched: "H.M.G. does not ratify terms of truce Dar-es-Salaam and Tanga. You should inform Governors of the two towns of this at a convenient opportunity shortly before any further offensive action is taken against either of the towns."[24]

To cancel the truce any earlier could provoke the Germans into strengthening their defenses. Accordingly, Aitken had concurred that the truce would not be repudiated until just before the British made their move on German territory.

The Navy's Lieutenant Commander Caulfield, a signatory to the treaty, felt honor-bound by his promise to give the Germans a full day's fair warning. Aitken shared Caulfield's sense of honor.

RM did not share it, as he asserts in a fury. British lives were going to be lost because of the private conspiracy that had been cooked up by the card-playing Naval Officer and his German cronies.

Then, RM wrote, "Aitken asked me to outline what we knew about the enemy; I . . . [gave] my opinion that there was probably very little in Tanga. . . . If the Fox went in and abrogated the truce that would destroy any chance of surprise."[25]

Aitken was fond of huffing that the Indian Army would make short work of a rabble of Africans. He dismissed the possibility of serious opposition. He said he intended to stampede the Germans in two days' time.[26] None of the conferees argued the point with him prior to the event. One must suspect they all—including RM—shared his preconceptions: Tanga was undefended and it was just a matter of marching in and taking the city. When things turned out otherwise, several of them later attempted to absolve themselves of responsibility. That was natural. But RM's concoctions were exceptional. Contradicting his own dismissal of Tanga's lack of defenses, he later wrote: "My intelligence report of 1 November [1914] said that 4,000 German troops might be expected [at Tanga] with numerous machine guns."[27] And: "If only Sheppard and Aitken had not ignored my Intelligence Reports."[28]

He submitted no such reports. Had he done so, he might have been rushed immediately into confinement as a dangerous lunatic. Everybody in the pre-attack conference knew there weren't four thousand troops in all of German East Africa, let alone at Tanga. In actual strength there were only about 125 *schutztruppen* in and around Tanga, of whom just a few dozen men were trained troops; they had two machine guns, and these would be augmented by only two more during the course of the battle.

In fact warnings were voiced and were heard. They were not ignored. And it was not RM who spoke them.

Aitken's chief of staff, Brig. Gen. "Collie" Sheppard, reminded the conferees that substantial German forces were concentrated near Kilimanjaro, on the frontier where the Germans had seized and were holding the strategic (formerly) British outpost at Taveta.[29] Sheppard asserted (correctly) that it would take the German forces about thirty-six hours to get from Taveta down to Tanga by train. His estimate was accepted, but it was agreed the invasion would proceed. Everyone felt the timetable would give the Force enough time to secure Tanga before the Germans arrived.

🖋 🖋 🖋

As the Mombasa meeting broke up, Governor Belfield took RM aside. There was a telegram from RM's sister in England.

His mother, Georgina Potter Meinertzhagen, had died.

RM left the meeting "almost in tears."[30]

It is the only mention of his mother's death in *Army Diary*, and not even in the full-length typescript diaries does he appear to have dealt with the loss until two years later when he was invalided back to England and found that what was left of the family seemed incomplete without her.

The relationship between mother and son had been contradictory at best. Evidently he had not seen her since 1911, and he later complained that even though his mother had been unpleasant toward him, he felt affection toward her. It is impossible to tell from his guarded writings how much of the professed affection is a dutiful recitation of what he felt was expected of him. His mother had been a woman of quick intelligence whose aims often were dismissed by the men around her. Those who knew her regarded her as one of the brightest of the Potter sisters (all of whom were far brighter than average) but she had not achieved as much as some of the others had done; hers had been a disappointed life.

🐦 🐦 🐦

It was true that General Aitken had no grasp of the situation, as RM complained.

The record shows that RM had none either.

Headed for Tanga on November 1, the British attack force steamed south, its eleven transport ships flagged by the converted P&O liner *Karmala* and escorted by the Royal Navy's cruiser HMS *Fox*.

The invasion began early on Monday, November 2, with several false starts that were caused by Caulfield's concern about nautical mines and by the Germans' shameless insistence on literal enforcement of the Governors' Treaty with its provision for twenty-four hours' warning. (As Sheppard had predicted, Lettow and his *askari* needed time to come in from the mountains.)

The British high command dithered aboard ship. Apparently it had not occurred to any of the senior officers of Force "B" to finalize a plan of action in case the enemy didn't simply surrender the town.

This does not seem to have troubled the commanding general. Aitken sat in a deck chair reading a novel. He beckoned Norman King forward to explain the system he had planned for Civil Administration in the colony after it became British. King was baffled by the way the general seemed unaware that his troops were preparing for a bullet-whipped landing on a hostile shore.[31]

When the 24-hour truce expired, Aitken sent the first elements of his army toward the beach about a mile east of Tanga, out of sight from the town under the shelter of a cliff. Apparently he thought the landings would be unobserved,[32] in spite of the fact that every German within a hundred miles knew he had given Tanga notice of his intention to attack if the city didn't surrender.

On shore five or six Germans manned the lookout points. They were mystified and amused by the agonizingly slow arrival of *Fox* and three troop transports as they inched through the water. (The rest of the thirteen-ship force would remain farther out at sea until the following morning.[33]) The effort to get soldiers from ship to shore was bedeviled by delays, reefs, accidents, misjudgments, and near-drownings.

Lt. Gordon S. Johnson's battalion was the first to be able to get ashore. He found no joy in the affair. "The disembarkation arrangements appeared to be extraordinarily mismanaged; the troops sat in lighters for hours [lodged on reefs far out from the beach] waiting for a tug to tow them ashore. The tugs cast off while still in water too deep to wade and there was another long wait for boats. Had the Germans resisted the disembarkation they could have destroyed the troops as they sat helpless in the lighters."[34]

Three or four German riflemen did manage to fire some potluck rounds from shore at extreme range (about six hundred yards) until *Fox* pumped a six-inch shell in their direction.[35] According to RM it deepened an unoccupied trench and could be heard for miles, alerting any Germans who may have remained unaware of the pending invasion.[36]

A scalding typhoon now descended.

Lettow was on his way from Kilimanjaro with trainloads of troops but he wouldn't arrive until late into the night of November 3. Meanwhile the preliminary follies extended from dawn of November 2 until noon the next day, by which time the weather began to improve, several battalions had made it to shore, and additional ships were disembarking troops into lighters.

On the beachhead some of the Indians were unfit to carry on. Disoriented and savagely ill, they had no idea where they were or what was expected of them. They had had no food in many hours and their legs had atrophied from the months of imprisoned inactivity.

German spotters were puzzled by the lunatic wobbling of the Indian troops, and by the way the British had chosen a landing beach that seemed extraordinarily unsuitable to their purpose. To get to Tanga from here the invaders would have to negotiate a swamp, climb a cliff, and then wade, jump, and hack their way through an abundance of mangrove reeds, plantations, and thorn bush.

Hadn't the English asked anybody about the terrain?

Finally on the morning of November 3, a handful of German defenders, knowing they must delay the invaders several more hours before Lettow could arrive with reinforcements, assembled on the heights. These few launched a clattering attack on Force "B."

Some of the British bearers immediately dropped their machine-guns and ran back to the water, yelling at each other in a cacophony of languages.

These who began the rout were bearers, not soldiers. But the hysteria of their flight infected the soldiers behind them, and soon the bearers were followed by dozens of limping Indian troops.

The handful of German *askari* took advantage of the confusion by shooting at the fleeing sepoys. German bullets hammered them up and spun them down, and the Indians' return fire was indiscriminate shooting of a very poor standard. General Wapshare wrote: "They were . . . pressed by the enemy. [At] 8:40 the Fox now fired some six inch shell into the beach which stopped [the Germans]."[37]

His colleague, General Tighe, wrote ludicrously of "[e]stimating enemy force of 2,500 rifles."[38] (The *schutztruppe* riflemen and a few indignant German civilians were in fact about eighty-five in number.)

Lt. Col. Charles Jourdain—a veteran officer who remained cool under fire—wrote: "A good deal of rain fell while the first few companies were landing. Information was received from Brig. Gen. Tighe that the 13th Rajputs & 61st Pioneers had had a reverse & were demoralized. There was a good deal of depression & jumpiness about, and a shot fired by a man of F Company caused a stampede of natives & Indians near General Tighe's Head Quarters."[39]

General Wapshare added: "The 13th Rajputs would not go [forward], and Tighe in consequence had to fall back. He and his Brigade Major had marvelous scrapes—one shot going through the leg of his trousers. His Staff Captain Walter was killed. Tighe's losses were heavy in officers & men."[40]

Whether or not Aitken had finished reading his novel, he remained aboard his flagship until late afternoon when he came ashore. He would have done better to remain at sea literally as well as figuratively. From the ship he had had contact with shore units by means of flashing lamps. Once he was ashore things moved too fast to allow for the stringing of telephone lines. Runners kept getting lost in the mangroves and bush. In the slashing rain it was impossible to use heliographs (which used flashes of the sun's rays to send reflected dot-dash signals). Aitken's communications officer, Malleson, had prepared no usable means of communication with the battalions. So no one could make contact with anyone else who wasn't actually within field of vision or earshot.[41]

Astonished by the sheer size of the enemy force, the Germans hesitated, and pulled back to regroup. As a result the two sides lost contact with each other. The howling downpour resumed, and several hours of groping ensued while the swampy land and furious insects made the invaders even more miserable. The Navy refused to send boats to pick up the fleeing Indian bearers, so they huddled on the beach all day in a miserable driving rain while Aitken's second brigade was landed from shipboard.

The fiasco was chaotic and grim. Pockets of fighting were fierce but disorganized because the companies were isolated and bewildered by the lack of instructions or information.

At this point the town was empty; Aitken could have walked in, but he didn't know that. It seems not to have occurred to RM or anyone else to probe the town with patrols.

During the early hours RM remained on shipboard. After he went ashore his role on the beach at first is unclear; he did not give, seek, or receive orders. He seems to have flitted from one point to another without evident purpose, and without producing useful information. In his observations of these hours we find little of significance other than his uncanny foreknowledge of things no one else was thinking at the time, such as his awe-struck admiration for the efficiency of the German army—he calls it "the world's finest military machine" (a phrase that clanks with connotations of Wehrmacht propaganda from World War II).

The rain stopped and Tanga became an airless steam bath. Colonel Jourdain, commanding the Loyal North Lancashires, revealed his gloom: "Very hot. Emerged into thick crops . . . lost touch . . . . Men lay down and appeared to take no further part in the fight." [42]

RM appears, at last—or at least he seems to be there:

> On the edge of Tanga, Tighe ran into an entrenched position strongly held by the enemy. Soon after, he was attacked and beaten back, his men breaking and disorganised. No amount of heroic example on behalf of the British officers availed. Officer after officer was shot down trying to rally the men and stem the tide of flight. Waller, Ishmael, and Carr Harris fell and if the enemy had pressed the attack the whole force would have been captured or driven into the sea. And the Fox never fired a shot.
>
> Tighe estimates the enemy strength at 2,500 rifles, but from what I saw, I should say it was more like 250 with four machine guns. From the local German press it appears the Germans had no intention of holding Tanga and I doubt if there was any [more] than a handful of police in the place yesterday.[43]

Next morning, RM adds acidly: "Aitken decided to attack Tanga today but not until after all the headquarters officers had a good breakfast."

Wednesday, November 4. RM describes a rabble of confused sepoys bolting from the line. He is compelled to stop them—to teach them a lesson with his boots and his pistol. He lays about him with abandon, clubbing and/or shooting to death large numbers of Indian soldiers from the 13th Shekhawat Rajputs who are fleeing or kneeling to pray. He is "forced" to shoot a Rajput Indian officer who tries to draw his sword on RM.[44] (One wonders how many British officers may have been stupid enough to draw their swords on other British officers who were armed with ready firearms. One also may wonder how an officer teaches "cowards" any sort of useful lesson by killing them. And one may wonder why none of these executions allegedly perpetrated by RM appears in anybody's accounts other than his own.)

At this point RM is at the rear of the British troops—because that is where fleeing troops would be. If we believe his assertions, therefore, we also must believe he is in no position to ascertain anything about enemy positions or strength, and is too busy slaughtering his own people to go near the enemy.

The general picture of the Tanga debacle that will be handed down to historians is of a handful of superhuman Germans and noble *askaris* making fools of cowardly Indians, sending them screaming in panic. That picture will be derived in part from RM's vitriolic and contemptuous faultfinding. It is not by any means a whole or balanced truth.

In reality the Battle of Tanga was not an unmitigated collapse of the Indian Army. Several spirited face-to-face encounters took place between Lettow's troops (by now about five hundred in number, and another several hundred were assembling, having come down by train from Moshi) and Aitken's lot, of whom thousands were willing and able to fight; we would not know that from reading RM and his beneficiaries.

Indians were not the only ones filled with fear. Lettow's adjutant, Captain von Hammerstein, was so enraged by the flight of a scared German *askari* from his post that Hammerstein threw an empty beer bottle at the man and knocked him out cold. This caused such hilarity among the *askaris* that Lettow and Hammerstein encouraged their men to throw beer bottles at enemy troops. How much beer-drinking was involved is an open question, but there's no question the bottle-throwing had a wonderful effect on *askari* morale and seemed to throw some of the sepoys into even greater confusion.

In spite of all this, most British formations held their ground in spite of ridiculous and contradictory commands from above.

Many German troops were brand-new volunteers—one rifle company was made up entirely of landlocked sailors from German merchant ships who had been marooned by the Allied blockade. Lettow's little force had not yet learned to work as a unified army. Most of his men were armed with obsolete black-powder 1871 rifles—relics of the Franco-Prussian War, some of them marked with an "X" as unusable.[45]

On the British side, some of the Indian units certainly were not physically or emotionally fit to serve. But, RM to the contrary, others gave a brave account of themselves—braver than their officers had any right to expect. At the same time, some soldiers of the great German machine behaved like fools. To green recruits on either side, the experience was an education in horror. They were learning that war was not glorious. It not only looked gruesome but it smelled dreadful—open latrines, accidents in pants, blood, rot, and the stench of burnt cordite. Lettow summed it up best when he pointed out later that many of those who served on both sides were very young and had had no experience of war before this.[46]

As for the story of Tanga that was passed forward, we should be aware that the two most important factors in measuring "panic" among sepoys were an observer's distance from the action and the direction from which he observed it. RM in the rear echelon saw troops bursting out of the bush and fleeing toward him, and may have believed he was seeing a rout. He certainly saw a disorganized crowd of terrified deserters in flight, but these were a minority. The men who stayed in the front lines and fought were not the ones who were seen and scorned by observers in the rear.

Late on November 4 RM asserts he gathered up two dozen courageous Kashmiris. There is no proof outside his own tales that he went near the thick of battle at any time, but he says he led his recruits into the town, where sharp fighting was in progress.

> German machine guns were deadly and swept every approach, every house spitting fire . . . .
> [Of the 25 men I had with me, nine] fell at the first attempt to cross. My men dwindled away or were shot and I found myself with two men in the Customs House and there was soon a lull in the firing.
> Keeping a sharp look-out for any chance of a shot I saw a small group of Germans peering round a house not 150 yards from me. Keeping well hidden, I hoped they might expose themselves more and give me a fair shot, which they soon did. One tall man with a fine face gave me a splendid chance, and I fired at him, but missed. I saw my bullet

splash on the wall just by him. So I gave him another and again missed. Never before had I had such an easy target or made such bad shooting. They then commenced to fire back and we had a duel lasting five minutes, one of my men being shot through the head, but for some unexplained reason, neither I nor those Germans could shoot straight. It annoyed me intensely for two reasons, it was my first fair chance at a German and, secondly, I had shot abominably. This party of Germans disappeared round the house and I saw them no more, and as I seemed more or less isolated I got back to Aitken with my one man and reported what I had seen, for I really had no business up in the firing line. Though I could not imagine what an intelligence officer's duties were in a fight like this, except to try and help.

On my way back I found seven Rajput sepoys cowering under a bank in deadly terror of their lives. I ordered them out and into a position whence they could shoot. Two obeyed, but the others demurred and finally refused to move, so I threatened them with my rifle, when they all got up and moved, but one man still refused and on threatening me with his rifle I shot the brute as he lay half-crazy with fear.[47]

These paragraphs are fraught with lies and inadvertent confessions. By the time the fighting got into Tanga some of it had become very nasty, as street battles tend to do; but Lettow's only machine guns were east of town attempting to stem the main British advance. There were no German machine guns in town.

RM's admission that he can't imagine what an intelligence officer's duties were is enough to give us pause. He was recently graduated from Staff College. The nature of his duties ought to have been clear enough: Determine the lie of the land, locate the enemy, enumerate his strength, ascertain his capacities and movements and if possible his intentions—and keep reporting this information promptly to field command so that HQ's decisions can be based on the most current knowledge.

His description of house-to-house combat in town is inaccurate because RM wasn't there. His report must have been cobbled together from second-hand information. The Loyal North Lancashires[48]—a battalion of Europeans raised in India—had seized the Customs House and, along with a party of Kashmiri Gurkhas, lived up to their reputations as first-class fighting men.[49] The battle was ferocious, and regrettable; there was great suffering. Lettow's soldiers were "staggered by the intensity of the enemy's fire." Finally the Germans tenaciously pulled themselves together to counterattack and drove the Lancs back to the east, out of the city. When Jourdain's battalion fell back outside town, German machine guns inflicted dreadful casualties on them,[50] much as Meinertzhagen's and Butler's Maxim gun had slaughtered the Nandi at Ket Parak.

The same horrendous crossfire outside the town was described by General Wapshare: "The enemy were [sic] able to get two machine guns onto them from both sides . . . & did terrible executions, one double company being wiped out."[51]

If we believe RM's account (above) of his own alleged movements, then before the main body of troops backed into that deadly crossfire, he personally had lost twenty-four of the twenty-five soldiers who came with him. That would be an appalling failure on any officer's record, if indeed it were true. He also purports to have killed at least two more of his own soldiers deliberately—"I shot the brute as he lay half-crazy with fear"—and this doesn't include the unidentified men earlier to whom he says he had taken boot and pistol.

Years later Lettow would write in his autobiography: "As darkness fell . . . the only people at the German front were myself and a few companions. We were fired upon by an enemy patrol. That was Captain Meinertzhagen, the leader of the British Intelligence Service, who was scouting out Tanga. My first sociable interchange with my friend Meinertzhagen!"[52]

The scene in which Lettow and Meinertzhagen try to shoot each other is charmingly incongruous, but it didn't happen. Lettow is not lying; he's accepting a fellow officer's generosity in filling in the blanks.

It comes clear in Lettow's autobiography when he reveals that a key source of some of his postwar information about the battle at Tanga was "Colonel Meinertzhagen, who had been the head of the British Intelligence Service in East Africa and had also fought at Tanga. I must thank him for important communications that only then made some events understandable to me."[53]

One can picture the two of them in 1926 at Lettow's table, sliding dinnerware around to represent the movements of each side's forces. Possibly Lettow mentioned to RM the luck with which he escaped injury from British rifles. It would take no more than that to trigger RM's solipsistic imagination. One imagines him leaping up in excitement. "Why, that rifle was mine! I was the one shooting at you. Isn't it uncanny how we couldn't hit each other?"

Lettow would have had no reason to disbelieve him. Later when he sat down to write the story of his life, he incorporated the RM version of the harmless duel at Tanga because he probably believed it (why shouldn't he?) and because it provided him with a ready-made literary device with which to introduce RM in the pages of his autobiography—a book in which RM reappears several times.

The battle of Tanga sank into its final calamity. General Wapshare wrote: "Wednesday 4th Nov.—A swarm of bees attacked us. This caused a good deal of confusion; I was badly stung myself and had to bolt into a dark tent for a moment to get rid of them. By now the Indian troops were getting shaken & the bees causing men to run about started the riot. Nothing we could now do would stop it."

Gordon S. Johnson wrote: "An attempt to communicate between Infantry and Guns was made by running a telephone [line] from the Infantry back along the road, up which we advanced, to the top of the cliffs and thence by flag to the ships. It appears to have been ineffective. I have heard that the signaler was stung to death by bees."[54]

Norman King wrote: "Saw a Tommy come in with a swollen face which looked like a sheet of linen sprinkled with black pepper . . . he muttered, 'Bees'. . . ."[55]

Farmers had been cultivating bees for their honey in the plantations on the outskirts of Tanga. Artillery, machine-guns, and rifles had unsettled the hives. The bees retaliated by swarming. The attack of killer bees was the last straw for Tighe's dazed sepoys. Their retreat was an unstoppable riot, and instantly a legend was born: that Lettow drew the enemy into position and fired his machine guns into the hives to provoke the bees into stinging the British back to their ships.

Lettow was delighted with this bit of mythology, and did nothing to discourage the legend until after the war: "I may now perhaps betray the fact that at the decisive moment all the machine-guns of one of our companies were put out of action by these same 'trained bees,' so that we suffered from this new 'training' quite as much as the English."[56]

The "trained bees" myth spread like a Serengeti wind. It was taken for gospel throughout Africa. It added new majesty to Lettow's fabled mystical powers. Nearly a century later people would still be relating—with conviction—the tale of "The Battle of the Bees."[57]

Years later, RM would claim that he and two other officers, being convinced that Aitken was unfit to command, proposed to toss a coin to decide which of them should kill Aitken.[58] Neither of the alleged co-conspirators

(General Sheppard, Colonel Dobbs) appears ever to have heard of this muti-
nous meditation. Dobbs was a transport officer and Sheppard was the Chief
of Staff who (RM later wrote) ignored RM's alleged intelligence reports.
He doesn't explain why he should pick these two for henchmen, but
both of them were dead by 1942 and couldn't deny the complicity he
imputed to them.

What actually happened was not a mutiny but an appeal to what little
common sense Aitken may have possessed. On the evening of November 4
he issued orders that the entire force was to attack next morning. In what
must have been a state of near-apoplectic desperation, Wapshare, Tighe,
and Shepherd buttonholed the commanding general, told him in no uncertain terms that he had already lost a third of his force and most of his line
officers and that his cause was lost, and implored him to get the men off the
beaches, back to the transports, and out of German East Africa.[59]

There was no mutiny, and no one threatened his life. His officers
asked, and Aitken concurred. He called off the order to attack. He ordered
a withdrawal.

Lettow put it in context with graceful simplicity: "The enemy felt himself completely defeated, and so he was."[60]

In hindsight, given even a rudimentary understanding of the nature of
the human beast, we can feel more sympathy than contempt toward the
troops of Force "B." The sepoys had been led into slaughter by a cocked-up
system that rushed itself off to war while giving them virtually no training,
respect, or leadership. As often happens in war, it wasn't the troops who
lost the Battle of Tanga. It was the generals.[61]

Whether RM actually took part in the fighting on the ground is an
open question. He says he was there. No one else reports seeing him there.

He comes on stage, for certain, on the afternoon of November 5, after
the expeditionary force has withdrawn nearly all its men to the ships. He is
sent ashore under a truce flag to negotiate for the repatriation of wounded
prisoners. He has been selected for this chore because he speaks German.

RM carries a letter to the German commandant from Aitken, apolo-
gizing for yesterday's errant six-inch shell that demolished part of the German hospital. He makes his way into an armed compound—*The British
Commandant's respects, and Captain Meinertzhagen is at the* schutztruppe's
disposal—and is welcomed by several friendly officers:

> . . . and we chatted away like old friends, talking about yesterday's
> fight. . . . Several German officers who were present at breakfast

expressed their admiration at the behaviour of the North Lancs, and we discussed the fight freely as though it had been a football match. . . . Whilst . . . we conversed freely about the war, just outside the window were a few Germans lying among the trees sniping at the *Fox*. . . . I handed over . . . all our abandoned stores, a revolting job. We also administered parole to all ranks in hospital and the evacuation commenced . . . . We had breakfast with Dr. Deppe—good beer, ice, plenty of eggs and cream and asparagus.[62]

Complaining that he is suffering painful headaches from being blown into a palm tree by a shell from HMS *Fox*, he offers a summing up: "Here we were now, out of sight of land and steaming for Mombasa, a beaten and broken force. My confidence in the leadership and personnel of the force was badly shaken."[63]

The Battle of Tanga was an inconsequential engagement in the cosmic sense, but so lopsided a debacle that it ranks as one of the most foolish and embarrassing military disasters in the history of the British Empire. Aitken's more than 1,500 casualties outnumbered Lettow's active force in all Africa. Aitken abandoned virtually all his weapons, ammunition, and supplies on the beach for von Lettow, who hadn't slept for seventy-two hours but still managed to limit his side's casualties to a total of sixty-nine, most of whom were to live to fight again.

News of the defeat was withheld from the public in both Britain and India for several months.[64] The War Office issued an order prohibiting any mention of the Tanga tribulation in officers' correspondence.

Dismally, neither Churchill nor the military seemed to learn from the experience, for in some respects the next year's catastrophic landings at Gallipoli would follow a fatally similar pattern.

On December 1, 1914, Maj. Gen. A. E. Aitken submitted a self-serving report. London's blistering reply pushed aside Aitken's lame excuses and relieved him of all duties.[65] Attached to it were remarks that singled out the Force's worthless intelligence work. No intelligence officer was singled out by name, but nothing excludes RM from a share of the blame.[66]

In the end, nearly the only useful information RM provided to anyone was what he gave to the Germans. In 1919 Lettow wrote:

> The whole Anglo-Indian Expeditionary Force of 8,000 men had been thus decisively beaten by our force of little more than 1,000 men. Not till the evening [5 November] did we realize the magnitude of this

victory, when an English officer, Captain Meinertzhagen, came under a flag of truce to negotiate with Captain von Hammerstein, my representative, for the handing over of the wounded.[67]

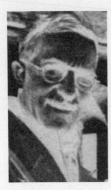

CHAPTER 6
NAIROBI

One of the features of the last week has been Brigadier-General Dealy, our Chief Engineer Officer. He is a charming fellow but constitutionally lazy. He also knows his work backwards. He made a lovely trestle bridge the other day and has spent the last seven days looking for a river over which to place it. The bridge turns up at all sorts of places, blocks the roads, gets stuck in the mud, loses its way in the bush, and visits every river in turn, seeking a home. It's a lovely bridge, just too large for some rivers, not quite fitting others, but Dealy has great hopes. . . . He is very keen that I should procure for him the bank-to-bank measurements of every river between here and Tanga in the hopes that his bridge may fit one of them.[1]

With such remarks RM captivated generations of readers—and writers.

By the end of 1914 he was in his prime at age thirty-seven. He had great charm along with the pious, bloodthirsty soul of a medieval knight. He was bold, conflicted, passionate, distant, deceitful, righteous, and ambivalent. His incident-prone life was an epic adventure that required no literary enhancement.

Compare the observations of one who served with him. Lt. Gordon Saffery Johnson came ashore at Tanga in 1914, was recruited onto the Intelligence staff in 1915, and remained in the office throughout RM's tenure and beyond. After the war Johnson wrote:

Meinertzhagen was a very efficient intelligence officer with lots of brains, no scruples, and quite unreliable; I was his "bottle-washer" (personal assistant) and got to know him very well. I admired his knowledge, ability, and skill as an I.O. and his courage in concealing for some months the pernicious anemia from which he was suffering. I would not trust him a yard or believe a word he said unless I knew that it suited his book to tell the truth in this instance.[2]

The legend: In 1914–1916 Richard Meinertzhagen builds a network of European, African, and Arab/Swahili agents who are able to move back and forth across the border into German East Africa. There they make use of RM's clever espionage invention, the "DPM" (Dirty Paper Method; the agent plucks valuable documents out of latrines, paper being in such short supply that it usually gets re-used as toilet tissue). They interview locals after plying them with drink; they pass tons of RM-created counterfeit money in order to undermine the value of the DOA rupee, they spread military disinformation to confuse the enemy, and they position dead animals around isolated healthy waterholes while erecting "Poison" signs at the water's edge.

This is the foundation of the RM myth, derived from his versions. They are not supported by accounts written by the men he served with, or by real-time records (including many of RM's own reports).

In the first of several head-rollings, Wapshare took Aitken's place. RM's views of this general's shortcomings, like those of Aitken's, have some merit. But RM did nothing to improve the job performance of "Wappy," whose diary sometimes reveals more than he may have wanted it to reveal: "3rd Jan. [1915]—Heard that the German had crossed frontier near the lake. Sent up two Co[mpanie]s of the L.N.L. & two guns. I then went out shooting with O'Grady & Meinertzhagen & got a zebra & Tommy."[3]

RM was an excellent safari guide for the generals; he made himself very popular in that role. And he spent quite a bit of time collecting birds and animals for his game bag. He hunted hippos[4] and all sorts of smaller game animals and birds, many of which he took the time to skin and stuff. Perhaps he did not allow his interest in wildlife to interfere with his military duties, but by the time he was ready to go home to England after two years in East Africa, he claimed he had accumulated three thousand specimens that he brought home. (He also said he had taken a great many wildlife photographs but, he wrote, all his exposed film was stolen from the hold of a ship in Mombasa in November 1916.[5])

Lettow kept raiding British outposts and blowing up British trains. RM explained that it wasn't his fault. "It is a curious fact that the authorities out here ignore my reports which are based on facts, and prefer to conjure up their own ideas which are pure imagination based on pure nonsense."[6] The record, however, shows that the authorities were working with what RM and his staff gave them. He never knew when or where the raiders would appear. Lettow's *askari*, with their *kofias* shading the backs of their necks and sometimes with camouflage vegetation growing out of their headwear, stalked their prey (usually railway trains), blew up bridges, seized supplies, and disappeared amid the acacia trees.

It was frustrating for British soldiers who caught only occasional and fleeting sight of the enemy. Lettow was determined to avoid pitched battles and not fight the British on their terms. (Lettow didn't like to listen to chaplains reading prayers over the dead, regardless who was dead.)

One night he blew up the Tsavo bridge—the most elaborate span on the Uganda Rail line. It had taken British and Indian engineers a year to build it in 1896–97 and had cost the lives of several British officers, about thirty Indian laborers, and more than a hundred Africans, many of them mauled to death by an infamous pair of man-eating lions. Now in a matter of moments Lettow had destroyed it.[7]

Large crews of Indian laborers protected by KAR troops were kept on the run to repair the railway. Although their improvised solutions often were ingenious, sometimes it could take a train more than a week to get from Mombasa to Nairobi.

Both the Imperial War Museum and the Public Records Office now have extensive collections of RM's neatly letterpress-printed reports. Examining them in comparison with his diary entries is a revealing exercise.

The British kept analyzing the campaign in their own lights. They determined which sectors the enemy would hold most tenaciously—key railway junctions, for example, or important towns or productive fertile areas. Once these places were identified, Britain's superior strength could drive Lettow back to one or another of those strongpoints and he must stop to defend it. And there, they knew, he could be defeated.

Lettow knew Germany was not going to win the World War on the plains of Africa. He did not think in terms of holding strongpoints. What mattered was that every soldier the British set against him in Africa was a soldier who couldn't fight against the Fatherland on the Western Front.[8] That was his purpose in holding the British to the wheel and grinding them against it by conducting a war of movement and lightning raids, and by whisking his forces out of harm's way as soon as his immediate objective was accomplished, thus keeping his small army intact.

RM later pretends to have known better, but in his reports he repeatedly and mistakenly assumes that Lettow will not give up territory or abandon his Central Railway because to do so would mean the abandonment of some important tract of *Deutsche Ost-Afrika*.

The British kept mounting huge operations designed to encircle Lettow—and invariably the pincers closed on abandoned campsites.

As the war continued, Lettow succeeded in drawing the British (and the French, Belgians, and Portuguese) out to the ever-lengthening ends of arduous supply lines, and exhausting them. If the British had understood his scheme they'd simply have cut him loose and let him drift on his own. That, for Lettow, would have been defeat. But it was the one tactic the Allies never attempted.

An observant intelligence operative might have become aware of Lettow's thinking early on, from interrogating prisoners and refugees and from reading the newspapers. Yet a thorough examination of RM's intelligence reports and the appreciations of GHQ reveals a stunning failure (shared by his fellow officers) to understand Lettow's intent.

By the end of the war no fewer than 137 British generals—more than the number of commissioned German field-combat officers of all grades in the entire *Schutztruppe*—had served against Lettow. None of them caught him.[9]

If one believes the diaries then RM alone was aware of Lettow's plan as early as November 13, 1914—just a week after Tanga: "Von Lettow is not going to fight it out. He will flit from pillar to post and occupy as many of us as he can."[10] Later he elaborates: "Von Lettow is slippery and is not going to be caught by maneuver. He knows the country better than we do; his troops understand the last word in bush warfare and can live on the country. I think we are in for an expensive hide-and-seek, and von Lettow will still be cuckooing somewhere in tropical Africa when the cease-fire goes."[11]

Outside his diaries there is no hint he thought or said these things during the war. Many years after the war he said them, and he was believed. No one seems to have asked the obvious question: Why is there no contemporary record of his ever having made this argument, or of a general reacting to it?

Each report and summary prepared for top command by Meinertzhagen and his Intelligence Staff, East Africa Force, had to be signed by an officer. From January 1915 to August 1916, except on dates when he was away from Nairobi, the distinctive signature is that of Richard Meinertzhagen.

These papers establish RM's whereabouts. Often they show—over his own signature—that at times when he later wrote he was off in the wilderness fighting Germans, he was in fact where he was supposed to be: at his desk in Nairobi (or out with generals in nearby parks on game-hunting day trips). They also establish a mark against which to measure the extent to which his reports were or were not ignored, and they give us a chance to examine the professed achievements of his spy network.

His then-aide, Gordon Johnson, later wrote:

> [Meinertzhagen] wrote a fictional account of his adventures in GEA[12] to suit his own prejudices and hatreds—e.g., of the Indian Army. You will notice . . . how often he claims to have corrected senior officers or ordered them about. Some of these stories are comic—e.g., on page 74 [of Leonard Mosley's book *Duel for Kilimanjaro*] Meinertzhagen says that he "told Dobbs to get back on board at once." Meinertzhagen was then a captain and Dobbs a Lt. Colonel who would not have tolerated such impertinence for a moment—nor would Meinertzhagen have tried it on him. Then, and afterwards when I knew him as a Major, he behaved before senior officers with the normal good manners exacted of all regular officers; he did not offer his opinions unasked![13]

RM made contributions. His maps and descriptions of the enemy landscape were superb. His reports are handsome[14]—he commandeered a printing press and provided his successive generals (Wapshare, then Tighe, then Smuts) with beautifully printed daily reports. These contained maps of German railways and road systems, gazetteers of water hole locations and the size and placement of enemy fortifications, expertly drawn contour charts, notes on seasonal weather expectations and disease belts, and— the feature for which he became especially admired—biographical information about every officer in the German army across the border, right down to each officer's food preference, shoe size, and educational background. He included photographic reproductions of each officer's signature (even Lettow's) for use by British officers who might care to identify or to forge German documents.

His generals, especially the celebrated South African Boer hero Jan Christiaan Smuts (who took command early in 1916), marveled at the thorough detail of Meinertzhagen's intelligence work. What they did not seem to realize was that his reports on enemy leaders were derived from pre-war information that Norman King and other British subjects had brought with them from German East Africa before the war started. Circumstances forced the Germans to be a consistent lot: all the Germans who were with Lettow at the end of the war had been with him at the beginning. No newcomers arrived after the war broke out.

In these circumstances it was not difficult for RM to parcel out rations of information from the documentation he had on hand right from the very beginning.

Other information seems to have been derived from the Royal Navy's East Africa *Handbook*.[15] Updated from time to time, this little pocket-size gem contained the most recent fragments of information about enemy activities that the Navy had been able to learn from wireless intercepts and from the capture of enemy cargo vessels.

Updates occasionally appeared in RM's reports; many of these seem to have come in by way of interviews with British soldiers who had been captured by the Germans and then turned loose on parole. Other bits came from interviews that Norman King—the soul of politeness—conducted with Germans who were taken prisoner in the succession of skirmishes that peppered the period of RM's service in the theater. Norman King was a congenial soul who had made friends with many German officers before the war and greeted them as old chums rather than as enemies when he went to visit them in the various stockades where they were held for a while before being shipped back to Europe. For their part, the Germans were happy to see him and to receive his generous gifts of food and beer, but they appear to have been fiercely loyal (perhaps more loyal to Lettow than to Germany) and they seldom gave up information of real significance, nor was King so discourteous as to try and pry sensitive information out of them if they were unwilling to share it.

It does not appear that RM took the time to interrogate many prisoners personally, although he spoke German. The brunt was carried by Norman King, usually in Nairobi where the former Consul hobnobbed with the Lord Delamere set.[16] Wapshare wrote, "King, Mackay's assistant, speaks & reads German like a native. Complimented me on my accent."[17] King was congenial and disarming, but from the tone of his diaries it seems unlikely he obtained much useful intelligence. The atmosphere was one of camaraderie rather than hatred; the war was an inconvenience to be endured by all, but let it not interfere with friendships or bridge tournaments.[18]

If RM had any difficulty with this arrangement, he does not seem to have mentioned it.

In his diary King repeatedly confirms that after these interviews he always filed his reports with RM. He expresses no impression or opinion of RM.

Most of King's reports have not survived. But we can see that few results of his interrogations found their way into the reports RM delivered to GHQ and the field commands.

In general, field officers of the East Africa Force were not shy about what they felt was slipshod work in the General Staff. South African Brig. F.

B. Adler wrote, "Intelligence work, especially in the Kilimanjaro operations, was poor."[19]

What RM did may have been an acceptable form of collation, but it was mainly library research and it was mainly useless. Just enough information seems to have come into his office, and to have been passed from his desk to the generals', to distract them from the fact that they were not getting what they needed. Where were Lettow's main forces? What were his lines of march? What were his intentions?

During his two years in the East Africa campaign, Captain (and then, at last, in the summer of 1915, Major[20]) Meinertzhagen submitted a great many Intelligence Reports.[21] In return he received very few orders, requests, or inquiries. Did his superiors not expect much of him? Between the lines of accounts written by civilians and fellow officers one gets the impression he was appreciated more as safari hunter, polo teammate, tour guide, naturalist, and social companion than as intelligence overseer.[22] The occasional comment about the poverty of intelligence seems to have skirted issues: no one wanted to insult anyone.[23]

He did make an effort to flood German East Africa with counterfeit currency. From banknotes confiscated from German POWs, he personally forged a sample of the 20 *Rupien* note issued at Dar es Salaam on March 15, 1915. He thought it fine work: "I have now had several million printed which I intend to introduce into German East in the hopes of discrediting their paper currency in which their men are paid. . . . I have been busy today spreading out my spurious notes in the sun to get them bleached and dirty. The Standard Printing Press printed them for me."[24]

In the year 2001 dealers in collectibles were asking $400 for one of Meinertzhagen's counterfeit *Deutsche Ost-Afrika* notes. That's eight times as much as they could get for a genuine German one—because not many of RM's forgeries remain. The counterfeits fooled no one. He printed his fake currency on paper that was as stiff as cardboard (the originals were on softer paper) and he used two separate German notes as the matrix for his printing plates, so that his counterfeit notes all had the same pairs of serial numbers, the one on the front being different from the one on the back.

His alleged "several million" notes was in reality probably a few thousand. These can seem difficult to picture, if indeed they were spread out to dry under the African sun with high-plains breezes coming up at frequent intervals.

However many they were, his counterfeits were detected by the Germans and put to suitable use as kindling or as wadding for their homemade artillery ammunition. So RM's surviving forgeries have become rarities, and command a high price today.[25]

Later RM would write about heat-of-battle adventures and his tireless round-the-clock work in building a network of thousands of intelligence agents. He quotes a passage about himself in the Official History that describes his estimates of enemy strength as having been ignored by the authorities. Then the Official History, as quoted by RM, describes how RM built up an Intelligence section of more than three thousand agents who provided vital information to the Army.[26]

These hallucinations have been perpetuated by generations of authorities on British Africa.

The Official History praises RM for his efficient organization of agents, but in a footnote it explains that the scouts in the field, in numbers that "eventually exceeded 3,000" were led by "Pretorius and others, particularly in the Lake area under Capt. J. J. Drought."[27] RM's versions disregard this footnote, and both writers deprive us of the fact that neither Pretorius nor Drought was under RM's jurisdiction. The celebrated hunter-guide Pieter Pretorius operated under a South African chain of command, quite separate from RM's authority, and the remarkable James J. Drought and his "Skin Corps"—a frontier unit of Ugandan *askari* scouts, organized under Uganda KAR command—was another with whom RM had no connection apart from the occasional pro-forma paperwork. Drought and RM struck up a sort of friendship after the war, but in 1915 they did not work together, in spite of RM's diary statements to the contrary.

Pretorius and Drought ran guerrilla units of scouts, not spies. Precisely because RM does not make the distinction, it becomes important for the rest of us to know that there is a difference between military scouts and intelligence agents. Agents by definition are undercover spies operating behind enemy lines and pretending to work for or with the enemy. Scouts, on the other hand, are soldiers, usually in uniform—a visible part of the army rather than an invisible force behind the lines.

On occasion the line between scouts and spies may have become a bit smudged: Drought's "Skin Corps" *askari* infiltrated enemy lines and they wore no uniforms (no clothes at all, virtually), but their missions were to engage the enemy and to drive him away from his positions—not to obtain information about the enemy's military secrets in clandestine fashion and sneak away unseen.

RM writes:

25th July 1916. Lukigura
    In July 1916 a War Office representative came out to report on our
"intelligence" service. I told him everything except the DPM method.
He was amazed at the small sum we spent on secret services and practically insisted on giving us more. My monthly bill for secret service
was barely £150 and this War Office man insisted we must spend more,
offering to open an account for £10,000, which I refused. A deliberate
attempt to make me waste public money.[28]

    RM's sense of fiscal responsibility may be commendable but if his
entire department subsisted on 150 pounds a month then how large a string
of agents can he have been running over there behind German lines? Such
agents are motivated by many things, but tangible rewards like money generally come well before noble sentiments like patriotism.

    In the winter of 1915 a handful of British scouts daringly ventured
into German country near Kilimanjaro. They braved perils and near-misses,
and eventually were looking at Lettow himself. Before they could decide on
an action, however, the party was betrayed into German hands by its own
African guide.
    One member of that scouting party, Lt. Arthur Wienholt, was interro-
gated by Lettow himself, personally and courteously. Wienholt loyally refused to give Lettow any significant answers and Lettow gently refused to
press the youth. Allowing Weinholt to keep his dignity, Lettow saw that his
injury was properly dressed. Soon after, when no infection appeared, Lettow
paroled Wienholt, releasing him to return to British lines.[29]
    The gentlemanly gesture on Lettow's part was practical. Wienholt could
be counted on to report back to his commanders on the excellence of German strength and morale. Similar vignettes appear in other officers' memoirs.[30] These accounts lead to unexpected markers on the RM trail. Wienholt,
for example, writes of his detachment's betrayal by a turncoat African guide.
This seems to be one of several instances of "treachery" on the part of tribesmen who worked for British intelligence.
    Both RM's intelligence reports and his later diaries complain of such
treason, and it is reflected in the notes of several commanding generals.
    Africans can be just as loyal and dependable as any other group of
humans. In this instance they may not have cared which European army
won the war, but those Africans who signed on (as "hired guns," so to speak)

could be expected to remain loyal to their hire. If they grew tired of one side, some of them would resign, cross the border, and sign up with the other side (or sit out the war), but most of them lived by a code of honor. So long as they took an army's pay, they served that army loyally.

So if large numbers betrayed their vows of allegiance, it was not whimsical. It had a cause.

Why, then, were British troops betrayed to the Germans by their own African guides?

As soon as the war began, Mackay and other officers of the King's African Rifles had begun to recruit frontier tribesmen into the military to serve as scouts and intelligence agents. The tribes who lived along the boundary between British East Africa and German East Africa were especially in demand, because they could move back and forth without arousing suspicion. A Maasai woman, for example, could amble from German territory into British territory with her husband's herd of cattle as well as an observant brain filled with information about German outposts. She would cause no alarm on the part of passing soldiers of either army. When she reached a British encampment she would be paid for her information about the Germans.

Mackay (not Meinertzhagen) initiated that system, in collaboration with Uganda officers like James J. Drought. Then at the beginning of 1915 Mackay, who seems to have suffered from a recurrent fever (probably malaria), was offered the governorship of Mafia Island. He was grateful for the chance to move to its healthy climate. His departure left a vacancy. That was when General Wapshare filled it with his hunting chum Captain Meinertzhagen, who by that time had impressed GHQ with his African expertise.

This brought the fledgling force of frontier spies under RM's command.

The penny began to drop when we learned that most of the British Force's border spies came from the Nandi tribe. Altogether nearly two thousand of these tribesmen saw service in the war, some as soldiers and scouts and others as outright spies who went over to the German side and collected information and brought it back and got paid for it.

The two thousand Nandi who served Britain were, in number, about 20 percent of the then-adult male population of the entire tribe. In proportion to its numbers, the tribe easily provided the largest and most enthusiastic delegation of recruits to British *askari* ranks. Their way of life was war, and many of them happily had signed up.

The recruits' enthusiasm seems to have stopped short of RM's doorstep, however.

Nandi culture included a warrior circumcision ritual and a series of initiations that occurred at roughly fourteen-year intervals. Since it didn't take place every year or even every decade, boys and young men of various ages took part.

One such group had been admitted into warrior ranks a few years before the Laibon met his death in 1905 in an ambush that had been set up—notoriously—by Richard Meinertzhagen.[31]

It was the men of that group who made up the majority of active warriors a bit less than ten years after the Laibon's death when RM took over the British intelligence network in Nairobi.

These Nandi agents ranged in age from about eighteen to about thirty. Some of the older ones had followed the shaman Koitalel (the "Laibon"); some may have helped to bury him and his companions after RM and Butler packed up their Maxim gun and went home to Nandi Fort.

Nandi culture taught history by means of oral tradition. There can be little doubt that every Nandi agent in East Africa in 1915 knew exactly who RM was and what he had done in 1905. (Today they still know who he was and what he did.)

Perhaps because he shared a racial arrogance with fellow officers, RM did not recognize that his paid secret agents must have loathed him—personally. Those Nandi agents must have felt horribly betrayed when they found they'd been placed under command of the very officer who had slaughtered their kinsmen at Ket Parak Hill.

As a result, RM's very presence in the post warranted that the Germans would get a great deal of help from the Nandi, and that the British would get little or none.

23rd December 1931 [*sic*] . . . :

On the 23rd I left Karungu with Drought and fifteen Intelligence scouts. . . . We crossed the border on the 25th and soon got news from natives of an enemy patrol at Kitambi Hill, so we continued our march and at 5 p.m. we located four tents, fires burning and by the mercy of God, no precautions, no sentries, and men lounging about. We . . . rushed them silently from not more than a few paces. We used bayonets only and I think we each got our man. Drought got three, a great effort. I rushed into the officer's tent where I found a stout German on a camp bed. On a table was a most excellent Xmas dinner. I covered him with my rifle and shouted to him to hold his hands up. He at once groped under his pillow and I had to shoot, killing him at once. My shot

was the only one fired. . . . Drought said he was hungry, so was I, and
why waste that good dinner? So we set to and had one of the best
though most gruesome dinners I have ever had, including an excellent
Xmas pudding. The fat German dead in bed did not disturb us in the
least nor restrain our appetites, but looking back on it now I wonder
we could manage it. After that excellent meal, I searched the German's
kit. He was a reserve officer and apparently by name _____, a letter on
his person being addressed to Graf _____. So I must have shot a
Duke. The first Duke I have killed.[32]

RM's version of the Graf's Christmas Dinner in the unpublished diaries differs from the passage quoted above in just one detail: In the published book (as cited above), the count has no name. In the typescript RM
identifies the dead German officer as Graf Wecklenburg.[33]

Why delete the dead count's name from the published book? Perhaps
because there was no such person in East Africa as Graf Wecklenburg, nor
is there any record of the death of any German officer or of any action like
this one in Africa at the time.

James Drought's reports to KAR headquarters in Uganda show he
was otherwise occupied with his Skin Corps, hundreds of miles away in the
lake country.[34] RM's official reports during the time of the alleged incident
show he was behind his desk in Nairobi to sign the daily Intelligence staff
reports and summaries on every day of the alleged December 1915 trek.[35]

🐦 🐦 🐦

By March 1916 the 26th Squadron, Royal Flying Corps, was serving
as a spotter for artillery in the Kilimanjaro region. Every serviceable plane
was kept in the air "all day except between the hours of 1 P.M. and 3 P.M."
(The midday groundings were ordered because on many days "weather was
extremely hot and flying difficult.")

The squadron diary reports: "March 11th, 1916, 12:25 P.M. to 3:50
P.M.—2Lt. Bertram took Major Minashagen [sic], chief Intelligence Staff,
on a reconnaissance over Himo."[36]

For his part, RM gives posterity a more detailed report on the same
flight:

11th March 1916. Mbuyuni
    Soon after dawn this morning I took my first trip in an aeroplane
and I shall never forget the experience. I asked the pilot, a South African boy called Bertram, if he would first take me up to the level of

Kilimanjaro snows and then afterwards fly over the enemy's position at Latema-Reata. He said he could easily do the latter but doubted if his machine would carry us up as high as the snows of Kilimanjaro. However, I persuaded him to jettison as much weight as he could and take an extra supply of petrol.

Soon after starting we flew low over the bush towards Chala, passing over several herds of hartebeest, oryx, and giraffe. The giraffe were the only animals who evinced alarm. They scattered in all directions, galloping away with their ungainly amble and were soon lost to sight in the bush. On approaching Chala we mounted steadily and made for the summit of Kilimanjaro, soon registering 12,000 feet and reached the large grassy plateau north of the summit. We still ascended, reaching 17,000 feet when we were close to the huge snow-clad crater, the summit of the highest mountain in Africa. Our highest limit was 17,400 feet. We flew close to the snow and had a wonderful view, but it was all too short and I had little time to take it all in. All I remember is a wonderful dazzling snow-field which we circled and intense cold. I did not feel any effects from the height. There was unfortunately a slight haze on the plains, but we could see them stretching for miles in all directions, all bush-clad and blue in the distance, gradually merging into the horizon. Lake Jipe was a conspicuous feature and much larger than I imagined.

Having had a good gaze at the snow the pilot told me he was going to descend to Taveta. Engines were shut off and we glided down slowly to about 5,000 feet over Taveta. There I could easily see our troops encamped, the horse lines being very conspicuous. From Taveta we made for Latema and Reata Hills held by the enemy. Moshi appeared deserted and I could detect no movement on the Usambara Railway, but I saw a large body of German troops at the railway bridge over the Lumi River. When over Latema we came down to 3,500 feet, but I saw absolutely nothing. A small gun opened on us with shrapnel, but the bursts were very wide. Some ten rounds were fired at us. It was curious to see the shrapnel bursting and not to hear any explosion, the roar of our engines drowning everything.[37]

The passage may have stirred the hearts of adventure-hungry readers. It may seem both thrilling and credible at first glance. It agrees with the Squadron's log on such essentials as the pilot's name, the date, and the place. And Bertram's phonetic attempt to spell "Meinertzhagen" is entirely believable. But RM just couldn't leave well enough alone.

Kilimanjaro stands 19,340 feet high. Every pilot's log indicates that the 26th Squadron's best aircraft had at most an effective ceiling of about 5,000 feet in the heat-thinned equatorial air. RM saw the snow-capped top of Kilimanjaro the same way everyone else did: from far below. Even in a more hospitable climate for flying, no airplane in existence in early 1916 could climb much above 10,000 feet. No pilot or passenger could soar with any rapidity to an altitude of more than 15,000 feet (even in a balloon) without risking passing out from lack of oxygen. And if a World War I plane did somehow manage to claw its way to "17,400 feet" and then cut its engine, the thinness of the air at that altitude would have assisted the aircraft in assuming the glide path of a falling safe.[38]

RM's flight—both the real one and his flight of fancy—took place during a week when the heaviest fighting of the season was occurring around the flanks of Kilimanjaro. After the war the opponent, Lettow, wrote:

Colonel Meinertzhagen told me later that he had personally scouted the German positions in an airplane and not learned a thing. The enemy was fighting blindfolded. Their losses were great. On the night of the 11th of March [1916], Meinertzhagen himself was in Taveta, which the surviving English had flowed back into after we defeated them. He said there was enormous confusion, as they believed the Germans could come at any moment. The situation was such that the tread of Germans in Taveta on the night of the 11th of March would have led to a panic.[39]

RM does not mention any of this when he describes his recon, which he inserts as a self-contained set-piece. Others, however, seem to have noticed his flight and seem to have regarded it as a dangerous joyride. It provoked caustic criticism from Flight Lt. Bertram's Squadron Commander (Major Wallace), who wrote to GHQ:

I would like it to be placed on record that . . . the Squadron has its full complement of trained observer officers, whose duties it is to observe. If other officers are allowed to go up untrained and without experience they are liable to make conflicting reports with the result that reliance cannot be placed on any reports. . . . It is usual for observer officers to be attached to the Squadron . . . after having satisfied the authorities that they are competent officers for observation in the air . . .

That . . . officers would be sent up on special work such as . . . to

obtain perspective views of certain parts of the country seems unnecessary, as the same results could be obtained by photography, and the
reconnaissances would not be interfered with. The economical use of
aeroplanes is essential, and it is impossible to maintain efficiency if
officers are sent over the enemy to substantiate details already supplied by the squadron.[40]

By the beginning of 1916 it was clear the East African Force needed a
fresh commander. The War Office toyed with the notion of getting Winston
Churchill out of their hair by giving him command of the theater. Churchill
campaigned eagerly, but ultimately unsuccessfully, for the job; it went instead to South Africa's Boer hero, "Grey Steel" Gen. Jan Christiaan Smuts.[41]
While the question was still open, however, Churchill's quick-witted cousin
and former personal secretary (and then-Member of Parliament), Freddie
Guest, went to East Africa as Churchill's advance man. Guest soon found he
had no advances to make in his cousin's behalf. He made himself useful by
joining the Intelligence staff. During the next year he made a significant
impression on the life of RM.

    Smuts, the new Commanding General, took a liking to RM. On Febru-
ary 22, 1916 he put RM's name in for the Distinguished Service Order. This
brightened things a bit for RM but he still seems to have been unable to tell
anyone where to find the enemy.
    Meanwhile the spring rains were exceptional—in some places cata-
strophic. They slowed all movement to waterlogged maneuvers and slug-
gish pursuit. Smuts advanced doggedly but the *schutztruppe* remained intact
and in good spirits. For the next two and a half years the strategy that
dictated operations in East Africa was not England's but Lettow's.
    In the late spring of 1916, during his last military action in the the-
ater, RM tells us how he broke the stock of his rifle across an enemy machine gunner's head, then yanked a knobkerrie out of a German officer's
grasp and beat him to death with his own club. RM says he then realized the
dead officer was Lettow's acting field commander, Capt. Friedrich von
Kornatzki. From then on, he carried a war club with him wherever he went,
and maintained it was the knobkerrie he took from Kornatzki. It is the club
that T. E. Lawrence mentions in *Seven Pillars of Wisdom*.
    There's no doubt Kornatzki was killed at Kondoa,[42] but no contempo-
rary accounts mention anything about clubbing or about RM's having been
there at all. We can either take his word for it or choose to disbelieve.

Many took his word. A colorful story well-told can prevail over one that's extracted from a glacial mass of official documents, especially when these have to be located, sifted through, studied critically, and cross-checked. RM saved those who accepted his accounts a great deal of tedious work.

🦃 🦃 🦃

Freddie Guest[43] was two or three years older than RM. Guest was a Winchester old boy while RM, like Churchill, was a Harrovian, but given their families' circumstances they must have had quite a bit in common on first meeting.

Guest was well known in his time. A sometime Army officer, he had served as private secretary to Churchill in 1906 (when RM had been making his name in Nandi country). In the period leading into the war Guest had become Liberal Whip in the House of Commons but all the same he went off to battle as aide de camp to Sir John D. P. French, who commanded all British forces on the Western Front in 1914–1915.

Guest and RM's father-in-law Hermann Le Roy-Lewis crossed paths at Headquarters in 1915, when Guest was serving not only as General French's ADC but also as a commutative figure for the exchange of unofficial correspondence between French and former First Lord of the Admiralty Winston Churchill—communications that became difficult after Gallipoli when Churchill was given the sack and Lord Kitchener forbade him to communicate with his friend French. Then French, too, was sacked, and those who had served on his staff were not welcome on General Haig's staff. So Captain Guest had been temporarily without a job until his cousin Winston revealed that he was being considered as the new military commander for East Africa. Guest immediately volunteered for active service in that theater. He arrived in January 1916. In Nairobi, he and RM seem to have struck up an immediate friendship and he soon became RM's valued deputy. By February 1916 Guest was signing or initialing the intelligence reports whenever RM was not in the office.[44]

Guest was a sarcastic cynic with a keen understanding of human weaknesses. He and RM found each other to be congenial companions, and when they both returned to London some months later, RM found him a useful contact.

Not everyone felt Guest was well suited to responsible office. Col. (later Brig. Gen.) C. P. Fendall was a field officer, not intimate with command circles, but he reported there frequently enough to form opinions about some of the officers who served in Nairobi in 1916. He expressed them candidly in his private diary, where he wrote that Guest was "a man of affairs, with very nice manners and has tact, also understanding. Question whether he is strong enough and leader enough to manage the somewhat unruly crew."[45] The "unruly crew" seems to have been RM's Intelligence staff.

For quite a while Freddie Guest was one of the very few people about whom RM had only good things to say. Five years later he began to notice flaws in Guest and began to criticize him, but that would be in a different context (international politics) and nearly a different universe.

🐦 🐦 🐦

By the summer of 1916, as British forces crawled south, RM made his withdrawal from active management of the Intelligence Office. He was fading into a haze of fevers and depression. Colonel Fendall wrote, "Meinertzhagen, G.S.O.2. Intelligence. A very clever, very hardworking man. He has worked the Intelligence very well, and has now more or less broken down under the strain of the responsibility."[46]

His aide, Gordon Johnson, identified RM's ailment as pernicious anemia; in his diaries RM refers to a general malaise—a depression to which he alludes amid increasingly strident diatribes about Smuts's "gross carelessness" and the incompetence of Smuts's South African generals, whom he calls budding Napoleons whose utterances are mere flatulence.[47]

By October his mind is wandering; he can't sleep; he's lost all interest in food; Freddie Guest and the doctors are worried enough to persuade Smuts to send him back to Nairobi for a rest.

During the next few weeks, he writes that he has devoted considerable thought to the situation in East Africa, about which he serves up several pages of complaints and insults, leading to this conclusion:

> I think the worst and most expensive error of the campaign was the employment of generals who were not first class; their quality was lamentable. I have no hesitation in saying that if we had had a general of the calibre of General von Lettow Vorbeck,[48] and if the Germans had had an Aitken, Wapshare, Stewart or Malleson—or even Smuts—the East African campaign would have been over by the end of 1914 and hundreds of valuable lives and millions of pounds would have been saved. For this I blame Simla and the War Office. Even Smuts was not an astute soldier; a brilliant statesman and politician, but no soldier.[49]

At the time when he supposedly was writing up these thoughts RM was examined by Nairobi medical staff who pronounced his condition shocking. On November 10, 1916, Smuts ordered him invalided back to England.[50]

Freddie Guest did not succeed him as chief of intelligence. He too was ill with hepatitis and intestinal maladies, and was invalided home.[51]

RM would depart in December. In the meantime he spent much of those last two months of 1916 in the comforts of the luxurious Rift Valley Hotel. Not for publication, but privately, he wrote that he'd rarely had such a wonderful time.[52]

CHAPTER 7
ZION

I n 1953 RM paid a two-week visit to Jerusalem.

At the time, Ariel Sharon was being vilified for having launched a massive artillery attack against a West Bank village called Qibia. The anger toward Israel was not limited to the hearts of her Arab neighbors. Israel, an infant state just five years old, not only needed its heroes but also needed to point out that it had important powerful friends who came from worlds altogether outside the Jewish and Middle Eastern worlds.

So RM was not treated like an ordinary tourist. Welcomed by governmental officials, he inspected the Israeli Navy, appeared on radio, and dined with the foreign minister, the British ambassador, and the then-president of Israel.

The retired British hero had become modestly famous in the Holy Land, where history is hugely misunderstood anyway. . . .

From RM's first arrival in the Middle East in 1917 he began to incite fictions that would become traditions. After a while, the Jews came to revere him because they believed he fought for them. (Some Muslims also admired him—for his admitted anti-Semitism and, later, for his unconcealed support of Hitler. He was a hero for all seasons.)

🕊 🕊 🕊

He reported in at Cairo on May 24, 1917. During the five months between then and the haversack incident, he became a Zionist. By his own admission he had arrived in the Middle East a casual anti-Semite, a WASP with no particular interest in Jewish politics. Almost instantly he became a dedicated supporter of the Zionist cause (the cause of establishing a Jewish state in Palestine). He attributes his conversion to his meetings with two extraordinary men: Chaim Weizmann, to whom he was introduced in London shortly before he left for Cairo, and Aaron Aaronsohn, whom he was to meet soon after he arrived in the Middle East.

This was the abrupt beginning of what was to be a decades-long relationship with Zionist leaders who learned to trust RM, and who came to rely on him in the decades that were to follow.[1]

Aaron Aaronson[2] understood that the Jews of the desert would survive only if Britain won the war. To further that outcome, he and his sister Sarah organized the NILI Ring to commit espionage and sabotage within Ottoman lines, and placed their information at the disposal of the British.

The Aaronsohns' NILI[3] Ring, a predecessor to the Mossad, had been in existence for a year before RM's arrival. Until its destruction at about the time of the Battle of Beersheba, it was to remain the Allies' principal reliable source of behind-the-lines information about events in Ottoman territory. Sometimes that information was sparse because the Aaronsohns' agents had huge difficulty in getting messages out. Sometimes they swam quite far out to sea to pass documents in waterproof cases to crewmen aboard French or British ships. Those documents were worth their weight in blood.

With a price on his head, Aaronsohn made his escape from the Ottoman world. In 1916 he slipped through eastern and northern Europe, got out by sea, nearly drowned, and finally made his way to shore in England, where he banged on doors at the War Office until a colonel named Gribbon agreed to see him. Gribbon[4] was an Operations staff officer whose areas included the defense of Suez and the appraisal of Turkish strength in the Levant. Gribbon's immediate superior was Sir George Macdonough, Director of British Military Intelligence, who listened to what Aaronsohn had to say, introduced him to Chaim Weizmann, and ordered Colonel Gribbon to do his best to sign up Aaronsohn and his spy ring because this looked like an excellent opportunity for both British Intelligence and the Jews of Palestine to achieve a common goal.

The partnership was formed virtually overnight. At Gribbon's request, Aaronsohn went to Cairo to coordinate NILI's work with that of British Intelligence.

After the war Gribbon expressed the opinion that in the crucial battle for Beersheba alone, Aaronsohn had saved thirty thousand British lives. At a dinner during the Paris Peace Conference in 1919 he stated that Aaronsohn had done more than anyone else to enable the Allied victory in Palestine.[5]

DMI Sir George Macdonough echoed those sentiments in a postwar lecture, remarking that Allenby's operations may have appeared risky and audacious, but in fact they weren't as chancy as they looked, because the NILI had supplied him with intelligence on the disposition and movements of enemy forces.[6]

Aaronsohn wrote that RM was an officer from the staff of General Smuts who was also a dedicated zoologist and ornithologist, and who had arrived from London to inspect the Intelligence Services.[7] This gives some idea of the fictions with which RM was already cloaking himself. Subsequently, with outstanding gall, RM was to identify "my best agent" as having been "a Jew Aaron Aaronsshon" [sic].[8] (It was Gribbon in 1915–1916, not RM in 1917, who established the relationship with Aaronsohn and worked intimately with the Jewish intelligence network in Palestine. RM, as usual, was wildly exceeding the facts when he called Aaronsohn "one of *my* agents.")

On the occasion when he first met RM in June 1917, Aaronsohn had come to Cairo to argue with the two British officers who thought of themselves as his military superiors: Murray (the commanding general) and the spymaster Wyndham Deedes.[9] Aaronsohn sought a more direct role in political control of developing events in Palestine, while the British executives appear to have seen him as a local native-type who ought to content himself with providing intelligence on Turko-German positions and movements.

RM had the good sense to treat him better than that, so the two men got along quite well from the outset. Historian Ronald Florence, a student of the Aaronsohns' lives and careers, wrote to me:

> Aaron Aaronsohn is a less appealing character than his sensuous sister (allegedly the first woman in Palestine to abandon the corset) . . . He was infuriatingly petulant, arrogant, and much too smart even for his rather large britches, but his intimate knowledge of the geography, geology, and hydrology of Palestine, and his considerable experience with the Turks from Djemal Pasha down to ordinary soldiers, was probably of great . . . importance to Allenby. . . . Others claimed to know Palestine; Aaronsohn had literally walked and ridden the country, cataloguing with the eye of an agronomist and scientist. . . .
>
> He gave them detailed weather information about Palestine, including wind direction patterns (speed, direction, temperature) . . .
>
> Deedes, who was sympathetic to the Zionists, was clearly frustrated by Aaronsohn's petulance. He brought Meinertzhagen, in [what Aaronsohn believed was] his capacity as Chief of Field Reconnaissance, into the office, knowing Aaronsohn respected Meinertzhagen because he was new to Cairo, not a rival, and not part of those elements of British intelligence Aaronsohn [mistrusted].[10]

Aaronsohn's information about desert winds and water sources was very helpful to RM in his map-making, but even if RM gravitated toward him at first because Aaronsohn was useful, there's no doubt the two men formed an immediate friendship. They shared an interest in natural science and a fascination with spying. These were enough to bring them together in the environment of a military encampment where the gossip of the officers' mess was largely limited to military speculation, sporting discussion, and lewd jokes everyone had heard fifty times.

Aaronsohn was a fascinating monologist. RM—sharp with sarcasm, abrasively dismissive of the "stupidity" of the officers around him, and eager to chat about matters beyond the Turkish trenches or the GHQ staff rugby game—gravitated as naturally to Aaronsohn in Sinai as he had to Freddie Guest in Nairobi. The man impressed RM with both his scientific knowledge and his political rage. RM came to see the Zionist Jews as sophisticated, cultured, educated, rational, and intelligent. In other words they behaved like Europeans, unlike the local Muslim lot whom RM dismissed: "The Arab is a poor fighter though an adept at looting, sabotage, and murder."[11]

The reasons for his sudden conversion are likely to be more complicated than he made them out to be—and more subjectively motivated—but it does seem clear that Aaronsohn gave him one thing RM always craved but rarely believed he was receiving: Aaronsohn took him seriously.

Zion is the name of a hill in Jerusalem. In 1896 the founders of a movement to re-establish a Jewish state in Palestine named their organization after that hill. When RM met his first Zionists their movement was barely out of its second decade; it was still feeling its way—it had an end in view, but its notion of a means to that end was pretty much limited to the idea of encouraging Jews to emigrate from places where they were mistreated (the ghettos of Europe, western Asia, and North Africa) and to settle in Palestine so that eventually there would be enough of them to form a majority.

As a policy this notion (it led to the "right of return") was naive because it did little to address the fact that Palestine was a subsidiary of the Ottoman Empire, an ill-tempered relic of feudalism that didn't permit local populations to make independent democratic decisions.

As a vassal of Ankara, Palestine was not looked upon by most European Jews as a friendly sort of place to move to. Regardless of discriminations against them and racist laws that forbade them to partake of many of the rights of other citizens of the countries in which they lived, still they felt a kind of safety in the familiar comfort of their ghettos; most felt little incentive to exchange it for the perils of an inhospitable stretch of desert that was run by Turks whom they viewed (in the common stereotype of the era) as Mongol horsemen of the Attila-the-Hun sort, straight out of the Middle Ages armed with scimitars and flintlock rifles.

So the Zionist idea was not a big success with Western European Jews. In countries farther east, however, pogroms were all too commonplace. In Russia the dreaded Tatar Cossacks were notorious for leveling Jewish villages (*shtetl*s) and dragging off girls and boys for a variety of unsavory purposes. So Jewish families from Lithuania to the Ukraine to Siberia were sacrificing everything they could, in order that their children (if not they themselves) could escape to sanctuaries where the life of a Jew was not in perpetual peril. Many of these emigrés found their way to England, France, the United States—and Palestine.

To encourage both Arabs and Jews to support them, the Allies made promises to both groups. The promises involved rewards to be provided after the war.

Some of these assurances overlapped each other. Unfortunately neither the British nor the French Government possessed the wisdom of a Solomon when it came to adjudging how the baby should be split. Palestine essentially was pledged, separately and totally, both to the Arabs and to the Jews. (Solomon didn't get off the hook by saying, "It's not my baby," but somehow Lloyd George and Clemenceau seemed to think they could.)[12]

Zionism, at the time, did not have the look of a winner. It was a dubious scheme not only to British and Arab eyes but to many Jewish eyes as well.

This was the cause to which RM, a non-Solomon, decided to dedicate himself. His allegiance to Zionism, however formulated, was a brave one, and it was not a fickle or short-lived enthusiasm; he remained a steadfast supporter of the movement throughout his long life, although he continued to provide reminders of his contrariness and inconsistency by issuing periodic anti-Semitic outbursts and by joining a number of pro-Nazi business organizations in the early and mid-1930s. Perhaps he felt these were expected of him. Perhaps he was reassuring himself that even though he had a lot of Jewish friends and relations (by marriage) he was still a member of the gentile ruling class.

There was some question whether his grandmother Mary Seddons had been Jewish, or perhaps of Gypsy descent; so far as is known, that question has never been resolved, nor does it appear to have been of much importance to Richard or other members of the Meinertzhagen family. They had arrived in England as Presbyterians and had become Church of England members before Richard's birth. He seldom exhibited much religious curiosity and seems to have had no passion for Christianity, except perhaps as he approached his death. He had been raised in the traditional English church of Henry VIII and he attended services with fitful irregularity, but his diaries reveal him to have been an unconvinced agnostic.

RM, in truth, was anti-Semitic only in the same way he was anti-anyone. He didn't approve of any group except his own, and since he was the only member of that group, it got rather lonely at times. Even that didn't bother him; he sang the praises of solitude, and sought it out, sometimes for weeks or months at a time.

Until 1917, he hadn't had much occasion to think about Jews as a category or as a topic for attention. There had been no Dreyfus case in the British army (and as a rule no British soldier gave a damn what happened in the French army). Until he came to Palestine, RM probably had no opinion at all about whether or not Jews ought to have the right to settle there and live in peace. It just wasn't an issue that would have engaged him.

Having been juxtaposed with T. E. Lawrence, and seeing the sort of publicity that Lawrence's exploits provoked, RM appears to have felt he had been given short shrift. Perhaps he wanted to be known as "Meinertzhagen of Palestine."

But it was no real contest. RM lacked the traits that made Lawrence what he was—the poetic soul, the intellectual curiosity, the agonized conscience, the quirky gift of leadership.

In the Sinai in 1917 he was, according to his later imagination, a heroic crusader with cloak and dagger. From his field-office tent at Deirel Belah he purported to have set up dozens of agents whom he ran behind Turkish lines.[13] This was at a time when Allenby's military intelligence was improving, not because of RM but because of British crypto-analysts in London's top-secret "Room 40" who broke the German and Turkish signals codes. At the same time, T. E. Lawrence and the Arabs kept cutting Turkish telegraph lines in the desert, so the Germans and Turks were forced to fall back on wireless communications that could be intercepted by British receiving stations like the one on top of the Great Pyramid at Giza. RM explains that he set up this receiver as one of his creative espionage stunts. In fact the receiver had been set up by the Royal Navy a year before RM came on the scene. Several other radio-intercept centers as well had been put in place before his arrival.[14]

Among the intercepts, RM tells us, were coded signals from German sources indicating that a Zeppelin airship was bound from Europe to East Africa carrying an enormous cargo—to re-supply Lettow's *schutztruppe*.

According to RM, as soon as he found out about the Zeppelin's mission he made it his business to prevent its getting through to East Africa. He did this, he says, by encrypting a message in the current German cipher and sending the signal by wireless to the airship. RM maintains that his signal informed the dirigible's captain that Lettow had surrendered, and that it ordered Zeppelin L-59 to return to Europe.

RM adds that he sighted the Zeppelin near Sollum, on the Mediterranean coast of Egypt, both during her flight south to Africa and on her subsequent retreat. He then generously compliments the Germans on their heroic effort.[15] At the same time he congratulates himself for single-handedly having prevented the re-supply of the entire German army in East Africa.[16]

The facts: on November 21, 1917, the huge ship—the largest Zeppelin ever built—lifted off from Jamboli (Bulgaria) under command of Kapitänleutnant Ludwig Bockholt. She crossed the Mediterranean and prowled south across Libya and the Sudan. Two days after takeoff she had reached a point not far to the west of Khartoum, having traveled some two thousand miles in two days. Her destination was the flat plateau at Mahenge in German East Africa.

The British, having broken Germany's wireless codes, were aware of the flight and its purpose. The Royal Navy alerted East Africa's Royal Flying Corps squadrons to watch for the approach of the airship. What turned her back, however, was a signal relayed from one of Lettow's little transmitters. The frail signal was amplified and forwarded by neutral stations in a few towns friendly to Lettow, and after some hours it reached German Naval Command. The signal informed headquarters not that Lettow had surrendered (neither L-59 nor anyone else would have bought that one; if Lettow had surrendered it would have made headlines on every radio program and telegraph key in the hemisphere), but that the *schutztruppe* had been unable to hold the flatlands around Mahenge and had been forced by heavy blanket-fire from British artillery to retreat back into jagged mountains where the dirigible would have no chance of landing without risking explosion.

With no hope of a place to land—intact and safe from the British— and with every likelihood of her being destroyed or falling into enemy hands, German GHQ had no choice but to order *marinezeppelin* L-59 to turn back.

The recall signal was sent from the German Admiralty station at Nauen (and not from RM's imaginary transmitter or any other British source) on November 23, 1917.

RM cannot have seen the ship in the air on either the outbound or the return voyage; L-59's course did not take her within sight of the British-held coast. In fact she was fortunate in that the cloud cover was thick enough to prevent repeated RFC squadron patrols from finding her, although even if they had seen her they might not have been able to climb high enough to shoot her down.

She returned safely to her starting point. The adventure of the L-59 was heroic both in scale and in spirit. Despite his protestations, RM had nothing to do with it.[17]

His few months in the Sinai were fraught with melodrama, if we accept his accounts. Some of the episodes can be ignored. One seems to beg investigation.

It includes a number of harrowing serial episodes across half a dozen years, so it is one of the more extravagant fancies in the Meinertzhagen canon. This is his lengthy and suspenseful feud with arch-villain Fritz Frank, German spy extraordinare.

RM writes that he became alarmed by the laxity of security in British ranks in the Middle East. There was far too much chatter in the mess tents and parade grounds. He resolved to put a stop to it.

From the moment of his arrival in Cairo he had heard rumors about a German spy[18] who was a master of disguise and deception, could shoot a gnat at half a mile, and apparently could leap tall pyramids in a single bound.

So far as Cairo's veteran Intelligence-*wallahs* knew, there was little or nothing to these yarns about the night-riding Teutonic terrorist, but the rumors were well in place by the time RM arrived on the scene. He saw in them a splendid opportunity.

He writes that General Murray gave him permission[19] to circulate a phony description of this nonexistent agent to the troops. RM set out to "leak" information that the master German spy was able to travel at will through Turkish and British lines, arriving usually on horseback and often disguising himself as an Australian cavalry officer, complete with boyish mannerisms and full Light Horse kit.[20]

RM saw to it that the shadowy super-spy's reputation grew to ever more awesome proportions. Fritz Frank was said to have blown up a ship in the Suez Canal. He was said to have helped cause the British failures at Gaza by hanging about British camps and chatting with officers.

The Intelligence Office's enlargement of this apparition was business-like in intention, and achieved its purpose: it helped teach the officers and men of Allenby's army to keep their mouths shut and their eyes and ears open. Whether RM had anything to do with it is another question. An extraordinary document was issued by GHQ. It's not clear whether RM contributed to the authorship of this shinplaster; he may have done; he adored this sort of prank. Published anonymously, with the straight-faced endorsement of EMSIB—Eastern Mediterranean Special Intelligence Bureau (Cairo)—the delightful document was printed and distributed throughout the command so as to be nailed to every tent pole. It went on at length about the "Particulars and Description of the Spy Frank or Franke or Franks." The spy must have been an awesome master of disguise, for at various places in the poster he is described as "not very tall . . . with scar on left chin" and as having "red face, green eyes, . . . spotted hands, speaks Arabic like an Arab (Bedouin)" and as having "very black towsy hair, ... very piercing dark eyes which he moves from side to side when speaking, . . . emaciated appearance, tattooed on the right hand just above the wrist with a dagger shaped mark."[21]

(In response, one unidentified officer noted "Fictitious Frank . . . is a distinctive-looking individual possessing one green eye and one brown, and a gray stubbly moustache, is of foreign appearance . . . and yet curiously enough we can't catch him."[22])

But RM insists he did catch Fritz Frank. During a visit with German prisoners at a POW camp near Alexandria, RM writes, he interrogated a prisoner who turned out to be not German but Greek, and who said he had done some work for the German spy Fritz Frank. RM was taken aback to hear someone from "the other side" claim to have been employed by a person RM believed was nonexistent, but he says the Greek gave him "ample documentary proof" that he did indeed work for Frank. (RM does not choose to describe the nature of this documentary proof.)

RM says he bargained with the Greek and "turned" him (into a double-agent) by offering to get the Greek released from prison camp if the Greek would join RM's network of spies.

Additionally the Greek had to promise to lure Frank to a meeting with RM.

There is no clear explanation of what RM had to offer Fritz Frank that would have enticed such a man to show up for such a meeting. But a *tête á tête* with Frank was scheduled to take place in the dark of night, in a wadi near Deirel Belah. Then, RM writes, he came to the rendezvous before dawn, but found the Greek intermediary was an even earlier riser. The Greek was there alone, apologetic, and a bit fearful, nervously insisting that Fritz Frank and his "orderly" would be along any minute now.

Then a lone rider trotted forward from the dark bends of the wadi. The rider was dressed in Australian uniform—a slender figure, presumably the "orderly"—and abruptly both the Greek and the orderly fired potshots at RM. His horse reared in panic, thus spoiling the two villains' aim. He heard the bullets whistle by.[23] He drew his revolver and returned fire. The horse continued to lurch but he made one shot count. It dropped the orderly to the ground, screaming, with his life spurting out of his neck while the Greek was gone in a flash.

RM stepped off his horse and approached the writhing figure of the dying orderly and discovered to his horror that the "orderly" was an attractive young German woman.

She expired just then, without speaking.

He was mortified, having shot a woman to death; he describes the feelings of gentlemanly guilt with which he buried the girl in the desert.

(He neglects to describe how he identified the dead woman as German.)

He told no one of the incident—no one except his diaries.

Months later, he writes, a tip led him to a house in Taffa. He searched the place and found the "true" story in an assortment of photographs. They appalled him. The Greek, he realized now, had been the elusive Fritz Frank himself. And the woman whom RM killed had been Frank's beloved young wife.[24]

There follows a series of episodes extending into a long shaggy-dog feud between Meinertzhagen and Frank. The aggrieved and vengeful spy hunts RM relentlessly for years, long past the end of the war. The two men lock glances across various crowded restaurants and black German forests. Frank sends threatening letters to RM.[25] In September 1919 RM spots Frank on a railway platform in Aleppo, shouts at him, then shoots at him, possibly wounding Frank.[26]

The villain survives and the feud continues. Its final episode occurs seven years after the first exchange of shots. In a crowded Cologne restaurant RM locks glances with Frank across the room; Frank gives a slight bow of recognition, then he disappears. RM seeks help from British consulate intelligence people, who inform him that Frank is now the head of a bureau of the German Secret Service. RM tells us the Intelligence office launched a search for Frank and assigned RM a plainclothes bodyguard. He says he began carrying a rifle or revolver with him everywhere, even to bed.[27]

At that point the Holmes-v.-Moriarty serial adventure comes to an end; we hear no more about Fritz Frank.[28]

We do, however, encounter the RM vs. Frank myth in subsequent literature, some of which has what appears to have respectable provenance. Take for example the book *Secret Service* (1933) by British Intelligence-*wallah* Sir George Grey Aston.[29] Here we find reference to the

Middle East in 1917 and "a British Intelligence Officer, whom we will call 'Mannering,' and his opponent in the German Secret Service, one 'Fritz'."

Sir George, who has convincing credentials in the annals of commando warfare and clandestine espionage services, has something of a field day in this book. The entirety of his Chapter XV is devoted to a detail-by-detail replication of RM's story of the "feud," including such particulars as the "Greek" POW, the British officer's inadvertent shooting of Fritz's wife whom he had thought was an orderly, and the postwar exchange of hard glances across a crowded restaurant. "Fritz . . . was neither a bogey nor a myth, but a formidable reality—probably the most efficient and resourceful German Secret Service agent in the whole of the Great War."[30]

RM didn't publish his version until 1960, and it's not possible to be certain of the decade (let alone the year) when he typed it up in his diaries. One estimate places the typing, if not the initial composition, sometime in the 1940s. But he had begun pushing some of his Frank fables at least as early as the 1920s in various media (letters, conversations, articles for bird journals, and early drafts of the diaries).

The RM and Aston versions are so alike—nearly word for word— that it would be impossible to argue that one of them was not copied from the other. As to who borrowed it from whom, there is no decisive evidence. At least one significant segment in the Aston version of the Fritz & Richard Show (the one in which the two men glare at each other across a restaurant in Europe some years after the war) appears in RM's full-length unpublished "original" diaries but did not appear in any of his published books, but either writer could have created it. RM could have read it in Aston's book, but he just as easily could have sent the yarn to Aston in a letter. RM wrote thousands of letters; he was astoundingly prolific.

So—once again to give our man the benefit of the doubt—we can assume that RM did not steal the story from Sir George Aston, but in fact gave it to him.

Regardless of all that, the story is untrue.[31]

Near the end of 1917, having participated in no battles, RM was ordered back to England for reassignment. He found office duty as dreary as ever. He catalogued birds. He visited friends. Evidently the most exhilarating achievement of which he could boast during the next few months was the shooting of an adult male carrion crow, *Corvus c. corone*, out of a tree in Hyde Park on April 1.[32]

As summer approached, Macdonough sent him across the Channel to join the intelligence staff at Allied Headquarters in France. At interval, he finished out the war there. He was temporarily promoted to acting colonel, delivered himself of methodological lectures, and presented himself as an expert in the theories and tactics of military intelligence. He was not involved in the planning or execution of any actual combat operations. He did manage a few extended leaves, back in England—to hunt birds in Invernesshire, for example, at the very time when he later pretended to have been attempting at the personal behest of King George V to rescue the imprisoned Romanov family from Ekaterinberg—a high-flying escapade that seems so implausible that it is relegated here to a footnote.[33]

From the spring of 1918 until August he commuted between England and France, delivering lectures on intelligence to groups of officers who had been selected for staff advancement. In September—the month when Lettow re-invaded German East Africa from Mozambique, while Allenby tricked the Turks and Germans yet again and routed them at Megiddo so that he could capture Damascus[34]—RM was sent to France to join the GHQ staff full-time.

The increasing importance of RM's assignments seems to have had to do in part with his imposing roster of lofty contacts. In letters written in July 1918 his friend Freddie Guest describes their gatherings at the Other Club, a Parliamentary dining club and informal political-action lodge—membership by invitation only—into which RM had been inducted in 1917 by the good offices of its honorary secretary who happened to be Freddie Guest. Winston Churchill was one of its founding members, Lloyd George belonged, as had Lord Kitchener, and in later years Field Marshal Lord Alanbrooke (a distinguished military leader during World War II) would join as well. The association included cabinet members, military officers, Parliamentarians, and business leaders.

In this company RM in fact had "arrived." Thus he was uniquely placed to put the case for his Zionist friends, and as the war approached its end his years of greatest influence and effect were just beginning.[35]

On the Western Front at the time of RM's arrival at GHQ, confusion still rampaged through the upper ranks: Allied generals and politicians continued to argue tactics while what was left of Europe disintegrated. Trench life was hip-deep in mud, a-crawl with lice and rats and maggots, and mortally temporary. At intervals ragged lines of men lifted themselves out of these living graves to fling themselves against enemy bullets out of patriotism, duty, morality, honor, revenge, relief, simple fear, or some human herd psychology that had not yet been defined, or perhaps simply out of the lack of anywhere else to be except back there in the stinking trench.

Some convinced themselves that valor in a meaningless war had value. Others learned that war was not so much as Clausewitz had defined it ("an extension of politics by other means") as it was a failure of politics and of good sense, and of civilization itself.

The war and its era were flushed with huge moral ambiguities and contradictory convictions but few of these seem to have distressed Colonel Meinertzhagen. He owned few doubts. Issues that were debated violently—about the arrogance or the virtues of empire, about the hideous folly or the righteous need for war and slaughter—were issues he dismissed with curt truisms. Perhaps he needed to be that way: soldiers are not at their most effective if they stop to reason why. He sometimes expressed, but seldom seemed to understand, the subtler pleasures, bleakness, and confusion of the nature of human affairs. He stood back, sometimes disengaged and all but inaccessible, complaining of other people's intolerance and cruelty and insensitivity while lacking the insight to recognize the same traits in his self. In his statements, then and later, one finds little sense of the desperate experience of war. Filled with melodrama and geopolitics, he seemed not so much heroic as aloft: an observer who looked down upon the action from the great height of retrospect. He described the war as if it were a movie set, aerially photographed, arranged, and lighted to capture individual commanders while—like a soundtrack narrator—he provided opinions on them and his theories about generalship, strategy, nations, and races.

Younger officers regarded him not only with the ease of fellowship that came with membership in the same social aristocracy, but also with professional deference because of his reputation. To them he was, at forty, a legendary eminence in the gamesmanship of illusive tactics: master of trickery, impresario of deceptions, and the Western Front's foremost authority on migrating birds. In his hawkish features they saw the proud menace and the lightning certainty of a bird of prey: a raptor.

Possibly the Great War ended too soon for Richard Meinertzhagen—he had established a reputation by having appropriated the haversack heroics unto himself, and during the summer of 1918 he served on the Western Front with what appears to have been a realistic hope of having been appointed one of Britain's top intelligence officers. As late as October 23[36] his section was still occupied with long-term plans for future intelligence methodology and for a formalization of practices within the Security Section, as if the war could go on for decades. In fact, it ended nineteen days later. The

way of the war changed because Germany finally ran out of food and because mutinies were crippling the German army, the front-line forces of
which were manned mainly by untrained conscripts. The final collapse came
with startling suddenness.

So did the shell that blew RM out of a scout car and sent him into
hospital for surgery.

Before dawn on November 11, 1918, Meinertzhagen writes, he was in
Marshall Foch's party at the signing of the German surrender, under instructions to pick up a copy of the surrender document once the Germans
had signed it, and to deliver it to Field Marshal Sir Douglas Haig, who did
not wish to meet with any Germans.

As Meinertzhagen set out with the precious document for Haig, his
car was blown up, he knew not by what. The explosion killed his driver. He
recalls that some object struck his abdomen with great force, at the same
point where a horse-kick had injured him in the water during the sinking of
the *Transylvania.*

In dreadful pain, he caught a ride on a lorry and fulfilled his mission
with the aid of a large amount of brandy,[37]delivering the signed German
surrender to Haig.

There is scant evidence to support RM's contention that he carried
the German surrender documents to General Haig to obtain Haig's counter-
signature. The truth, like the teller, is elusive. RM was in fact an officer on
Haig's staff at the time, but no mention of him appears in Haig's journals for
the day.[38]

CHAPTER 8
ADRIFT

From the spring of 1919 to the fall of 1921 Richard Meinertzhagen was one of the most important Englishmen in the Middle East.

He returned to duty—still on crutches—in the spring of 1919, when he went to Paris for the Peace Congress that argued for months before finalizing the terms of the dismal armistice that officially ended the Great War.

Shortly after the conference began, RM flew back to London and spent a chaste night with a "revolting" prostitute in the Charing Cross Hotel, for the purpose of being observed by a chambermaid in order to give his wife Armorel grounds of adultery on which to divorce him.

Court records bear out Meinertzhagen's story about the hotel and the hooker, describing the co-respondent as "an unknown female." In the diaries he states this was the only basis on which Armorel was willing to grant it, but that is his personalization of a generic fact of life: in England until well after World War II, the charade he employed was the traditional, and virtually the only, way a couple could agree to obtain a legal divorce.

He may have been embroidering when he insisted that he spitefully forced Armorel's lawyer to serve him with the papers in the Monkey House of the London Zoo. In one of the typescripts he snarls that this service took place at four in the afternoon on February 17, 1919, with the monkeys as witnesses.[1] It may have happened that way; or he may have wished it had.

In Paris he was seconded to the War Office and, for the purposes of the Peace Congress, attached to the staff of Lords Balfour and Curzon; officially he was counted among the four hundred members of Balfour's staff.[2] His assignment had to do with mapmaking, his forte—he was to help draw boundaries for the newly carved-up Middle East. Later, in one of his many melodramatic but harmless fancies, he gave the impression that he was in Paris on the Intelligence Staff, perhaps acquiring secrets from shadowy sources. He was not.[3]

While Meinertzhagen and T. E. Lawrence were attending the Congress, Lawrence was writing busily away at night at a manuscript that was the first version of what was to become his literary master work, *Seven Pillars of Wisdom*.

Ironies seem to lurk at every Meinertzhagen turning. One of them shows up in his claim that during these evenings Lawrence showed chapters of the manuscript-in-progress to him.

Publicly Lawrence and Meinertzhagen must have had a mutually respectful "correct" relationship—both were capable of displaying impeccable manners. Off and on, between 1917 and 1921, Lawrence and Meinertzhagen worked together; or, more accurately, they worked adjacently. They represented opposing "clients" and their mentalities were as distinct from each other as were their loyalties.[4] During the war Lawrence frequently could be found in the thick of battle;[5] the best evidence suggests Meinertzhagen seldom engaged in actual combat—he was brave enough, but his offices were not front-line postings. The two officers were not close friends. A simple illustration of the distance between them is that Lawrence's friends and peers called him "Ned" and RM appears to have been ignorant of that.[6]

Years later, long after Lawrence had died, RM published a number of demeaning comments about him.[7] Given all this background, some Lawrence students seem to assume therefore that Lawrence never would have shown his book to RM.

But it is a fact that Lawrence showed his original manuscript of the first (later lost)[8] draft of the book to three men: David Hogarth, Guy Dawnay, and Richard Meinertzhagen.[9]

It takes only a moment to understand why Lawrence allowed these three to read his passages: they were with him in Paris, they had been his fellow officers in the Sinai in 1917, and they had served in Allenby's headquarters and were familiar with the locales and personalities. Lawrence naturally would have wanted to know whether any of the three might have been able to correct inadvertent inaccuracies in his book.

In that light, the extraordinary privilege that Lawrence seems to have granted to RM becomes much less mysterious.[10]

To help win support in the Paris negotiations, Dr. Chaim Weizmann armed himself with "a letter from Colonel Meinertzhagen describing the pogrom and the period leading up to it, and stressing the blindness (real or willfully induced) of the administration which had refused to see the danger after their attention had been repeatedly called to it."[11]

Weizmann came to Paris only two or three times during the Congress.

The rest of the time RM spoke up for Zionism at every opportunity. He accomplished quite a bit, for a junior officer. He managed to keep reminding officials of the importance of the Zionist position. When politicians tried to give away the whole Middle East to the French or the Arabs, RM was there to complicate things.

He did not achieve victory for his friends any more than T. E. Lawrence did for his, but the record shows that RM's efforts were genuine. Years later, Sir John Shuckburgh wrote:

> Meinertzhagen put forward his proposal which might involve the transfer of Arabs from Palestine. He felt that the only solution of the problem was "the gift of Palestine to Jewry" and this needed to be implemented immediately. "Those Arabs who dislike the solution can be compensated and moved elsewhere," wrote Meinertzhagen in his diary, adding that . . . a settlement of the Jewish Question which would affect World Jewry would cause only a slight injustice to a handful of Arabs who already had "a country many hundred times greater than Palestine."[12]

Meinertzhagen was a powerful voice and a genuine influence. Yet he enhanced his importance with further fiction. He wrote that the northern boundary of the British Government's proposed Palestine Protectorate was to be called the Meinertzhagen Line. The phrase has become another touchstone of RM mythology. It is as unreal as many others. The term appears in no primary records other than a map, to which RM had access, where the notation "Meinertzhagen Line" is entered in pencil.[13]

He expressed vividly his contempt for the terms of the misbegotten Treaty of Versailles that emerged from the Congress. His analysis of the politics was simplistic but his vitriol seems justified by subsequent events. The formal politeness exhibited by delegates was a statesmanlike mask that ill disguised a snarling bitterness that followed the slaughter of millions. In taking their revenge on the defeated Germany the conferees imposed their vindictive wills and aroused ancient hatreds. Whether they intended it or not, they stirred up dreadful hostilities that would lead to World War II and would continue to rage a century into the future.

Muslims and Jews in the Middle East were consistent about one thing. Each side believed the British betrayed it in favor of the other. The truth, by contrast, was that London betrayed both sides with equanimity.

London had one point of view and the British who served on the ground had another. In the Middle East most British officials wanted mainly to get out. They weren't fond of either side in the disputes.

In London, the Arabs had their partisans—industrialists with an interest in oil, romantics like Lawrence, leftists who felt the Arabs had got a raw deal—and the Zionists had theirs: men of power, both Jewish and non-Jewish, who believed Zionism was more likely to bring civilization (i.e., better relations with Britain) to the region than was the medieval atavism (in their view) of Islam.

But these partisans were few. To policy-makers in Britain, the Middle East was of political concern (as it became later to American policy-makers) only strategically. Its disputes might affect their interests in oil fields or the Suez Canal. Beyond a general, huffily righteous belief that violence ought to be discouraged, Europeans generally felt the Zionists and the Arabs were being unfair in dragging Britain into their feuds. Let them take care of their own problems. They had created the mess; let them resolve it. The responsibility was theirs, not London's.

Sir Edmund Allenby, now a knighted field marshal, accepted appointment as High Commissioner for Egypt and the Sudan (an office in which he would serve from 1919 until 1925). He remained in command of the British Army's occupation forces in the Middle East, charged with defending not only the Suez Canal but also Britain's growing attentiveness to French imperial designs.

The undeclared turf war against the French meant that sometimes Allenby felt a need to appease the Arabs of Transjordan, Syria, and Lebanon in order to keep them from defecting to the French side.[14] The Foreign Office, under Balfour and then Curzon, knew that such militarily motivated appeasements would tend to recoil against the interests of Zionism. They tried to counterbalance the weight of military interests with their own favoritism toward Zionism.

Chaim Weizmann had written to Lord Balfour on August 17, 1919: "Things are brighter now . . . Colonel Meinertzhagen has been appointed C.P.O. [Chief Political Officer, Palestine.] He is an honest, fair-minded and clever man."[15] It was Weizmann who was responsible for the selection of Meinertzhagen to replace Brig. Gen. C. Gilbert Falkingham Clayton as "political officer"—a post created in an attempt to bridge the differences between civilian government and military administrators.[16]

(Posterity seems to have been confused by the fact that Clayton was a founding father of British Intelligence in Cairo. Historians assumed that as Clayton's successor RM took on the mantle not only of a political adminis- trator who happened to be in uniform, but also of Britain's intelligence- *meister* in the region. RM did nothing to disabuse the historians of this assumption.)

Balfour, Curzon, and Weizmann felt that Meinertzhagen, with his widely known partisanship and his purported willingness to argue with generals (plus his connections in high places that protected him from reprisal) would be the perfect man for the job, especially since he and Allenby were old comrades in arms who shared a keen scientific interest in the study of mi- gratory birds.

And so, in the fall of 1919, RM became Political Officer in Palestine. The assignment gradually proved to be a disaster, since he had minimal political skills. His mediations seem to have been limited mainly to his blam- ing "Hebraphobes" (his word for anti-Semites) for all the troubles of the region.

But at first his assignments and duties were important; he was Britain's spearhead in Palestine. His service to the Crown from 1919 to 1922 was undoubtedly the most significant period of any in his military career; he held center-stage, and the after-effects of his actions were conspicuous.

His assignment was related to intelligence-gathering, but not in a melodramatic sense.[17] He supervised no spy network and committed no known acts of sabotage or violence. Officially his work had to do with Brit- ish military establishments in the region. Semi-officially he represented the Zionist viewpoint. Unofficially he watched and collected birds and informa- tion about wildlife.

Some histories have proposed that without Meinertzhagen's intricate schemes and bold interventions during the early years of the Mandate (1919– 1923) the Arabs might well have overrun Palestine—that it was Meinertzhagen's clandestine sabotage and overt support that kept alive the dream of Eretz-Israel and made migration attractive to many European Jews.

The overt support was real. The clandestine work was not.

In Cairo, RM served under orders to report both to Allenby and to the Foreign Office. This dual allegiance would have caused great difficulties even for an officer far more diplomatically inclined.[18] He made impressions— not always the kind he would like to have made—on fellow expatriates. The celebrated Gertrude Bell, slender "queen of the desert" with her defiant red hair and bold green eyes, out-ranked him (although he seemed unable to acknowledge that). She encountered Meinertzhagen quite a few times in her sorties through the Paris Peace Congress and the Middle East, and never learned to spell his name, but as to the rest of him she was in no way short of opinions. In 1919 she wrote:

29 September 1919:

Col. Meinetzhagen [sic], . . . P.O. [Political Officer] for Palestine and Syria, said . . . that it would be of [great] value to him if Col. Wilson would appoint an officer here to tour in Palestine and Syria and send up exactly what was needed, but he was visibly discountenanced when I said that owing to the lack of personnel the officer, if appointed, might be myself. . . .

[He] knows . . . nothing about such subjects as exchange, justice, finance, revenue etc. He strikes me as being very rigid, not at all receptive and as taking no kind of interest in anything outside his rather narrow job. He used to be a strong Zionist; Gen. Clayton believes that he has considerably modified his views on this head.[19]

RM had not modified his Zionist views at all, but he may have learned to tell Clayton what he thought Clayton wanted to hear. Meanwhile RM didn't like Miss Bell any better than she liked him. He wrote in his diary typescripts that she had an excessively high opinion of herself and a narrow pro-Arab view of things. He expressed indignation that she tried to deflect him with eyelash-batting feminine wiles from the opinions dictated by his conscience. When she traded on the fact that she was a woman she was being unfair, he complained, and in any case he found her rude and intolerant.[20]

Interestingly, Gertrude Bell was both anti-feminist and anti-suffrage. She believed most women (other than her) were lesser beings. In that view she and Meinertzhagen might have found common ground, but they never seem to have made much attempt to appreciate each other's feelings. She wrote, "General Bowes's office suffers as much as I do from the rigidity of Col. Meinertsthagen [sic]."[21]

She seemed to feel she personally owned the Middle East; she wanted and expected to rule over Mesopotamia.[22] When she did not achieve that goal, the brilliant Miss Bell proved to be more fragile than anyone had thought. In 1926, lonely and disappointed, she committed suicide. She was fifty-seven years old.

According to Miss Bell's diaries and letters, she met Meinertzhagen fairly frequently in various locations around the theater throughout his terms of duty there. With a few minor exceptions, the only records of these meetings seem to be those that occur in her diaries and letters. She has few kind words for him, and she was not alone in such judgments. Sahar Huneidi writes:

> Of the senior staff, only Colonel Richard Meinertzhagen, the military adviser, was a declared Zionist, though his passion was such that the Palin Commission, set up to look into the causes of the 1920 Easter riots in Jerusalem, saw fit to devote long passages to him in its final report of July 1920. Among other things, the report called Meinertzhagen the 'chief support of the Zionists' and 'Dr. Weizmann's nominee' whose 'definite anti-Arab bias and prejudice in favour of Zionism . . . reveal him as an agent who, however capable of doing good work in other spheres, is singularly out of place in the East.'[23]

Events in the deserts were as unsettled and reversible then as now. It seems pointless to describe or analyze the details of RM's travels and observations. Some remarks seem on point today and some do not. (Those who read his published "diary" books in the late 1950s and early 1960s may have taken them too seriously because they took him at his word when he said the entries dated 1919 or 1921 were actually written at those times, rather than sometime during subsequent decades.)[24]

The job gave him ample opportunities to go birding around the eastern Mediterranean. He turned up at Malta, Damascus, Aleppo, Jerusalem, Beirut, Haifa, and so forth. His inspection tours and information-gathering visits lasted about a fortnight; he spent half of each month at GHQ. So the Government placed at his disposal two cars—one for his transport within Cairo and the other for his trips across the desert. The latter was fitted with extra fuel and water tanks, plentiful food storage, and a bed so that he could sleep overnight on the road, as there were few hotels along the routes he must travel. The two cars were both Rolls Royces, and each had its own chauffeur-mechanic.[25]

His diaries record "My first visit to Damascus, in 1919"; "Conference in Damascus with Faisul [sic], King of Iraq, and the French"; "I visit Aleppo, Syria"; "Second visit to Damascus and trip into desert"; "I cross the Range in Lebanon in 1919"; "First visit to Sollum, Western Egypt"; "trip to Siwa Oasis in Libya and the Western Desert"; various other long and often hazardous trips through Palestine and Syria; an interview with Monsieur Picot in Beirut; and a Christmas 1919 holiday in Helwan with the celebrated ornithologist Michael Nicoll and his wife.[26] He was leading an exciting life; no one else seems to have traveled so widely in the region at the time. He observed, he recorded, he reported. For some, this would have been satisfaction enough.

At work he felt he was the lone hold-out against strong pressures to appease the Arabs at any cost. Zionists kept peppering him with expressions of concern about what they saw as the unfriendly attitude of the Administration.[27] Typical of the majority view was this one, expressed in the heat of events by Allenby's chief military administrator, Maj. Gen. H. D. Watson: "The antagonism to Zionism of the majority of the population [i.e., the Arabs] is deep-rooted—it is fast leading to hatred of the British—and will result, if the Zionist programme is forced upon them, in an outbreak of serious character."[28]

Meinertzhagen behaved in contradictory fashion, both overestimating and underestimating his own significance. Even though he was a mere major in the temporary uniform of a lieutenant colonel, in his unhesitating defense of Zionist interests he behaved as if he had a field marshal's stars on his epaulets. When his views were not honored he would express shock and outrage—at least to his friends; the self-created reputation to the contrary, he did not engage in frontal arguments with superior officers. But even without confrontation, he was known to have friends at court. Because of his membership in the Other Club and such affiliations, he wielded far more sway than did any other line officer in Cairo.

Even so, he felt—incorrectly—that everybody in the British administration was dead-set against him. This was not the case. He and Zionism had enemies but they also had allies. If he had been Zion's only champion in Allenby's realm, that realm would have dumped Zionism—and him—early on. RM had support, not only in the corridors of power in London but also on the ground in the Middle East, where a few of Allenby's officers and an articulate Jewish leadership provided support for his efforts.[29]

Still, he was in the minority. An example of the petty obstacles that cluttered his way can be found in an account by Chaim Weizmann, who set sail from Europe for Palestine in the fall of 1919 at a time when Allenby was away in the Sudanese desert and Gen. Walter Congreve (commander of the troops stationed in Egypt) was in temporary command of the theater. Weizmann wrote: "While we were still on the high seas, General Congreve, Acting High Commissioner in Egypt during Allenby's absence, was informed that a Zionist by the name of Weizmann would shortly be arriving in Alexandria, and as his coming would certainly make trouble, he had better not be permitted to land." Weizmann said he later learned that his old friend Meinertzhagen had got wind of Congreve's attempt to head him off. Congreve ignored RM's insistence that Zionism was an arm of official British policy and that Weizmann was traveling under the authority of Allenby and the Prime Minister. So RM, not for the last time, went over the commanding general's head (and behind his back) by cabling London. The Foreign Office and the War Office issued direct orders to Congreve, and Chaim Weizmann was allowed to complete his mission.[30]

RM was neither cashiered nor exiled for having gone over Congreve's head. This confirms that his clout in Whitehall extended much farther than his rank might suggest.

But the same dedication to Zionism that thrust him into prominence also isolated him not only from crusty generals like Congreve but also from old friends in the Army. Among many he had become *persona non grata* because of the depth and sincerity of his dedication to Zionism, and his unwillingness to tolerate compromise. He was one of the very few British officers who were committed to carrying out the policy of the Balfour Declaration.[31]

At the same time he felt an urgent need to fend off the blatant (but weak) advances of the French, who always, in RM's opinion, were up to no good.[32]

Militants in both the Jewish and Arab camps kept stirring the pot. British administrators reared back on their dignity. Meinertzhagen felt something must be done before it all deteriorated into atavistic bloodletting, which would be not only a bad thing in itself but also a convenient opportunity for French and Arab ambitions. He pressed the authorities in London to split their military administration from the civilian authority—bring in civilians to deal with the domestic problems of local populations. "I fought Allenby and his administration on the Zionist question, exposed the lamentable state of affairs to the Foreign Office, [and finally] succeeded in removing the heads of the Administration and transferring responsibility from the War Office to the Foreign Office, thereby bringing into Palestine a civil Government under Herbert Samuel."[33]

RM exceeds reality in asking us to infer that he was the cause of all this or that he was the sponsor of Herbert Samuel, but he certainly played a part in it all.

Sir Herbert Samuel was a Briton, a Jew, a left-wing Member of Parliament who was not admired by RM, and a prominent member of the "Rainbow Circle" of intellectuals with H. G. Wells, George Bernard Shaw, and Beatrice and Sidney Webb. (RM was the Webbs' nephew.) Sir Herbert was a compassionate classicist steeped in history, and was the first unconverted Orthodox Jew to have served in a British Cabinet office. He felt deep sympathy for both the Arabs and the Jews; he saw both groups as peoples who had been oppressed for many centuries. It was to be his misfortune to be burdened with the blame for much of the violence and mischief that would plague the Middle East during his tenure there. Each grew to see him as a tool of the other. (To the Jews he bent over backwards much too far in his efforts to show the Arabs his lack of bias. To the Arabs he was, simply, a Jew.)

His arrival in Palestine was not a factor in RM's military career. By the time Sir Herbert set foot in Palestine in June 1920 to the welcome of a seventeen-gun salute, RM had departed the region.

His leave-taking was more like a forcible ejection. He finally had gone too far.

The "Bloody Passover" Jerusalem riots of March 1920 caused more carnage than any that had gone before.

Afterward most observers held that British military authorities gave Arab rioters a free hand. They arrested a few but turned them loose almost immediately, while they arrested and held a number of Jews who had displayed the effrontery to fight back. The leader of these defenders, Vladimir Jabotinsky, was sentenced to fifteen years' imprisonment by the presiding military court—a sentence that would be lifted only after Colonel Meinertzhagen interceded.[34] (It is unclear whether, or how seriously, RM's intercession actually changed the sentence; various political factors were in play.)

All this was too much for Meinertzhagen. Convinced that "Hebraphobes" in the Army had betrayed London's interests—that they had set off the riots as a way of demonstrating the hopeless impracticality of Zionism as policy—he reported to Allenby on the alleged betrayals. He named names. He accused Gov. Ronald Storrs and Colonel Waters-Taylor of having organized the anti-Jewish riots. Later he accused them of having supported the schemes of Arab terrorist leader and confidence artist Haj Amin al-Husseini.[35] Amin had been sentenced by a British court to fifteen years' imprisonment, but Waters-Taylors and others persuaded Sir Herbert Samuel to appease the Arabs by giving him amnesty and having Amin appointed Grand Mufti of Jerusalem[36]—an appointment Meinertzhagen reviled as "sheer madness."

Allenby's refusal to take action was what infuriated RM most, but a coup was taking place in Damascus at the time—it would end with the enthroning of Faisal as king of Syria—and in spite of the widespread bloodshed and the wholesale arrests of Jews, Allenby told RM he could take no action until he saw which way things settled down in Syria.[37]

At that point RM went behind Allenby's back and over his head. He sent a detailed cable to Lord Curzon. It accused Allenby of failing to carry out official British policy even though RM had given him ample advance warning of the riots.

Meinertzhagen's report to the Foreign Secretary, dated April 14, 1920, reached Lord Curzon at San Remo where he was attending an international conference, one of whose topics of discussion was the Palestine mandate. David Lloyd George, Chaim Weizmann, and Lord Balfour were there as well.

They all saw the Meinertzhagen cable. It virtually frothed with rage:

"The officers of the Administration are, almost without exception, anti-Zionist. . . . If our British Administration were imbued with an understanding of and sympathy for Zionism which your Lordship has a right to expect, the risk of anti-Jewish riots might have been minimized, if not altogether avoided."[38]

Allenby's immediate and inevitable reaction was to sack Meinertzhagen.[39]

Later, General Wavell recalled it this way:

Allenby's Political Officer, Colonel Meinertzhagen (who was an Intelligence officer in 1917 and had been responsible for the famous 'haversack ruse' at the Third Battle of Gaza), considering that Allenby was not carrying out in Palestine the policy of the Foreign Office in furtherance of the Balfour Declaration, sent a dispatch to this effect to the Foreign Office. A friend, to whom he showed the letter, warned him that Allenby would not allow such criticism by one of his staff. Meinertzhagen agreed that this was likely, but persisted in what he held to be his duty. His dismissal was even swifter than the friend had prophesied, and followed immediately on Allenby seeing a copy of the letter. But Meinertzhagen had no fear of Allenby and always met him on equal terms. "I suppose you realize that you would have had to give your housemaid longer notice," was his only comment. Allenby laughed, and they parted friends. They had always had a common interest in the study of birds.[40]

Everyone, even Meinertzhagen himself, seems to have accepted the inescapable: Allenby must be appeased.

With that cable to the Foreign Office, Meinertzhagen made his point with enough effectiveness to influence British policy for several years to come, but he also seemed to have brought an end to his career in the military. He wrote, "My work automatically ceased and my appointment became

impossible. Allenby clamoured for my removal and I go, but meanwhile I
have done what I set out to do, namely I have set Zionism up in Palestine."[41]
He was patting himself on the back of course, but in this instance credit
was due. He had taken a risk by whistle blowing; he knowingly had jeopar-
dized his career. It was a brave and gallant act.

RM took extended leave. He visited friends in Scotland and South
Uist and worked in Lord Walter Rothschild's bird rooms at Tring. He met an
enchanting young woman, Annie Jackson. She possessed a sweet face and
an easy smile of warm amusement, a helmet of dark hair, a trim athletic
figure, and a glint of witty intelligent mischief in her otherwise kind eyes.
He began to take her to theatres and dinners.

Behind these surfaces, wheels were grinding in the War Office and
other burrows. For a while it looked as if the Army wished that RM would
be sent far away where he could be kept out of mind; military attaché to
Tokyo—that would be just the spot for him.

The idea met with jeers from the Foreign Office: "The proposal to
send him to Japan merely reflects a desire to have him out of the way. I think
we ought to renew our objection. I will not budge."[42]

Fifteen years earlier, after the Nandi massacre, the Foreign Office had
reviled him while the War Office defended him. With a nice irony, their positions now were reversed.

The insult to his career seems to have provoked his imagination: he
wrote that he was offered a seat in Parliament and the office of Assistant
Commissioner of Police—both on the same day.[43] (Aside from RM's own
claims, no record of either offer has surfaced.)

He may have been trying to distract himself not only from his abrupt
dismissal but also from the discovery that on at least four occasions staff
members of the British Museum (Natural History) had reported to their
superiors that birds seemed to be missing after visits by Colonel
Meinertzhagen. On the fourth occasion a supervisor in the Bird Rooms, C. F.
Regan, confronted him.

Inside Meinertzhagen's dispatch case Regan found nine birds that RM
had been in the act of carrying out of the Museum.

RM said he was borrowing the bird skins to work on at home. However,
many other birds that he previously had "borrowed" were also missing.

The Trustees stopped short of making a public accusation, but they
barred RM from the Museum and especially from the bird collections. Thereafter the bird rooms remained closed to him for a year and a half. It was not

until the spring of 1921 that the Trustees ordered "that the privilege of making use of the Bird Room be restored to Colonel R. Meinertzhagen."

RM was readmitted to the Museum not because of second thoughts regarding his guilt, but because an influential friend interceded for him. This was confirmed years later when the Museum's Keeper of Zoology, Norman Boyd Kinnear, recalled: "After Colonel Meinertzhagen married Miss Annie Jackson, who was a regular worker in the Bird Room, Lord Rothschild, after talking the matter over with Dr. Lowe, suggested to the Trustees that the ban on Colonel Meinertzhagen should be lifted, and this was agreed to in 1921."[44]

Miss Annie Jackson was the daughter of a to-the-manor-born Light Horse officer, Maj. Randle Jackson, who had died some years earlier. At age thirty-two she was warm, affectionate, bright, and outdoorsy. Annie and her sister Dorothy would inherit a sizable fortune and two landed estates at Swordale (Easter Ross, in northern Scotland) and at Upwell (near Wisbech, in Norfolk). Their mother Emily had allowed the two daughters to grow up as wilderness tomboys with more interest in wildlife than in drawing room chatter. Both girls read zoology at Imperial College, South Kensington (London), and became zoologists, an unusual achievement for women of their generation. In 1915 Annie, just twenty-six years old, had been elected one of the first female members of the British Ornithologists' Union, and by 1920 she had become a noted authority on ducks and wading birds and had contributed a number of articles to the scientific literature on freshwater fowl.

Miss Jackson and Lt. Col. Meinertzhagen were smitten with each other. She was a striking woman—he found her to be "ideal"—and he was a tall, dashing officer at the peak of his fame as warrior and intelligence hero, and just coming into the first of what were to be five decades' renown in the eyes of some of his fellow birders as the greatest ornithologist of his era.

He confessed to Annie what a botch he had made of his first marriage. He dithered: he said he did not know whether to go mountaineering in India or stay home and woo this altogether too-wonderful woman. She was much too good for him. Now into his forties he had yet to possess a clue to romancing women but he knew he wanted this one; he wanted home, family, a house full of raucous children to whom he knew he would be a wonderful father. But he told Annie, with all the candor he owned, that he probably would make a dreadful husband.

Annie was willing to chance it. She was a gentle woman, the soul of kindness and generosity. Meinertzhagen seemed comfortable with her from the very first moment. She was a naturalist, an adept outdoorswoman, and the daughter of a soldier: a perfect match for him. They spoke the same idioms. He was able to let his guard down in a way he had not been able to do with anyone since the death of his brother Dan twenty-three years before.

From their first meeting near the end of 1920 onwards, "Dick and Annie" were inseparable in London and in the bird rooms at Tring. Their courtship was of the whirlwind variety but, unlike his previous marriage, this relationship was not to cause him immediate regret or anger—quite the reverse.

Just weeks after they had first met, Annie accepted his proposal on February 8, 1921. Many of Meinertzhagen's vast extended family fell in love with Annie. British birding's pre-eminent journal, the *Ibis*, announced the unprecedented betrothal of the two "well-known ornithologists," both of whom were members of the British Ornithologists' Union (which happened to be the publisher of the *Ibis*).

Quickly, as though to make up for lost years, Annie and Dick presented themselves to the South Kensington registry office on March 3—his forty-third birthday—and were married.[45]

The wedding-day photo of the couple shows Annie as a lovely woman illuminated by a vivacious expression of happiness. Unfortunately the groom looked stiff as a board, awkward in his medal-adorned dress uniform, mouth uncertain beneath his mustache, and eyes adrift as if he were suffering this politely but would rather be off hunting birds. As in many photos, he managed somehow to look simultaneously stern and childishly uncertain of himself.[46]

Freddie Guest, who was just about to accept an appointment as Britain's first Air Minister, did service as an usher. Chaim Weizmann gave Annie her first wedding present. Afterward they went out for a celebratory wedding breakfast with Lord Willy Percy and other friends.

Churchill would have been there but he and his wife Clementine had embarked on a steamer for Alexandria that day. Churchill had hoped the newlywed Meinertzhagens would advance the date of the wedding so they could accompany his party, but they had a quieter sort of honeymoon in mind—a hiking holiday over the moors and fens of Annie's ancestral castle at Swordale, in a remote corner of northern Scotland near Inverness.

Meinertzhagen's refusal to change the date of his wedding on Churchill's account, and Churchill's refusal to change the date of his sailing on Meinertzhagen's account, would prove to be indicators of a standoff that would characterize Britain's affairs in the Middle East during the coming two years.

🐦 🐦 🐦

On February 13, 1921, Churchill had changed hats. With the wave of a Lloyd-Georgian wand he had become Colonial Secretary. Then Churchill informed the War Office: "I shall want Meinertzhagen for the Middle East department."[47]

Palestine was a protectorate set up under the authority of the League of Nations. It was not a British colony, but that didn't stop Churchill from annexing the Middle East to the bailiwick of his Colonial Office.

Lord Curzon complained in a letter from the Foreign Office: "He wants to grab everything in his new Department & be a sort of Asiatic Foreign Secretary."[48]

Rivalries and confusions kept swirling. By the time RM reported for duty on May 9, 1921, about two months after his wedding to Annie, he was bitter about the way he felt Churchill had betrayed RM's idea of fair play. RM found that his assigned office-mates included his old colleague Lt. Col. T. E. Lawrence who, abetted by sweeping suggestions from Gertrude Bell, had drafted a set of official position papers for Churchill at the 1921 Cairo Conference—a conference RM had not attended.[49] Churchill had patched together the two-and-a-half-day meeting in Cairo very quickly, in an attempt to reach compromise between Arabs and Jews—a compromise he achieved (briefly) by creating Arab kingdoms in Mesopotamia and the Trans-Jordan,[50] thus reducing by 90 percent the acreage the Zionists had expected to have as part of Israel.

When RM heard about the Cairo Conference, he denounced it as a betrayal of Zionism and of Britain's promises to the Jews. None of this, though, prevented him from taking Annie around to visit his old home Mottisfont Abbey in Hampshire, his friends the Portals at Holywell, the hunting estate at Possingworth, the reservoirs at Tring (where he shot ducks), and the Templeton home of Freddie Guest.

In May there were outbreaks of violence throughout Palestine. RM says he was sent there on a tour of inspection, but he wrote elsewhere that at this time (RM, "Conquisitio Mea") he was exploring the Sudan and Somaliland. Simultaneously his typed diaries state that he was traveling in the Ahaggar Mountains of northwest Africa.

In fact he did spend a few weeks touring Palestine, trying to get the feel of things, and then returned to England to report his findings to Churchill. Nothing in the available records indicates he was investigating anything other than military posts and their equipment.

All the same, in the Colonial Office under Churchill and Sir Herbert

Samuel, RM once again was to record himself as the lonely steadfast voice of Zionism in British military councils that were otherwise dominated, he believed, by pro-Arab anti-Semites. In the diaries he depicts himself as the sole gallant front-line defender of the Jews in Churchill's Colonial Office.[51]

As usual the truth was more complicated—RM was hardly the only voice for Zionism, and based on its actions the British government was not at all one-sided; it tried to remain on the fence but on various occasions, and in telling ways, it showed favor toward the Zionists at the expense of the Arabs.

The actual record shows that RM spent most of his Colonial Office tour of duty in England, occupied with military budget matters and logistics rather than regional or ethnic politics.

In 1919–1920 he had represented the Foreign Office in Allenby's military camp. Now in 1921–1922 he was the War Office's military man in Churchill's civilian camp. Department records show that he spent much of his time in London or in the British countryside on leaves that were long enough for him and his bride to visit friends all around the British Isles. Only occasionally did he make an inspection tour of bases around the Middle East, where he appraised the usefulness of the installations and reported to his economy-minded government whether certain posts might be closed, reduced in strength, or consolidated.

In Churchill's Middle East section, RM's desk was next to that of T. E. Lawrence. RM could not help but look down upon Lawrence—not only was Lawrence unusually short while RM was unusually tall, but RM came from a moneyed (therefore quasi-aristocratic) background while Lawrence, though far more cultivated, was an illegitimate son of socially undistinguished parentage. To some people this would not have mattered, but RM in his peculiar, rough way was quite a snob about such things. In his diaries RM refers to Lawrence as "the little man."[52]

Lawrence's version was a bit different. Liddell Hart made notes from a chat with him: "T. E. joined Colonial Office in 1921 on Churchill's promise that he could do entirely what he liked, could quit any time, but meantime have free hand. . . . [Churchill] allowed him to have Young and Meinertzhagen as assistants."[53]

In their recollections both officers fudged reality, and Liddell Hart does not seem to have noticed the contradictions between their stories.[54] RM was not Lawrence's assistant. The Colonial Office List for 1922 is headed by Secretary of State for the Colonial Office: The Right Hon. Winston S. Churchill, MP, appointed February 14, 1921. His name is followed by two Under-Secretaries, then by a variety of assistants—about forty-five names in all. Among the forty-five is Assistant Under-Secretary of State Sir John E. Shuckburgh ("Seconded temporarily from India Office for service in connection with the Middle East"). Shuckburgh's Middle East Division includes twelve named individuals. Of these, the very last two are "Col. T. E. Lawrence (Specially attached as Adviser on Arab Affairs)" and finally "Lt. Col. R. Meinertzhagen (Military Adviser, Seconded temporarily from the War Office)."[55]

During his forays into the Middle East RM kept encountering the redoubtable Gertrude Bell. For Meinertzhagen-watchers the most intriguing thing about the arm's-length, sword's-point relationship (if it can be called a relationship at all) between these two is the glancing illumination it reflects upon a third party—a close and long-term friend of both Miss Bell and RM, the remarkable if baffling archaeologist/ornithologist/spy Jack Philby.

The vituperative Harry St. John Bridger Philby, BA, FRGS (1885–1960) had served before the war as a political officer in the Indian Civil Service. He then became director of a company called Sharqich Ltd., in Jeddah (Arabia). Thereafter he lived most of his life in Arabia; he became a Muslim (in those days "Moslem") in 1932.

He mapped much of the country, wrote several books and numerous papers, collected and identified a lot of birds, kept a home in London, and was a member of the Athenaeum Club and the Royal Geographical Society.

Known to acquaintances as "Sinjin" (traditional pronunciation of the name St. John), he was called Jack by a few friends, Meinertzhagen among them. Philby's MI5 files were released from the PRO in November 2002. Many members of the Meinertzhagen circle appear in them—Lord Lloyd, John Shuckburgh, and others. Philby is difficult to parse. He was a staunch Arabist and a convert to Islam. In England he associated with fascist leader William Joyce and was a founder of the extreme right-wing British National Party, but most of his friends including RM thought of him as a fuzzy-headed duffer and perhaps even a leftist.

It seems amazing that Meinertzhagen and Philby became friends. Philby was regarded as a "rabid" anti-Zionist. He was to serve as an adviser to Saudi Arabian ruler Abdul Aziz ibn Saud, and subsequently it was Philby who brokered the arrangement by which King Ibn Saud sold the concession in Arabia's oil to the United States—possibly the most lucrative acquisition in the history of commerce up to that time. And of course Philby's son Kim was to become perhaps the most notorious Communist spy of the twentieth century.

Nevertheless, Jack Philby and Dick Meinertzhagen formed an immediate friendship that lasted the rest of their lives.[56]

Second son of a struggling boarding-house proprietress and her absent gamekeeper husband, Jack Philby was urged by his mother to take up a diplomatic career. He found one, in the Political and Secret Department of the India Office. Jack grew up ashamed of his "worthless" father and resentful that his parents' financial expectations had been wiped out early by a coffee blight in Ceylon, where they had met and married. The stage was set from the outset for his betrayal of his class and his country (he harbored but usually concealed a lifelong bitterness toward those of his contemporaries who had private incomes) but in youth he was a dutiful—even outstanding—scholar: an accomplished classicist and a brilliant linguist in Westminster School and then Trinity College, Cambridge.

At heart Jack Philby was an autocrat who resented any meddling in his affairs by those he regarded as his intellectual or moral inferiors—a class to which he consigned just about everyone he ever met. In India during his first years of Imperial Government service he preached radical socialism and further offended his messmates by marrying a beautiful young red-haired woman who was socially "beneath him." Their first child and only son, Kim, was born in India on New Year's Day 1912, just two years before Jack's appointment as a District Commissioner—high office for a man not yet thirty.[57]

In 1914 in India, Philby entered the shadowy world of the British Secret Service. When the Great War broke out, the Indian government summoned him to its summer capital at Simla. He was placed in charge of press censorship and was given a position in a special branch in which, as Anthony Cave Brown puts it, he "became the radical whose job it was to hunt radicals"—a precise and eerie parallel to the position of trust that would be given to his son Kim three decades later. He disliked Indian service, however, and seized upon the earliest opportunity to have himself transferred to Cairo.

In the Middle East, by 1917, with the help of new friends, his quick wits, and expert applications of deceit (including the systematic theft of government secrets), Philby had climbed the ladder of power to become His Majesty's Government's Imperial Agent to Basra, Riyadh, and the Arab kingdoms. His goal, he later admitted, was not so much to achieve power or wealth as it was to achieve fame, and in that aim he succeeded. The perils and courage of his camel treks across Middle Eastern sands made good newspaper copy. Philby soon was awarded a Founder's Medal by the Royal Geographical Society—an honor previously reserved for posthumous presentation to dashing (if foolhardy) heroes like Scott of the Antarctic. It is in eclipse now, but at the time St. John Philby's fame as lone-rider British conqueror of the Arab wastes became even greater than T. E. Lawrence's. His was a household name in England and the Colonies.

But then came the sensational "Lawrence of Arabia" publicity barrage, perpetrated mainly by the American journalist Lowell Thomas. Both Philby and Meinertzhagen got buried under the debris of that broadside. Perhaps, after all, it is no wonder they became friends.

RM left London in the fall on a tour of inspection around the Middle East. It was to consume several months.

In the desert, when he was not meeting with Philby, Meinertzhagen carried on with his bird work. In a later issue of *Ibis* he recorded "An account of a journey across the Syrian Desert from Amman in Transjordania to Ramadi on the Euphrates,"[58] in which he reports he visited the Qa Al Azraq Oasis—he describes it as "a perfect paradise for birds, with green meadows, pools, and bushes."

Colonial Office files contain a multi-page typed memorandum from RM to Shuckburgh dated October 18, 1922. It rambles on about conditions in the places through which RM was traveling, with emphasis on details of supply, transport, regulations, and logistical matters of interest to military stations in the vicinity. Reading it, one can infer more about RM's attitudes than one can about the Middle East. RM saw the landscape clearly but saw its peoples and cultures through lenses that were framed, colored, and distorted by the attitudes of a colonial officer of Victorian vintage. The overriding good, in any consideration, was that of the Empire; indigenous peoples ought to have no rights other than those the Crown chose to grant them. This indelicacy was in part a pose he had decided to adopt, for he felt that it gave additional strength to his advocacy for Zionism.[59]

Annie joined him for a good part of that trip in 1922–1923. It began in Jerusalem with a visit to Sir Herbert Samuel at Government House. A week later RM visited Jack Philby, who at the moment was serving as political commissioner of Transjordan, and then on October 24 the Meinertzhagens set off in an armored car for Baghdad.

It does not seem to have been the most productive of trips. A British officer wrote in his 1923 diary that he sat next to Colonel Meinertzhagen at a dinner in the Allenby Hotel in Palestine: "I unburdened my heart to Meinertzhagen on the subject of the abuse of religious power by the Moslem authorities. . . . He entirely shared my views."[60]

Sharing views with fellow officers was one thing; solving the unsolvable was another. The trip was not completely unproductive—he sent memos several pages in length to Wyndham Deedes dealing with all sorts of topics, like the military situation in Transjordan and the Palestine Garrison[61]—but much of it must have struck him as ephemeral and unimportant.

At Baghdad he learned the six-year Lloyd George coalition government had fallen. A general election had brought in the Conservatives with Bonar Law as the new prime minister. Churchill even lost his seat in Parliament—standing as a Liberal, he came in fourth in the Dundee election. So he gave up his Liberal Party affiliation. Thus exiled to the "wilderness" and having had recent surgery, Churchill found himself, as he put it, "without an office, without a seat, without a party and without an appendix."[62]

Churchill's replacement in the Colonial Office was the Duke of Devonshire—a peer about whom Meinertzhagen knew nothing.

In the absence of orders to the contrary the Meinertzhagens continued on their journey. They examined bird habitats in northern Arabia. They made unofficial visits to Kurdistan and the fringes of Turkey. Then it was Christmas in Baghdad with Lady and Sir Percy Cox;[63] then India, then back to Aden, where he inspected the Yemen Infantry, then to Egypt and back to Palestine. Richard and Annie, with the Philbys and sometimes with the Nicolls, went birding around Amman, Petra, and Jerusalem. They studied the avian wildlife of Beersheba and Gaza.

He was being paid by the army, and presumably was not listed as being absent without leave, but most of RM's travel in those seasons can be described as personal junketing.

Finally in April 1923 he returned to England and the new regime.

He met his new boss, the Duke of Devonshire, a stuffy Conservative whose ignorance, in RM's estimation, was boundless.[64] He continued to work a while on the Middle East Desk under Shuckburgh but the department was no longer a place familiar to him. The previous December the Churchills had left England for Villa Rêve d'Or near Cannes in the south of France, and T. E. Lawrence too had left—pestered by celebrity-hounds and journalists, he had resigned his position with the Colonial Office and secretly enlisted in the RAF under an assumed name.

Like so many others in the hangover that followed the ghastly bloodshed of a dreadful war and the additional millions of deaths inflicted by the 1918–1919 influenza epidemic, Meinertzhagen seemed directionless. His diaries for the period often drift without transition from the cosmic to the mundane. He could begin a page with, "The muddle in the Middle East" and end it with, "A duck shoot at Tring."[65]

In his office, his friends were gone; his purpose seemed nullified by the way Middle East affairs now were set in concrete. RM recorded no triumphs or losses, and soon sought a way out.

His first move was a return to the deserts. Once again he spent much of 1923 traveling—in the Middle East, North Africa, and India. Annie again joined him for a good part of that time.

Colonial Office archives are heavy with files concerning the last major effort in which RM was involved—the matter of extracting British Army troops and replacing them with local levies and Indian Army troops in garrisons in Palestine. This caused reams of political argumentation but it sheds less illumination than heat, and in retrospect it seems as it must have seemed at the time—an exercise in petty economizing.[66]

RM's devotion to Zionism was undiminished. Now and then he dipped a clumsy toe into political waters. A year or two earlier, on August 2, 1921, back in London, he had posted a memo to Shuckburgh. Evidently the memo caused consternation even though he couched it most carefully in what he believed were polite and reasonable terms.

Shuckburgh's anger was partly caused by the stunning insensitivity of RM's timing. A report had arrived on RM's desk informing him that two or three dozen machine guns were on their way to the Zionists of Jerusalem,[67] but at the same time a delegation of Christians and Moslems from Palestine was visiting London to press an anti-Zionist view on Whitehall. The sensitive moment was the worst possible time for RM to discuss *favorably* the Zionists' persistent gun-running into Palestine—but that is just what he did.

To RM the overriding issue was the need for such an escalation of armament. His memo emphasized that the Jews in Palestine were not being protected by the British army as they ought to have been; that this failure of protection was due in part to the indifference of British officials in Palestine who didn't approve of Zionism and who therefore should be removed from the place; that Allenby's lingering influence (Cairo military command) on the civilian administrator of the Palestine Mandate (Sir Herbert Samuel) was counterproductive; that once and for all, as he'd suggested, Palestine should be divorced not only from Allenby's military command but also from Allenby's influence, which Meinertzhagen believed to be pro-Arab; that Zionist immigration ought to be encouraged rather than hindered; and that the then-informal Jewish administration of areas in Palestine be given Most Favored Nation status.

It was hardly the most propitious moment to drop such a ticking memo on the desk of the Assistant Under-Secretary of State for the Middle East.

Shuckburgh, a sensible fellow, seems to have filed the memo away without mentioning it to Churchill, for there were no immediate repercussions.

It was not until three months later that the Colonial Secretary sent down a written cautionary note about the need to discipline the unruly RM, and the issue this time was not Zionism. It had to do with Meinertzhagen's actual assignment. Churchill wrote, in a memo to Shuckburgh, "Please caution Colonel Meinertzhagen that he is not to express to the War Office opinions in regard to military matters contrary to my policy. Yesterday the Secretary of State for War told me that Colonel Meinertzhagen was quite agreeable to the removal of the armoured cars from Trans-Jordania. I have definitely forbidden this, and it is wrong for any officer in the department to give to other departments opinions contrary to my decisions."

This was not a mere slip. In the context of departmental rivalries it was the next thing to outright treason. RM, a Colonial Office man, had taken it upon himself to countermand a Colonial Office directive in favor of the desires of the War Office.

RM was on thin ice—and militarily on his last legs.

He seemed unaware of the peril to his career. He had a more important preoccupation: the birth of his first child. In December 1921 Annie gave birth to a daughter whom they christened Anne Margaret. For the veteran Meinertzhagen, who thought of himself as middle-aged at forty-two, the arrival of his firstborn was a triumph rather on the order of Allenby's victory at Beersheba.

On July 22, 1922, the League of Nations formally recognized Britain's Palestine Mandate. It was good news for Zionism. Annie and Dick Meinertzhagen celebrated it at dinner with the Weizmanns.[68] As things turned out, it may have been an impolitic dinner for RM to attend. By that summer it had become evident in the Colonial Secretariat that information was being leaked from the Middle East Desk to the Zionist office in London. RM insisted he had nothing to do with this; he said he always refused to discuss confidential matters with Weizmann or anyone else outside his own office, and he said Weizmann understood his position and did not try to influence him to break that confidence. According to Meinertzhagen, he felt he was being framed, and he seemed to feel Shuckburgh was behind the frame up—Shuckburgh suddenly had become "saturated" with hatred of Jews and Zionism and was, according to RM, a vile saboteur of the Jewish interests he was supposed to protect.

Agitated about the escaping information, Churchill hauled RM on the carpet on June 14, 1922. RM snapped an offer to resign on the spot if Churchill was not completely satisfied with his integrity. He says Churchill refused to accept his resignation, but at the same time emphasized the need to exercise extreme care during any contact with Weizmann.

RM then tells us he had a good idea who was leaking the information—a Jew, a minor clerk in the Middle East office, who claimed not to know Weizmann but had been seen coming out of Weizmann's house.[69]

Whether in fact RM leaked information to Weizmann is a question to which no answer has come forward. He must be presumed innocent. But from that point forward he was on his way out—superannuated, unpromoted, a twenty-three-year veteran with no general's tabs in sight.

RM's expressions of his attitudes toward Shuckburgh appear to depend on when he wrote or rewrote a particular diary page. Early on (1918–1920), and then again much later (1930s), Shuckburgh was helpful to RM in interceding with Churchill on RM's behalf. But in November 1921, when Churchill told Shuckburgh to discipline Meinertzhagen, RM's position of trust seems to have eroded. He doesn't blame Shuckburgh for his subsequent departure from the Colonial Office, but the events of mid-1922 seem to have marked a final ruination of his career and he probably saw Shuckburgh's sly hand in it. Clearly his feelings toward both Shuckburgh and Churchill underwent a marked change.

Churchill switched to the Tories and made his way back into Parliament a couple of years later; he became Stanley Baldwin's Chancellor of the Exchequer in 1924 and that might have been in time for him to do RM some good but Churchill wanted nothing further to do with the dangerously outspoken Major. They may have remained on polite speaking terms, willing to nod to each other at large social gatherings—perhaps in part because of the Meinertzhagen–Freddie Guest friendship—but Churchill was no longer RM's friend at court; in fact no affiliation seems to have survived at all.[70]

Things deflated rapidly. RM found himself reassigned to what he felt was a degrading job. By this time even his old regiment seemed unwilling to acknowledge him. After a postwar downsizing of the Royal Fusiliers he was found redundant. He found himself abruptly reassigned to the Duke of Cornwall's Light Infantry Regiment.

As a sop to himself he insists he was placed "second-in-command"[71] of the Regiment but the record shows no such thing.

Around this time he holds, in his diaries, that he was offered various lofty positions, and to have turned them all down—inspector general of

British Forces in West Africa; chief of the British intelligence service for Ireland; governor of the Falkland Islands. If one accepts the premise that RM's assertions cannot be accepted without confirmation by independent sources, then no such offers were made. No known records support any of these assertions.

On June 1, 1924, Meinertzhagen reported for duty, as ordered, to the temporary billets of his battalion. It happened to be on a training tour of duty in Cologne, Germany.

Cologne was not the Regiment's usual domain; the French, with their African troops, were the occupying power in the sector. Meinertzhagen's visit there, along with the Battalion's, was to be a temporary affair, so Annie did not accompany him.

His work at the Cologne barracks consisted not of spying (as his diaries intimate) but of training troops and maneuvering them through war games.

The emphasis in his recollection of the period seems to be on a bitter comparison between the conquered German heroes and the conqueror French cretins for whom Meinertzhagen's most oft-repeated adjective is rotten.

He returned to London at the end of September 1924 to be with his family (and to take up playing the harmonica, much to the consternation of his infant daughter Anne who hated the sounds it made).[72] Restive and confused, he dragged Annie with him on overnight and weekend visits to birding and hunting friends and to some of his army intelligence cronies. Among others they visited the Benson brothers at South Uist, where RM went egg collecting with the Hon. Guy Charteris, whose daughter Ann later would marry Meinertzhagen's friend and spy/writer protégé Ian Fleming. They met the celebrated German ornithologist Erwin Stresemann at the Rothschild Museum in Tring, and they tried to relax and enjoy a bit of home and hearth until in December he was posted out to India.

By then Annie was expecting a second child. She did not go with him.

He joined the relocated battalion at Lucknow in January 1925 and did not like what he saw of the place or the regiment. He wrote that he had "black dog"—in those days a familiar phrase for depression.[73] At this point, between the lines we can picture a man near the end of his rope—separated by thousands of miles from his family, tossed onto a veritable rubbish heap by the army, not too long before barred by the British Museum, and probably feeling ill-used and ill-prepared.

He was in Lucknow on January 7, 1925, when, back in England, Annie gave birth to their second child, Daniel. RM's distance from the boy's birth may have been the trigger that set him off. He consulted by wire with Annie in England to make sure he had her approval; then he wrote and delivered on January 26, 1925, his resignation both from the regiment and from the British Army.[74]

Without objection he accepted a reduction to a Major's pension—£420 a year.[75] It didn't matter; Annie had money.

Rather than return home he set out on a bird-sighting expedition to Kashmir and Tibet. Perhaps he felt incapable of facing people in England. His emotions must have been in turmoil. The world had fallen down around his ankles. The career of his entire adult life was gone—disappeared as if it had never taken place. He had no way of knowing that half his lifetime still lay ahead of him—but he did know he felt ill-used and ignominiously discarded by the portion that lay behind him.

It seems evident that for the first time in his life of solitary traveling he felt unhappy to be alone in the wild. He missed Annie. He asked her to come out and join him in a grand Asian bird-hunt.

CHAPTER 9
FAMILY

On active service RM's annual salary had been good but not princely: about £900 before it was halved by his retirement. In previous years he had enjoyed gifts from Uncle Ernest and some additional income from the family bank, which was being managed (not terribly well) by his younger brother Louis, with whom RM was on the outs.[1] The estrangement seems to have been due, at least in part, to what RM regarded as Louis's effrontery in having named his firstborn son Daniel. For more than six generations, Meinertzhagen patriarchs had named their firstborn sons Daniel. RM was the eldest surviving son of the most recent Daniel Meinertzhagen, and he held that it was his right—and his alone—to bestow the name on his first son.

Louis's attitude was that in 1915, when his own first son had been born, Richard had been off in Africa and had been married to Armorel for several years and had produced no offspring and anyway it was clear RM was not interested in carrying on as a banking member of the family. Louis couldn't see what the fuss was all about, but RM insisted on his prerogative. When his first son—second child—was born in January 1925, the baby was christened Daniel. This led to confusion, what with two first cousins, ten years apart in age, both named Daniel Meinertzhagen. Louis seems to have taken the confusion in stride, though: he and RM resumed cordial relations not too long after the birth of RM's son.

Annie's sister Dorothy Jackson had died in Scotland in 1921. Their mother and Richard's bride became heirs to the Jackson estates. Annie received a good income and her inheritance was the principal source of his livelihood for the remaining forty-six years of RM's life; he earned little or nothing from his scientific work and book publications, and except for a few months early in World War II he had no further government salary after 1924. It is not clear whether he received financial support from his family, but if so it probably was meager. When he was preparing to trek across half the world on one of his extravagant expeditions, he would apply to the government and/or the museums for stipends, but these applications may have had less to do with money than with his need to legitimize the scientific purpose of his explorations. He needed approval, not money. In virtually every case, he went ahead with his planned expeditions whether or not he received grants.

In his writings, the absence of references to income and expenditures may not be a deliberate attempt to obfuscate the issue. Most of the time RM seems to have been uninterested in money. One might suspect otherwise, given the evidence of his penchant for stealing birds, words, and other collectibles, but those who knew him seem to feel RM's copious thefts had nothing to do with financial profit. In the end, they point out, he gave all the bird specimens away, and he may never have thought about the tremendous amount of time and work that scientists would need to expend in order to correct his frauds. On the other hand, Scottish national files show that in 1937 RM obtained a decree granting him authority to sell properties from Annie's estate.[2] Which properties he sold, and what he did with the proceeds, are facts not in evidence.

Sometimes he spent lavishly. But it was bad form for gentlemen of his class to speak (or even think) about money. His mother had driven into him a contempt for greed. (The usual ironies applied: mother Georgina had been a child of privilege and as a married woman she'd lived in relative splendor thanks to her husband's large income—but she was above all that.)

The end result is that when RM writes, "I had no desire to . . . contaminate my soul with commerce and all the greed of moneymaking,"[3] one does not know whether to believe or disbelieve him.

Despite the subdued aspect he presented during his months of depressed confusion after he left the army in 1925, RM's outsize qualities impressed many Asians and Europeans whom he met along the way. In an age when travel was still physically demanding and dangerous, he trekked relentlessly from the snows of the Himalayas to the rainforests of Burma and the plains of India. He made notes, eerie in their objective detachment, on the effects of extreme altitudes upon his body. He nearly died of cholera in Baltistan but kept plunging forward, confused and doleful but unwilling to be stopped by anything short of death.

From boyhood on he had been in tune with nature; now he took photographs, made drawings, and provided armchair tourists with keen descriptions of rain forests and snowy mountains, of Buddhist ceremonies and the characteristics of yaks; he discovered new (previously unrecorded) species of bats, birds, and *mallophaga*.[4]

As soon as their newborn son was old enough to be looked after by a nanny, Annie steamed out to meet him in Bombay. He went eagerly to meet her ship.

They visited or traveled with some of the noted hunters and itinerant natural scientists of the age: V.S. La Personne (of the Bombay Natural History Society), Cyril Mackworth-Praed, RM's old friend Frederick "Hatter" Bailey of the heroic mission to Tashkent—with whom, we must assume, RM shared yarns about their mutual former boss Sir John Shuckburgh—and Dr. Sálim Ali who was to become the dean of Indian ornithology, a leader of the Bombay Natural History Society, author of many books (including the original and numerous updated editions of *The Book of Indian Birds* (1941ff), and founder-director of several wildlife preserves including what is now the Sálim Ali Bird Sanctuary in Kerala on the Periyar river. Sálim Ali had a special interest, which Meinertzhagen shared, in vultures.

The two men formed an immediate bond despite Meinertzhagen's habit of belittling Indians as he belittled all groups. He expressed unabashed contempt for "wogs" (Westernized Oriental Gentlemen). As the years passed, he and Sálim Ali managed to become not only scientific peer-colleagues but close personal friends.[5] One must attribute this friendship to Sálim Ali's extraordinary patience and tolerance, for Meinertzhagen often treated him outrageously. The good-natured Sálim Ali (who said Meinertzhagen was easy to find in a crowd because he was as tall and thin as a flagstaff[6]) was amused by it; in his autobiography he seemed pleased that RM had referred to him as "a rank seditionist and communist . . . [who] is prepared to turn the British out of India tomorrow and govern the country himself. I have repeatedly told him that the British Government have [*sic*] no intention of handing over millions of uneducated Indians to the mercy of such men as Sálim: that no Englishman would tolerate men being governed by rats."[7]

It was Sálim Ali, not Meinertzhagen, who published those remarks. The Englishman's ringing racism seemed to amuse him; he felt RM's outrageous expression of bigotry was a pose contrived for its shocking effect (like the smoking revolver at the dinner party). We see, not in the quotation but in Sálim Ali's reaction to it, an indication of the captivating charisma that RM projected. In person he meant to shock but not to assail; he meant his affronts to be seen through.

RM and Sálim Ali were to work together and visit each other's homes over many years; they obviously and genuinely liked each other. Sálim Ali was a distinguished scientist—erudite, brave, dedicated, sensitive, and proud. If he had felt that RM truly regarded him as a "rat" he would have had nothing to do with the Englishman. He regarded RM's blustering as friendly insults—inverted compliments. Who among us has not greeted a dear friend with humorous abuse?

A cold record of RM's transgressions can make a monster of him; but, to most of the people around him, he was no monster; he was personable and eccentric—a thoroughly enchanting rogue.

In his autobiography Sálim Ali recounts set-piece RM myths as RM told them to him (the "treachery" of the Nandi Laibon, the triumph of the haversack ruse). He seems to accept those without challenge. So did most people who heard the stories direct from Meinertzhagen. But Sálim Ali's face-to-face view of RM's personality is sharp-eyed. He found RM to be extremely courageous:

> Meinertzhagen seemed to be as indifferent to physical pain as to personal danger. While we were collecting in a reedy marsh near Kabul, he, wearing khaki shorts with legs uncovered, accidentally stepped on a barb-pointed reed which broke off, leaving about three-quarters of an inch of its length within his flesh. Regardless of this, he continued splodging through the marsh while his blood flowed freely. Finally, after some persuasion, he agreed to return. As he was limping back to the car to get back and have the barb removed by the embassy doctor, he noticed a Bearded Vulture—a wanted species—some 300 yards away in a different direction. Ignoring the projecting reed and the flowing blood he limped up to the bird and shot it before getting back to the car. . . .
>
> Though possessed also of many admirable qualities, he had a distinct streak of the bully in his make-up and could be unreasonable to the point of brutality at times. . . . [Sometimes a mere trifle] sent him off the deep end into a paroxysm of insensate rage.[8]

Sálim Ali seems especially illuminating on the subject of RM's attitude as it expressed itself in his penchant for appropriating things without permission:

> Before the expedition started, looking over the list of stores and equipment I had brought, he was jeeringly contemptuous about my having been so sybaritic as to bring two Petromax lamps when he himself had managed well enough without this luxury and with only hurri-

cane lanterns all the forty years or more he had been collecting. I said that the Petromaxes were really meant for myself because I was used to them and could not work at night in poor light. He made some snooty remarks about people getting soft and so on, and there the matter ended. When we got going in our first camp and the Petromaxes were lit, what did I find on return from the evening round of collecting but that Meinertzhagen had calmly monopolized both the lamps for himself, one on either side, seeming to enjoy their brightness rather than missing his old accustomed hurricane lanterns. This set the pattern; thenceforth, and all through the expedition, if I wished to work after dark I had to sneak up to the Petromaxes which had become inseparable from him.[9]

To trace the route of Meinertzhagen's 1925–1926 journey is to compile a catalogue of exotic place-names some of which would remain relatively unexplored by outsiders even into the twenty-first century. The pleasure of having his wife's company during part of the trip, and the excitement of exploration, brought him up out of his despond.

For more than a year he traversed about a thousand miles a month in the rain forests, open plains, and rocky, wooded mountains of India and Burma, wearing gaiters and plus-fours, shooting birds, boars, antelopes, leopards, and tigers. Hunting in the gentle English countryside or the veldt of Africa might not seem to have offered sufficient preparation for these rough shoots in the secret places of Asia but it had taught him tracking and marksmanship, along with the patience to hide up and wait, absolutely still, regardless of heat, cold, insects or other discomforts. In this manner he accumulated the collections for which he became famous—animals, butterflies, plants, insects, and birds. He or his hired skinners cleaned and stuffed all his specimens with intricate care, then mounted the animals on armatures, the insects on slides, the plants in pressboards, and the birds in shallow-drawered cases.

Only one wildlife form seems not to have appealed to his collecting passion. "I always kill snakes on principle."[10]

RM, Annie, and Sálim Ali started the year 1926 in Darjeeling; they traveled along the Phalut Ridge, from which they could see the peak of Mount Everest. Then Annie returned home because her mother was ill. RM pressed on. He relished the challenge presented by each new mountain to climb and each new river to cross.

After Annie's mother died, RM returned to Calcutta and said farewell to Sálim Ali. He set sail from Bombay and, by way of Port Said, arrived back in London on February 13.[11]

After the funeral Annie and RM visited friends in Gloucestershire, then rented Rose Hall (Sutherland) "for the season," then attended an Ornithological Congress in Copenhagen. On June 1 they stopped in Hamburg then visited Bremen to see his relatives. On June 5 they visited the eminent German ornithologist Erwin Stresemann. Then they checked in with RM's former German opponent from East Africa, Generalmajor Paul von Lettow-Vorbeck. It seems to have been a cheerful and intense visit; both Lettow and RM discuss it in their memoirs. The two men became friends, and would keep in touch for decades.[12]

Col. R. Meinertzhagen's reputation had grown among natural scientists and wilderness explorers—it preceded him back to England, where not long after his return he was elected to the councils of both the British Ornithologists' Union and the Royal Geographical Society.[13]

Later that summer, at Rosehall, Annie and RM entertained birders Hugh and Joan Whistler and other visitors. RM went shooting, here and there, with Brooksbank and with Maurice Portal. He and Annie went up to Scotland in August. Later, he visited Gilbert and Maud Russell at Mottisfont Abbey—they were the new owners. RM still behaved as if the place belonged to him, but the Russells didn't seem to mind this eccentricity. They introduced RM to their circle of weekend guests. He must have made a hit with them, for he was frequently to be invited back.

🕊 🕊 🕊

Early in 1921, shortly after their daughter's birth, Annie and Richard had bought the house at 17 Kensington Park Gardens (London) that was to be their primary residence and in which he would live out the rest of his life. They paid £3,750—a high price in those days. The house, to which they usually would refer simply as "KPG," still stands in a white row of elegant dwellings in Notting Hill. (Unfortunately for RM-watchers its interior has been extensively remodeled.) A large three-story attached Georgian structure with attic and basement and a deep back garden, it was built with a connecting foyer that adjoined the house next door, so that both houses shared the entrance and it was not necessary for the occupant of either house to go outdoors in order to enter the other.

The adjoining house—number 18—was the residence of Meinertzhagen's first cousin Rachel Hobhouse Clay and her husband Sir Felix Clay, who had bought it several years earlier. Rachel's mother was one of the Potters—a sister of Meinertzhagen's mother. She had married Sir Felix Clay, who had been a close friend of Richard's father.[14] The Clays had five children of whom two daughters, Janet and Theresa, soon were to become central to Richard's life.

In the diaries he is vague about when he first met the two young sisters. He seems to want us to infer that he was not aware of them until the late 1920s. In fact, however, they all lived under the same roof from 1922 (when Theresa was eleven years old) on.

In light of subsequent events it seems safe to assume that Theresa and her sister were called upon to look after the Meinertzhagens' children from time to time.

His marriage to Annie had begun as a romantic love-match and by all external indications appears to have been "normal." But he was skittish in his relationships with nearly all women. They were, to him, minefields. Some watchers describe him as having been "innocent"—i.e., repressed. There was a wide but inconsistent prudish streak in him. A century later he might have become a television network executive, reveling in fantasies of ghastly violence but horrified by any hint of sexual irregularity. Occasionally, though not consistently, he tried to insist that his first marriage (to Armorel Lewis) had never been consummated.[15]

To describe him as a misogynist is barely to scratch the surface. His grand-nephew recalls, "He hated things feminine. If he went into a shop, and this goes right up until the [Second World] War, if he was waited on by a woman who had makeup on her face, or colored nails, he'd send for the manager and say he wouldn't be served by a painted woman."[16]

He had grown up in a family dominated by exceptional women. His aunts and sisters were outspoken leaders of the Suffrage and Socialist movements.[17] They must have been an intimidating lot. The women of the Potter-Hobhouse-Meinertzhagen clans seem to have been born to be activists; Beatrice Webb was only the most famous of them. In 1900 during the Boer War it was RM's aunt, the crusading Emily Hobhouse, who alerted the world to the horrors of the Kitchener concentration camps in South Africa, into which thousands of Boer families had been herded like livestock while children died before their own mothers' eyes. Emily Hobhouse was joined in these demonstrations by her sister-in-law Kate Meinertzhagen, another aunt of Richard's, and together they helped bring an end to the shabby and bitter South African war.

Through it all, RM's response was to rebuke both women as disloyal to the British Army and possibly unbalanced. Emily Hobhouse, in addition, was in his opinion dangerously perverted.[18]

During the first two-thirds of RM's lifespan these women's battle was yet to be won; in fact it had barely started. In Britain, women only gained the vote in 1918, and even then it was restricted to those over the age of thirty. RM abhorred the development in any case. With apocalyptic certainty he declared that it could mean the end of the civilized world, because women were creatures of unreason and unfettered, childish emotional outbursts. When—sometimes at the top of his lungs—he put such arguments to the women in the family, they did not retreat. They retorted that he sounded as if he were describing not them but himself.

Since his pronouncements, and the tone in which he delivered himself of them, were so sure to provoke just such reactions, one cannot know how much of his reactionary radicalism was a pose designed for his own wicked amusement. He was not above stating that there were three kinds of women— those who were satisfied to be married, those who had to be seduced, and the third kind for whom nothing would do except rape.[19] (So far as we know, he never raped nor attempted to rape anyone, nor seriously advocated rape; his jokes may have been in bad taste, and sometimes could be appallingly unfunny, but they were only that—jokes.)

In effect, he was surrounded and often intimidated, although he never would admit it, by what he heard as a cacophony of women. They were leaders; they kept charging passionately onto new battlefields many of which they eventually would conquer: social reform, theoretical investigation, human rights, artistic creativity, and philosophical inquiry.[20]

None of these things made much sense to him. RM's understanding of such battlefields was poor at best. He saw them fitfully, as if they were illuminated at night by distant artillery flashes, and whenever possible he turned away because he did not care for subtleties.

Annie, a woman of remarkable character, appears to have seen through his exaggerated Victorian male chauvinism as if it were clear glass. She refused to take his tirades seriously. Behind the bluster, she probably felt, was a vulnerable and lovable man.

That was true until some point in 1926 or 1927, when evidently her feeling changed. That was when he chose to publish his article about Asian birds without correcting it—and it was when she changed her will.

The reasons for her change of heart are easy to infer but difficult to prove.

After RM left government service, specific incidents of his life became more difficult to track. Government bureaucracies, for all their failings, are wonderful keepers of paper. A great deal of that paper, as it applies to Richard Meinertzhagen, has become available. Therefore it has been possible to compare and thus to confirm or disprove the alleged adventures in his military career (including his actual and considerable importance in the Middle East after the Great War).

Accounts of his civilian activities during the ensuing four decades can be found in his own writings, but independent sources are more scattered and more difficult to find. Fortunately quite a few are accessible that were not available to previous biographers, but gaps remain.

The chill that began to separate Annie and Dick in 1926 is believed, by some, to have been caused by his preparation of a long two-part *Ibis* account of the year-long safari around Asia. Here is how one key ornithological source, who has asked for anonymity, summarizes suppositions:

> RM took a trip after retirement from soldiering to Ladakh and Sikkim in 1925–6. . . . Later that year, RM and Annie published a quick paper together naming new subspecies from that trip. Then RM sole-authored a big "ornithological results" paper on the whole trip, which came out in *Ibis* in two parts in 1927.[21] In this paper he describes in vivid detail encountering and collecting numerous rare birds, which are in fact most of his Indian subcontinent frauds. But RM, in no uncertain terms, describes having collected these, so it is not a simple mix-up, or forgetfulness, or carelessness, etc. . . . Almost certainly [Annie], as an ornithologist and trip participant, realized what he had done: RM had filled in the true trip collection with fraudulent specimens.[22]

As this correspondent points out, it would have been virtually impossible for Annie not to have realized the fakery her husband was perpetrating.

But did she confront him? We don't know.

We do know that RM persisted in writing his fictionalized history of their trek.

Why did RM pretend he had found birds in new places? The probable answer: reputation. A man can become famous by discovering a new species in a place where it previously wasn't thought to exist. When he makes similar discoveries several times over the years, he becomes a titan in the community of peers.

He pretended he didn't care what people thought of him, but nearly everything he did seems to have been driven by a need to draw attention. His diaries, their pages so coyly protected from public view for so many years, stood racked in handsome rows on the bookcase in his foyer, where they were the first things people noticed. These were not the hidden memoirs of a colorless secret agent keeping daily histories for the benefit of a handful of future spymasters. Like their author they were as inconspicuous as skywriting but as revealing as a London fog.

In 1926–1928, he traveled quite a bit, but seldom did Annie accompany him. He visited new friends Maud and Gilbert Russell at Mottisfont Abbey, where he was acquainted with many among their eccentric set, including the young then-journalist Ian Fleming. He seems to have been away from home just about every weekend—to John O'Groats, to Langwell, to Abernethy (Perthshire—deer hunting), to Kilmory, to Harrow. (During these same months, in "Conquisitio Mea," he purports to have been exploring Szechwan.)

There was no public estrangement but a definite shift was occurring in their relationship. At times Annie and Dick still played gracious hosts. They entertained Sir Felix and Lady Clay at Swordale. This fact suggests another proposed reason for Annie's growing estrangement from him. During 1927 RM wrote at length in his diaries about the Clays' daughters, the young cousins Theresa (then fifteen) and Janet (sixteen). The latter gave him some bed socks. But it was the former about whom he waxed passionate in the diaries. As usual we cannot be sure these pages were written when they purport to have been written, but they are accompanied by his photographs of the happy teenage cousins, some of them nude pictures, pasted onto the backs of the typed pages. These seem contemporaneous with the text.[23]

In diaries attributed to earlier years, he described a vivid dream he remembered from when he was far away on Mauritius—a dream he says occurred during the actual birth of Theresa in 1911.[24] Now he writes at some length about Cousin Theresa ("Tess"), who—he believes—is that very dream child: a garden-fresh vision of perfection. In 1927, he writes, she is a cheerful, sensible, and energetic outdoor girl with a fine sense of humor and a rare ability "to play the game (rare attribute among women)."[25]

He rambles on, page after page, about how his dream-child of 1911 has turned into a real person. Forgetting how he has claimed elsewhere in the diaries that he really didn't notice Cousin Theresa until the later 1920s, he remarks how at the moment he first met Theresa in 1922 he saw something uncannily familiar in her face. He feels a mystical bond with her.

He worries that he's too "dull" for her, but then takes comfort in a sense that she shares with him a close unspoken bond. When he sees her off, with her brother Anthony, on a train for London, he bends to kiss a golden strand of her hair.

On the same page he remarks, with unemotional detachment, that Annie is expecting her third baby in March.[26]

Did Annie know about his odd infatuation with his fifteen-year-old cousin?

A definitive answer to that question has not surfaced. We know that Annie changed her will in 1927. The new will no longer left her estates to her husband. Now it left various things in trust for her children, with an income to her husband, but he was to receive the income only so long as he did not remarry. ("£100,000 Lost by Remarriage," gossiped one of the tabloid newspapers after Annie died.[27])

We found no mention anywhere that Annie had ever explained why she changed her will.

But this sequence of events seems interesting. For whatever reason, she signed the new will shortly after RM published his long two-part article.

And she signed it at about the same time when young Theresa Clay became a sudden and substantial presence in RM's diary entries.

🐦 🐦 🐦

RM's friend Michael Nicoll, the ornithologist, had died in 1925.

The two had met not long after RM first arrived in Cairo in 1917, when the newly arrived RM had gone to see the noted "bird man of Egypt" to peck at Nicoll's brain about local birds. On occasion thereafter he traveled with Nicoll and his wife Norrie to various points in Egypt and had spent the 1919–1920 holidays with them in Cairo and Helwan. In 1922 the Nicolls had visited "Dick and Annie" at her family estate of Swordale in Scotland. A few months later, back in the Middle East, Dick and Annie had gone birding with the Nicolls and with Jack Philby.[28]

Now, as 1927 ran toward its end, RM fled from England on a long trip to Egypt, ostensibly to complete his late friend's book as a favor to Nicoll's widow.

It would be published in 1930 as *Nicoll's Birds of Egypt* "by Colonel R. Meinertzhagen."[29] Unarguably he did quite a bit of independent research before completing the book, and he provided quite a few of its illustrations, and the title seems appropriate—but within its text RM's references to Nicoll seem inadequate at best.

Norrie Nicoll remained on cordial terms with him for years after the death of her husband, but nonetheless, assertions of plagiarism hover around the book to this day. I'm told by a correspondent who requests anonymity, "RM only acquiesced in putting the latter title on the earlier book out of fear that Nicoll's widow would sue him"—a statement at two degrees of separation or more, and therefore to be taken as opinion rather than fact.

With more substance, similar accusations were leveled against him regarding his later tome *Birds of Arabia*.[30] But, for the most part, RM was not a literary plagiarist by the usual definitions. He wrote an enormous number of scholarly articles and several books about wildlife, and while they often drift into the fanciful and the unscientific, they unquestionably were his own work. He seems to have preferred stealing birds to stealing words.

While in Egypt in 1927–1928 RM had very little to say in his diaries about Annie's pregnancy but he did manage to gush about Theresa Clay's seventeenth birthday.[31] Then, upon his return to England on April 16, 1928, he stayed with Sir Felix and Lady Clay at Burnt House.

That was when he first met his new son, Richard Randle Meinertzhagen, "Ran," now three weeks old.

On June 4, 1928, he recorded Annie's displeasure with their hired nurse. She took the children to Edinburgh to see if she could find a nurse in Scotland. He saw them off at King's Cross. Should we infer she was getting away from him as quickly as possible?

His account of those days appears on the top half of a diary page. Below, filling out the rest of the page, are two photos of Theresa Clay holding a small dog. On the facing page are pictures of Theresa and Janet. Their poses may seem provocative. Perhaps the girls, who were very pretty, were mischievously teasing the photographer.

After another fortnight in London RM went north by train to join Annie and the three children at Swordale. Soon they were visited by the Clays. He enjoyed their stay and was depressed by their departure. He records his resentment toward the mundane chores he had to perform because Annie was still breast-feeding the baby. The weather was terrible and the mood he reflects is dismal.[32]

A few days later, on July 6, 1928, Annie was shot in the head and died.

A local newspaper stated that Mrs. Meinertzhagen "had finished revolver target practice and was returning to the castle—her husband a short distance ahead—examining her revolver in the belief that the live cartridge had been expended. The revolver discharged a bullet which penetrated her head."[33]

The version in RM's diaries holds that he and Annie had finished sighting-in the handgun and he was walking down to retrieve their target when he heard the gunshot behind him, wheeled, and saw Annie dead on the ground.[34]

No inquest or enquiry took place. The findings of the post-mortem examinations by two physicians are cited in the death certificate itself: "Injury to spinal cord & lower part of brain from bullet wound at short range."[35]

The only eyewitness to the event was Richard Meinertzhagen. In the absence of compelling evidence to the contrary, the death of his wife was ruled an accident.

Suspicions ramified. Some of his family members, and some of the same friends who had been charmed and intrigued by RM, became convinced he had driven his wife to suicide or had murdered her. One lady ornithologist told me that some years later Meinertzhagen had tried "in a deadly voice" to ask her out on a date—to climb an Alp. She said she had declined on grounds of abject terror: she believed he was a madman and had murdered his wife. "He was the only true Jekyll-Hyde personality I've ever known."[36]

In a recorded interview one of Meinertzhagen's relatives, who knew him quite well, told me, "He had no scruples. He'd eliminate anybody. . . . She [Annie] was a crack shot. Somebody said it was sort of a duel. They gave each other a chance. 'If you shoot me, then I'll take my secrets to the grave. But otherwise I've got to shoot you.' So they had the duel. So the story goes."[37] Similarly, dodologist Ralfe Whistler recalls that on one occasion RM told him that he had killed his wife Annie "in some sort of duel."[38]

To those who believe Annie's death was no accident, the circumstantial evidence seems persuasive. The path of the bullet would seem to create doubt as to whether she could have inflicted the wound on herself. RM was at least a full foot taller than his wife, so a downward shot through her head and spine—especially if she were leaning forward a bit—could have been fired much more readily by him than by her.

It is argued that Annie would not likely have shot herself by accident. She was an expert with firearms, having grown up with them in the landed hunting set and having spent years hunting birds all over the world and providing specimens to the leading museums.

Those who believe she was murdered point out that if ever in RM's long and bloody career there was a smoking gun, this was that case—literally, with its bullet driven through Annie's head and spine at point-blank range. They cite the standard homicide trinity: method, opportunity, and motive. Annie was shot to death at close range; her husband was the only witness; she died under suspicious circumstances at a time when her death was very much to his benefit because, they point out, it kept her from exposing his bird thefts, it freed him to carry on with his pubescent cousins, and it left him a large income for life.[39]

Opinion is not proof, and no one was ever charged with or convicted of murder in the case of the death of Annie Meinertzhagen. For the record, RM is innocent until and unless he should be proven guilty.

The case for RM's innocence derives in part, and with irony, from his habit of lying. Much of his reputation as a bloodthirsty killer seems to have been a bluff of his own manufacture. It is typified by the story he enjoyed telling party guests about how he and Ewart "Cape to Cairo" Grogan once killed a young Kikuyu man, roasted him over a spit, and tried to eat him in order to find out what human flesh tasted like. Grogan later mentioned that it hadn't tasted very good, so they set the half-cooked man aside and ate waterbuck instead. The gruesome story was related at different times in different locations and separately by both Grogan and RM.[40] All the same, one feels safe in spurning it: Grogan was widely reputed to be one of the greatest liars in all Africa, and as we have seen, RM was hardly a font of reliable truths. Both creators of the attempted-cannibalism story were men who adored making outrageous statements purely for their shock value. They knew each other over several decades, so they had plenty of time to concoct the yarn, toss it back and forth, and embellish it.

The slaughters of various African villages, the beating death of RM's polo syce in India, the numerous shootings and clubbings of deserters and enemy troops—history has laid these and many other homicides at RM's door, but we may seriously doubt any of them occurred outside his own fancies.

It leaves a frustrating question: If he wasn't really the killer he pretended to be, then why should we suspect he may have murdered his wife?

The only replies—tentative ones—are the arguments given above: motive, means, opportunity, and what we believe we know about the character of RM.

Annie was buried at Swordale four days after her death. Not long after, RM attended St. Martin's Church in Trafalgar Square where Theresa Clay was baptized, at the age of seventeen. RM was her sponsor. He seems uncertain whether that meant he was her godfather.[41]

In the months that followed Annie's death, the Clay girls stood like Canute against the force of RM's bereavement. They protected his three children, kept the ongoing transactions of his life in order, and tried to cheer him up. He expressed wonder at the kindness with which Janet and Theresa treated him. He describes walks and bird watching, ocean swims, and driving lessons that caused howls of laughter.

All the same, by the time RM returned to London in mid-September he sank into a deep depression from which he did not emerge until the next spring. His next diary entry is dated March 3, 1929 and is filled with bleak complaints—in loneliness and despair he had taken to his bed, could not concentrate, could not eat or sleep.

Few independent records seem to survive regarding RM's activities during the rest of 1929. By his own account, a friend took his children to Cornwall for a while; RM stayed with various friends and in August visited the old school where he once had been happy—Aysgarth. According to his recollection in one of his books,[42] he visited the Spurn Head Lighthouse. In "Conquisitio Mea" he asserts he was in the Marismas and the Sierra Nevada of Spain. (The latter assertion is untrue, as is much of the material in that curious typescript.)

His depression became even grimmer. He felt he was losing his memory and perhaps his mind. Finally on September 11 he voluntarily checked himself into the psychiatric sanatorium in Ruthin, Wales.[43]

He does not reveal what sort of treatment he received in the clinic, and our earnest hunt for records has been foiled by the interval of too many decades.[44] It seems safe to infer he was trying to come to grips with Annie's death. He may seem to have had a borderline personality disorder in that respect—not manic-depressive but subject to occasional lengthy fits of despair when he felt unappreciated, ignored, and ill-treated by life. But the jargon clauses of personality type-casting, even when they seem to be a perfect fit, can only describe Richard Meinertzhagen in silhouette. He does not stay comfortably in them, and they do not explain him fully.

CHAPTER 10

ESPIONAGE

Now and then Richard Meinertzhagen's name has been linked in some fashion to the murder of his brother-in-law Alexander "Sandy" Wollaston, who was shot to death in his rooms at Cambridge on June 3, 1930. In fact RM had nothing to do with that. It was a dreadful crime of multiple-murder; it ended the life of the prominent world-traveling explorer and teacher.

Alexander Frederick Richmond "Sandy" Wollaston, DSC, MRCS, LRCP, was a doctor, a botanist, and a celebrated explorer and climber who had braved the savage mountains of New Guinea and participated in one of the earliest attempts to climb Mt. Everest (Mallory's first expedition, 1924). Wollaston had explored parts of India and Tibet with Frederick M. "Hatter" Bailey, the lifelong friend of Meinertzhagen. And Sandy Wollaston had served as a surgeon in the Royal Navy in East Africa during Meinertzhagen's tour as chief intelligence officer in that theater.[1]

They had been friendly for some years when, in 1923, Wollaston married Meinertzhagen's then twenty-four-year-old sister Polly (aka Mary Amelia Meinertzhagen—the sister who allegedly had provided RM with one of the documents that went into his famous haversack in 1917).

By 1930 Polly and her husband Sandy had three little children, of whom their uncle Dick Meinertzhagen was quite fond.[2]

Sandy Wollaston had taken a position at Cambridge as a senior tutor in order to earn enough money to support his family. A brilliant but de-ranged student named D. N. Potts, whom he had been trying to help, came to Wollaston's rooms in Gibbs' and shot him with a stolen revolver and then shot the police detective-superintendent who had come to arrest him, and then turned the revolver on himself. All three died.[3]

RM and Theresa Clay were in London entraining for a bird congress in Amsterdam when they received word of the triple homicide. RM was stunned by the death of Sandy Wollaston. On the London railway platform RM was so overcome by the news of Wollaston's death that he could not bring himself to go to his sister or to help with funeral arrangements.

Relying on the lame excuse that he had committed himself to appear at the ornithological meeting in the Netherlands, he got on the train and went. Theresa Clay, who feared he might plunge back into the depression from which he had only recently been plucked by the sanatorium doctors at Ruthin, stayed close on that trip. Tess's sister Janet represented them at Sandy Wollaston's funeral several days later.

The murder of Sandy Wollaston was an open-and-shut case. The murderer was identified without any doubt. None of this had any traceable connection to Richard Meinertzhagen, but he had invited gossip with his widely known outrages. Questions began to circulate—had Wollaston been killed for some secret foreign reason that had made him a target for his brother-in-law's "other work"?

That it all had begun to backfire against RM was hardly surprising.

🐦 🐦 🐦

According to Meinertzhagen and those who were bamboozled by him, from the mid-1920s until the 1940s he took part in numerous espionage and counterespionage capers.

It is alleged, for example, that he played some part in an anti-Bolshevik ARCOS raid in London. ARCOS was a Russian trade venture that provided clumsy cover for a Soviet spy ring; its headquarters at No. 49 Moorgate were raided by British government forces on May 12, 1927. Special Branch and Intelligence officers came away with a valuable haul that included a precious list of Russian agents, by name and by cover-name, and locations of blind-drop points in not only Great Britain but the Commonwealth, the United States, and several South American countries. The 1927 ARCOS raid itself was well publicized and caused a breaking-off of diplomatic relations for a couple of years between Britain and the USSR—an effect that pleased a great many Tories, including RM.[4]

There may have been an earlier secret raid on ARCOS (one in which it is said RM participated) but it would have taken place while he was still in India.[5]

After he left the army he devoted himself to his family and his bird work—and he liked to pretend he was spying ("my other work"). Some of his bird cataloging took place in the British Museums of Natural History, in London and in Akeman Street at Tring in Hertfordshire (Lord Rothschild's museum, which subsequently was annexed to the British Museum system), and in the zoological collections of world capitals. These trips, along with his collecting safaris, took him (sometimes with Annie or, later, with Theresa Clay) to Africa and the Middle East. He claimed later, rather vaguely, that his work also took him to parts of Western Europe where the industrious ferrets of the Russian secret police were busy establishing cells from which to recruit discontented workers and foment sabotage, political or physical.

His own recollections to the contrary, RM made very few trips to the Continent in the 1920s. Of the few he did make, all had to do with bird work, and few took him anywhere near places where a spy could learn anything useful. His most frequent destination was Germany, and the only side trips he seems to have made (other than to visit ornithological museums and collectors) were brief visits to his German relatives or to spend a day or two in the home of his friend Lettow.

Lettow despised communism,[6] and there is no indication RM's relations in Germany had any love for the Bolsheviks, so one may find it difficult to determine where he found any Russian spies.

That portion of his "other work" reached its climax, according to RM, when he wiped out a nest of Bolshevik spies in the Andalusian hills of Spain in February–March 1930.

His "Ronda incident" made a stirring tale. It received fairly wide circulation at dinner parties during his lifetime; it seems particularly to have impressed his friend Ian Fleming.

RM's version went something like this:

As a part-time agent without portfolio (he has authority but not a title), Colonel Meinertzhagen is employed by the British Secret Service for years to track Bolshevik infiltrators and identify their cells.[7] He does not mention a three-digit code name (like "007") but he makes very clear the assertion that he is licensed to kill.

Early in 1930 he is in pursuit of one particularly vicious group from Amsterdam along a circuitous route that leads finally into Spain, to an isolated Andalusian farm near Ronda, where the Soviet agitators make rendezvous for purposes unknown but apparently sinister.

Ronda—where the bullfight in its modern form was born in 1726—is in a country of orange-growing orchards in the mountains not far from Seville, Malaga, and Cadiz. The location is dramatic, the scenery overwhelming. (Perhaps fittingly, Orson Welles is buried near the town.)

RM goes in along a craggy ravine at night accompanied by a detachment of Spanish policemen, two of whom are shot to death by Russian lookouts, whereupon Meinertzhagen in a cold fury stalks the villains through the dark house and kills several but then is driven back by gas grenades that are hurled at him and at the soldiers by the surviving Reds.

With the soldiers' blood in his shoes he strikes back by burning the house to the ground. He and the surviving Spanish soldiers shoot those survivors who emerge only to become targets silhouetted against the flames. The blaze consumes the living and the dead together.

In the end the charred farmhouse contains at least nineteen bodies—two Spanish policemen and seventeen Russian and Spanish Bolshevik agents.

The rubble is buried and the cowboys-and-Indians battle is hushed up by the British and Spanish governments, but the latter awards Meinertzhagen a medal, the Order of King Charles III, which later will adorn the souvenir hall of his house at 17 Kensington Park Gardens along with the bookcase containing his leather-bound diaries, his well-worn knobkerrie war club, and the battle ensign of the German raiding cruiser *Königsberg* that he brought back from Africa in 1917.[8]

All this was quite exciting. There is no record of the incident anywhere in the government or intelligence files of the British or the Spanish or the Russian governments, but true believers in hush-hush conspiracies can explain all that away. What seems harder to dispute is that on the occasion of the alleged battle, RM was not alone.

The trip was a birding expedition and he was accompanied by good friends and London titans Guy Benson, Ben and Lindy Pollen, and several others. Guy Benson (a brother in what was to become the Kleinwort-Benson banking dynasty) kept a meticulous daily log of events—the emphasis was on birds seen and birds taken, but the handwritten diary also lists the names of the parties who participated in each day's hunts.[9] Meinertzhagen's movements are accounted for, day by day and often hour by hour, in that log, and after they returned to England various members of the party discussed the trip with their ornithological friends. Unless all the hunters along with their wives and servants were part of a massive conspiracy to cover up facts, one must draw the conclusion that Meinertzhagen had no time or opportunity to sneak in and out of a camp that was in the middle of a trackless wilderness in order to meet with Spanish guardsmen and then organize and commit an atrocity a hundred miles away.

It may be significant that RM's alleged Ronda massacre occurs not long after he came out of the sanatorium at Ruthin. He had been released from the Ruthin clinic—or had discharged himself—in October 1929, after a stay of no more than six weeks. His social calendar became busy immediately. In London he played host to General and Frau von Lettow-Vorbeck at his house in Kensington Park Gardens when they arrived. He escorted them to a celebratory dinner given by Lettow's former opponent (and RM's former commander) Jan Christiaan Smuts. Lettow recalled:

> In December, 1929, I accepted an invitation from the British East Africa fighters and travelled with my wife to London.
>
> I arrived on time to the minute at the Holborn Restaurant in London, where 1,100 former soldiers had assembled, and where for the first time I met face-to-face my long-time opponent General Smuts.
>
> We lodged at Colonel Meinertzhagen's, who had unfortunately become a widower in the meantime.
>
> . . . I had the opportunity to marvel at Meinertzhagen's ornithological successes and I determined that he really was a serious naturalist. A large room was filled with cases in which prepared bird skins, pheasants from the Himalayas, etc., were stored.
>
> When a fire broke out, caused by an iron stove in the room where the bird skins were kept, my wife quickly jumped up and smothered the flames. This danger to his prized possessions apparently did not concern the Colonel at all; he scarcely got up from his chair. I had to conclude that, within the course of a few generations, his Bremen origins had taken in an imposing dose of British phlegmatism.[10]

"Phlegmatism" wasn't RM's normal manner but these weren't normal times for him. His own diary entry for that same evening suggests he was still in the throes of a collapse of "nerves."

So perhaps the Ronda adventure actually did take place—in his beliefs.

Throughout the twenty years preceding World War II RM claims to have carried numerous torches, not to mention cloaks and daggers, on behalf of both the Foreign Office and Chaim Weizmann, and in the effort to stamp out Bolshevism and to foster Zionism. He fantasized that he brightened a few of Winston Churchill's wilderness years as well, and that he and T. E. Lawrence set about attempting to reorganize British Intelligence right from the top down (an attempt that was cut short by Lawrence's death), and that later, when he was seventy, he fell in with a band of Israeli youth to shoot Arabs on the streets of Haifa.

So far as can be determined from reliable primary evidence, once again none of these adventures really happened. No basis for any of them can be found in any documentation other than those written, dictated, or influenced by Richard Meinertzhagen himself.

Georgie and Dee Meinertzhagen (center) and their ten children at Mottisfont Abbey, in 1893. Richard is at top right. *Photo courtesy of Sir Peter Meinertzhagen.*

The Meinertzhagen home at Mottisfont Abbey, Hampshire, c. 1897. *Photo courtesy of Nicholas Meinertzhagen.*

Richard Meinertzhagen (with his dog "Baby") and one of his kills in British East Africa, c. 1902. *Photo courtesy of Sir Peter and Nicholas Meinertzhagen.*

"Sammy" Butler (left) and Richard Meinertzhagen, 1905. *Photo courtesy of Sir Peter and Nicholas Meinertzhagen.*

Richard Meinertzhagen in East Africa in early 1906, shortly after the Ket Parak massacre. *Photo taken by Lt. Seymour "Sammy" Butler, courtesy of Sir Peter Meinertzhagen.*

Richard Meinertzhagen in local garb, Mesopotamia, 1914. *Photo courtesy of Sir Peter and Nicholas Meinertzhagen.*

The infamous beehives of Tanga, 1914. *Photo courtesy of Nicholas Meinertzhagen.*

Richard Meinertzhagen in the Highlands, 1922. *Photo courtesy of Sir Peter and Nicholas Meinertzhagen.*

Richard and Annie Jackson Meinertzhagen at a picnic, 1922.
Photo courtesy of Sir Peter and Nicholas Meinertzhagen.

Richard Meinertzhagen dressed for a "hunt" in central Europe, 1936. *Photo courtesy of Sir Peter and Nicholas Meinertzhagen.*

Theresa Clay searching for mallophaga, 1938. *Photo courtesy of Sir Peter and Nicholas Meinertzhagen.*

Gen. Paul E. von Lettow-Vorbeck and Colonel Meinertzhagen, Germany, 1939. *Photo courtesy of Nicholas Meinertzhagen.*

Richard
Meinertzhagen,
1962. *Photo
courtesy of
Nicholas
Meinertzhagen.*

Richard Meinertzhagen and his sisters Beatrice and Lawrencina. *Photo
courtesy of Nicholas Meinertzhagen.*

He exhibited two consistent political traits. The driving forces behind most of his political notions after 1917 were pro-Zionism and anti-Communism. Such motivations did not set him apart from others, but his particular anti-Bolshevik rants were unusual in that they seemed based not only on economics or ideology (he wrote reams of indignation about strikes) but on ethnicity as well: he expressed a hatred for Russians even more vitriolic than his contempt for the French. RM's revulsion toward Bolshevism and its more moderate cousins (socialism, trade unions, Labor, even Liberalism) was of the frothing-at-the-mouth variety.

As usual he made a few exceptions to this prejudice. The most notable—another connection that he barely mentioned in his writings—was his long friendship with Soviet Ambassador Ivan Maisky.

Naturally some think this odd alliance is a sure sign of Meinertzhagen's involvement in the traffic in high-level multinational secrets. It probably is true that RM made use of Maisky in keeping abreast of happenings at diplomatic levels in both Moscow and Berlin so that at parties he could sound well informed and so that he could make the occasional self-important report to Chaim Weizmann or to his highly placed dinner companions. RM seems to have taken pride in the information he wormed out of Maisky, but none of it was of real use to anyone; the Russian was a canny diplomat who never allowed anyone to glimpse a secret unless he wanted it disseminated.

The actual nature of the RM–Maisky friendship was divined by his amused aunt, Beatrice Webb. She wrote:

> [Our nephew] Dick Meinertzhagen—a tall, handsome, elderly colonel—made love to Madame [Maisky] as he desperately wants to get a visa for a remoter part of USSR, in search of rare birds.[11]
>
> . . . The sequel to the courting of Madame Maisky at Barbara's dinner was the presence of the Maiskys at Dick's "To the Derby" party—a company of fellow officers, among them Lord William Percy and a certain Captain Bennett, who had been caught by the Bolsheviks while fighting with the White Armies in South Russia—but he escaped from the prison. When the Maiskys' chauffeur appeared on the scene to take them back, there was an instantaneous recognition between former gaoler and escaped prisoner—the Soviet chauffeur turning out to be a GPU [Soviet military secret police] official. They chummed up and were joined by Dick and Lord William Percy—both of whom were connected with the British Secret Service—whereupon the four "mystery men" strolled off together for a friendly glass and a smoke—much to the astonishment of Their Excellencies and the other guests!

... I [said to Oliver Baldwin] that: "Dick got his visa."

"More due to the GPU official than to Madame Maisky," said Oliver Baldwin.[12]

Historians and biographers were hamstrung by the Official Secrets Act, which kept their noses out of the official records of the intelligence services. Only lately has it become easier to examine RM's extravagant cloak-and-dagger hints and declarations. Beginning in the late 1990s, under the auspices of a new Freedom of Information law, the British government began to release large numbers of files that previously had remained closed. By the time of this writing (2006) many archives of the intelligence services from the 1920s and 1930s have become available. As for those that remain "locked up," their summaries make clear that none of them has anything significantly to do with Richard Meinertzhagen.

On the other hand his name does appear in several documents recently released. In the main, these confirm his active involvement during the 1930s in Nazi-front "Anglo-German fellowship" organizations.

As early as November 1929, just before the Lettows came to visit RM in London, leaders of the then-called Anglo-German Committee had approached Meinertzhagen about bringing Lettow to a meeting of their group. Apparently Meinertzhagen tried to persuade the German hero to join him but, for whatever reason, Lettow did not attend.

Nevertheless the approach created a contact between the Anglo-German Committee and Meinertzhagen—a contact that soon became a fast connection.[13]

It was to become the Anglo-German Association—a group of British business and military men. It did not see its intentions as sinister. No Nazis had taken power when it was inaugurated. Germany's government had collapsed several times; her people lived hand to mouth, if at all. It was as if the entire nation had been turned into an island penal colony, isolated and starving and trying to feed on nothing but dirt. The group hoped, by encouraging "the promotion of rapprochement between Germany and Great Britain," to help business and industry in the battered nation crawl back to their feet, from the gutter into which they had been flung by the punitive terms of the Versailles Treaty.

The clubby businessmen wanted to relax the restrictions of the Treaty in order to do more business with people in Germany. Their motives may have been dictated by self-interest but they saw nothing ignoble in their actions. They were trying to create employment in Germany, which in turn would create a market for goods amongst the German people, and allow them to feed themselves. No one believed these actions constituted a criminal conspiracy.

It would be a few years before the Society and its successors were to take on the militant fascist and anti-Semitic trappings of the Nazis who, from 1933 on, were their primary sponsors.

Among the drafters and early members of the Anglo-German Association—all of whom were or soon became social companions of Meinertzhagen—were famed thriller writer John Buchan (*The Thirty-Nine Steps*), Gen. Sir Ian Hamilton (late of Gallipoli), Sir Charles Hobhouse (noted Conservative, related to Meinertzhagen by marriage), Adm. Earl Jellicoe (former Admiral of the Fleet), and German-Jewish banker Erich Warburg.[14]

On November 26, 1934, RM dined at the Savoy with Ernest Tennant, Nazi Germany's Joaquim von Ribbentrop, and several British businessmen.[15] They decided to reorganize the Anglo-German club, the better to further business connections between the two countries. RM wrote, "I pointed out that we wanted something wider than that, some organisation to combat the lies and misrepresentations now being spread in this country by the press and socialist and Jewish propaganda. . . . It was agreed to widen the scope of the new organization to include both economic and political matters."[16]

In a similar vein he wrote for publication, without any sense of irony, that he regarded Zionism as just another form of Bolshevism.[17]

At the same time he continued to dine, at intervals, with the Weizmanns.

With hindsight it may be too easy to overstress his hypocrisy. Until the late 1930s it was not clear that Zionism and Nazism were mutually opposed or mutually exclusive. The Anglo-German clubs were formed by bankers and businessmen, Muslims and Jews among them, who dreaded Stalinism far more than they feared Nazism. Some of these organizations professed Christian beliefs—a factor that put them at odds with Hitler, who disdained Christianity as "a Jewish religion."[18] They saw Bolshevism as their most perilous common enemy. They believed only Hitler and Mussolini could save Europe from the Red Peril.[19]

RM's fulminations against socialism—a catch-all concept in which he included communism, Labor, and liberalism—were highly emotional. They begin in his entries for 1909 on what he perceives to be pernicious trends toward socialism[20] and they persist right through to the end of the diaries. He writes of bureaucracy gone mad; of the selfishness, obstructionism, sabotage, and tyranny perpetrated by Labor; of the bad manners of the lower classes and the lack of common decency or patriotism in the Trades Union Congress; of extortion and profiteering by the proletariat; of disgusting socialist propaganda; of the offensiveness of the plebeians, the parasitism of Socialists, the irresponsible apathy of workers, the retreat from Empire and Colonialism, the myth of social equality, the deterioration of English character and the decline in intellectual standards, the drift toward Sovietism, the blackmailing arrogance of taxation, the stupidity of union leaders, the increase in strikes and an increase in crime which RM blames on the unions, the surrender of Britain's weak government to trades union dictatorship, the menace of higher wages and lower output, socialism and inflation, mass hysteria, the devaluation of currency and wealth, the death of thrift, inefficiency everywhere, Labor's love affair with lies, the abdication of the ruling classes and the end of Conservatism, political "drift," world depression caused by socialism, the discontented folly and the political decadence of the Left, and always the impending economic crisis with civilization collapsing and the world heading for ruin.

He was outspoken about all those conventional ideas, but with the exception of a few diary entries, RM remained cagey about his affiliations with the Nazi front organizations. He seems willing to reveal only that he was present at a dinner or a soiree or a chamber meeting; usually he does not tell his diary what transpired in the meetings.

He was, in fact, a co-founder of the Anglo-German Fellowship.[21] This may have been social as much as political. A cross-check of the directorships of leading British companies of the era produces a roster of Meinertzhagen-connected names which appear repeatedly on boards that had become, de facto, interlocked. A number of the Fellowship members belonged to the extended Meinertzhagen family—Potters, Huths, Booths, Hobhouses, Holts, and Rothschilds, important persons nearly all of whose names appeared regularly on the guest lists of RM's parties and whose dinner tables RM graced (or sometimes disgraced) with his presence. They all served as officers (often chairmen) of powerful companies in banking, shipping, insurance, and construction with interests in Germany, Japan, and Italy.[22]

The intelligence services reflected the conservative views of these business people. They consistently treated Soviet Communism as a much greater threat to British security than Nazism, and they acted accordingly. But because of frequent needling by the minority (led by Churchill) who saw great danger in Hitler's brutality and Germany's rearmament, they could not altogether ignore what was going on in the fascist-dominated countries. The intelligence offices may have regarded the Anglo-German clubs as being "on our side" but this did not discourage them from infiltrating the clubs and maintaining records on their activities. Circumstances forced them to redouble such efforts after Italy invaded Ethiopia in 1935 in precisely the sort of naked power-grab that anti-fascists had predicted.

Within two or three years all the noteworthy pro-fascist organizations had been infiltrated by Secret Service agents who were not sufficiently in sympathy with them to keep their secrets from their reports to the Home Office. Some of these reports have become available recently.[23]

While a few of the more wild-eyed club members may have tried to pass what they thought was significant advice to Berlin, they stole no secrets of value and seem to have committed no other acts of espionage or sabotage. They may have been misguided; most of them were not treasonous.

It is tempting to surmise that these organizations were ideal for Meinertzhagen's tastes—they smacked of intrigues but required little of him.[24]

During the same years, RM became part of a group whose objectives were opposite to those of the Anglo-German clubs. This was the Focus, a sort of successor to the Other Club. It was a discreet lobby that grew up around Winston Churchill and fellow back-benchers, some of whose benches were not back far enough to suit the Chamberlain Tories. The Focus, whose design was to fight the Nazi aggression that the group believed was inevitable, was peopled by influential Britons who ranged from communists to royalists but had in common a profound distrust of Meinertzhagen's then-hero Adolf Hitler. Historian Mike Hughes describes the Focus as "an example of the singularly unholy alliance between anti-Semites and Zionists."[25]

Among the members were the diplomatic wizard Sir Robert Vansittart, influential publisher Victor Gollancz, intelligence master Sir Joseph Ball, Churchill's shadowy espionage aide Desmond Morton, young Reuters correspondent Ian Fleming, and the high-spirited Maud Russell.

Mrs. Russell's husband Gilbert—a sophisticate, and a cousin of the Duke of Bedford—had earned a fortune by co-founding a merchant bank that had moved into close alliance with the City firms that belonged to the Benson Brothers, the Churchills, and the Flemings. Maud was the daughter of a German-born Jewish stockbroker in London, one of whose clients happened to have been Winston Churchill; Winston's banker friend Gilbert Russell was quite a bit older than Maud, but he was witty and charming and they soon formed an easy alliance that led to a wedding. In the 1930s the Russells, who had been married since 1917, continued frequently to entertain friends like the Churchills at their country estate in Hampshire, where casual meetings of the Focus occurred from time to time.[26] That country estate was Mottisfont Abbey, where Meinertzhagen had spent his childhood and to which he returned whenever he could.[27]

Ian Fleming—whose name Meinertzhagen in his diaries consistently misspells as "Flemming"—and Meinertzhagen became friends in the 1930s after meeting at one of Maud Russell's dinners.[28] Fleming was, like Meinertzhagen, the son of a prominent banking family. In those years prior to his Naval Intelligence career and his creation of James Bond "007," he worked as financial correspondent for the Reuters wire service. At a social level equal to that of Richard Meinertzhagen, but a generation younger, Fleming became a fascinated protégé of the older man; ironically Meinertzhagen, fully thirty years the elder, was to outlive Fleming by several years.

The two men had been friends for years, and would be drawn even closer by Fleming's marriage in 1952 to Ann Charteris, who was a member of the Benson family, the powerful banking dynasty in which the three ranking brothers—Rex, Con, and Guy, celebrated heroes of the Great War—were among Meinertzhagen's closest lifelong friends and political companions.

RM stubbornly continued to regard Mottisfont Abbey as his home right up to his death in 1967. He took a highly personal and resentful view whenever changes were made to it, especially in the early 1900s when the game-protective rules were changed by various residents in order to allow what he thought of as indiscriminate poaching, and then in later years when some of the thousands of acres began to be sold off for development. But during the 1930s, when the Russells owned and occupied the venerable pile, he seems to have approved of their stewardship—possibly because they always made him feel welcome even though he did not always agree with their political views or their taste in art. (Maud was a patron of Matisse and Picasso. Meinertzhagen had no affinity for that sort of thing.)

The Russells knew Ian Fleming's parents through business connections (the family bank, founded in 1908, was—and still is—Robert Fleming and Company). Ian Fleming had become a Reuters correspondent in 1931. He was tall, lean, hawk-beaked, and exceptionally clever and droll, the sort of man with whom women fell in love at once, and with whom men immediately felt comfortable because of his easy manner—a lazy, offhand style that masked not only considerable courage but also his nagging secret: he had a fragile heart and was never quite sure he wouldn't die at any moment. This did not prevent his gentle, tireless womanizing. In 1933 or thereabouts, when he was just twenty-three and she was in her forties, he and Maud became lovers (a liaison of which her husband apparently was aware and to which he did not strenuously object).[29]

It was at Mottisfont Abbey, sometime in the mid-1930s, that Maud Russell introduced Ian Fleming to Sir Joseph Ball, with RM looking on. Ball was a pioneering practitioner of political dirty tricks against Labor. The man behind the Zinoviev Letter (a contrivance that had caused the fall of the Labor Government in the 1920s), he had become an early member of the Executive Committee of the Anglo-German Fellowship. He had reorganized the Conservatives' intelligence apparatus while he worked as the editor of *Truth*, a pro-Nazi paper advocating peace with Germany.

Ball was an old, and sometimes odd, intelligence hand—recently he had become involved in the complicated process of clandestinely working with international banks to rescue Jewish property from Germany on behalf of its expatriate owners. Meinertzhagen felt at home with him. Ball saw young Fleming as just the sort of recruit his department always needed. RM played into Ball's hands by fascinating young Fleming with his dashing tales of swashbuckling adventure.[30]

(RM had quite an influence on Fleming. The latter's biographer reports that the novelist decided "mere stories were just not good enough after books like *Diary of a Black Sheep* by his . . . hero Colonel Richard Meinertzhagen." That was when Fleming stopped writing fiction.)[31]

RM's interactions with the Russells and their circle were a predictable, if not necessarily logical, part of his pattern. Despite his complaints about his own family he often spent time with its members, even though many of them were leaders of what he saw as the enemy camp. He was the resident conservative at many of his Aunt Beatrice and Uncle Sidney Webb's socialist gatherings.

Despite being well fixed, he had no qualms about imposing himself on such prominent members of the working-class opposition as his first cousin Sir Stafford Cripps, who had been an outstanding figure in leftist movements for years and eventually was to become one of the major mavericks of British politics—Labor's postwar Chancellor of the Exchequer.

Cripps, who like Meinertzhagen was a nephew of Beatrice Webb, made contact with the Communist Party and thus drew the unfriendly attention of MI-5. That peaked in 1934 when it looked as if the owlish but curiously magnetic Stafford Cripps might become Britain's next prime minister by leading the Socialist wing of the Labor Party to power. That bubble of expectation was deflated quickly by more realistic politicians who provoked the recklessly outspoken Cripps into proposing the granting of emergency powers to a "temporary" dictator in order to raise a working-class army to bring down British capitalists.[32]

Issues, for armchair warriors like RM who preferred to view things in black-and-white, were confused. He saw opposite blocs overlap. Those on the far left sometimes seemed to march in lock-step with those on the far right. He saw the right-wing describe itself as "socialist" (the Nazi party was a socialist body according to its own lights). He could not make sense of the oddly shifting loyalties of people who in RM's opinion should have known better—people like Cripps and Cripps' crony Aneurin Bevan, the populist working-man's leader who for a while allied himself with notorious British fascist leader Oswald Mosley. RM and his fellow dedicated Tories were hard pressed to know what to make of the wildly somersaulting allegiances, alliances, and affections of these political leaders.[33]

In spite of his protestations to the contrary, Meinertzhagen was willing to make use of his contacts in high office even when he found their politics anathema, provided he felt he had a sound reason to do so. At the beginning of the 1930s, when his uncle Sidney Webb was appointed Secretary of State for the Colonies, Meinertzhagen immediately set about writing letters to Uncle Sidney, taking up the Zionist cause and offering his services. When he received no response he went down from Yorkshire to London to buttonhole his uncle. They met on October 4, 1929, at Meinertzhagen's old stomping grounds in the Colonial Office, and chatted most of the day. According to RM, Sidney Webb agreed with him on the points he made, but seemed weary of the whole Jewish business.[34]

Seeing no advance to be made there, RM began to barrage the newspapers with letters to the editors. Eventually he made quite a pest of himself, but as he was careful to keep up his social ties to the publishers and senior editorial staffs, his letters continued to appear with some frequency over quite a few years. They are, almost uniformly, vehicles carrying heavy loads of outrage.

Much of RM's time in the 1930s, as in the second half of the 1920s, was devoted to bird work and the cataloging of *mallophaga*. Here and there he kept dropping hints about alleged secret projects—"my other work." Nick Meinertzhagen recalls: "He was involved with Lawrence of Arabia in setting up a Middle East Intelligence section—some sort of directorate— and Lawrence used to come to our garden and play blowing up trains. But he [Uncle Dick] stopped that when Lawrence was killed in May 1935. That's one clue as to what he was doing in the Thirties. . . . There was apparently a secret service that was more secret than even the Secret Service."[35]

Nick Meinertzhagen believes it firmly. So did John Lord, in his biography of Meinertzhagen, when he confirmed that T. E. Lawrence used to visit Meinertzhagen at his house in the 1930s. And Rodney Legg's *Lawrence Of Arabia In Dorset* contains a chapter titled "Lawrence: Director Designate of proposed Intelligence Directorate" in which he states that Lawrence and Meinertzhagen headed a review panel that was sifting proposals and making recommendations for a thorough overhaul of the entire British secret intelligence structure.[36]

It troubles some researchers that a man assigned to reorganize the entire British intelligence apparatus could at the same time have been writing indignant letters to newspaper editors on behalf of road-killed rodents, Zionism, Germany's brave struggle against socialism, and the plight of migratory birds whose resting places on Heligoland Island had been disturbed by the construction of naval facilities. (The latter—an issue he first had raised at the Paris Peace Congress in 1919—was a crusade in which RM persisted until he won it in the early 1950s.) But then, one is told, such are the marvelous eccentricities of the British upper classes.

The release of any government files that may even remotely support such contentions is still awaited. Unlike RM's, T. E. Lawrence's life has been sectioned, examined microscopically, and accounted for—nearly minute by minute—by numerous biographers and by professional and amateur scholars, many of whom belong to the T. E. Lawrence Society. Virtually all of them seem agreed that neither Lawrence nor Meinertzhagen did any such work in 1935, nor would anyone in authority have been interested in recruiting either of them for such a purpose.

Some students of the Meinertzhagen mysteries seem to want to believe RM had a hand in the 1933 death of T. E. Lawrence's friend the Iraqi King Faisal, when he was undergoing medical treatment in Switzerland. Arabs believed the Europeans would not allow him to return, and as if to confirm their belief, Faisal died on September 8, 1933. Officially the King died of natural causes. Conspiracy theorists divined he had died of an assassin's clever and silent intrusion. At first glance it appears Meinertzhagen may have been there—Switzerland: he traveled a good deal in 1933, on birding and social adventures throughout Syria, Turkey, Lebanon, Palestine, Transjordan, and Iraq (where he was a guest of the Iraq Petroleum Company and its "Syrian Desert Pipeline"); he returned to Europe by way of

Bulgaria, and from there stopped over in Switzerland on his route home.[37] All this seems to fit into the circumstantial charge against him.

The trouble with the theory is that the calendars do not match up. After his bird-hunting sweep of several months through the Middle East, Meinertzhagen met Janet Clay in Sofia in June 1933 and they returned to England from there, and by July he was in Scotland, at Swordale with Tess Clay, the Pollens, and the Newalls. He noted, "Second visit to Bulgaria in 1933 postponed," and then five pages later added, "My interview with Hitler postponed." Partly as a result of these postponements, his restless travels during the rest of that year were pretty much confined to the British Isles, with occasional forays no farther out than Ushant (a bird-rich island in the Atlantic off northwestern Brittany, where the French and British navies had battled twice during the Napoleonic Wars). Birding friends accompanied him on all these trips, so he was not alone to go rushing off to Switzerland or the Middle East, and in sum he was nowhere near the site of the death of Faisal.[38]

🐦 🐦 🐦

Benjamin Netanyahu (Prime Minister of Israel, 1996–1999) wrote in 2000, "No one argued [for Zionism] more forcefully than Col. Richard Meinertzhagen, the British chief of intelligence in the Middle East."[39]

When Israel sought statehood in the late 1930s, British prime minister Neville Chamberlain—fearful of a reaction from Hitler—announced that his government would no longer honor the Balfour Declaration. The event provoked an exasperated RM to declare that he could see no distinction between the actions of His Majesty's Government in Palestine and those of Hitler in the Sudetenland. Attempting to shame his government into reversing its course, he buttonholed his friends in power on both the right and the left, and broadsided the world press with fiery letters-to-the-editor in which he flatly accused both the German and the British Governments of mass murder.[40]

Then, after having exploded in reaction to Chamberlain's betrayal of the Jews, RM became the man who didn't shoot Hitler.

The accepted legend—the Meinertzhagen version—is this:

During the 1930s RM makes several trips to Germany where he pleads the case for Jewish emigration to Palestine. Unfortunately he has to return to Chaim Weizmann in London without many successes to report.

On his final visit to prewar Berlin, in 1939, he has a loaded revolver in his pocket when he meets Hitler to make one last appeal for the lives of

Jews. Ever thereafter he curses himself for not having had the courage to use it: he dismisses out of hand the reassurances of everyone who reminds him that if he had used the pistol he would have been killed instantly. He doesn't seem to think his own life could be of much importance in the circumstances.

He attempts painfully in his diaries to analyze his failure to act; but his efforts at introspection are clumsy and wide of the mark—the best he can produce is something that reads like an awkward description of stage-fright.

Why didn't he use the gun? Was it a matter of honor—something a gentleman simply does not do? Was it in his mind, at the last minute, that perhaps Hitler and Chamberlain deserved each other? Was it something in a portion of him that was aware of the military maxim that it was unwise to kill the enemy's chief because there might be no one left with whom to negotiate and the ensuing chaos might be harder to handle than the chief was?

Or was it something else?

RM wrote of three meetings with Hitler, all in Berlin—October 17, 1934; July 15, 1935; and June 28, 1939.

At the first meeting, RM writes that he was hugely impressed by Hitler's fire, flash, intensity, and dedication; he listened to Hitler's rationalization of various Nazi policies, including systematic anti-Semitism; he was baffled when Hitler raised his arm in the Nazi salute and said, "Heil Hitler." After a moment's thought, Meinertzhagen says he raised his own arm in an identical salute and proclaimed, "Heil Meinertzhagen."[41]

That bit of slapstick is too fatuous to deserve serious attention. Hitler never "heiled" himself. RM's descriptions of the conversation that followed and of the Fuehrer's glorious personality emphasize RM's pro-Nazi state of mind; they seem accurate enough but they contain nothing he couldn't have read in a magazine.[42]

"Heil Meinertzhagen" is absurd, but bird-related meetings show that RM definitely was in Berlin on the three dates when he says he was meeting Hitler.

That is when another question suggests itself. What was Hitler doing on those three dates?

RM says the first meeting occurred on October 17, 1934. That was the day when the Ministers' Allegiance Act was passed. It was a milestone of executive-branch and parliamentary surrender, requiring all ministers of the German government to swear personal allegiance and obedience to Hitler.

Quite a bit of suspense had been worked up as to whether the ministers would kowtow or whether they would revolt. Hitler was pretty well secured behind locked doors in the Chancellery that day, accompanied by only the most loyal members of his entourage. One may suspect the Fuehrer had other things on his mind that day than heiling himself and meeting with an eccentric retired British military officer. Nevertheless, of RM's three meetings with Hitler, this is the only one that cannot be conclusively examined from independent sources.

An industrial delegation from England had met with Hitler just a few weeks earlier but it had not included Meinertzhagen.[43] Indeed, quite a few members of the Anglo-German groups were granted such introductions at one time or another, but Meinertzhagen's name was never among them.[44]

Two facts are important here. First, no foreigners were allowed into the presence of Hitler until the meeting had been authorized by an agreement between the Nazi regime and the foreigner's Embassy, which had to vouch for the visitor. Second, various branches of British Intelligence kept a keen eye on the movements of their countrymen when they went anywhere near the Nazi leaders. Spies were everywhere.

The British Embassy and the Foreign Office kept bundles of records showing that meetings took place between Hitler and various visiting members of the Anglo-German clubs. Men like Tennant, Mount Temple, Rykens, and Lord Willy Percy met with Hitler, sometimes several times. (Unlike the others, Percy was not welcomed back after he created a bit of an incident by refusing to propose a toast to the Fuehrer.)

Every British visitor to cabinet-level German offices or officeholders was logged.

No records show RM as having been cleared for, or having attended, such a meeting in 1934. No surveillance reports indicate there was any contact between Hitler and RM in 1934.

It is possible, though not plausible, that he managed to slip through the cracks, but his next two alleged visits can be examined more conclusively.

On July 14, 1935, a delegation of retired British colonels was welcomed to Germany with panoply and extensive press coverage, and on the following day—the day of RM's purported second meeting with Hitler—the Chancellor and Rudolf Hess personally welcomed five of the officer-delegates, who were led by Maj. Frances Fetherston-Godley. The meeting was very brief, and Hitler hastened away on what his aides explained was pressing business.

If one stops at that point, it is reasonable to infer that Meinertzhagen was one of the other four. But he was not.

In fact that July 15, when RM says he was pleading for Jewish emigration with the Fuehrer, was a day of extremely violent anti-Jewish rioting in Berlin. The visiting British officers were put off by it. RM in his diaries does not even mention having noticed it. More than two hundred thugs—in partly civilian clothes, but wearing the boots and sometimes the trousers of Nazi storm troopers—smashed windows, wrecked shops, shrieked anti-Jewish slogans, battered bleeding civilians to the curbstones, ransacked passing automobiles, and placed a number of Jews "under protective arrest" from which quite a few of them never reappeared. In the *Kurfurstendamm* (Berlin's equivalent of Fifth Avenue) the doors of the fabled Kempinski Hotel were closed and locked. While young hoodlums chanted the Horst Wessel song, shocked foreign visitors took cover wherever they could find it; some were wounded, and a British Embassy worker rescued a man who fled blindly along the street, his eyes filled with blood.

The Berlin riots continued for a full week, out in plain sight on the main boulevards. The pogroms caused widespread bloody casualties among Jews and Catholic clergy (the latter because the Vatican had protested the Reich's encouragement of neo-pagan attitudes; the Church particularly had objected to the Reich's threats to use Nazi sterilization laws against Catholics.)[45]

As for Hitler, he did not spend much of his time that week in Berlin. After hurriedly leaving the five British officers behind, he traveled quickly and unexpectedly to lower Saxony—to Braunschweig, where he visited the centuries-old tomb of Henry the Lion in St. Blasius Cathedral in order to pay his respects to that blood-soaked predecessor.[46]

Like Hitler, Meinertzhagen does not seem to have noticed the disturbances. Perhaps, rather than meeting with Hitler, he was on the outskirts of Berlin in a museum, peacefully cataloging birds.

Did he later appropriate his story of the meeting with Hitler from one of the five who actually had been there? To ask the question seems legitimate; to answer it, unfortunately, seems impossible.

Once again, however, no British or German documents describe any encounter between Meinertzhagen and Hitler.

Nor, in fact, is any such meeting mentioned in any documents for *any* year, other than by Meinertzhagen in his diaries and by those who have relied on his diaries for their histories.

By this point it may be anticlimactic to suggest that Meinertzhagen never met Hitler at all, but that does seem to be the case.

His third and final alleged meeting with Hitler—the one to which he took a loaded revolver in his pocket—occurred on June 28, 1939. He went there, presumably, to make one last appeal for the lives of Polish and German Jews. Theresa Clay accompanied him on the trip to Germany, but not on the alleged visit to the Chancellery—a visit to which (as usual) no witness other than Meinertzhagen has ever come forward.

For a while after that trip, Meinertzhagen seems to have remained undecided as to whether or not he actually had been armed at the time. Dr. Ernst Mayr, one of the world's pre-eminent natural scientists, wrote, "He used to brag [to me] that he once stayed in a [hotel] room the window of which faced Hitler's living room. With a good rifle and optical equipment he could have killed Hitler, he claimed."[47]

In RM's diaries he meets with the Nazi leader in the Chancellery at 11:00 A.M. on June 28, 1939 (with pistol in pocket). The meeting lasts nearly three-quarters of an hour. "I had ample opportunity to kill both Hitler and Ribbentrop and am seriously troubled about it."[48]

Hitler's movements made news; he was covered by the world's press. A reading of the daily issues of the *Times* from June 26 to July 1, 1939, confirms that Hitler spent that entire week at his mountain retreat at Berchtesgarten in Bavaria, far from Berlin. He mapped out his war plans and made occasional forays down the mountain to Munich to make public appearances and attend the opera; he was seen every day, and can hardly have made a round-trip to Berlin in total secrecy merely to meet with Richard Meinertzhagen. In fact he was not terribly popular in Berlin or anywhere in northern Germany. He preferred to spend as much time as possible in the south, in Bavaria from which he drew his main strength and support.

So at the time of RM's purported meeting with him, the two men were hundreds of miles apart.

His bravado about rushing back and forth between Weizmann and Hitler, carrying messages and negotiating for endangered Jews, seems empty. Sadly, it seems to have been an emptiness that impressed the Zionists.

RM may have persuaded his Zionist friends and a great many others that he was performing "other work" and was an important figure in the worldwide fights against Bolshevism and for the establishment of a Jewish state in Palestine—but very little of that was true.

It all implodes into darkness.

CHAPTER 11
BIRDS

In 1931 RM wrote to Hatter Bailey, "I go to Iceland with my little Cousin Theresa."[1]

RM saw to it that Tess Clay, thirty-three years younger than he, received a good scientific education. Within a few years she would become a respected scientist. She earned a Ph.D. at Edinburgh and by the 1950s she merited a worldwide reputation as one of the foremost students of bird-related *mallophaga* and their hosts. Quite a few birds are named for her (e.g., the Afghan *Montifringilla theresae* and the Moroccan *Riparia rupestris theresae*. The names were assigned by RM; he had the right to do that, but the fact that a dozen birds were named after Theresa in one short paper written by RM seems to have given some ornithologists reason to think its author was very cranky if not seriously disturbed).

"Tess and Dick" traveled together and worked together. She was his housekeeper, nanny, secretary, and scientific partner.

They seemed inseparable for more than thirty years. They loved each other. But no one is certain whether they shared a bed. She continued to live in the attached house next door to his, with a connecting passage between. When they traveled they sometimes took separate rooms. RM usually introduced Tess as his housekeeper or cousin or sometimes, inaccurately, as his niece.

Even those who knew them at close range were uncertain whether their relationship was physical. The only person who seems to have had enough nerve to ask RM outright about it was Lord Victor Rothschild. RM "told him in no uncertain terms to shut up."[2]

At first—1930 and a few years thereafter—both sisters were in his retinue, alternating as nanny-nurse and housekeeper. RM's grand-nephew recalls: "Rachel, Tess's mother, lived with the girls next door to the [Meinertzhagens] in the 1920s. It was all very incestuous. Later [after Annie died], Tess went on living next door, but the houses were connected."[3]

The arrangement did not meet with the approval of the girls' mother. Hermione Hobhouse writes:

> My reflections of Dick Meinertzhagen are anecdotal and more than slightly scurrilous. He was a cousin of both my mother, through her Huth relations, and my father through their mothers, both Potter sisters.
>
> He was very much a figure of legend. One version said he had shot his wife in a gunroom accident; and he lived with two of my (much older) first cousins in succession. He lived in a house in respectable North Kensington next to their mother [Rachel Hobhouse Clay], with whom he "did not speak." On one occasion I was visiting the aunt in her garden, and they solemnly addressed each other through me, *viz*:
>
> "Hermione will you tell your aunt Rachel...?"
>
> "Will you tell your Cousin Dick...?"[4]

Once again the general social acceptance of RM's eccentricities won the day, and after a while the girls' parents came to accept the odd unity of the three cousins. The parents, Rachel and Sir Felix Clay, continued to live in the house attached to RM's, and they became regular guests at RM's celebrated Derby Day parties as soon as he inaugurated that tradition in the mid-1930s.

It was convenient for RM to have both young women in his entourage because it meant he could leave one at home to look after children and household while he traveled abroad, or socialized around Britain, with the other.

The process involved scrupulously fair alternation. In 1930 RM took Tess to the Ornithological Congress in Amsterdam and thence to Hamburg and Flensburg; then after the children's school holidays (in Wales) he took Janet to Haverford. He accompanied Janet to Inverary, and Tess to Aberlady. Near the end of the year he went off with Janet to explore the Ahaggar Mountains in North Africa.[5]

Most of their journeys were not to places so far away. By the 1930s RM—who professed a desire for solitude but rarely put it into practice—had laid down a well-tamped trail to the country homes of numerous relations and friends, each of which was within stalking distance of birds and game animals. Hardly a fortnight went by without his dining and sometimes staying the weekend with moneyed and/or titled hosts, especially the Russells at Mottisfont Abbey. They all seemed to take his posturing in stride; he seems to have been a welcome addition to any party.

Both Clay sisters remained in his employ and under his various roofs until Tess completed her studies at Edinburgh. Then Janet suddenly, at age twenty-three, went away on an extended trip to Ceylon. By the time she returned, RM had rented Grey Friars, Suffolk, for the summer of 1935, and Janet went there to help him with the children while Tess was away hunting birds and bugs in Poland with their friend Billy Payn (who was more or less openly homosexual and therefore "safe," in a time when chaperones were still customary).

As soon as Tess returned from Poland, Janet went off to France to work as an *au pair* and nanny. She never returned. RM confided to his diary that he felt bereft.

He was famous for his bombastic displays of temper toward women, and Janet may have fled after she had had enough of that. However, more than one family member believes the sisters had a falling-out because Theresa thought Janet had seduced him or tried to seduce him. One relation recalls that Tess seemed to believe it was all Janet's fault. In any event Janet suddenly was gone and RM did not mention her again in his writings except to drop the offhand comment in 1948 that he had learned she had got married.[6]

RM went back to London and escorted Lindy Pollen (wife of his friend Ben Pollen—they all were friends of Freddie Guest) to the ballet. Then he and Tess carted the children out to Brendon, Exmoor. For RM it was a decade of almost constant restless movement.

The story of Richard Meinertzhagen and Theresa Clay is an intricate one, full of unexpected turns and unanswered questions. The reality of the relationship remains out of focus. Short on facts, it became long on conjecture.

Several men in the family had their difficulties with regard to the other gender. Some seem to have been unusually attracted to young girls. Richard's younger brother Frederick "Fritz" Meinertzhagen spent a great deal of time with prostitutes, most of them quite young. He had taken some medical training, and made numerous drawings of prostitutes that were academic in style. He made a study of women's diseases among the prostitutes—allegedly he would visit the same young women regularly to find out how much they were earning, how many times they were ill, which diseases infected them, and how they treated these ailments. By most accounts his interest was both academic and sexual. He may have gone too far when he married Florence Maxwell-Barnes, variously described as a waitress or an actress, who was taken or mistaken for a fallen woman by some in the family. (Only after her death, around 1940, does Fritz seem to have been welcomed tentatively back into Meinertzhagen family gatherings.) RM's father "Dee" is said to have had his favorite prostitutes in London, and the lore of the family is that another close relation of RM's died after being run down in the street at night on his way home from a visit to a brothel.

A few ornithologists seem to accept the notion that on his expeditions, when Tess was not accompanying him, RM occasionally would get dressed up like a dude and depart night camp to visit exotic hotspots, perhaps to seek out their young ladies. Since no companion seems to have gone with him on such nocturnal prowls, the scenario can only suggest possibilities; it is doubted by many, but has been reported by several sources.[7]

It seems safe to conclude that wild, dangerous places were within his comfort zone but women were not. He believed he had been the subject of women's scorn throughout his childhood, and after he achieved his full growth he was not terribly comfortable in any situation that made him relate to women on terms other than his own.

Years later, after RM died, did Tess find postcard pictures of seductive pre-pubescent nudes hidden under the pajamas in his drawer? Probably not, but it was by no means unusual for widows to find just that sort of thing hidden amid the belongings of elderly Victorian gentlemen recently departed.

Grand-nephew Nick recalls Theresa Clay:

> When she was quite young she'd have been his ideal picture of a tomboyish pubescent girl.
>
> Like most Englishmen of his generation—well, quite a few of them got married just for appearance, and had the obligatory children but they were clearly homosexual. I certainly don't think *he* was homosexual, but he was odd. Perhaps asexual?
>
> I think once you get delving into the sexuality of people, you know there are so many English men who are half-half, because most boys go through a homosexual period in the schools. Some of them end up as the greatest womanizers, and others turn into homosexuals, and some of those are turned by their wives into heterosexuals. So I don't know.[8]

The record seems to confirm Nicholas Meinertzhagen's surmise. RM may have been relatively asexual; he probably was not bisexual or homosexual. Nor was he homophobic. On several occasions he traveled on bird-collecting safaris in company with Billy Payn or other taxidermists, employees, or friends who were (sometimes openly) gay. No accounts of mutual attraction have appeared, even in gossip. With RM nothing ever seems absolutely certain, but to the extent that he responded to stimuli, all signs point to his having been heterosexual.

Until the chill came between them, he seemed to have a warm (for him) marriage to Annie. After that, the exception in his life was Theresa Clay. Many observers were surprised by the intensity of RM's obvious feelings for Tess, and hers for him. If she became even a slight bit ill, RM would ring a sister or a friend and weep down the phone about the situation—a curiously powerful reaction in circumstances that usually proved to have been trivial. (Aside from one surgical operation to remove a benign growth during World War II, Theresa was extremely healthy. She lived to a ripe old age, and remained stunning in grey hair. Photos bear out what several people who knew her have described—she was very attractive, and rather boyish both of figure and of clothing.)

Dame Miriam Rothschild said, "The explanation seems to be in her sheer devotion to him. Tess simply believed what she was told. Tess may never have looked at the diaries and therefore may never have seen the violence recorded there or spotted the inconsistencies that they carry."[9]

Recently it has become evident that Theresa knew RM was falsifying specimens.[10] He probably fed her various denials and rationalizations, but she was accustomed to being his supporter—and thus his enabler.

One fact seems suggestive, if not conclusive: during most of their lives together, at least when they were in company Tess addressed him or referred to him as "Uncle Dick."

As for RM, in his diaries after about 1931 he usually did not gush about Tess. The best he could do was to see to it that *Montifringilla theresae* and at least a full dozen other species were named after Theresa, and to note that she was "an ideal companion. And incidentally a first rate bird skinner."[11]

During the 1930s, after *Nicoll's Birds of Egypt* had been published to much acclaim among ornithologists, RM secured the backing (sometimes nominal) of geographic organizations and museums, and embarked on several lengthy safaris. In 1930 it was the Baltic—Latvia and northwestern Russia—and then near the end of the year he took Janet on an extended tour of Algeria and Morocco; they returned to England in March 1931. In July and August he and Tess explored Iceland. In 1932 he hiked the Pyrenees with Tess. In 1933 he went back to the Middle East—Constantinople, Beirut, Damascus, and home by way of Sofia. (In his diaries he writes that he was accompanied by Theresa Clay; in "Conquisitio Mea" he was accompanied by

Janet Clay.) In 1934 he visited Estonia and then met his sister Bardie in Moscow and his uncle Sidney Webb as well. In 1935 he remained in the British Isles except for one trip to a bird convention in Germany (when he claims to have met Hitler for the second time). In 1936 he and Tess, with Ben and Lindy Pollen, set off on a major safari in Kenya, Uganda, Sudan, and Egypt. Later that year he made a brief trip to Hungary with Rex Benson. In 1937 he set off on another grandiose expedition—four months in India, the Deccan Plateau, Burma, Peshawar, Nepal (where he stayed with the Hatter Baileys), and Afghanistan. Sálim Ali joined him again on part of this trek. In a time when travel was still strenuous RM was suitably impressed by the Taj Mahal, the Khyber Pass, and other landmarks. In 1938 he and Tess went to Leningrad, then Helsinki, and then up through Lapland; after a few months back in England, RM and Tess, with W. H. ("Billy") Payn and a chauffeur-guide, journeyed to Marseilles, Tangier, Casablanca, and Marrakech. For six weeks they were birding in the Atlas Mountains. They faced not only cliffs and chasms but blizzards. At the end of the trek they emerged from the rugged range and descended to the fabled exotic city of Fez. Along the perilous route they had taken and skinned 812 birds. In his near–book length article about the trip for *the Ibis* RM was uncharacteristically kind—even obsequious—toward the French authorities who provided indispensable help (and even politeness) throughout Morocco.[12]

Then in the early months of 1939 they made their first visit to the New World: they steamed aboard the *Aquitania* to New York, visited Niagara Falls, and then went to Washington, D.C., where they stayed with their friend Alexander Wetmore of the Smithsonian Institution. They traveled, mainly by train, to Chicago, the Grand Canyon, Pasadena, San Diego, Tijuana, and Tucson. On this trip they met with scholars and birders. After about six weeks in the States they embarked on the *Queen Mary* back to England.

In 1940 the British Ornithologists' Union elected Hugh Whistler and Richard Meinertzhagen as its two vice-presidents. The issue of the *Ibis* that first posts their names on its masthead is the same issue in which appears RM's oft-celebrated piece "How Do Larger Raptorial Birds Hunt Their Prey,"[13] which to some extent is the basis for his later book *Pirates and Predators*. The brief article shows how particularly he was fascinated by the behavior of both groups—the Predator (say, an osprey) and the Pirate (say, an eagle, which waits for the osprey to do the hard work and then, as the osprey heads for home with the prey clutched in his talons, swoops through in a high-speed dive and, without slowing, plucks the prey from the grasp of the unsuspecting predator).

He could display an appetite for frivolity. In 1934 he inaugurated what was to become a raucous tradition: Col. Dick's Derby Day Bus Party.

The Derby Day horse races take place on the first Saturday in June, at Epsom. The Royal Family often entered horses in the trials. The occasion brought out the best of British society in its finery. RM enjoyed turning this pretentiousness on its head. He hired a red double-deck bus, stocked it with his friends and relations, and took it to the races. In the 1930s equivalent of a tailgate picnic, he hosted his party around the parked bus. Everyone would climb to the second story to watch the races. Between contests they would come down to eat—and drink.

From the mid-1930s to the early 1960s RM's bus party became an annual event to which invitations were prized. Right from the beginning, the guest lists included a marvelous selection of blue-bloods, adventurers, entertainers, and relatives.[14]

RM's nephew Nicholas Wollaston writes: "In the 1950s I was on his invitation list. The drink at his parties was usually a poisonous cocktail of his invention called Mau Mau."[15]

Sálim Ali recalled it as a day of "sybaritic feasting and jollity. . . . I wouldn't have imagined till then how light-hearted and jolly Meinertzhagen could be: he led in all the fun, rode on the merry-go-round horses, slapped his thighs in delight, and seemed to enjoy himself thoroughly."[16]

With a break for World War II, the Derby Day parties continued for about twenty-five years, taking place whenever he happened to be in England on Derby Day; because of his addiction to travel, the parties took place on average every two years.

Beatrice Webb—endlessly inquisitive, endlessly dissatisfied—observed the behavior of people at parties. In passages that throw light on the curious interlacing of the socialist and conservative wings of the Meinertzhagen mentality, she wrote:

> At the Soviet Embassy the Maiskys entertained at dinner some forty admirers of the Webbs' work—half of our own family and friends, the others mostly Soviet officials, diplomatic and trade, with their wives. It was equally informal and homely—with no ceremony or glamour—a sort of family gathering of brainworking men and women inspired by a common purpose. Stafford [Cripps], John, the Drakes, and Dick Meinertzhagen attended by Theresa Clay (Dick has become, in spite of his reactionary opinions, a personal friend of the Maiskys) represented

our relations. . . . [Guests also included George Bernard Shaw and Victor Gollancz.]

. . . . Finished up at Barbara's for dinner and the night, talking to nephews and nieces of the Meinertzhagen clan, more especially the Louis Meinertzhagen family—a conservative and decadent group—elegant young people of uncertain outlook and casual code of morals. They may turn out better value than the young people of their environment. Indeed Luke, now in a stockbroker's office, refused to stay on at Oxford for a fourth year, because he disliked the atmosphere of homosexuality plus financial recklessness which dominated the group of undergraduates to which he belonged. The only well-conducted and serious-minded youths, he said, were communist—and he did not approve of this anti-faith; he was cynical about public affairs, and had not made up his mind to which party he belongs. His elder brother is a convinced conservative and is trying to get into the Treasury; if he fails to be a top man in the Civil Service exam, he will be well placed by his father in an important financial house in the City.

. . . . The late Huth firm yields no profits, now in the hands of American financiers (I hear from Barbara that the firm is being absorbed into an international bank, that Lewis [i.e., Richard's younger brother Louis Meinertzhagen] is reduced to £1500 as a winder-up, which will cease presently when he will have only £500 as a Director). He has a great contempt for his brother Fritz who has been an ardent communist for some time; and he disapproves of Dick. He himself is in the black books of all his brothers and sisters as he is accused to having agreed to the confiscation of all their holdings in Frederick Huth and Co. in return for his own £500 a year salary! Altogether Louis Meinertzhagen is not a scrupulous or generous-minded sample of the City financier—he is a decadent and a parasite, just as Dick is a bold adventurer. Louis's wife [Gwynedd] is a Llewellyn—daughter of the president of the Royal Academy (sister of the Air Pilot), a large handsome woman, of no intelligence and pleasure-loving, belonging to the artistic bohemian corner of London society.

The women of the Meinertzhagen family are better than the men. . . . One fact is clear. From being a wealthy family allied to wealthy families, the Meinertzhagen family have fallen into relative poverty, which is also true of the Booths. The Daniel Meinertzhagen who married an R. P. in the early seventies, though not a millionaire, seemed on the road to be one. . . . Today I doubt whether the total income of the eight families of the Meinertzhagen clan of over thirty persons mounts up to ten thousand a year. It is to be noted that both the Huths and the Booths functioned in the international sphere of business and finance.[17]

The drop in Louis Meinertzhagen's fortunes was partly the result of panics and the Great Depression, but ironically the black sheep, Dick, ended up in better financial fettle than did some of his banker siblings and in-laws. Annie's estate continued to provide him with a comfortable living, and he was able to conduct his worldwide safaris in a grand style otherwise nearly forgotten since the days of Edwardian grand tours.

He tried to present his life as a sort of allegory with himself in the heroic role of a Gawain who quests the world, faces one frightful test after another, and teaches everyone the value of chivalry and honor. He succeeded, instead, in stylizing and glorifying himself in a simplified, yet superhuman way, thus presenting his romantic delusions as a sort of life. A great many people have accepted these idealizations as facts.

Physically he was monumental but behaviorally he was mercurial, a shape-shifting figure whose image changes in every mirror.

Miriam Rothschild's *Dear Lord Rothschild* contains a chapter section about a pompous bird-thief to whom she assigned the false name "Cunningham." Late in life she admitted Cunningham actually was Richard Meinertzhagen, who frequently flew into monumentally indignant rages whenever some other poor sod got caught committing the very same kind of offenses that RM himself committed. She was afraid to use his real name because, one may infer, he was apparently bomb-proof and quite willing to retaliate against those who displeased him. She said, "I think he had a serious medical/mental/emotional difficulty. . . . He lacked a sense of reality."[18]

The tapestry of embellishments, facts, exaggerations, truths, and lies began to unravel as early as 1919, but RM managed to maintain control over its fraying threads during his lifetime and for a surprising length of time afterwards. The entire fabric did not come apart until the 1990s. Its disintegration began not with challenges to his military or espionage allegations, but with revelations of his disservice to bird science. The first major publication that attracted widespread notice was in the *Ibis* in 1993—Alan Knox's "Richard Meinertzhagen—A Case of Fraud Examined," in which Knox concluded his preliminary study of the Meinertzhagen birds by saying: "The collection . . . was, and remains, deeply flawed."[19]

Not long after Knox's publication, the case went into the popular press:

The British Ornithology Union is revising its records after learning that Colonel Richard Meinertzhagen, one of the world's most prolific bird collectors, routinely misidentified birds killed abroad as having been killed in the British Isles; stole birds from other collections and relabeled them as his own discoveries; and altered remains to credit himself with finding new subspecies. Meinertzhagen left his collection to the BOU in 1967. It is displayed by the National Museum of History, along with a second Meinertzhagen collection of more than half a million lice, fleas, and mites. A decorated veteran of World War I, Meinertzhagen is perhaps best remembered neither for his collections, nor his wartime exploits, but for escaping punishment after beating a groom to death with a polo mallet because the man allegedly mistreated Meinertzhagen's ponies.[20]

By then Pamela Rasmussen—a leading American ornithologist affiliated first with the Smithsonian Institution and now with Michigan State University—had consulted with Robert Prys-Jones, Head of the Bird Group at the Natural History Museum, Tring, and with Nigel Collar, an encyclopedically knowledgeable scientist with Birdlife International. Finding that many of the birds had been stuffed with various taxidermic contents and techniques that were unique to ornithologists who were not RM, the scientists (singly and together) proceeded with an examination of RM's specimens that continues to this day. It has employed such devices as X-rays, microphotos, and even fiber tests carried out by the forensic laboratory of the Federal Bureau of Investigation.[21]

In some cases the original material and stitches had been replaced by RM. To the eye of the expert, every taxidermist has his own signature. RM, an accomplished forger in many fields, knew how to doctor evidence. But forensic examination has found traces of the original materials in the odd cavity here and there—enough to prove that RM was not the original taxidermist, and in some cases enough to match up the stolen bird with other collectors' records of missing specimens.

After several years' painstaking study by Rasmussen and himself, Dr. Prys Jones concluded:

The bird collection of the "soldier, scientist, and spy" Richard Meinertzhagen, largely held by the Natural History Museum, comprises over twenty thousand specimens and was long regarded as of exceptional importance. However, over the past decade it has become clear that much of it was fraudulently acquired and is fraudulently labeled.

. . . [We have learned] how slow and difficult the path may be from
well-founded suspicion to a reasonable level of proof.[22]

These announcements took the case public but they were by no means
the first challenges. The British Museum's records of his "borrowings" went
back to 1920. Some contemporaries regarded him as a common thief, and
said as much in print—one, Charles Vaurie, wrote in a letter that "upon my
oath" RM had stolen skins from the Paris and Leningrad Museums as well
as the American Museum of Natural History on Central Park West in New
York. Vaurie insisted that RM had replaced the skins' original labels with
new tags of his own making, not only to disguise the thefts but also to
support his singular theories of distribution, habitat, and behavior.

Vaurie added: "Macdonald . . . asked me one day what should be done
with Meinertzhagen's collection. I forget what I said, but not what Macdonald
said, which was that 'it should be burned.' He was very serious but probably did not dare to antagonize the trustees of the BM."[23] Even then, seven
years after RM's death, Vaurie's remark revealed how other contributors'
fear of antagonizing the Trustees was precisely the weapon RM had employed during his lifetime. He had been one of the BMNH's biggest "names."

At the time, Vaurie's statements were unconfirmed allegations, even
though they had the force of his own eyewitness observation. Vaurie, a respected scientist who had accompanied RM on safari, knew and expected
that his letter would be shared amongst members of the birding fraternity.
But there was no public response to his accusations of theft.

Alan Knox's 1993 paper—thirty-six years after RM's death—was the
first that openly questioned the collection's authenticity. Since then, Pamela
Rasmussen, Robert Prys-Jones, and Nigel Collar have devoted years to their
painstaking studies of RM's birds in order to prove that, as the earlier ornithologists had stated privately, many of RM's "rarest" birds were frauds and
that, indeed, some had been stolen from the British Museum itself.

The cataloging of RM's collections remains an unfinished work-in-
progress. The researchers continue to uncover thefts and frauds by compar-
ing (a) the birds themselves, (b) RM's diary entries and other writings, (c)
independent evidence of his travels (shipping schedules, letters, etc.), and
(d) the labels RM attached to the birds he stole from other collectors and
restuffed—labels that he contrived in an effort to distract suspicion by claiming he'd shot the birds hundreds or thousands of miles (and sometimes
several dozen years) away from where they actually came from.

Nigel Collar has edited several books on threatened birds. Endanger-
ment and extinction are all too familiar to him. He puts it mildly: "The

damage the man did to the ornithological collection is not easily pardoned."[24]

He did the damage over an incredible span of years. After RM was barred from the Museum in 1919, only to be reinstated a year and a half later at the request of Lord Walter Rothschild, the museum's staff knew RM was still stealing specimens.[25] They kept watching him until in 1931 an irritated RM wrote in a huff to Lord Rothschild: "I have no alternative and shall remove the whole [Ahaggar] collection from the Museum this morning. I am exceedingly sorry that this collection which Capt. Benson and I took such trouble to get together and which we always hoped would fill a gap in the national collection, has been so peremptorily refused by Mr. Regan."[26]

Evidently that was enough. Charles Tate Regan (Director of the Museum) again was muzzled and RM calmed down without removing the collection. But a few years later the Trustees found reason to suspect RM of having stolen at least two bound volumes of the journal *Parasitology*. This was around the time when Theresa Clay was taking up her doctoral study of *mallophaga*. The investigation that followed the disappearance of the rare and expensive books eventually involved the Director of Public Prosecutions and the Commissioner of Metropolitan Police (New Scotland Yard), with the attendant accumulation of paperwork.[27]

In 1936 the Director reported that the police had produced a bound copy of the *mallophaga* paper from *Parasitology*, vol. IX, which had been found in the possession of Col. R. Meinertzhagen. On its first page were partially obliterated marks, exactly the shape of the Museum's Zoological Library stamp and date stamp.

Sergeant McBain's dogged inquiries unearthed the fact that RM had sent the document out to have it re-bound in new covers. The bookbinding company was in liquidation, with its records in disorder, and—after having been "cautioned" by the detective—RM blithely stated he had bought the book from some second-hand bookshop in the neighborhood of Long Acre or Charing Cross Road. He couldn't remember the name of the shop, but he remembered having taken the book to the binding company to have it rebound.

RM agreed grudgingly to the Detective Sergeant's request that the volumes be returned to the Museum but he insisted upon various provisos including a statement in writing from the Superintendent of Scotland Yard (RM's old friend Hugh Trenchard) in which it was to be made clear that if RM had acquired stolen property he had done so unknowingly.

He brazenly added the stipulation that he should be reimbursed by the Museum for the cost of having had the book re-bound.

Then he added the further stipulation that if the Museum accepted his explanation, he would drop his request for reimbursement.

In the end, with rueful formality the BMNH and Scotland Yard allowed the case to drop for lack of sufficient evidence.

Keeper of the Zoology Department N. B. Kinnear later wrote that another ornithologist (Dr. D. A. Bannerman) had been a personal victim of RM's bird thefts. Kinnear added, "The late Hugh Whistler, my greatest friend and a regular worker in the Bird Room, had to be warned by me as he had a large collection of his own, which Colonel Meinertzhagen sometimes visited."[28]

The files of the British Museum (Natural History) contain a letter dated 1940 from Claud Ticehurst (editor of the *Ibis*) to the noted ornithologist Hugh Whistler: "On going through the rest of Dick's skins I found 6–8 Mandelli's skins. He is a queer lot. This stealing of B. M. skins leads to faked records, not only on labels but in print."[29]

Hugh Whistler[30] was an author and birding chum who had been on several ornithological expeditions with RM—he was a son of the painter James McNeill Whistler. Forewarned by both Ticehurst and Kinnear, Whistler examined his own collection shortly after a visit from RM. He noticed that some birds were missing from his collection.

But there was no Whistler whistle-blowing. He wrote to Ticehurst, "Dick asked me to come up and spend the night for the dinner next week— to meet Jourdain—but I don't like to go on accepting hospitality from a man I believe to be a th..f. A pity as I was quite fond of him." Yet, perhaps intending to keep the dirty laundry within the "family," neither Whistler nor Ticehurst made any public accusation.

Both men died shortly thereafter. Their deaths seem to have occurred from natural causes. But Whistler's son Ralfe recalls that Meinertzhagen continued to visit his mother for some time afterward, flirting with Hugh's widow and invariably making off at the end of the visit with several bird skins in his coat pockets. As previously reported, Ralfe Whistler says that on one occasion Meinertzhagen told him and his mother that he had killed his wife Annie "in some sort of duel."[31] This story was commonly repeated amongst ornithologists, many of whom seem to have believed that RM liked to mention the "duel" if the subject of purloined birds came up, in order to encourage collectors to keep their mouths shut about the latter lest they risk the former.

"The Trustees gave instructions that records, with dates, should be kept in all Departments of all books used by Colonel Meinertzhagen, and that steps be taken to check all papers dealing with *mallophaga* in the Museum Libraries, with a view to discovering whether other losses had occurred."[32] RM kept getting in trouble with the administrators and kept being rescued by friends of high station. These did not include the Museum's Sir Clive Foster Cooper (Regan's successor as Director of the BMNH), Norman Boyd Kinnear, or J. D. Macdonald. RM's ongoing relationship with those three over several decades can best be described as a series of angry feuds interrupted by occasional moments of icy courtesy.

> [Re] Colonel R. Meinertzhagen. I have to report that there is evidence which appears very strongly to imply that one of our visitors has removed a registered specimen from the collection.
>
> I had instructions from you to watch Col. R. Meinertzhagen as carefully as possible without causing offence, but it has been very difficult to do that in view of the freedom which is traditionally allowed to students in the Bird Room.
>
> Colonel Meinertzhagen has been in several times in the past year. He usually comes just before the lunch hour, during which the Bird Room remains open but with only one of the staff in attendance. Recently he has been asking to see birds from the Turkestan–Kurdistan area. I usually get them out for him myself . . . and as I handed the box to him I was able to count the contents: there were eight specimens. We had a very busy afternoon and the box was not replaced in the cabinet until the following morning. I asked Usher to get it out again and count the specimens; there were only seven.
>
> It is important to note that this is the only box of specimens the visitor had so that there is no possibility of the missing bird being misplaced.
>
> . . . [The missing bird] is number 565, a male, obtained at Tang-I-dorg, Dohut, Kurdistan, on 23/10/22, and presented by Sir Percy Cox & Capt. R. E. Cheesman.
>
> [Signed] J. D. Macdonald[33]

Once again—this was 1947—Scotland Yard was brought in to investigate. The Museum's assistant director wrote, "Detective Inspectors Fluendy and Townsent . . . made arrangements with [staff] with the object of catching Colonel Meinertzhagen red-handed if he again abstracted any specimens from the Bird Collections. [Signed] F. W. Woodbine."[34] But the Trustees backed away from setting such a trap, and once again the issue was dropped on alleged grounds of insufficient evidence. The Museum's failure to take stronger action was mitigated by the fact that the alleged criminal was easy to suspect but difficult to accuse, both because of his standing and because proofs were elusive.

Sir Clive Foster Cooper wrote in exasperation to Lord Macmillan: "Colonel Meinertzhagen . . . regards himself and his collections as being above the law or at least exempt from the limitations which the Trustees have devised to protect their collections from the undesirable attentions of lesser mortals."[35]

Macmillan's reply was diplomatic and appeasing. As it happened, Lord Macmillan had been Britain's first Minister of Information. He too knew RM. He believed RM had been a valued member of the Ministry's antecedent organization, MI-7 (in which RM had served early in World War II). Reinforcing RM's position was a key advisor to the Museum, Gavin De Beer, a scientist who had served with RM in the MI-7 intelligence section. De Beer seems to have become to RM in World War II as Freddie Guest had been in World War I: a supportive and uncritical friend at court. Later, in 1950, De Beer joined the Museum's staff and was the director with whom RM negotiated the gift of his collections. Through De Beer's efforts RM was awarded the title Honorary Associate of the Museum in 1954; RM was even issued a house key.[36]

On one occasion several large color plates which had gone missing from an ancient and very rare bird book in the Museum library turned up in RM's collection. Once again the police were called in. Once again no public action was taken.

Finally, with the pulling of quite a few strings, RM's testy relationship with the Bird Room was resolved by an agreement that henceforth birds would be examined and "shaken out" for *mallophaga* by Theresa Clay in lieu of RM.[37]

That, too, seems not to have deterred him. During her lifetime, Theresa Clay's name as a respected scientist was unsullied by her connection to Meinertzhagen, but recent investigations by Robert Dalgleish and colleagues show that she must have collaborated with RM in falsifying *mallophaga* data by discounting and discarding specimens from some of the birds she "shook out" for him.[38]

Theresa Clay's unquestioning support for RM, as a subject for inquiry, is one to which there are no simple answers. The relationship, whether platonic or otherwise, has been described as a great love story. She gave him her unconditional loyalty.

All who knew her feel she was not the sort of person to compromise her principles. It should be remembered, however, that she had lived under the same roof with him from her eleventh year on,[39] and that his was a hugely forceful personality to which anyone might have found it difficult to summon lifelong resistance.

Robert Dalgliesh writes: "In 1970, while I was a dinner guest at her Kensington Gardens home, another dinner guest asked Theresa about Richard Meinertzhagen. The typically composed Theresa almost leaped out of her chair and wanted to know '. . . what have you heard . . . why are you asking?'"[40]

After the war ended, Jack Philby suggested to RM that they could work together to update and complete the handbook on the birds of Arabia that had been begun by George Latimer Bates, the transplanted American who had lived most of his life in Africa.[41]

In 1933, when Bates had explored Arabia to make preliminary notes for the study, he had gone into partnership on the project with Philby, who continued to send notes and specimens to Bates for study. Together the two men had provided the British Museum with more than two thousand bird skins, and Bates had begun to compose the typescript text for his book. But Bates had died in 1940, at age seventy-six, with the work uncompleted.

In 1946 Philby came to RM with the notes he and Bates had made. Philby—who in some ways was quite lazy and preferred to get others to wait on him—wanted a new partner who could take over the actual writing; RM was widely regarded as the best ornithologist of his time; and the two were old friends. It all seemed ready-made for them. RM agreed, and the onetime handbook turned into a full-scale definitive study.[42]

During the several years of the book's preparation Philby and RM were rarely in the same place at the same time. They did contrive to get together now and then, either in England or in the Middle East or in North Africa. Most of the time their collaboration took place by post. Thus the Philby correspondence archive (at St. Antony's College, Oxford) provides an especially rich resource for the study of how the book came to be.[43]

While they pursued their separate researches for the book, Philby in 1949 suggested to RM that the only effective way for them to exchange information would be through A. C. Trott in the Foreign Office diplomatic pouch.[44] Some of RM's devotees take this as evidence the two were up to something sinister in the foreign-intrigue line. It seems more likely that mail service was unreliable in the sections of the world where the two men traveled, and that sometimes they would be writing to each other across the unbridgeable gulf that separated Israel from the rest of the Middle East—

so their use of the diplomatic pouch was simply a way to make sure communications got through to each other.

In 1951 with the backing of a grant from the American Arabian Oil Company (Aramco), RM made his last major research visit to Arabia for the book. He had been working on it, off and on, for about five years by then. It took both men a great deal of patient travel and study, and endless comparison of sometimes conflicting reports from various ornithological sources, but finally in 1953 the cross-checking was done, the manuscript was finished, the illustrations were assembled, and in 1954 bound copies of RM's enormous *Birds of Arabia* arrived in bookshops.[45]

Charles Vaurie immediately reviewed it unfavorably in the *Ibis* and set about complaining to fellow scientists that RM had plagiarized the book from the "Birds of Arabia" manuscript that had been completed in the 1930s by George Latimer Bates.

RM retorted that he no longer had a copy of Bates's manuscript when he wrote his own book and that in fact he had not seen the Bates manuscript in years and did not know what had become of it.

When he died, RM left the Bates manuscript—the one he did not have and had not seen in years—to the British Museum Library. The museum still has it.

In 1997 the case for plagiarism against RM was dissected by Graham S. Cowles in a long and detailed article. Cowles shows that RM did not steal more than a small portion of the text (an amount RM may have felt was permissible), but Cowles concludes that RM, who had promised Jack Philby that he would give Bates co-credit in the authorship of the book, not only lists himself as its sole author but mentions poor Bates just once, and very briefly, in an appendix at the back.[46]

In *Birds of Arabia* and some of his other publications the scientific reliability of Meinertzhagen's observations is problematic. He tended to anthropomorphize animal and even insect behavior to the point where he might have been writing about newly discovered New Guinea tribespeople rather than birds. A flavor of childlike marveling wonder sometimes creeps into his publications.

All the same, his bird writing, even if sometimes factually wrong, usually tends to be much more dependable and certainly more plausible—therefore less irritating—than his military or political memoirs. The former may be compared with Disney wildlife-movie narrations but the latter are Indiana Jones fantasies.

Aside from his claims about meetings with Hitler, he seems to have set those adventuresome fantasies aside for a time in the late 1930s when he was at the top of his birding career. But then came the Second World War.

CHAPTER 12

WARFARE

A t the beginning of September 1939—the eve of World War II—
Richard Meinertzhagen was at Swordale in Scotland. He received
a telegram: "Anxious discuss possibility appointment under General Wavell
would it be possible for you make early call on Warburton room 171 War
Office."[1]

Forced to leave the children behind with Tess, he was plucked from
Shetland by a seaplane. He explained in a letter to Hatter Bailey: "I was
ordered down by the War Office last Friday but as all boat and air services
had been suspended owing to a fleet of U-boats in the vicinity, it was not too
easy to comply. [It took] the help of the Navy [destroyer] and a Bomber Sea
Plane. . . ."[2]

At Inverness he boarded a train for the long ride south to London. He
arrived there on the morning of September 5 and went home to get his old
uniform out of the wardrobe. Then he reported to the War Office, where
Warburton told him his old friend General Wavell had asked to have RM
assigned to him for "intelligence work in Cairo."

RM then was introduced to "Prof. Rushbrook Williams who runs the
Foreign Office Political Intelligence. An able man. . . ."

The invitation from Wavell may have been one of RM's fantasies. He
was not rushed to Cairo. Instead, he wrote, "They have asked me to stay on
in the War Office and not go abroad."[3]

He settled in to work but was not happy about it. "I reached London
last Tuesday and am now working in the War Office. My further movements
are uncertain. I had to leave the children [behind]."[4]

His further movements were as uncertain as the state of the war. It
was a chaotic time. The storming of Poland that began on September 1,
1939, was the first full-scale demonstration of the swiftness and might of
the new German war machine. *Blitzkrieg*—"lightning war"—was meant to
impress the world. In that aim it succeeded. It brought Poland to its knees.

British Prime Minister Neville Chamberlain reluctantly declared war; France followed suit.

Some conservatives and fascists believed war was a communist tool backed by Jews who wanted to bring down the free market structure of the European economy. The latter advocates (RM among them) had tried to prevent war with Germany because they—both those who supported Hitler and those who opposed him—did not want to see the Crown's remaining wealth dissipated in another costly war that perhaps could not be won, possibly would exhaust both Britain and Germany, and probably would lead to the loss of both the Empire and the German Reich while it would enable the ascendancy of socialism in Britain and Bolshevik communism on the Continent. (To some extent their fears were justified by the outcomes—in the end, all those things happened to one degree or another, but none turned out to be quite as catastrophic in the long run as RM and his fellow prophets anticipated.)

No one came right out and challenged RM's loyalties, but his widely known connections with Ribbentrop and his unconcealed right-wing sympathies may have encouraged the War Office to keep him close at hand where they could watch him. (Later it would seem they had not been watching him closely enough; but he never betrayed Allied security—his transgressions were more infantile than that.)

The Army List inserted him as a reinstated lieutenant colonel in Military Intelligence, G.S.O.-3 (General Staff Officer, 3rd Grade)—a catch-all category that could include anyone from an office worker to a secret agent who returned from fiery fields once a year to be debriefed.

He allowed people around him to believe he was working at the command level in planning and outfitting a variety of enterprises, ranging from an American intervention in the Russo-Finnish War of 1939–1940 to Zionist-led expeditions that blew up German oil barges in central Europe.

Within ten days after the war began, he was able to acquire—through his brother Louis and other City contacts—information about clandestine London banking relationships with Germany. He said Special Branch used the information to shut down a Dutch bank and several London brokers. Like many of his claims, this may have been wholly or partly true, but we have only RM's word for it. Still, he had changed his mind about Germany so drastically that sometimes he nearly began to sound like one of the hated Bolshies—he complained indignantly about his brother Louis's war profiteering.[5]

In October 1939 he wrote: "I have initiated a scheme for forging German notes with a view to discrediting their paper currency. We are also forging ration cards to disorganize their food supply."[6] If these forgeries were distributed, one may assume they must have been a bit less amateurish and ineffectual than the ones he had circulated in East Africa.

Then, he wrote, he visited Robert Vansittart in the Foreign Office. Vansittart and RM had first met in 1919 at the Paris Congress. Since then Vansittart had become a powerful figure. An embedded civil servant and seasoned behind-the-scenes manipulator, he was for years the de facto head of the Foreign Office. As permanent Secretary for Foreign Affairs for many years, he wielded great power in the murky world of Whitehall. He was noted for his flirtation (like Churchill's) with the espionage world: he had his own "private agency" to which prominent Germans passed information. In the 1930s he was a frequent guest at Mottisfont Abbey, where RM was a regular as well.

RM does not dwell on Vansittart in his diaries but it is clear they maintained an uneasy acquaintanceship. During the 1930s Vansittart and Churchill had tried to convince the government of the seriousness of the Nazi menace, but they were disregarded by a majority of "appeasers;" prominent among those was Richard Meinertzhagen, who thought Hitler far preferable to Stalin. In his oddly naive way, Meinertzhagen seems to have regarded Vansittart as a well-intentioned but duped Communist sympathizer if not a Stalinist agent. His willingness to tolerate Vansittart's wrong-headedness may have had to do with the fact that Vansittart was deeply pro-Israel as well (although Vansittart's position was rendered even more complicated by a quiet, sustained dedication to Britain's interests in the oil fields of the Middle East).[7]

RM and Vansittart had met with RM's old friend Soviet Ambassador Ivan Maisky (at Mottisfont Abbey) in the spring of 1939. Vansittart was trying to persuade Maisky to discuss with his superiors a British–Soviet alliance against Germany. Maisky duly reported these meetings to Moscow, and even though he had not committed his government to anything, he was rebuked for having exceeded his authority by having discussed such matters at all.[8] Whether RM played any active role in those talks is open to question. It is possible he did. By 1939 his views toward the Nazi regime were changing rapidly.

His own account of the attempt to "turn" Maisky is different from the one in the official records. He claimed he had contrived to meet Maisky at the latter's home, where (RM wrote) he secured from Maisky a personal commitment—despite the Hitler–Stalin pact—of a British-French-Soviet coalition against Germany; RM wrote that he immediately filed a report on this conversation with the War Office.[9] Unlike the Vansittart discussions, which left a paper trail, there is no record of any Maisky–Meinertzhagen discussions on the topic. (A year later, of course, such an alliance did occur—but it was the result of Hitler's sudden invasion of Russia rather than anything said to or by Maisky.)

Meinertzhagen's mentions of Vansittart are brief, oblique, and not informative. But years later, when he read Vansittart's memoir,[10] Meinertzhagen was disturbed by its dismissal of him as an "unremembered" man. (Vansittart had referred to RM when discussing his second cousin T. E. Lawrence—Vansittart had listed RM as one of three men now forgotten who noticed that Lawrence had something about him.) In his diary RM railed against such references to himself—clearly it bothered him immensely to be regarded as obscure or insignificant.[11] Yet on the occasion of Vansittart's death in 1957 he wrote: "Vansittart was a valued friend of mine."[12]

According to RM, he met with Vansittart at the end of September 1939 to discuss the need to keep the Dardanelles open—a goal that meant bringing Turkey into the Alliance or at least keeping Turkey neutral. RM boasted that he had to knock heads together—the DMI, the CIGS, and then the Secretary for War himself, Hore-Belisha. RM claims he brought all this together in a matter of minutes. He wrote in his diary that he hoped Hore-Belisha would argue the matter strenuously at the same day's cabinet meeting.[13] He succeeded (according to him): single-handedly he had done what the Royal Navy and Allied Armies had been unable to accomplish in the previous war—secure the Dardanelles. Diplomatic pressure was brought to bear on Ankara, and as a result the straits remained open.

Again, regarding RM's actual involvement in the Dardanelles machinations, we have no one's testimony other than RM's own.

His friend General Wavell made a short trip home from Cairo. Wavell came directly to RM and "complained that everything went to France and nothing to him."[14] RM promised him immediate action—and Wavell got his reinforcements.

No evidence, aside from RM's diary typescripts, supports his involvement in that one, either.

There is, however, evidence to support the belief that Vansittart consulted RM with regard to the employment of propaganda behind German lines,[15] and that his strategic and tactical ideas were eagerly invited by several war leaders.

By the late 1930s he had become something of a celebrity among senior British authorities. (In hindsight one may be tempted to scoff that a crackpot Nazi sympathizer could have been so well regarded—but consider the standing that was achieved during the same time in the United States by the equally crackpot Nazi sympathizer Charles Lindbergh.) In Whitehall, RM and his ideas were solicited. His fire burned brightly in September–October 1939. Then, as we shall see, it flamed out very quickly.

From the outset he encountered difficulties. He wrote:

> Too many personal contacts [and therefore I] was not allowed to . . . fill a high post in the War Office. This is the result of my going straight to the fountain head when I want anything done in the slow War Office. Many of the senior officers are great personal friends of mine and in all Government offices I know most of the big men. If I want any line of policy from the Foreign Office I go to Halifax or Vansittart; if I have an Admiralty question I go to Winston, and so on. . . . I do not resent in the least a minor position in the War Office . . . [and] I am of more use in doing little odd jibs [*sic*, for "jobs"] of intelligence which a more senior officer might have difficulties in doing. . . . [Unfortunately] our little Hore-Belisha is not on good terms with either Winston or Halifax and he resents my seeing them atall [*sic*].[16]

There is a certain amount of fiction in the foregoing statement—RM never went to "Winston" about Admiralty matters or any other matters; Churchill no longer trusted him, and wanted nothing to do with him—but in those early war days, RM's ease of access to the big men in many (not all) government offices was real.

As Geoffrey Household suggested in his 1939 novel *Rogue Male* (a work of fiction about a big-game hunter who did not shoot Hitler when he had Hitler in his sights), espionage was a British game-preserve the patronage of which was restricted to members of the higher social classes. They all knew each other. They had a common language. In the 1940s Richard Meinertzhagen, though too senior to remain active in field operations, was entitled to feel he was participating in events at the strategic level. He met regularly with London's elite. He dined on occasion with the CIGS (Gen. Alan Brooke, later to become Lord Alanbrooke) and with Col. "Johnny" Bevan, Churchill's master of deception. (A member of the Barclay's Bank founding family and son-in-law of the Earl of Lucan, Bevan was an old Etonian well connected to the three banking Benson brothers who were among RM's closest friends, and to such ranking secret service executives as Stewart Menzies and Lord Victor Rothschild.)

Under Churchill's premiership the top offices of the wartime secret agencies were dominated by a socially interlocked group of prominent financiers, industrialists, scientists, artists, and statesmen, all of whom had extensive connections and the sort of ruthless imagination that was required by a need for "special means."[17]

It was a fraternity in which RM, less blustery than he had been in more casual times, seemed to fit quite well, so long as he stayed away from Churchill himself. By now his hair was white and his weathered face was cracked like a drought-stricken desert but he was all the more arresting for it, still erect and wide-chested and powerful of bearing. He strode the corridors of Whitehall in the uniform, and with the air, of a grand old soldier. He met frequently with the officials who had charge of informing and constructing British preparations for the coming war effort—his calendar was crowded with lunches, dinners, weekends, and cabinet-office meetings with such men-at-the-top (most of whom he had known since the previous war) as Gen. Sir John Kennedy (director of Military Intelligence), Alexander Cadogan of the Foreign Office, former prime minister Neville Chamberlain, Brig. Orde Wingate of Burma, old friend Lord Hugh Trenchard (of the Air Staff), veteran super-spy Guy Dawnay, South African leader Jan Christiaan Smuts, RM's old-time diplomatic nemeses Wyndham Deedes and Ronald Storrs, and Field Marshal Bernard Law Montgomery of Alamein.[18]

According to his entry for November 1, 1939, he had become coordinator for several entities whose work was related to the School of Chemical Warfare: his friend Weizmann, his future in-law Lord Victor Rothschild (who now was MI-5's executive in charge of detecting and preventing sabotage on the home front), and the War Office. They set out to learn what could be expected if the Germans dropped gas bombs on London, and how Britain should prepare to protect its citizens from them and to retaliate with similar weapons.

Ten days later he reported that Weizmann had just returned from Switzerland, bearing information about German respirators and German arsenic gas.[19] RM collated this information and brought it to the attention of the War Office. Then, RM wrote, he threw himself with special zeal into a project to destroy the enemy's barge traffic on the Danube, in order to curtail shipping of food and oil into Germany.[20] He describes an operation that involved specially designed bombs and mines that could be detonated at their targets by members of a Jewish underground sabotage unit, made up of expatriates from Palestine. These missions were commanded by the ferocious and fearless Zev Jabotinsky, who owed RM one because RM had managed to free Jabotinsky from a British prison after the man had been slammed into it for alleged infractions committed during the Jerusalem riots twenty years before.

He wrote that he and Weizmann tried to sell the idea of raising a Jewish army in Palestine, but General Ironside killed it by insisting the army be a mixture of Jews and Arabs.[21]

He wrote that he provided impetus and inspiration to then-Commander Ian Fleming who was helping draft plans for the development in the United States of that country's first full-time Intelligence agency, the OSS (Office of Strategic Services, forerunner of the CIA).[22]

Hatter Bailey turned up in London that December, looking for war work. He stayed as a house guest at 17 KPG where, over breakfast coffee, he growled about how the weakness of the Russian attack on Finland was showing the rottenness of the Bolshevik spirit. (Bailey, having been chased through the Himalayas by Red soldiers in his younger days, had a special dislike for them.) After a while Bailey obtained a prestigious post as King's Messenger in the Americas, as a cover for his intelligence operations under William "Intrepid" Stephenson. Whether correctly or not, Meinertzhagen took credit for getting Bailey this assignment.

It may have been the presence of "The Hatter" that encouraged RM to involve himself in the Finland issue.

After the Soviets and the Nazis had divided the carcass of Poland between themselves, Stalin had decided to eat Finland. The Finns resisted the Red Army's attempt to invade. In December 1939, as a Christmas present to the Finns, RM says he managed after heroic lobbying to get a few thousand hand grenades sent off to them, along with a paltry one hundred anti-tank rifles, a similar number of machine-guns, some ammunition, and a few dozen obsolete biplanes. Every bit of it required great struggle and he complained of the frustrations.[23]

The matériel was provided by private connections, mainly Canadian; we have no way to be sure to what extent RM was actually involved, although it is clear he played some sort of role in Britain's silent attempts to support Finland. Early in 1940 he wrote wistfully, "I should love to go to Finland."[24] His sentiments were consistent: he believed Communist Russia was the enemy of civilization. Just as he believed the world would be improved when the Zionists got their Jewish state, he believed with equal fervor that the world would not be safe until Bolshevism was crushed.

Beatrice Webb wrote:

> The Maiskys looked in about 6:30, in excellent spirits, confident that the Red Army is going to win through in Finland. He believes that the conservative government does NOT want to go to war with the

USSR but may find it difficult to resist pressure from the Labour Party in that direction.

Dick Meinertzhagen for dinner, arrived in full uniform looking dignified and discreet, but tired, from the Foreign Office Intelligence Department where he is working long hours for seven days a week, an entry which rather disconcerted the Soviet Ambassador. We gathered from Dick that the ski-ers are for Finland and are going immediately: I assume as volunteers under Major Roosevelt. Dick refused to discuss Peace terms: no one knew who was going to win, and how far there will victory [sic] on either side. He was gloomy, though he asserted that all would be "as usual" after the war.[25]

As usual RM was disregarding political facts of life. In the war between the Axis and the Allies, both Finland and the USSR were officially neutral at the time. The British government had no desire to provoke Stalin into coming into the war on Hitler's side, which they believed he might do if the Allies were to provide visible support to Helsinki in its resistance against the Red invasion. So in the coming few months the only support that reached Finland came from "volunteer" sources, officially (if not actually) unaffiliated with any of the warring governments. Some of these volunteers, like Maj. Kermit Roosevelt's brigade, were made up of troops who looked as if they could be of use even to the superb fighters of the Finnish armed forces, but before the volunteer forces could be trained and shipped to the battle fronts, the short war ended. On March 12, 1940, Finland reluctantly signed a peace treaty with the USSR in which Finland ceded part of its territory, including a few airports and a naval base. Nevertheless the Red Army had been mortified and the Finns were able to maintain most of their land area and their precious independence. The vigor with which they had defended themselves had left Stalin with the knowledge that he might defeat them, but only at enormous cost; in effect, the armistice was a victory for Finland.

RM was, in effect, one of the conduits between the War Office and the Zionists. But the nature of his duties was confined mainly to public relations work.

Until recently, information relating to his work in the years 1940–1945 was difficult to pin down. The activities of his section (and of all sections) of the wartime secret services were kept under wraps by official decree for several decades after the end of the war. As a result, RM's work in Intelligence during World War II has been reported on the basis of the claims he made in his diaries. The realities have been examined very little.

Recent release of formerly classified documents sheds light on these realities, at last.

The early spring of 1940 was as beautiful as any in memory. The more perilous and dismaying the news from all quarters of Europe, the more glorious the weather. A good many meetings devoted to deadly issues of war took place on sunny lawns. RM attended many of them. Even if his diaries are disregarded, we can assume he actually chatted with a large number of important people.

Little wonder that in the midst of it all (including the Battle of Britain and the London Blitz) he would be writing: "I have had little spare time for birds; in fact I have not looked at one since the war started."[26]

He liaised frequently with his friend Lord Victor Rothschild, who had become head of MI-5's anti-sabotage section, and who employed RM's cousin Teresa Mayor as his good right hand. (After the war Victor Rothschild would marry her.) For an undisclosed length of time, Theresa Clay worked in MI-5 as well—RM wrote to a friend: "Theresa still works in the War Office, very high up and drawing a huge salary. She has taken to military intelligence as a duck to water. . . . She is going to have difficulty after the war in switching back to zoology."[27]

Lord Victor's sister Miriam Rothschild was in Intelligence as well. These inter-related officers saw one another frequently in the dank hallways of the Intelligence warrens.

The world inhabited by RM, the two Tesses, and Lord Victor was one that sometimes erupted in melodrama of an order that would have been implausible even in the most harebrained pulp fictions. By 1942, for example, Victor Rothschild had to test Winston Churchill's cigars to insure against the possibility "that if anybody were to attempt to do any funny business it would take the form of painting a virulent poison on to the end [of a cigar] which would ultimately go into the mouth."[28]

In the years before the war, RM's cousin Teresa Mayor (1915–1996) had been working for the book publisher Jonathan Cape. In 1939 she was RM's house guest for a while at 17 Kensington Park Gardens. After Tess and RM returned to London from America, Teresa Mayor moved into a house that belonged to Lord Victor Rothschild at 5 Bentinck Street. That house, in which Gibbon reputedly had written his *Decline and Fall of the Roman Empire*, was to become notorious for the uninhibited social life of Teresa Mayor's fellow lodgers, Anthony Blunt and Guy Burgess, who threw gay sybaritic revelries with scandalous abandon. Among their frequent visitors were Kim Philby, Donald Maclean, and Guy Liddell—all rising stars of British Intelligence. Practitioners of guilt-by-association conspiracy theories have used these facts to rationalize theories that Victor Rothschild or Teresa Mayor was "the fifth man" in the complicated nest of Red spies that included Philby, Maclean, Guy Burgess, and Anthony Blunt, and satirists have had field days with the fact that the top British counterspies of the 1950s who commanded the effort to dig out Soviet moles were themselves Soviet moles. But lengthy investigations seem to have established firmly that Victor Rothschild was never a Soviet agent, nor was Teresa Mayor. Nor, certainly, was Richard Meinertzhagen.[29]

One of the actual moles, Kim Philby, had dropped his right-wing rhetoric by 1940. Gone and forgotten were his days of Anglo-German fellowship.

Between May and August 1940, about fifteen hundred people were "detained" as suspected security risks under Defense Regulation 18B. One of those detainees was Kim's father Harry St. John "Jack" Philby, who was even less adept than RM when it came to keeping his opinions to himself.

Jack Philby was initially jailed in Liverpool and soon was moved to a detention camp in Ascot. Unlike Oswald Mosley and other suspected Nazi sympathizers who were held incommunicado in camps for years, the elder Philby was freed some months after his arrest. Did RM play a role in his release?[30] It seems likely. Philby dined with RM almost immediately after being freed from detention.

RM seems to have found it necessary to amuse himself with impish exercises. Dame Miriam Rothschild recalled:

> He played a game with the Ministry, pretending he was trying ever so desperately to get back into the Secret Service. He kept doing application forms and putting them on the Ministry's desks, when all the time he [already] had an office of his own—it was right next door [to theirs]! But the Ministry wasn't even aware he was there. He kept carrying on as if he hadn't been taken back in—he *so* enjoyed having them on.[31]

MI-7 was the branch of military operational intelligence responsible for propaganda and censorship. RM had served under that directorate during part of his service as a staff officer during the last twenty months of the

Great War.[32] The MI-7 office was shut down shortly after the end of the
Great War; some of its operations continued into the 1920s within the
shrunken MI-5 and MI-6 departments.

MI-7 was revived in September 1939. Once again its fields of enter-
prise were limited to propaganda and censorship.

Not long after RM was recalled to active duty, he was assigned to a
desk in the department.

On September 6, 1939, he reported to Warburton in Room 171 of the
War Office. Warburton was director of MI-7.[33] He did not publish most of
these recollections but RM's own typescript diaries for 1939–1940 describe
the work he actually performed, and kindly show us where a researcher
may look in official files for amplification.[34] Such a search confirms that he
worked in the propaganda department, sifting incoming news stories from
around the world, "placing" the most encouraging ones with British newspapers and censoring the most discouraging ones (i.e., forbidding the newspapers from publishing them—a power that Warburton's department wielded
under wartime emergency legislation).

The section was short-lived. On April 15, 1940, MI-7 was disbanded
and its duties were parceled out to other sections.[35] Much of its propaganda, directed at the enemy and often in the form of leaflets dropped from
bombers, continued to be produced in enormous numbers by the new Political Warfare Executive (by the end of the war more than a million publications had been distributed). RM was not reassigned to that department. In
effect, he was retired in the spring of 1940.[36]

He continued to draw a paycheck but his only official connection with
government war work was his membership in the Home Guard, that valiant
organization of civilians who provided superb work during German air attacks in watching the skies, in shepherding citizens to safe shelters, and in
assisting emergency services in the care of the wounded and the disoriented. He rarely reported for duty with the Home Guard, however. His physical
disabilities were trouble enough, but also he may have been embarrassed by
such a politically trivial posting. He preferred to let people think he was
guarding not merely the sandbags in the streets of Westminster but the soul
and leadership of the nation that was housed behind its doors.[37]

He continued to put on his uniform and circulate in the buildings of
Whitehall. But he had no job there. By the summer of 1940, he was virtually
an impostor.[38]

Within his network of high-ranking cronies he remained "in the loop,"
kept abreast of developments, although it is clear that he was no longer

entrusted with any sort of classified information. He dined fairly frequently, right through the war, with "Pug" Ismay and Gen. Alan Brooke and other very top-level war leaders. His opinions were valued, partly because of his lingering reputation as the mastermind and hero of the 1917 haversack ruse.

He was treated that way by many, but not by all. By 1922 Winston Churchill had washed his hands of RM and thereafter wanted nothing further to do with him. No meetings between the two old school-mates were recorded at any time for any reason in any place after 1922. Churchill's authorized biographer, Sir Martin Gilbert, confirms that Churchill—a notorious pack-rat who never threw a scrap of paper away—neither wrote nor kept any communications with RM. To Churchill, RM had become a nonperson.

Thus, lacking the good opinion of the strongest prime minister in British history, RM was given no job of high responsibility (clandestine or otherwise).

Some of his partisans still insist on believing he was part of a secret intelligence cabal that ran World War II from behind the scenes. With all due respect to those aficionados, one must disagree. Churchill for one would have forbidden it absolutely, and he would not have been alone in that.[39]

Even within his circle, among some of his clubby friends RM appears to have been regarded as untrustworthy, perhaps on account of his willingness to spout outrageous opinions and perhaps because of his reputation—widespread among family and acquaintances—as a possible but never charged or openly accused wife-killer, who in full British fairness had to be regarded as innocent until and unless proven guilty, but who in full British common sense was not necessarily to be trusted.

For those or other reasons, after the spring of 1940 there is no evidence (other than his own diaries[40] and the stories he inflicted on friends and relatives) that any senior official ever consulted him about matters that were not openly known and published.

RM's life in retrospect is chock-full of irony. In 1942 in Burma and India after the fall of Singapore, a replica of RM's most famous ruse was initiated—by Gen. Sir Archibald Wavell, who had been transferred to the Far East:

> Operation "Error" . . . [was] virtually a re-run of the famous ploy that Wavell had described in his life of Allenby, when Col. Richard Meinertzhagen, scouting in front of the British lines in Palestine in

September 1917, had drawn Turkish fire and fled, dropping as he gal-
loped away a saddle bag containing a complete set of marked maps
and orders which successfully misled the Turks as to the location of
Allenby's forthcoming attack. This time the misinformation indicated a
formidable defensive build-up of British forces in India, more than sufficient to block any further Japanese advance. The documents were
contained in a brief-case which, together with other items of the Commander-in-Chief's personal effects, was left in a staff car ditched on the
further side of the Ava bridge over the Irrawaddy river, a few hours
before the bridge was blown.[41]

The man who devised the details of the "Error" scheme for Wavell was
his Intelligence staff officer, world-traveling author Maj. Peter Fleming—
the brother of RM's friend Ian Fleming.

Another replication of the haversack trick, on a heroic scale, took
place in 1943 with the deception code-named "Trojan Horse." It was devised by Col. John Bevan's LCS (London Controlling Section).[42] False papers
were planted on the dead body of a British "officer" (actually a sailor who
had drowned after a torpedoing) and the body was allowed to wash up on a
Spanish beach, where the "neutral" local authorities brought it to the attention of German intelligence officers, as Bevan had known they would. Bevan's
naval intelligence liaison officer, Lt. Cdr. Ewen Montagu, directed the scheme,
and it worked brilliantly. After swallowing the dead man's documents whole,
the Germans busily committed their resources to the defense of Greece
against an attack that never came, while Allied forces invaded Sicily.

RM had no direct role in the Trojan Horse caper (popularly known as
"The Man Who Never Was"—the title of Montagu's postwar book and the
movie based on it), but his having inspired it was acknowledged later by,
among others, John Bevan and Field Marshals Lord Wavell and Lord
Alanbrooke. All three officers knew RM; the latter two were his friends and
the former was an in-law and a close chum of RM's comrades the Benson
brothers, all three of whom carried on extensive Intelligence work not only
with Stewart Menzies ("C") of MI-6 but also with Colonel Bevan of LCS.[43]

None of them was conspiring in any sort of cover-up. They believed
Meinertzhagen had created and carried out the haversack ruse. It was a
matter of history. Besides, Wavell had been there. (Wavell had been in
Allenby's headquarters and had known a bit about the haversack scheme
but clearly did not know enough about it, or its effects, to cause him to
disbelieve RM's version.)

Thus Richard Meinertzhagen's most celebrated exploit, which in fact had been both a failure and a lie, became the inspiration (one war later) for two real exploits both of which were genuine successes.

The lie continued to have a life of its own. In the late 1950s RM's friend from Nandi Fort and Cambrai, Maj. Gen. Sammy Butler, typed up a recollection by Field Marshal Lord Archibald Wavell about the exploit for which both generals best remembered Meinertzhagen:

I dined one night with Archie [Wavell, in Cairo in 1940]. . . . He related many of his experiences in the 1914–18 war. As regards Meinertzhagen's exploit, when he dropped faked orders (in front of Turks) which were picked up, he [Wavell] said—quote:

"In the haversack he let fall purposely, when shot at by the Turks, were faked orders, some money, some letters from his wife and the haversack was blood spattered (to give the idea he'd been hit)—He himself flopped in the saddle as if wounded, Turks picked up haversack, then followed a great discussion as to whether it was a fake. Liman von Sanders, the German C. in C. was sure it was not a fake, the Turks thought it was. However, it was decided to accept it as genuine and dispositions were made accordingly—Result, our victory at 3rd Battle of Gaza. When the haversack was captured, the Turks published an order to the troops, pointing out that this was gross carelessness and warning officers against carrying written orders in the field, and also an order rewarding the corporal who picked up the haversack!"[44]

🐦 🐦 🐦

He was in his sixties and complaining of aches and illnesses that he blamed on the approach of old age. He said a German bomb injured him during his efforts to evacuate troops from Dunkirk on June 1, 1940, while he was crossing and re-crossing the Channel to bring British troops home.[45] His seamanship and purported heroics at Dunkirk seem to have been witnessed by no one except himself, and as for the injuries, there were two and they both seem to have been related to London taxicabs. The first took place in January 1940 when he was hit by a taxi; it injured his leg. A year later, a bomb explosion blew up the London taxi in which he was riding. His reaction to that one was indignant and personalized: "Hitler scored a direct hit on me."[46]

In fact the injury was serious. The explosion nearly blew the helmet off his head. He wrote to Hatter Bailey: "I was hit by a pound or two of something which dented my tin hat and knocked me out," and explained to another friend, "I was unfortunately struck down on March 4th, and am not yet right. Concussion for three weeks and am not allowed to work again for another six weeks. At my age these things take time."[47]

He was bedridden for weeks and partially incapacitated for months. Tess lived with him ("her family having evacuated themselves [sic] to the country") and took care of him.

The bomb set him aside, but it seems to have preceded an extraordinary burst of energy in which he wrote at top speed over many months. In fact he was so busy writing the memoir *Me* (never published) and revising his diaries that his contemporaneous bird manuscript, "Conquisitio Mea," had to be typed by someone else—probably Theresa Clay—as it was not produced by his usual italic-face machine or with his habitual misspellings.

Both *Me* and "Conquisitio Mea" were completed in 1942.

From then on occurred the truly creative period of his life: the rehabilitation of his diaries.[48]

The brain injury may help explain some of the outrages he perpetrated upon plausibility in and after 1942, but they were not so different in scope or content from the preceding fictions.

CHAPTER 13
KENSINGTON

The war years were traumatic for everyone. RM was no exception. By 1944 he was sixty-six years old. His injuries were not inconsiderable but he was alive and relatively sturdy, while at an increasing rate his family, friends, and contemporaries were dying off, some from warfare and some from the maladies of advancing age.

Each death took a bit of the starch out of him but he carried on. Even though restricted by wartime shortages he managed to keep up his habit of traveling around the British Isles, sometimes with the children, to stay with friends. He turned up frequently at Mottisfont Abbey. He complained sourly of the BMNH's delays in evacuating its collections from London, remarked acidly upon the bomb damage to the museum, and took a photo of his sister Bobo's house, which had been bombed.

The loss that broke his heart was that of his elder son Dan, who was killed in action by mortar fire while serving as an officer with the Coldstream Guards. He was killed in the battle that later was described as "a bridge too far," at Arnhem, on October 2, 1944. Dan was nineteen.

The boy—the eighth successive eldest son of the eldest son to be named Daniel Meinertzhagen[1]—had been Richard's favorite, to the detriment of the younger two children. Dan had been bright and brave, upright and forthright— an excellent young man, by the account of everyone who knew him—and the loss left Richard inconsolable. He brooded on the dark and enraging coincidence by which his own brother Dan had died in 1898, suddenly and unexpectedly and at about the same age as, and with the same horrible effect on, Richard the survivor. (Sometimes immune to irony, he does not seem to have noticed how he blamed his own parents for having made a favorite of *his* older brother, at Richard's expense.)

He lost himself in the wilds of Scotland for a while that winter, hiking into wind-whipped fogs of icy solitude, perhaps hoping the harsh northern winter would cleanse his soul of its demons. He broke ribs (either from a fall or from coughing) and was taped up over the year-end holidays, which would have been miserable enough for him without the bandaging, but when he came home for Christmas he did his best to put on a good face for his children Anne and Ran. The staunch Tess helped see him through the grief.

He traveled desperately in 1945 as the war in Europe was ending: he couldn't sit still. Peregrinations took him to Mottisfont Abbey; to the Scilly Isles (with daughter Anne); to Norfolk; to Cornwall; to Exmouth with Tess; back to the Scilly Isles; to his in-laws the Booths at Funtington; back to Catfield in October; then to Hartley Windney; to the Henley Regatta; to the Rex Bensons' (Drovers); to the Carlyons' (Tregrehan); across the Irish Channel with Tess to County Kerry and Dublin. He and Tess climbed to the top of Snowdon—the same climb RM had made years earlier with Tess's sister Janet—and he became spry enough, in mind and spirit, to plan a safari to Arabia and Egypt.

But what brought him out of depression, in the end, was writing. He said his "diaries" were a safety valve. Now he withdrew into a self-created cave and wrote an account of his late son's life, based on his own diaries and Dan's diary and the trove of letters Dan had written home from schools, travels, and military assignments. He wrote furiously, reconstructing the entire (but all too brief) track of Dan's passage through the years. He meant the book to be a memoir and a tribute. He introduced it with mention of "my love and admiration for the boy. . . . I want others to share with me the glorious pride and gratitude I feel, not only for Dan, but for that whole gallant band of youth who have given us so much without complaint."

When the book was complete, he published it in 1947: *The Life of a Boy*.[2]

Those who know a bit about Richard Meinertzhagen tend to associate his name immediately not only with "haversack" but with "diaries." RM's leatherette-bound diary volumes had their own display bookcase in the entranceway to his home at 17 Kensington Park Gardens in London. He lived there, between expeditions, from 1922 until his death in 1967. He was not in the habit of allowing visitors to thumb through the volumes, but when coaxed he might open one of them and select a page or two for the visitor to examine.

These unpublished diaries are now housed at Rhodes House (the Bodleian Library), Oxford. I was given free access to them, thanks to the generosity of RM's son Ran Meinertzhagen.

The diaries are in top-class blue Walker's T-103 loose-leaf three-ring binders, flexible and heavy-duty (cover number 1008, paper size 1080). There are eighty-two volumes, including the Index. Each volume holds more than one hundred sheets (two hundred pages); some contain two hundred sheets or more. The binders are trademarked 1905. The first few volumes, purporting to have been typed in 1903 (or 1907) from earlier handwritten ones, are typed in an ordinary pica font. After the first few the rest of the volumes are presented in a distinctive italic typeface so neat it looks as if it came out of an electric typewriter, on very heavy linen-paper that must be at least 30-weight stock.

There are very few typographical errors and very few tipped-in text additions. Of the latter a few are handwritten but most are typed.

The left-hand margins are wide, so that brief topical descriptions can be typed there, both to identify the content of the paragraph beside them and to provide a heading that reappears in the astonishingly thorough and well-organized Index volume.

The diaries consist mainly of pages typewritten on one side with objects pasted onto the reverse side and captioned: maps, flattened bugs, dried flowers, clippings from magazines and newspapers, military dispatches, personal letters and postcards, Meinertzhagen's own precise and often wonderful drawings, and above all, photographs. Some are by the diarist, some by others.

Of hundreds of photo prints, quite a few appear to be picture postcards but I can't be sure because it's not the visiting researcher's right to peel inserts away from the opaque paper backing to which they are firmly pasted. I left the typescripts as I found them.

A few of the photos and maps are labeled as having been taken off German officers alive or dead. Some of these are suspiciously intact and pristine—never a rip or a bloodstain.

More than ten thousand pages in length, the full-length seventy-seven volume memoir is amazingly tidy, a very professional-looking presentation and hardly the kind of document you would expect from an ebullient man of action and self-described poor scholar. Except for a few consistent misspellings or eccentricities with certain words—"atonce" for "at once," for instance—the spelling, typing, and syntax are expert, uniform, and by all evidence unhurried.

Interestingly, the page numbers (at the top of each right-hand page) are not typed. They are entered in pen or often in pencil. Some are smudged, showing that they have been erased and changed.

At the beginning of the first volume are pasted-in polite letters of regret and rejection from major publishers to whom the author submitted the gigantic work. Generalized, their response was something on the order of (I paraphrase): "We like your tale very much and please bring it back to us after you've edited it down to perhaps three percent of its present length"— a notion Meinertzhagen seems to have taken to be a vile personal insult.

In the end he was able to pare sections of the mass down to materials that were published in his four "Diary" books, plus a fifth volume about the brief but admirable life of his son Dan.[3]

To my layman's eye some of the pages appear to be typed on fresher paper than others, and there's something just slightly different about the typeface on those pages. I'm not the first observer to point out how some pages are typed with much smaller margins and crowded line-spacing to make room for twice the amount of text that must have appeared on an earlier version of the same page. In several instances page-numbers are out of sequence and/or inconsistent with references in the Index.

An over-all examination suggests that many of the first revisions were revised again and yet again.

Even the earliest of the present volumes are revisions rather than an original draft. They are not what they purport to be—i.e., the daily or occasional fresh and firsthand experiences and observations of a true diarist.

I have tried, and failed, to imagine a man toting a heavy typewriter through jungles, deserts, Himalayas, and combat. Even if one should assume the sacred machine was carried for him by bearers, pack animals, or baggage columns—all of which were lacking on some of his earlier trips— one would have to accept the notion that RM's noisy typing would have kept awake not only his traveling companions but alert prowling panthers and enemy scouts night after night in the bush.

Some students—both admirers and detractors—feel that RM probably wrote many of his original diary notes in handwritten pocket notebooks and then, weeks or months or even years afterward, rewrote them on the typewriter. This is plausible and acceptable with the proviso that we remember how often he rewrote them yet again, sometimes many years later.

He tells us in his introductory note to the typescripts that he had kept diary notes by hand since 1899 (when he entered army service). He avers that after acquiring the typewriter he transcribed those eight years' back-entries into typescript without altering anything except grammatical mistakes. In view of the accuracy, or lack of it, in the diaries as a whole, we need to take such statements with skepticism.

During World War II he gathered whatever remained of his childhood diaries and wrote a memoir of his early life, up to and including his experiences in Africa during the first years of the twentieth century.

The title was *Me*. It was never published. After writing it, he destroyed the original handwritten childhood diaries because, he said, he felt they contained wicked flippant comments about various people and he did not wish to preserve such unkindnesses. In fact he assiduously destroyed any previous version as soon as he had superseded it.

He appears to have used some of the *Me* material as a basis for entries in his final book, *Diary of a Black Sheep* (1964), but there are large discrepancies between the contents of those two works, and further discrepancies with the typescript diaries.

Questions became inevitable about the typewriter on which he created his letters and diaries.

He later stated he had bought his distinctive typewriter in 1906. The typeface in all the RM typescripts after the first few volumes (after those bearing dates up to 1907) is a Garamond pica italic font. The particular style of Garamond on RM's typewriter appears to be a sub-strain of Goudy Modern that was designed in 1918. Frederic Goudy further refined the font in 1921; it then became known as Monotype Garamond and no longer resembled the font of the RM typescripts.[4] So we may be dealing with a fairly narrow period of manufacture.

Forensic typewriter specialists advise that the use of italic fonts on retail typewriters did not become usual until 1920; that year has become the cut-off date for investigators of "questioned documents" (usually wills, codicils or other legal documents), who hold that prior to 1920 italic typewriters were unavailable to the public. They could be obtained only by special order, and on those rare instances they were purchased by firms that used them for restricted purposes.

Circumstantial data seem to narrow the most likely date of manufacture of the RM typewriter to the years 1920 or 1921, although this is a judgment based on the opinion of experts who have not actually seen the machine. Its whereabouts are uncertain. There is a possibility that RM in 1906 or 1907 just happened to buy an off-brand typewriter with an unpatented customized font that just happened to resemble Garamond Goudy Modern 12-point Italic at some sixteen specific comparison points; that the typewriter miraculously survived the sinking of the *Transylvania* in 1917, when RM barely escaped the torpedoed liner with his life,[5] and that he managed to keep the same typewriter operating for the rest of his lifetime and well beyond, for Theresa Clay to use in answering mail in the 1980s.

Other than the diaries, only three documents allegedly produced by the typewriter prior to 1920 are known to exist. All three are letters that

RM purportedly wrote from East Africa in 1914 and 1915. All three are typed on the machine in question. The salutation of one is to "Jack" and of the other two to "Jeffer." All three letters were given to the Imperial War Museum in 1980 or shortly thereafter by the widow of Col. Jack Dunnington, who had been RM's friend and a fellow officer of the Royal Fusiliers. It was believed, naturally enough, that Dunnington-Jefferson had been the addressee of all three letters.

RM had first met Lt. (later Lt. Col. Sir) J. A. Dunnington-Jefferson in 1907 in South Africa when Dunnington-Jefferson was a young officer attached to the Mounted Rifles. A year later he transferred to the Intelligence staff. He and RM kept in touch over many years. They crossed paths in Durban, Natal, in 1911 (and in different locations on the same diary page RM makes an unclear pair of references—"To Rheims from Paris, 1919, with Col. Sir John Dunnington-Jefferson" and "A visit to Rheims with Jack Jefferson 1918"—is he referring to one trip or two?). Elsewhere there are notations of visits to Dunnington-Jefferson in York (1936) and of dining with him in London (1944, 1946, 1947 [twice], 1954, and 1955).[6]

RM's friendship with Dunnington-Jefferson assumes special significance because of those three letters in D-J's papers posthumously donated to the War Museum. They purport to have been written from Nairobi, December 15, 1914; Nairobi, May 28, 1915; and Mombasa, October 18, 1915.[7]

They assume crucial importance in dating the diary typescripts because, if authentic, they are the earliest known documents to have been typed on the distinctive italic-faced machine. On the other hand if their provenance should show them to have been typed after (rather than during) the Great War, then the last of RM's threadbare claims for the contemporaneity of his wartime diaries would fall apart.

The letters contain standard Meinertzhagenia, chastising military command for its idiocy. One of them describes the British fiasco at Tanga in November 1914. From their habitual misspellings there is no question they were written by RM, but they do provoke some suspicion as to when he wrote them, and why. They are without envelopes. They do not identify their addressees except by casual salutation; if they hadn't been among Dunnington-Jefferson's papers, it seems probable no one would have been able to identify their addressee.

RM's epistolary description of the cock-up of the Tanga assault is straightforward, but one may be skeptical toward the date of its origin because the Crown kept a heavy lid on all information about that debacle for more than a year afterward, and the War Office expressly forbade its officers to mention Tanga in any correspondence. The embarrassment was acute, and it was possible to contain news about it (as opposed to the disaster at Gallipoli which was so huge and so public that it couldn't be denied). Such letters as RM's, about the stupidity of his general officers at Tanga and afterward, never would have passed the military censors.

In one letter RM tries to get around the censorship question by mentioning he knows he's not supposed to talk about the fiasco so he's sending the letter via outside channels. Did he? If so, why? And what exactly could "outside channels" mean? In two out of three cases he purports to be in Nairobi, where he would have had no access to ship captains. The letters could not have gone out by diplomatic pouch because there wasn't a diplomatic pouch from British East Africa—it wasn't a foreign country. RM himself was in the chain of command of officers who supervised censorship, but the top man in that chain was his nemesis, Brig. Gen. Wilfred Malleson, CIE, who heavily out-ranked then-Captain Meinertzhagen and hated him bitterly. If Malleson or any of his sycophants had spotted an outbound letter from RM it probably would have been opened and, given the inflammatory nature of the letter and given Malleson's temperament, RM would have been court-martialed within an hour and had the epaulets stripped off him before dawn the next day.

It is not at all impossible that RM might have found a way around Malleson in getting these chatty but unimportant letters out, but in the circumstances one must question whether he would have taken such a risk to such small purpose. He would have known what it could cost him if Malleson caught him.

All his other letters sent home during the Great War, from Africa and later from Egypt and Palestine, were militarily circumspect and largely obedient to the censorship regulations of the day (regulations he was sworn to enforce). Those other letters of the period were handwritten or typed on standard-issue military typewriters.

The letters to Dunnington-Jefferson are unique. Thus they seem to provide an opening for one to plunge into conjecture. What if RM gave two or three "old" letters to Dunnington-Jefferson in, say, 1947, explaining that wartime censorship had prevented his posting them thirty years earlier and he had just come across these and thought his old friend might find them amusing? This hypothesis is admittedly a bit far out, but it's utterly consistent with his methods and notions. He prided himself on being a master of deception.

A clue in the letter to "Jack" lies in its reference to the addressee's son Kim. RM's friend and sometime co-conspirator Jack Philby had a son, later infamous, named Kim. Dunnington-Jefferson's estate may have ended up in possession of the letter, but Dunnington-Jefferson had no son named Kim.

If not deliberately, did Meinertzhagen give it mistakenly in the same parcel to D-J rather than to Philby, sometime in the 1940s?

Those are questions, not facts. A fact is that by 1921 he had begun to pepper ornithological societies and other recipients with letters composed on the italic machine. There is no question he used the machine regularly from then on, in both personal and business correspondence. Nor did he leave it at home when he went traveling. His post-army bird-hunting safaris were luxurious affairs that involved battalions of bearers and carloads of comforts; one has no difficulty picturing some poor sod carrying the type-writer from one camp to the next, keeping the thing clean of dust and insects, and setting it up on a camp desk whenever RM wanted to type up his notes on birds or lice. From 1921 on there are innumerable examples of his italic-typed correspondence from far-away outposts to ornithologist Hugh Whistler, to the BMNH, to Philby and to Hatter Bailey, and to his other cronies who didn't throw anything away.

But prior to 1920, so far as we have been able to determine there are only the voluminous diaries, and the three letters in the IWM.

The typewriter he allegedly acquired in 1907 was still in use long after his death by his cousin (often called his niece) and heir Theresa Clay, who had been his constant companion since 1929. Until the 1990s much of her correspondence, including letters in answer to historians' requests for permission to read the Oxford diaries, is typed on the same machine that produced the diaries.

The eighty-two volumes contain heaping catalogs of flora and fauna seen, collected, or both. These run on in serial form over scores of pages. The Index alone contains ten single-space typed pages under the heading "BIRDS," with references to pages in every volume from 0 (1899) through LXVI (volume 66, for the year 1956; some of the numbered volumes are too thick so they're divided into more than one binder; he continued typing new diaries after 1956 but those are not indexed). A great many of the faunal and floral notations do not agree with his journal publications or bird books, or with the tags he appended to some of the stolen birds and plucked plants in his collections. Perhaps when he was cobbling together the tags for the collections he didn't have the diaries at hand, or didn't feel like looking things up in them. And there are diary entries placing him on a certain ship or in a certain port on a certain date—entries that do not agree with published shipping records or independent accounts of Meinertzhagen's whereabouts.

Some of the plants are forgeries as well—cobbled together out of pieces of two or more types of plant: take for example a buttercup stalk topped with a daisy flower. These seem to be regarded good-naturedly by museum curators as practical jokes rather than willful frauds. Many still give him credit for his good work, along with the benefit of the doubt; they are correct, because after all he collected thousands of valued specimens for the museums and made valuable contributions to science, some of which were valid. But the question that remains—*How many?*—continues to frustrate scientists. The hidden costs of RM's counterfeits can be enormous. If we're misled by falsified information about species, we cannot document historical changes and predict future changes, and therefore we can't know how to deal with them.

Why was it so important that he mislead us?

The question has no simple answer. Actions and events are subject to discovery and description, but motivations are subject mainly to speculation. Years of back-and-forth discussions among scores of RM-watchers show mainly that he is a spectacular specimen under the microscope of just about any sort of psychological, social, genetic or metaphysical examiner.

The accepted method of studying the pathology of an individual is to gather the facts and see what pattern they assume. Traditionally, such a study begins with the facts of the subject's background and upbringing. The method is as valuable in the case of RM as in any other, but RM presents a special difficulty because we know surprisingly little about his early years other than what he wrote or said about himself.

In his writings he draws a portrait of himself as a neglected, abused, and molested child. It is hard to tell how much of this self-portrait we should accept. Is the inveterate self-dramatist sensationalizing an otherwise normal (if adventuresome) childhood?

We have glimpses from the points of view of others who knew him. If we gather those glimpses together and compare them, they help give us a picture that is more accurate, but it is sometimes inconclusive and frequently out of focus.

In June 1946 he threw his first postwar Derby Day bus party. Then after the marriage of his daughter Anne to John Payn (no relation to Billy Payn), RM visited the honeymoon couple in Cornwall. After that he got back into the old swing of things. In 1947 one of his grandest safaris set out for a five-month birding trip to North Africa.[8]

The others flew home but RM stayed behind to shepherd the fauna they had bagged. He stopped off in Cairo (April 18, 1948) and spent some time with Boodie and Rodney "Bill" Searight. These were old friends of RM's. Bill was a director and general manager of the Anglo-Egyptian Oilfields and Shell Refining & Marketing Co. Ltd. In the past he had secured berths for RM aboard oil ships plying the Middle East. Years later, after Boodie and RM had died, Bill was to marry Tess.

After visiting the Searights in Cairo in 1948, RM—and the specimens from his recent safari with Tess and Lord Willy Percy—left Egypt by ship. The ship called in at Haifa.

This 1948 visit to the infant Israel later became quite famous after RM said he had stepped ashore with a borrowed rifle, waded into a firefight between Jews and Arabs, and fought side-by-side with Haganah youths, picking off Arabs at two hundred yards until he exhausted his ammunition in the battle that brought independence to Israel. At the time he was seventy years old and arthritic from old injuries but he made his bullets count. Subsequent legend, still current, insists he proved himself a Zionist hero by fighting on the beaches of the birthing nation.[9]

Yet just a few days later from London he wrote to his friend "Hatter" Bailey, relating how he had witnessed the conflicts in Haifa—witnessed them, not participated in them. He does not mention going ashore at all.[10]

The ship was the *Empress of Scotland*, home-bound out of Alexandria, and the date of her stop at Haifa was April 25, 1948. John Patrick Domvile, an acquaintance of RM, was aboard ship, with a companion named Sharif Saif. Domvile had been identified by the British Consul in Haifa as one who was suspected of breaking the arms embargo—i.e., selling guns to the combatants in the conflict between Arabs and Jews. So he was under surveillance by the Secret Intelligence Service.[11]

Neither the SIS nor J. P. Domvile reported having noticed RM's heroic gunfight in the streets of Haifa. Nor, so far as can be determined, was it witnessed by anyone else aboard the ship or on shore. Nor did any Haganah soldier mention having seen it.

Later that same year, when Tess was confined to an uncertain convalescence after surgery, RM embarked on yet another big birding trek. He went to Arabia and Africa, traveling with ornithologist Philip A. Clancey. Theirs was not to be a happy collaboration.[12]

RM's refrain, "Am terribly distressed about Theresa" or words to that effect, is repeated frequently in his writings of the time. Nevertheless the expedition carried on according to plan. They met Ibn Saud, the King of Saudi Arabia. They bird-watched their way into Somaliland and dined with the governor before trekking on to Nairobi where RM did some work in the Coryndon Museum, met Dr. Louis Leakey, and had nice get-togethers with his nephews Nicholas Wollaston and Peter Meinertzhagen (the latter was then in the Foreign Service). Then RM and the Scotsman Clancey rambled round Mount Kenya and steamed from Mombasa to Zanzibar, Dar es Salaam, Mozambique, and finally Durban (Natal, South Africa), where he and Clancey parted ways. (Clancey lived there.) RM then flew to Cape Town, picked up cars and drivers, and toured the Namib Desert of southwest Africa. He finally left Africa from Johannesburg and returned to England in June 1949 just in time to host his Derby Day bus party.

Around that time he met young David Snow in the British Museum (Natural History). Snow recalls, "I had then no reason to suspect that any of his beautifully made skins were fraudulent." He was welcomed into the Meinertzhagen circle with a standing invitation to drop in at KPG and have lunch whenever he was nearby. Obedient to the gracious invitation, Snow invited himself every now and then. When RM was not in residence, his butler would welcome Snow and make sure the light lunch was to his liking.

Snow was a guest at RM's annual Derby Day parties and birthday parties as well. He found the latter memorable for their "lavish eats and drinks, and [their] ornithological quiz of twenty puzzling specimens of birds, or parts of birds, with a prize for the winner. . . . [The usual] winner was Derek Goodwin, a young assistant at the Bird Room who was the most generally knowledgeable ornithologist, I think, in the world, with an extraordinary memory for detail."[13]

In December 1950 RM embarked for the Persian Gulf in a Shell Tanker, courtesy of his friends the Searights. He was heading to Arabia to complete the research for his latest project.[14]

On this visit, King Aziz ibn Saud ceremoniously made RM the gift of three ostrich eggs from a species that had gone extinct.[15]

Then he flew to meet Harry St. John "Jack" Philby at Jeddah. They were preparing the book *Birds of Arabia*.

Aside from the work of completion he had done in preparing the two volumes of *Nicoll's Birds of Egypt* for publication in 1930, the recent biography of his late son had been RM's first book. He was well and frequently published in ornithological journals, and had provided a number of papers on intelligence and military affairs to branches of the official services, but until now he had never mentioned "being a writer" in the professional sense.

He was in his late sixties—and quite ready to embark on a new career.

The relationship between RM and Harry St. John Philby has drawn little attention from historians or biographers. By 1948 their lively friendship dated back across three decades. It appeared to be a strange pairing: Philby in many ways was RM's opposite. He was a convert to Islam—in Riyadh he was known as Abdullah Philby—and had served as an adviser to Arabia's King Aziz ibn Saud. It was Philby who brokered the arrangement by which the King sold the concession to drill for Arabia's oil to the United States (possibly the most lucrative acquisition in the history of commerce up to that time).[16] Philby was considered an anti-Semite[17] and a rabid anti-Zionist. In arguments about their respective political allegiances, he and RM frequently resorted to loud epithets (usually characterized by adjectives like "stupid" or "idiotic") but most of the time they seem to have kept it on a friend-ribbing-friend plane. And after 1941 Philby may have felt a powerful tug of gratitude toward RM because of the role RM professed to have played in getting him released from political detention at Ascot.

Philby's Arab connections were useful to RM in his birding expeditions. In the spring of 1951 RM was in Jeddah, whence a roving British official sent a message to the Foreign Secretary, informing the minister that Colonel Meinertzhagen, "this courteous and well-informed old gentleman, of about the same age as the King Hafez Saud," had received as a gift from the King three precious fossil eggs from a species of ostrich that is now extinct. The eggs had been found just recently near Rub'el Khali ("The Empty Quarter"), and were of a fair value (both monetary and scientific).[18] Both to the King and to RM, the fossil ostrich eggs were objects of ornithological interest; there was nothing inherently political in them. But the King undoubtedly felt he was making a good impression on a European who could be expected to carry good feelings away with him and report it back to London. (In that he was incorrect; RM in his diaries had a field day sarcastically describing in forensic detail the inedible meals he had been fed.) RM seems to have felt no qualms about traveling in an Arab country, and there is no indication he came back with any reports for British or Israeli Zionists.

He did keep up his alliance with Philby, however.

The publication of *Birds of Arabia* provoked spirited reaction. To some naturalists the book was a breath of fresh air in a library of musty volumes written in deadly scientific prose. To others it was irresponsible in its anecdotal descriptions and in the way it assigned human characteristics to birds.

RM jousted vigorously with his critics but he apparently enjoyed the controversies because he then set out to write the four volumes about his own life that have become the basis for the RM story as most students have known it. These were *Kenya Diary, 1902–1906* (published 1957); *Middle East Diary, 1917–1956* (published 1959); *Army Diary, 1899–1926* (published 1960); and *Diary of a Black Sheep* (published 1964).

As Malcolm Muggeridge suggested, the four books give us an account of the life of Richard Meinertzhagen as he would have liked to have it remembered. When first published, they stirred up a fair amount of interest. For the most part they were well reviewed (especially for the author's courage in confessing his violent misdeeds), and when the prestigious Eland Books reprinted RM's *Kenya Diary* in 1983 it became the top bestseller of all the books Eland had published up to that time. In the meantime his *Birds of Arabia* had been joined by his *Pirates and Predators* (1959) on the shelf of ornithology's must-have books.[19]

Honors came at an accelerating rate. He had served as a vice-president and medalist of the British Ornithologists' Union and as president of the British Ornithologists' Club, and he had been elected to the Council of the Royal Geographical Society; then in 1957 the Queen made him a CBE for his services to science.[20] An Honorary Associate of the British Museum, he received in 1951 the rare (and therefore much prized) Godman Salvin medal of the British Ornithologists' Union.

None of that seems to have been good enough. He told friends, and confided fictitiously to his diaries, that he had refused a knighthood.[21]

Frequently complaining about his health and his age, he nevertheless continued to strike out on arduous expeditions to various corners of the world, some of which still were on hardly any maps.

He kept writing bird books, papers, and introductions. He contributed a laudatory foreword to his friend Jack J. G. Mavrogordato's comprehensive 1960 study of falconry, *A Hawk for the Bush*.[22] And he kept up his ongoing stream of indignant letters to the editors of various newspapers on various topics of irritation.[23]

Always restless, he kept moving and kept trying new ventures. Nicholas Wollaston recalls: "He bought a harpsichord in old age, but he was quite unmusical and his fingers wouldn't work. Possibly he got more fun out of litigation with his neighbours whose dogs annoyed him."[24]

During the same years he pondered the disposition of his lifetime's vast collections of bird skins, plants, insects, and other artifacts. The natural choice was the British Museum (Natural History). But the hot furies of RM's youth did not grow cooler as he aged. He was frequently embroiled in quarrels with the administration of the BMNH. He began to put out feelers to other repositories, among them the Smithsonian in Washington and the American Museum of Natural History in New York—he had friends in high places at both, and much of Lord Walter Rothschild's collection was in the latter. The feelers produced responses that he found very gratifying. One came from Prof. Ernst Mayr, head of the American Ornithologists' Union and bird curator of the American Museum of Natural History. Mayr wrote: "In our eyes you are the dean of British ornithology, and it is you, and only you, who is maintaining in Great Britain the continuity between classical and modern ornithology."[25] It wasn't empty flattery. Several years earlier Ernst Mayr had written:

> The Meinertzhagen collection is by far the finest and largest private collection of birds now in existence anywhere in the world. It consists of some 25,000 to 30,000 specimens, nearly all of them exceptionally fine skins. The collection is particularly rich in material from type localities from all over the world and, specifically, from such inaccessible places as Arabia, Afghanistan, Somaliland, Bechuanaland, as well as parts of Russia that are now closed to us.[26]

In the end, however, perhaps out of guilt (because he had pilfered so many of its birds) or perhaps because of his friendship with Gavin De Beer, RM gave it all to the British Museum (Natural History). The collection was incredible—it included not only the birds described by Mayr but also nearly six hundred thousand specimens of *mallophaga* (bird lice), flies, fleas, and mites, many of them mounted on slides and carefully catalogued by Theresa Clay. The collection also included thousands of plants neatly displayed in herbaria cabinets. As for the birds, they comprised the largest collection known to be in private hands anywhere in the world. They were splendidly prepared, each bearing a neat legible label, arranged in the shallow drawers of cabinets specially made for the purpose.[27]

He formalized the gift of his birds in 1954 but it by no means marked an end to his travels and acquisitions. For several years RM continued to roam the world and send back specimens to the Museum.

He was gaunt, erect, striking, and still fiercely powerful. Young ornithologists, soldiers, and writers—in England, in Europe, in Africa—who met him for the first time found him to be majestic, and were awed.

In the 1950s he continued to visit the Lettows in Germany. He attended ornithological congresses in various capitals. He returned to the Himalayas (in 1951, with Tess and Sálim Ali) and went on a tiger shoot—

they were in Sikkim for RM's seventy-fourth birthday (he complained of bronchitis and a "heart attack"), then back to Calcutta whence Tess flew home to London. RM went off to Beirut ["Beyrouth, Syria"] and tried to cross from there to Israel without success—the Syrians allowed no travelers to cross the frontier. He got back to England in time to throw his Derby Day bus party.

Shortly after his seventy-fifth birthday in March 1953, RM set off to Israel. He was treated like a visiting head of state. The young country's press made a big deal of his visit.

He continued to visit far-flung hosts, and to host his notorious Derby Day parties, until he was past eighty. In 1956 he took himself off to Nairobi, where he met Ewart Grogan and other old cronies. He visited Lake Nakuru to see the flamingos and took note of the regrettable absence of big game on the plateaus. A year later he made another trip to East Africa, this one lasting nearly two months.

But he was fading steadily. In 1957 he managed to attend the Helsinki bird congress. One observer described RM as "gaunt, appeared sad and withdrawn, and kept in the shadows. I tried to question him about the Raza Lark, but he appeared genuinely very deaf, and I do not remember him talking much to anyone . . . and suspect he was living in a fantasy world."[28]

He managed to return to Israel one more time, and in 1959 visited Kenya. After that he shrank into crankiness. "I have been overwhelmed by a six-day law suit with two hours in the witness box which has been most exhausting."[29]

In 1961 he traveled with Theresa to British Guiana and Trinidad.

In 1956 RM's friend David Snow had come to Trinidad to work as Resident Naturalist at the Arima field station for the New York Zoological Services. He recalls that RM and Theresa "went to stay at the Spring Hill estate at the head of the Arima Valley. . . . He called to see William Beebe at Simla, the N. Y. Zoological Services house a few miles down the valley. They had of course both heard of each other, but had never met. I well remember how Beebe greeted him at the door, shook hands, and said in his quavering voice, 'I'm 84,' to which Meinertzhagen replied 'I'm 85.'"

In fact Meinertzhagen was eighty-three that year, but as usual seems to have been compelled to top the other.

David Snow writes further:

Asa Wright, a formidable Icelandic lady, owned the estate and supplemented her income by taking occasional paying guests. (It is now the Asa Wright Nature Center, visited by hundreds of birdwatchers every year.) One of its attractions was that a small colony of birds inhabited a gorge quite close to the house. As it happened, I was making a detailed study of them at the time. He was rather doddering by then, but was keen to get down to see the birds; so with one or two local helpers we got him down the steep path to the mouth of the gorge. He could not possibly have got down the small waterfall into the "cave" itself, where the gorge was roofed over and the birds lived; but he could see the birds and hear their extraordinary calls, and was very pleased.

That night he had a fall. Asa kept two chows [dogs], which slept on the first-floor landing. He had got up in the night, and crossing the landing stumbled over one of the dogs, fell, bruised himself rather badly and cracked a rib. They cut their visit short; Theresa took him back to London a day or two later. . . . The visit to the seabirds was the last of his field trips.[30]

The fall in Trinidad cracked his hip, broke a rib, and injured his back. The great heroic body no longer would do his bidding. He was all but immobilized for the rest of his life.[31] The year after the crippling tumble, RM wrote to Derek Goodwin: "I apologize for bothering you but my age and inactivity prevent my doing it [picking up four bird specimens at the BMNH]."[32]

He managed to pull himself together enough to attend the Oxford International Bird Congress in July 1966, in a wheelchair, but for much of the time in his final years RM became increasingly housebound. He seems to have remained intermittently lucid (though increasingly deaf). Tess managed virtually all aspects of his life, and kept strangers at bay; by then he had become moderately famous, but she allowed few outsiders to question him. The last face-to-face interview occurred in the spring of 1967, when RM had just entered his ninetieth year; journalist Colin Rickards visited 17 KPG to interview him for an article and found RM to be fully in command of his memories—or fictions—on the topic of Rickards' article (the Legion of Frontiersmen in East Africa in 1916–1917).[33]

At least for visitors like Rickards, RM was able to keep up appearances, but he was bedridden most of the time.

On June 17, 1967, having outlived Winston Churchill by two years, Richard Meinertzhagen died. Twelve days later a memorial service for him was held at St. Sepulchre's, Holborn. It was attended by his family and friends—an honor roll of political, financial, and social leaders.[34]

♪ ♪ ♪

Theresa Clay[35] continued to live in Kensington Park Gardens, even after her marriage in 1974 to the widowed Rodney G. "Bill" Searight, who had retired from the oil business. Bill Searight had spent much of his life in the Middle East and had become an important collector of Middle East watercolors.[36] He died in 1991, leaving an estate estimated at one million pounds sterling to his widow.

Theresa Clay Searight died at Brecon House Nursing Home in Sherborne, Dorset on March 17, 1995.

♪ ♪ ♪

Like falling dominos the beneficiaries of RM's assistance have been used in turn as reliable sources by subsequent historians and essayists. To whatever extent they relied on RM as a basis, they all are open to challenge. This is not merely a matter of correcting the personal record with regard to whether RM did or did not serve in a high position in World War II intelligence, or drop a haversack or slaughter a house full of Red spies in Spain. The major historical events remain unchanged: the battles still took place, the wars and their outcomes occurred, Bolshevism rose and fell. But their causes and/or results may have been misreported. Thus, for example, historians who relied on RM's accusations of incompetence among British generals in East Africa ought to be reconsidered (were the failures caused by the Intelligence officer rather than the commanding generals?). And those who have relied on the accuracy of RM's *obiter dicta* to explain Britain's flaws in administering the Palestine Mandate may not know that RM's obnoxious behavior on Zionism's behalf may have done more harm than was done by the anti-Semitic "hebraphobia" he complained was rampant in Whitehall. At the same time he clearly misled the Zionist leadership, as he has misled posterity, into believing his assertions that he argued Zionism's case vigorously with Hitler during several meetings in the 1930s.

Some would like to believe the only thing standing between Chaim Weizmann's loyalists and their eviction from Palestine was the heroic, lonely Richard Meinertzhagen. In fact, however, a part of what the radical Zionists saw as a betrayal on the part of the British government was the result not only of two-faced official policy or intentional double-dealing, but also of the deceit with which RM glossed over his own failures to act. He did not sell out his Zionist friends to the Hitler gang, but when he claimed to have tried to intercede on Zionism's behalf while actually he had done little or nothing, his inaction may have produced results that were just as calamitous for the

Jews of Europe (and for Weizmann) as those that might have been caused by an actual Nazi spy in Zionism's ranks. Fortunately the Zionists did not put all their eggs in the Meinertzhagen basket; nevertheless they were unknowingly injured by his failures.

Those of his intelligence reports that were filed on their actual dates, and many of his letters, can be confirmed because of their immediacy, their context, and their later inaccessibility to an author who otherwise might have been motivated to make changes after the fact.

When those real primary documents are combined with independent sources and weighed against RM's claims—only then does systematic comparison become possible. Sometimes the comparison is useful even when the primary source is filled with lies, like RM's statement to Ernst Mayr that he could have assassinated Hitler with a rifle from his hotel window.

Such comparisons tell stories quite different from the ones that RM told, and the ones in the histories are based on the latter.

Scientists must work from the same premise as historians. When a person has been caught repeatedly telling lies, nothing said by that person can be trusted until and unless it has been verified by evidence wholly independent of the person. On the basis of what is now known about RM, without confirmation from other sources we cannot fully accept *any* of his statements.

RM's legend is a cautionary lesson for an age in which the willingness to accept a good story tends to trump the need for truth. The most fertile soil for lies is gullibility. Even the sophisticated can be gullible—RM's lies at first were sewn not amongst the naive but amongst those who ought to have known better. These were the powerful, to whom position was all-important.

The legends were allowed to become currency by people to whom he was "one of us." They themselves often may not have taken him too seriously—"Oh never mind, that's just Dick"—but they kept this private knowledge within the circle while they made no effort to disabuse outsiders (reporters, scientists, biographers, and historians both popular and academic) who unquestioningly accepted even the most outrageous chapters of the RM mythology.

Some challenged it; most did not. Some of his peers were amused by the way he pulled the wool over so many eyes. But their amusement came at the expense of science and of historical accuracy, and sometimes the expense turned out to be huge.

It all seems to offer an object lesson for an age when mainstream journalism has become the province of tabloid sensation-mongers ("If it bleeds it leads"). The RM investigation also offers important cautions to those who would erect monuments or name landmarks in honor of self-promoters, and to those who would believe the accepted legends of heroes and faiths simply because these litanies have been repeated often enough.

In short, while "history" should provoke neither automatic denial nor cynicism, it ought to be greeted with a grain of skepticism and, when questions arise or plausibility seems dim, it should be subjected to verifiable tests before it is broadcast.

Women usually saw through him. Men usually did not. What does that signify?

Why did he do it? And why did so many influential people cooperate with him in the cover-ups?

The compulsions that seem to have driven RM are, in their way, more fascinating than the adventures he pretended to have lived. His achievements were genuine, but somehow he was obsessed with gilding each lily in ornate filigree so byzantine and heavy that it suffocated the flower within.

One must stand in awe before the solipsism of a man who persisted in spinning yarns about himself that seem designed to bring down on him the scorn of both those who disbelieved—because to them he was a liar—and of those who believed—because to them he was a vicious killer.

The nature of his derangement is unclear. He was one of ten siblings, and none of the other nine displayed traits similar to his. He was given much, and forgiven much. Yet sometimes he behaved as if he were a visitor from a parallel universe. He seemed unable to tell the difference between the mirage and the oasis.

Part heroic and part mischievous, he seems to have been compelled to find out just how much he could get away with.

One of my colleagues quipped that RM had as many personalities as a psycho ward.

Was he delusional? Or was he toying with us?

It is all too easy to be "had"—this is a common failing among most of us, probably a genetic trait that helps define the nature of our species. In order to be curious (our most rewarding, productive, and troublemaking characteristic) it seems we also must be trustful, sometimes to the point of total gullibility. Richard Meinertzhagen was a man who seems to have understood these notes instinctively, and who became a virtuoso on their instrument.

The roots of a person's behavior are myriad. Motivations lie beneath the level of consciousness. The same causes will lead to different effects in different individuals. We may see the record of a person's actions and reactions, but we may not know what provoked the reactions. Given our present limited knowledge of the workings of the human mind, any attempt to subject it to logical analysis is a minefield: therapists find it difficult to comprehend the pathology of a living patient who sits face-to-face with them and reacts to the therapist's skilled questioning—so how can we expect to reach a definition in the case of RM, who cannot answer questions and who left us with no record of his childhood except his own colorized version of it? (The occasional insight that shows up in his writings—about the death of his brother Dan, for example—appears to be an afterthought; none of these passages seems spontaneous—they feel as if they've been written shortly after he happened to read an article about psychology in the *Times*.)

Judged on his behavior, he seems to exhibit a syndrome for which there is a technical name. His grandiosity of fantasy and behavior, his abnormal need for admiration, and his routine lack of empathy appear to conform to the textbook definition of Malignant Narcissistic Personality Disorder (a term that didn't exist, for a pattern of behavior that had not been classified, during his lifetime).[37] But giving it a name merely assigns it to a category. It does not explain RM's pathology.

One tries to approach history with the discipline of a scientist—observe the evidence, induce a conclusion that fits the evidence, then test the conclusion against every possible measure to see if its validity holds up and if it fits all the available evidence. But the biographical historian cannot know all the variables and therefore cannot be an exact scientist. He can see only partial indirect reflections. He gathers as many facts as he can and tries to understand them in the context of influences upon, and prejudices of, those who have provided them. If he does his job properly he can reasonably induce a good deal more than the bare data. The argument for such extrapolation may be regarded with skepticism, but it also may be regarded as analogous to the case of a paleontologist who excavates scattered bits of fossil bone and—given not only the structure of the bones but also the context of the find—provides information about the animal and about the period in which it lived. The paleontologist may be looking at a few bone fragments but what he can see is the whole animal and its world.

That does not seem to be the case here. The bone is visible; the creature remains a mystery. In the end I can only join the scientists who know that sometimes we can observe phenomena without being able to explain them.

From a sociological angle the Meinertzhagen story makes for a fascinating study of ruling-class dynamics. From a psychiatric angle it makes for an eye-popping case study in narcissistic pathology. From a historical angle it's humbling: we thought we knew things, but what—and whom—can we trust?

Richard Meinertzhagen was a man of many contradictions. To me he remains utterly fascinating and often inexplicable. To some extent, perhaps the latter contributes to the former. He was a mystery, and that is where we must let him rest.

What remains to be said is what one of his well-known in-laws, Malcolm Muggeridge, wrote about RM in 1971:

> Anyone who knew Richard Meinertzhagen (as I did; he was a connection of mine by marriage) realised that even more than most of us he was two people. There was a fantasist full of tall stories which varied in the telling and were often, to me, totally incredible, though all calculated to make him appear a man of stupendous courage, resourcefulness, and ruthlessness. There was also a reflective, highly intelligent melancholic who turned on the world a somewhat sombre eye, and derived considerable satisfaction from disconcerting others, particularly his nearest and dearest, with the savagery of his ironical reflections and observations.
>
> I found the former a tiresome bore, and the latter an entertaining and sympathetic companion.
>
> . . . [RM was] the sour sage of Kensington Park Gardens. [His tales of his own adventures] would strain the credulity of schoolboy readers of Henty and Haggard. . . .
>
> [Of note to the biographer were] Meinertzhagen's own copious diaries, which I remember well because, in elegant leather bindings, they adorned the walls of his study. If they were referred to, he would glance at them with a complacent smile, giving me the feeling that they would prove to be a monument to his fantasy self. I gather from Mr. Lord's narrative that before Meinertzhagen died they were revised, some portions destroyed and others re-written. In any case, the final text represented, presumably, Meinertzhagen's definitive account of his own life.
>
> . . . His obsessive belief that his mother hated him has gone into an autobiographical volume of his own, characteristically entitled "*Diary of a Black Sheep*," but no attempt is made to investigate the validity of this from other sources. One would like, in a biography, to know more about it than just Meinertzhagen's own bald statements and highly coloured anecdotes.

... [More unlikely than] these African adventures, more even than Meinertzhagen's interviews with Hitler, at one of which he says he kept a revolver hidden in his coat with the possibility (untaken) of knocking off both the Führer and Ribbentrop, is the project he was engaged in with T. E. Lawrence for the unification of all British political and military intelligence services in a single directorate, spinning into one strand the organisations of the Foreign Office, the War Office, the Air Ministry, and Scotland Yard. Anyone familiar with the ferocious internecine strife between these bodies at the height of the 1939–1945 war will marvel indeed at Mr. Lord's statement that, when Lawrence died, their plan was worked out, and they were just applying to the Treasury for funds.

... I shall go on thinking of Meinertzhagen as he was on the last two times I saw him. The first, in the large lounge of an ultra-respectable Tunbridge Wells hotel where he used to stay each summer when his housekeeper was away. There he sat, wrapped in an Abyssinian blanket (given him—need I say it?—by Haile Selassie in return for some hair-raising service), glowering at the other blameless hotel residents. He continued to berate them as we contentedly munched our cucumber sandwiches and toasted tea scones together. The second occasion was on his death-bed. His beard had grown long and luxuriant, and he looked like a strange old patriarch. According to his sister Beatrice, who was also present, he had been blessed with beatific visions. I sincerely hope it was so, but she had some difficulty in inducing him to acknowledge them. Rather, his mind seemed to be turning on difficulties which had arisen over holding his funeral service in the church in which he had been christened, it having been turned over to the Russian Orthodox rite. All he wanted, it seemed, was an assurance that "Home Sweet Home" would be included in the service. This was not forthcoming. Shortly afterwards he died.[38]

GLOSSARY

BMNH: Files of the British Museum of Natural History in London.

CHAR: Files of the Churchill Archives Centre in Churchill College at Cambridge University.

HL: Files of the Hartley Library, University of Southampton, Highfield, Southampton.

IOL: Files of the India Office Library (96 Euston Road, London).

IWM: Files of the Imperial War Museum in London.

LHC: Files of the Liddell-Hart Centre for Military Archives, King's College London.

PRO: Records of the [British] National Archives housed in the Public Records Office at Kew, Richmond, London.

RM: Richard Meinertzhagen.

RMD: Typescript diaries of RM at Rhodes House (the Bodleian), Oxford.

NOTES

PREFACE

1. British members of the family pronounce the name "MINE-ert-ZAHG-'n." Meinertzhagen Square is in Jerusalem southwest of Mount Scopus at the intersection of Shalom Road, Nablus Road, Levi Eshkol Boulevard, and Hebrew University Boulevard. Meinertzhagen Square was dedicated in 1997 just a few months after Richard Meinertzhagen's life and adventures had been the subject of a Tel Aviv University conference.

2. *The Lighthorsemen*, written by Ian Jones, directed by Simon Wincer (1987: RKO Pictures). This action movie featured Anthony Andrews as Richard Meinertzhagen—dashing, brilliant, all-knowing. The RM legend seems to persist even more stubbornly in Israel than in Britain—see for example Jay M. Shapiro's book *The Colonel's Team* (Ginot Shomron, Israel: Palphot, Ltd., 2002).

3. The United States Central Intelligence Agency: *The Meinertzhagen Haversack Ruse* (Washington, D.C.: Mathtech Inc. and Everest Consulting Associates, 1981). Only two copies are known to exist in libraries—in the National Imagery and Mapping Center Library, and the CIA library, both in the Washington area. The 110-page book includes various illustrations and maps. The book's author is unidentified but may have been Lt. Cdr. Andrew W. Eddowes, USN, who is also the author of *The Haversack Ruse and British Deception Operations in Palestine during World War I* (Newport, RI: Naval War College, 1994).

4. Andrew Lycett, *Ian Fleming: The Man behind James Bond* (London: Orion Books, 1996), 438; and Michael Occleshaw, *The Romanov Conspiracies* (London: Orion Books, 1994), 179, referring to Buchan's adventure novels *The House of Four Winds* and *Hunting Towers*.

5. Rex Dalton, "Ornithologists Stunned by Bird Collector's Deceit," *Nature*, 437 (15 September 2005): 302–303. A flurry of news articles appeared around the same time; see for example Tom Spears, "The Phony Bird Collector," *Ottawa Citizen*, October 3, 2005. An AP wire-service story datelined Washington, D.C., appeared on September 7, 2005, with the title "Mystery Bird." Finally the balloon went up entirely with publication of Pamela Rasmussen's two-volume *A Guide to the Birds of South Asia: The Ripley Guide* (Washington, D.C.: Lynx Edicions/Smithsonian Institution, 2006) and John Seabrook's "Ruffled Feathers: Uncovering the Biggest Scandal in the Bird World" (*New Yorker*, May 29,

2006, 50–61). It should be noted that the museum in question has changed its name and location a few times. Officially it is now "The Natural History Museum," in Cromwell Road, South Kensington, London; in Meinertzhagen's lifetime it was "The British Museum (Natural History)," and to this day is called the "BMNH." Some years after Meinertzhagen's death, the ornithological collections were moved from London to the bird museum at Tring. His birds can be found there, but the documents used for this book's inquiries are in the library of the Cromwell Road building in London.

CHAPTER 1: LEGEND

1. As Oscar Wilde observed (in "A Woman of No Importance," 1893, Act III), "A man who can dominate a London dinner table can dominate the world." The anecdote about Richard Meinertzhagen and the smoking revolver, with minor variations, is attested to by several sources independent of one another. One version is reported in Mark Cocker's *Richard Meinertzhagen: Soldier, Scientist, Spy* (London: Secker & Warburg, 1989), 276, Note 22. In another account, the woman who agreed to hold the handgun said she had popped its cylinder open and seen that one cartridge had been fired (telephone interview by the author with Dame Miriam Rothschild, 17 April 2003). Lionel Jackson—well-known cricketer, friend of E. M. Forster—recounted the same "revolver ploy," which he said took place in his own house; context suggests this most probably was in the 1940s. It was reported by Nicholas Meinertzhagen in an interview with the author and Mark Cocker on 27 June 2003. With regard to his great-uncle and the smoking revolver, Nick added, "Whether he'd shot somebody or not I don't know."

2. Alan Knox, "Richard Meinertzhagen: A Case of Fraud Examined," *Ibis*, 135 (1993): 320–35; and Gail Vines, "Bird world in a flap about species fraud," *New Scientist*, 142, no. 142 (7 May 1994): 10.

3. Nigel Collar, Letter to author, 19 February 2002. Knox's and Vines's articles were not the first, but they were noticed. After them came quite a few, including Paul Recer, "Researchers Uncover Scientific Fraud," *Washington Post*, December 28, 1997, A03; Robert P. Prys-Jones and Pamela C. Rasmussen, "RM and Fraud: Removing the Mystery from a Flawed Collection," in *Proceedings of the 22nd International Ornithological Congress*, N. J. Adams and R. H. Slotow, eds. (Durban), 1998; Pamela C. Rasmussen and Nigel J. Collar, "Major specimen fraud in the Forest Owlet Heteroglaux," *Ibis* (Jan. 1999): 11–21; Scott Weidensaul, *The Ghost with Trembling Wings: Science, Wishful Thinking, and the Search for Lost Species* (New York: North Point Press, 2002); "Indian Owl, Considered Extinct, is Captured on Film by Americans," *New York Times*, January 6, 1998, 6; and Graciela Flores, "Impact of Bird Fraud Unclear," *The Scientist*, October 17, 2005.

4. Rex Dalton, "Ornithologists Stunned by Bird Collector's Deceit," 302–303.

5. The author has had exceptional assistance from several historians, investigators, researchers, ornithologists, intelligence agents, and fellow writers; without their contributions this book could not have been completed. I'm profoundly grateful to them. They, and their areas of expertise, are identified in the acknowledgments.

6. "Memorandum by Col. R. Meinertzhagen for Brigadier General, General Staff, GHQI, 23 October 1918: *The Security Section,*" PRO file AIR 1/1155. It is reproduced, in full, in John Ferris's book *The British Army and Signals Intelligence during the First World War* (Avon, UK: The Bath Press/Alan Sutton Publishing Ltd., for the Army Records Society, 1991). Ferris calls its author "the leading practitioner of deception during the First World War, Colonel Meinertzhagen."

7. Peter Capstick's *Warrior: The Legend of Colonel Richard Meinertzhagen, 1878–1967* (New York: St. Martin's Press, 1997) relates many cloak-and-dagger deeds that were easily disprovable by the time Capstick wrote that one, his last book. Michael Occleshaw's *Armour Against Fate: British Military Intelligence in the First World War and the Secret Rescue from Russia of the Grand Duchess Tatiana* (London: Columbus Books, 1989) is in large part about a purported heroic adventure led by Richard Meinertzhagen. Occleshaw adds further accounts of Meinertzhagen's undercover anti-Soviet exploits in *The Romanov Conspiracies* (London: Orion Paperbacks, 1994). Occleshaw maintains his faith in Meinertzhagen's authenticity. Occleshaw writes (letter to author, 10 February 2005): "Meinertzhagen was subjected to fierce criticism in 1994 over the alleged theft of bird skins and for claiming to have sighted birds in places where he had supposedly never been. . . . [but] whenever a credible new 'breakthrough' in the Romanov case appears, there is a systematic move to discredit it or the source upon which it is based. . . . The attempted character assassination of Meinertzhagen was started shortly before the publication of the paperback version [of my book *The Romanov Conspiracies*]." I don't know if it is sufficient comfort to Occleshaw to know that my work here is not an attempt to assassinate Meinertzhagen's character but an attempt to understand it. I suppose this book is in the nature of an autopsy. It is not written to settle scores or to right personal wrongs. It is an examination of a life that was lived and then revised and then believed.

8. For the sake of most readers who do not have convenient access to the tens of thousands of pages in the seventy-plus volumes of typescript diaries secured at Oxford ("RMD"), wherever possible the source for information from Meinertzhagen's diaries is cited from the *published* account in which it appears— usually one of his four "Diary" books: *Army Diary, 1899–1926* (London and Edinburgh: Oliver & Boyd, 1960); *Diary of a Black Sheep* (London: Oliver & Boyd, 1964); *Kenya Diary, 1902–1906* (Edinburgh: Oliver & Boyd, 1957); and *Middle East Diary, 1917–1956* (London: Cresset Press, 1959; New York: Thomas Yoseloff, 1960). The typescripts are cited only on those occasions when their information does not appear in the published works, or when the two differ widely.

9. According to Nicholas Meinertzhagen (interview on 27 June 2003), Richard actually concocted such a phony family tree, on paper.

10. Meinertzhagen's fiction of his alleged Danish family tree appears at the very beginning of his *Middle East Diary*.

11. David Lloyd George, *War Memoirs* (London: Odhams Press Ltd., 1937) 2:1923.

12. Meinertzhagen later claimed to have met several times with Lloyd George; he implies they were virtually on a first-name basis. More likely they met only once.

13. Richard Meinertzhagen, *Middle East Diary*, 159–160.

14. All these words of accusation appear in a single letter to the editor written by Richard Meinertzhagen in 1939—and it is only nine lines long. [*Ibis*, Fourteenth Series, 3, no. 4 (October 1939): 797–798.]
15. Generalmajor Paul E. von Lettow-Vorbeck, *Mein Leben* (Biberach an der Riss: Koehlers Verlagsgesellschaft, 1957).

CHAPTER 2: HAVERSACK

1. Miriam Rothschild, letter to author, 3 March 2002.
2. His maps were first-rate, but RM's legend does not include his map work. A few of his battlefront maps from the Gaza campaign are tipped into his *Army Diary*. Others can be found in PRO file WO 95/4472.
3. David Lloyd George's demand of Allenby—"Jerusalem. By Christmas."— is reported in the former's book *War Memoirs*, 2:1923.
4. Allenby's interest in bird-watching was typical of military men serving in remote lands. On the Gaza front he had little time for it. The joint Allenby–RM enthusiasm for birds seems to have been limited to rare occasions when there was time to go out and look. A mythology about Allenby's and RM's longtime bonding through birding is spread through the biographies and many of the articles about his service in the Middle East—see for example Tom Segev, *One Palestine, Complete: Jews and Arabs Under the British Mandate* (New York: Metropolitan Books, 2000), 23—but is not supported by tangible evidence.
5. Sir Maurice Wyndham Portal (Viscount of Laverstoke) served with British Military Intelligence in Palestine in 1917. Lord William Percy was an acknowledged expert on ducks, who later became author of *Three Studies in Bird Character* (London: Country Life, 1951).
6. In informal use the terms "cavalry" and "light horse" (or "mounted infantry") seem interchangeable, but there are distinctions. Cavalry troopers carry heavy sabers and saddle-scabbard rifles or carbines. Except when battle is imminent they usually carry their own bedding and provisions tied to their saddles. They are fully equipped not only for fighting but also for travel, and are trained to fight on horseback, with emphasis as much on slashing sabers as on rifles. In contrast, light horsemen (or mounted infantry) carry no swords or scabbards. Their equipment is spartan. They wear rifles strapped across their backs. Their horses carry them at speed to the enemy, where the soldiers usually dismount and fight on foot.
7. T. E. Lawrence, *Seven Pillars of Wisdom* (1926; repr., New York: Anchor Books, Random House, 1991). It is important to note that Lawrence was not at headquarters during the time when RM supposedly was hatching his plans with Allenby; at the time of these events Lawrence was in the desert with Arab guerrillas.

  Maj. Gen. Louis Jean Bols, English son of a Belgian diplomat, was Allenby's Chief-of-Staff. Brig. Gen. Guy Dawnay was one of several "intelligence chiefs" on Allenby's staff. The theater's formal hierarchy was vague, as Cairo crawled with overlapping intelligence agencies that operated under authority of the India Office, the Suez Canal directorate, the Egyptian Expeditionary Force, the Middle East Expeditionary Force, the Arab Bureau, and other entities.
8. RM, *Army Diary*, 283–284.

9. RM, *Army Diary*, 284.
10. Maj. Gen. Baron Friedrich Anton Carl Freiherr Kress von Kressenstein (1879–1948), a Bavarian, was ambitious and strict. He won the Blue Max for his successful defenses of Gaza 1 and 2, and was regarded as a brilliant and inspirational leader by historians, including Cyril Falls and Liddell-Hart. Some students of military history feel his career was built on unimaginative exercises in brute force, and imaginative excuses in passing the blame for disasters like his failure to take Suez in 1916 and his loss of Beersheba in 1917. He blamed both on weaknesses in the Turkish armies. (He may have been unique in accusing the feared Turks of being weak.)
11. Kress von Kressenstein, *Mit den Tuerken zum Suezkanal* (Berlin: Otto Schlagel, 1936), 268–269.
12. For details of the run-up to the Third Battle of Gaza, see entries of 15–22 October 1917 in PRO file WO 95/4472.
13. The charge at Beersheba was re-enacted by some of its original participants in the 1941 Australian film *40,000 Horsemen*, which can be found in various video formats. The movie as a whole is dreadful but the climactic action sequence is accurate and stunning.
14. Since Light Horsemen technically are not cavalry, one hesitates to qualify the charge at Beersheba in that category. Anyway it was not the last mounted charge in history: subsequent cavalry actions took place during the Russian Civil War, several Latin American revolutions, the Japanese invasion of China in the 1930s, the Spanish Civil War, World War II on the Eastern Front, and other twentieth century conflicts in places to which modern technology had not yet spread.
15. Among many readable and well researched accounts of these actions is David L. Bullock's *Allenby's War: The Palestine-Arabian Campaigns, 1916–1918* (Poole, Dorset, UK: Blandford Press, 1988). A most interesting contrarian view can be found in Matthew Hughes's *Allenby and British Strategy in the Middle East, 1917–1919* (London, UK, and Portland, OR: Frank Cass Publishers, 1999).
16. Cyril Falls, *Military Operations—Egypt & Palestine from June 1917 to the End of the War*, vol. 2, part I, (London: H. M. Stationery Office, 1930; Nashville, TN: The Battery Press, 1996), 62 (footnote). Falls's citation of Hussein Husni's comment refers to the book *Yildirim* (Istanbul: Remzi Kitabevi Press, 1920), in Turkish, by Lt. Col. Hussein Husni Emir Bey, Chief of Operations for the Turko-German forces at Gaza.
17. RM, *Army Diary*, 283–286.
18. When a lie is reported as fact in the accepted standard texts, it may be too late to correct some of its damage. See for example Sir Martin Gilbert's *The First World War: A Complete History* (New York: Henry Holt & Co., 1994), 370, or Randall Gray's *Chronicle of the First World War*, vol. 2 (Oxford: Facts on File, 1991), 94. For the legend's ongoing persistence see, among others, Harold E. Raugh, Jr., "Intelligence," *Military Heritage*, April 2001: 18–23—a lengthy article under the subtitle "Meinertzhagen's haversack ruse helped break the stalemate at Gaza and led to the capture of Jerusalem." All the RM myths are firmly in place. At the time he wrote his article it hadn't occurred to Raugh (an experienced and respectable military historian) to question the exploit. Like the rest of us, he was inclined to take the word of an officer and a gentleman at face value.

19. Sir Philip Walhouse Chetwode (later Baron Field Marshal Chetwode) was by all accounts a brilliant tactician.

20. PRO file WO 158/611/69. See also Papers of Gen. Sir William Henry Bartholomew, GCB, CMG, DSO (1877–1962)—"Papers relating to Bartholomew's service as Brig. Gen., General Staff, 20 Corps, in Palestine, including material concerning planning prior to the Third Battle of Gaza, 1917–1922," in the LHC, reference code GB99 KCLMA Bartholomew. On June 17, 1917, Allenby's Chief-of-Staff, Guy Dawnay, sent a memorandum to Chetwode in which he concurred with Chetwode's proposals and added his authority to the idea of attacking the enemy in strength at Beersheba rather than Gaza, while making use of manifold deceptions. On June 21 Chetwode gave Allenby his formal memorandum—it followed up on Dawnay's recommended surprise attack on the enemy's left flank at Beersheba. RM's name is not mentioned in either memo; they preceded his involvement. All the documents show that the haversack ruse and an accompanying strategy of deceptions were in place before RM was informed of them.

21. RM, *Army Diary*, 219. Allenby's urgent requests for additional forces—in an increasingly strident series of "SECRET" ciphers to London's Chief of the Imperial General Staff (CIGS)—were scams. Allenby knew no forces could be spared from the Western Front. His requisitions for reinforcement were meant to be intercepted and deciphered. They were part of the overall scheme to deceive the enemy. Obviously they also deceived RM.

22. Several exchanges between Allenby and CIGS's "Wully" Robertson, bundled in the 40388 cipher (which, Allenby knew, the Germans and Turks had broken), mentioned (nonexistent) plots for a French invasion on the coast north of Gaza and other ruses; other exchanges contained Allenby's requests for additional forces and Robertson's regretful refusals. These are in PRO file WO 106/724. The content of these signals is very different from that in the genuinely secure messages (in the same file) that were transmitted on the new undersea cable that had just gone into service by way of Cyprus. The latter show that GHQ knew that its 40388 cipher had been compromised by a theft in Cairo. They knew the Germans could read it; they used that knowledge.

23. RM, *Army Diary*, 223.

24. Lt. Gen. Sir George Mark Watson Macdonough (1865–1945) had served on the General Staff in France in command of field intelligence from 1914 to 1916, when he was brought back to the War Office to become Director of Military Intelligence. He had taken charge on January 3, 1916, shortly before RM reported for duty in his office.

25. Weizmann, four years older than RM, was born in Russia, earned a Ph.D. in chemistry, moved to England, and in 1904 became a senior lecturer at the University of Manchester. In 1906 he convinced Lord Balfour, the former Prime Minister (later author of the Balfour Declaration and a close friend of Lord Walter Rothschild) that a Jewish national home should be founded in Palestine. In 1910 Weizmann was naturalized as a British subject. His knowledge of both chemistry and industry proved vital to the British war effort when he solved an acute ammunition shortage by devising a method of isolating organisms found in horse chestnuts and cereals, and converting them into a form of acetone (a primary ingredient in artillery gunpowder). He showed the government how it could make use of existing breweries to manufacture the synthetic acetone—a step that

saved the military many months of construction. Weizmann's contribution allowed the Royal Navy and the Allied armies to keep their artillery supplied with
shells. See Chaim Weizmann, *Trial and Error: The Autobiography of Chaim
Weizmann, First President of Israel* (New York: Harper & Brothers, 1949).

26. Recently released documents pertaining to MI-7 and its operations can be found
in "History of M.I. 7(b) March, 1916–December, 1918,"—in PRO file INF 4/1B.
The section's work included censorship and propaganda.

27. RM's rank was Major until March 6, 1918, when he was promoted—temporarily—to brevet lieutenant colonel. After that, on GHQ Staff in France, he was
given another field promotion, this final one to temporary (full) colonel. But he
was a major when he resigned from the Army in 1925. See *The Army List* (London: H. M. Stationery Office, 1925 edition), 195. Upon retirement, officers routinely are granted title and pension commensurate with the highest rank they
held on active duty. Hence RM had the right during the rest of his life to bill
himself as "Colonel."

28. The formerly SECRET file "Military Press Control: A History of the Work of
M.I. 7, 1914–1919" is now accessible in PRO file KV 4/183. Farceurs and conspiracy buffs have applied the designation MI-7 (aka M.I.-7 or M.I.7 or MI7) to
everything from Monty Python-esque parodies to presumably serious descriptions of sinister government sections that allegedly conceal and deny purported
UFO sightings. In fact MI-7 did exist, briefly, on two occasions. Its operations
were earnest but prosaic. The first MI-7 office was shut down shortly after the
end of the Great War; some of its operations continued into the 1920s within
the shrunken MI-5 and MI-6 departments. MI-7 was revived in 1939, on the
eve of World War II, and when RM was recalled to active duty he was assigned
to a desk in that department.

29. Lt. Col. James Dacres Belgrave was born on September 27, 1896, in Kensington,
son of an Old Bailey barrister. He was commissioned in the Oxford-and-
Buckinghamshire Light Infantry in 1914. In July 1917 he was made a lieutenant colonel and assigned as GSOi (General Staff Officer, Intelligence) to Allenby's
Egyptian Expeditionary Force. (PRO file WO 339/23620.)

30. PRO file WO 95/4368. All this, as well as notes for several other ruses, can be
found in "Operations notes from GHQ EEF GSO," which include a "Memorandum from Lt. Col. J. D. Belgrave to Commanding General, EEF" and endorse-
ments of Belgrave's proposals, including Allenby's approval.

31. *Yildirim*, the memoir of Lt. Col. Hussein Husni Emir Bey (aka Hüsseyin Hüsnü
Emir), was published in Istanbul in 1920 by Remzi Kitabevi Press as an Ottoman text in the old form of Arabic script. A subsequent reissue was published
in the modern Latin alphabet (but still in Turkish), which may account for inconsistencies in translations. *Yildirim* was published contemporaneously with
The Secret Corps by journalist Ferdinand Tuohy, who had been one of RM's
fellow Gaza intelligence officers. Tuohy's chapter "The Lost Haversack" does
not mention RM by name but it does describe the ride, the feigned injury, the
dropped haversack, the escape of the heroic "staff officer," and the alleged
effect of the false documents on Turko-German high command. See Ferdinand
Tuohy, *The Secret Corps: A Tale of "Intelligence" on All Fronts* (London: John
Murray, Ltd., 1920), 283–285.

32. Kressenstein's 1938 book refers to RM as Allenby's Chief of Intelligence. Obviously he obtained that whopper directly or indirectly from RM—it has no other

primary source. By the time Kressenstein wrote the book, RM had indeed served as Allenby's political officer in the Middle East (*after* the war, and not in Intelligence). Later he slid the record backwards by two years so as to pose for civilians as having been Allenby's wartime chief of intelligence. By the late 1920s this inaccuracy had become a "truth" regarded by RM's club-mates (including historians and members of the press) as self-evident.

33. Hussein Husni Emir, *Yildirim*, 112–114.
34. von Kressenstein, *Mit den Tuerken zum Suezkanal*, 268–271, specifies that a bag belonging to British Chief-of-Intelligence Meinertzhagen had been dropped during a skirmish between cavalry patrols. This clearly came from RM, because (a) earlier versions on the German/Turkish side had identified the officer as "Weinertshagen" or variants thereof, and (b) none of the earlier Turkish or German accounts promoted RM to the office of Chief-of-Intelligence to Allenby. Kressenstein obtained neither the correct spelling nor the incorrect office from the Turks. It leads straight back to RM.

   Several Turkish history books describe the episode. One insists Kressenstein believed the papers were meant to fool him: Fahri Belen's *Ottoman Empire in the Twentieth Century* (Istanbul: Remzi Kitabevi, 1973), 334. An opposite theory appears in the quasi-official history, Birinci Dunya's *Harbi'nde Turk Harbi Sina-Filistin Cephesi* (The Turkish War in the First World War, the Sinai-Palestine Front) (Ankara: Genelkurmay Basimevi, 1986), 155–156; it maintains the Turkish commanders disbelieved the documents and wanted to reinforce Beersheba but Kressenstein overruled them. Yet another opinion is expressed in Yusuf Hikmet Bayur's *Turk Inkilabi Tarihi* (History of Turkish Revolution), vol. 3: *1915–1917* (Ankara: TTK—the Turkish History Foundation, 1957), 456; this one reports that an automobile dropped or left or forgot a bag near a Turkish camp; that the bag contained war plans for an assault on Gaza that was to be masked by a feigned attack at Beersheba; and that Kressenstein transferred significant bodies of troops to the Gaza area because he believed the English documents were genuine.

   Unlike those versions, Kressenstein's account conforms with what actually happened (if we discount its promotion of RM). The Turks and Germans around Gaza and Beersheba were not stampeded into rushing hordes of troops in either direction. The orders of one or two minor elements were changed a day or two prior to the attack, but that may have occurred for any of several reasons and did not materially affect the effectiveness (or lack thereof) of their defenses.

35. The British failed to mention the ruse in their early post-campaign trumpeting. The ink was still wet on the Turkish surrender when the first "official" record of the campaign—containing no haversack ruse—appeared over the by-line of General Sir Edmund H. H. Allenby himself. It is *A Brief Record of the Advance of the Egyptian Expeditionary Force, July 1917 to Oct 1918, Compiled from Official Sources* (Cairo: The Palestine News, 1918; London: H. M. Stationery Office, 1919). This book (actually written by Lt. Col. H. Pirie-Gordon, military editor of the *Palestine News*) acknowledges a long list of contributors by name. RM's is not among them. The typescript of the book is archived as a PRO document, subtitled "The Advance of the EEF," in PRO file CAB 44/12.

36. Tuohy, *The Secret Corps*, 289.

37. In yet another version, on January 4, 1921, Gen. Harry Chauvel wrote to Sir Henry Somer Gullett, who at the time was writing Australia's official history of the war: "I think that somewhere in here might come the story of the half finished letter to his girl, dropped in a haversack during one of our reconnaissances by a light horseman, saying that they, the mounted troops, were having a rough time constantly reconnoitering towards Beersheba to hoodwink the Turk, who was really going to be attacked at Gaza." (Letter from Gen. H. Chauvel to Sir Henry Somer Gullett at Canberra, in the Australian War Memorial collection, file AWM 40/97.) The book by Sir Henry Gullett for which Chauvel offered his comments is *The Australian Imperial Force in the Sinai and Palestine*, vol. 7 of the seven-volume *The Official History of Australia in the War of 1914–1918*, (Sydney: Angus & Robertson, 1923). Chauvel wrote an unpublished memoir as well: "General Sir H. G. Chauvel: Autobiography," n.d., Australian War Memorial Files, Canberra: ADFA Special Collection No. 254613; it does not mention the haversack, and neither account mentions RM. Chauvel would never have called RM a "light horseman." Chauvel would have referred to Capt. Arthur Neate that way, however, as Neate was Intelligence officer for Chauvel's Desert Mounted Corps.

38. RM's own words from the typescript diaries as they appeared in 1926 or 1927 are being quoted back at him in a letter to him from Cyril Falls, Historical Section (Military Branch) CID, dated April 27, 1927. RM preserved the original Cyril Falls letter—it is in an appendix to his unpublished diaries at Rhodes House, Oxford.

39. Neate's holograph letter (the original) is pasted in RM's typescript diary, vol. 23, pp. 76ff. A copy of the *Times* (London) piece of October 31, 1927, is pasted in near Neate's letter, facing the diary date 8 November 1927.

40. Maj. H. C. H. Robertson, DSO, was GSO3-Intelligence with the Ninth Regiment, Australian Light Horse; no relation to Gen. "Wully" Robertson of CIGS in London. (*The Army List*, 1917 and 1918 editions.)

41. Mrs. Hall retains Neate's original diary. She may bestow it on the Imperial War Museum or another public repository.

42. RM's tale of the crash-landing is exciting and heroic. Its gist: On the morning of October 6, 1917, RFC pilot Sandy Machintosh (RM's spelling) and his passenger (RM) take off and approach the enemy front. They are jumped by a German plane. Machintosh is gravely wounded. With no hand at its controls, the scout plane spirals into a death spin. RM climbs out of his open cockpit, clambers over the bit of fuselage that separates the two cockpits, settles into the cockpit (sitting on top of the injured Sandy), grasps the stick in his powerful grip and manhandles the airplane under control, pulling it out of its spin and leveling off. He steers for the aerodrome at Gafa, and while he circles over the field he drops a handwritten message over the side: the pilot has been hit, the untrained observer is flying the plane, and how do I land this thing? Furious action explodes on the strip beneath his wings—people wheeling, fire engines and ambulances charging, and men laying out strips of cloth that spell out landing directions: an arrow and an instruction to land at 80 degrees. He expresses great shame at the clumsy, clunky landing he executes, running the plane all the way off the edge of the field into a palm tree. He emerges shaken but still able to help evacuate the wounded Machintosh. Then, when he is

assured the pilot is in good hands, RM accepts a large draught of whisky. (RM, *Army Diary*, 221–222.)

A Lieutenant Macintosh (*sic*) did fly in 111 Squadron at the time. No doubt RM knew him. But, significantly, all serviceable military aircraft based near RM at the time, including Lieutenant Macintosh's, were Se5a biplanes—fast, efficient, deadly, and *single-cockpit single-seat planes*. There would have been no place for RM or any other passenger to sit. (Also worth noting is the fact that Macintosh occasionally encountered enemy aircraft, but never reported any damage or injuries. He survived the war intact.)

43. Arthur Charles Burnaby Neate (1885–1976) was commissioned in 1907 in the Royal Artillery. When the war began he was promoted to Captain and given command of a battery on the Western Front. He commanded another in Salonika before he was assigned as Intelligence officer to the Desert Mounted Corps in 1917. Neate was observant, thorough, and—well, *neat*. His information was of great practical value to commanders at all levels. For an example of his excellent work see Desert Mounted Corps intelligence report, "Intelligence Summary No. 1.5/2 for 24 hours ending 0800—29/9/17," in PRO file WO 95/4472.

44. C. G. Hancock and A. C. B. Neate, "The Situation in the Balkans," document dated March 17, 1930, in PRO catalog collections # RIIA/8/1, RIIA/8/569, RIIA/8/77.

45. *The Army List*, July 1926, 471.

46. *The Spectator*, March 23, 1956. Neate's appraisal of the haversack's effect on the German intelligence officer and "the Turkish Commander" is incorrect but understandable; it is based on the opinion that prevailed in British intelligence circles.

47. RMD, vol. 20, letters pasted to unnumbered sheets inserted loose-leaf between numbered pages 36 and 38.

48. His destruction of earlier versions is confirmed in his own "A Note on the Diaries" at the beginning of vol. 0 (Zero) of his bound typescripts, where he admits he destroyed some earlier material. But he does not begin to concede the real extent of his revisions and discards.

49. The objectionable "War Office man" may have been the Royal Marines' Maj. Gen. Sir George Aston, who came through Allenby's headquarters on a semi-official visit at the time to which RM refers. Aston's book *Secret Service* (London: Faber & Faber, 1933) relates the haversack story in abundant detail and is virtually identical to RM's account. Cyril Falls's official account of the haversack deceit appears in vol. 2 of his *Military Operations—Egypt & Palestine*, pp. 30–32. He writes of it as a feat "hardly to be matched [in] the annals of modern war."

50. RM, *Army Diary*, 222–223.

51. There also existed other calendars that didn't quite coincide with one another. Among them were the Hebrew, the Julian, the Persian, and the Coptic calendars. The Islamic calendar was the official calendar of the Ottoman Empire, but only until the end of 1917.

52. Husni Emir, *Yildirim*, 119.

53. Personal Record of Lt. Col. J. D. Belgrave, PRO file WO 339/23620.

CHAPTER 3: NANDI

1. "An Act for Naturalizing Daniel Meinertzhagen," Records of the Parliament Office, House of Lords—Private Bill Office: Original Acts; Local, Personal and

Private Acts, 7 William IV & Victoria I; file ref. HL/PO/PB/1/1837/7W4 &1V1n108; year 1837.

2. Norman and Jeanne Mackenzie, eds. *Diary of Beatrice Webb*, 4 vols. (Cambridge, MA: Belknap Press of Harvard University Press, 1982–1985), 2:29. Other citations herein from the diaries of Beatrice Webb are drawn, with permission, from the full-length unpublished Diaries of Beatrice Webb, 1873–1943, microfiche of pages in the British Library of Political and Economic Science, London. In those instances references are by date rather than page number, because the pagination is not consistent or always legible.

3. Barbara Caine, *Destined to Be Wives: The Sisters of Beatrice Webb* (Oxford: Clarendon Press, 1986).

4. The Season, as Barbara Caine points out, was "a conjunction of political, business, and social interests [which] coincided with the Parliamentary Session [and] points very clearly to the complex interactions between political and social life for the English upper- and upper-middle classes." (Caine, *Destined to Be Wives*, 51.)

5. *Times* (London), March 5, 1878.

6. RM, *Diary of a Black Sheep*, 101.

7. RM, *Diary of a Black Sheep*, 99. His remark has become a popular one in illustrating the constricted nature of Victorian marriages. It is reproduced both in Helena Michie's "Victorian Honeymoons: Sexual Reorientations and the 'Sights' of Europe," *Byline* 43, no. 2 (1 January 2001): 229; and in Caine's *Destined To Be Wives*, 95. Aside from blanket skepticism there seems no reason to disbelieve his account.

8. RM, *Middle East Diary*, xi.

9. Pat Morris, "From the Archives," *The Linnean* 17, no. 1 (2001). The Linnean Society is one of Britain's oldest and most prestigious natural history organizations.

10. RM, *Diary of a Black Sheep*, 164ff.

11. Benjamin Spock, M.D., published *The Common Sense Book of Baby and Child Care* in 1945. Its enormous readership encouraged torrents of pop-psychology and sexual pathology books.

12. RM, *Kenya Diary*, 324.

13. Miriam Rothschild, letter to author, 3 March 2002.

14. In his *Middle East Diary* (pp. 41–42) RM mentions that he has read Richard Aldington's *Lawrence of Arabia: A Biographical Enquiry* (London: Collins, 1955). The book caused a furor. It had previously been printed in France under the title *Lawrence L'Imposteur*. It attempted to debunk the heroic legend by emphasizing Lawrence's illegitimate birth and his alleged homosexuality. It caused great controversy (Lawrence's brother attempted to prevent its publication) and forced later biographers to address the questions it raised, but when they did so, most serious scholars concluded that Lawrence was largely asexual. He also was brilliant, shy, heroic, and very sensible although sometimes eccentric. Over the years Lawrence practiced various kinds of deception, but none of them seems to have caused serious gaps between the reality of his life and the understanding of a majority of peer-respected biographers and historians. The same cannot be said of RM.

15. Most of these diary passages refer to the period 1917–1923, when the two men worked together, occasionally in cooperation but often at cross purposes. At

their first meeting, according to the very tall RM, he took one look at the very short Lawrence, who was dressed in white Arab robes, and asked, "Boy or girl?" Lawrence blushed. "Boy." It goes downhill from there. (RM, *Middle East Diary*, 28–29.) Various scholars, including Lawrence's authorized biographer Jeremy Wilson, have stated their belief that RM wrote these accounts no earlier than the 1950s, and that they are preposterous.

16. RM, *Diary of a Black Sheep*, 210.

17. RM, *Pirates and Predators: The Piratical and Predatory Habits of Birds* (London and Edinburgh: Oliver & Boyd, 1959), 97.

18. RM, *Diary of a Black Sheep*, 175–176. The Harrow School Register shows that Churchill attended the school from 1888 to 1892 and that RM was enrolled there from 1891 to 1895.

19. RM, "Conquisitio Mea: A Record of My Ornithological Activities and Collections," unpublished typescript, 66 pages, in the library of the Smithsonian Institution, Record Unit 7006: Collection Division 1: Alexander Wetmore Papers, Meinertzhagen correspondence, Box 40, Folder 5. On March 29, 1942, RM wrote to Alex Wetmore in Washington that he wanted to publish "the best paper I have ever written on my collections and my ornithological history" and, in view of England's wartime paper rationing, asked whether Wetmore might find a publisher for it in the United States. When Wetmore volunteered to try, RM sent him a copy of his typescript "Conquisitio Mea." Wetmore found no publisher for it, and in 1944 RM wrote to him to ask that Wetmore return the typescript to him. Wetmore did so, but against the chance that it might get sunk on a mail-transport ship, took the precaution of making a photocopy, which remains today in the Smithsonian archives. It is a valuable tool for comparison with the Meinertzhagen "diaries" because it is one of the few documents of length from the period that he did not have an opportunity to destroy or revise beyond recognition.

20. D. Meinertzhagen and R. P. Hornby, *Bird Life in Arctic Spring: The Diaries of the Mottisfont Birds and Their Master* (London: R. H. Porter, 1899). A copy is held in the library of the BMNH.

21. Richard Bowdler Sharpe, "Birds," in Trustees of the British Museum, *The History of the Collections Contained in the Natural History Departments of the British Museum* (London: British Museum (Natural History), 1906), 2:426.

22. Cocker, *Richard Meinertzhagen*, 33.

23. Nicholas Meinertzhagen, interviewed at his home by the author, with Mark Cocker, 27 June 2003.

24. Richard's father Daniel (1842–1910) was the eldest son and the fifth of eleven children born to Daniel and Manuela Huth Meinertzhagen. When he married Georgina Potter in 1873 he instantly became not only a son-in-law of the prosperous Potter family but also brother-in-law to nine different British clans, most of them belonging to the ruling classes.

25. RM, *Army Diary*, 10.

26. RM, *Diary of a Black Sheep*, 214. RM insisted his father and Cecil Rhodes (founder of Rhodesia) were acquainted, and that his father's resistance to the rough frontier reputation of "the Rhodes gang" had made Dee forbid Richard to accept Rhodes's invitation to join him in Africa in 1895. RM's assertions about his personal encounters with Rhodes are open to question. One can picture him years later scouring old steamship arrivals pages in newspapers for the correct

date so that he then could write up a diary entry about having run down to Southhampton in 1899 to meet Rhodes at the pier. (In fact he got it wrong anyway. Rhodes was arriving, not departing, on the steamship in question.)

27. The *Times* (London), January 16, 1899.
28. Like many of the well-born set, RM often arranged his trips to India, Africa, or the Middle East to include a leisurely boat-train ride to Paris and thence—with side trips—by train to Marseille, a few days on the Riviera, and from there an upper-deck steam voyage through the Suez Canal and into the Indian Ocean.
29. RM, *Army Diary*, 11–12.
30. The Port Said archive, containing consular records and the Viceroy's papers, is held in PRO files FO 566/1009 and FO 78/5036.
31. RM, *Army Diary*, 18.
32. Sir Ernest Louis Meinertzhagen (1854–1933) was a brother of Richard's father. His papers are in the Templewood Papers collection, Cambridge University Library. He seems to have had genuine affection toward his nephew. He indulged Richard in his desires, including—when Richard was still a teen—a top of the line £200 Holland & Holland shotgun for bird-hunting.
33. RM, *Army Diary*, 381. See also RM, "The speed and altitude of bird flight (with notes on other animals)," *Ibis* (September 1955): 81–117.
34. Test information from *Natural History*, March 1974.
35. RM, *Army Diary*, 13–14.
36. RM, *Army Diary*, 20.
37. RM, *Army Diary*, 15. The Battle of Agincourt, between the English (led by King Henry V) and the French (led by Charles d'Albret) was a victory for the English, who were outnumbered four to one—but RM's point is that it took place in 1415.
38. RM, *Army Diary*, 16.
39. Bailey's service affiliation is discussed in correspondence from him to his father, circa 1902, in the Bailey files at the IOL.
40. Letter from RM to Frederick M. Bailey, 26 December 1932, in Meinertzhagen-Bailey correspondence, Foreign Office documents section, IOL. The exchange is prolific and friendly, but in his diaries and published books RM barely mentions Bailey. Both men served later under the aegis of Sir John Shuckburgh—who, if he didn't invent the cloak or the dagger, certainly seems to have found new uses for them. The publicity-shy Sir John Evelyn Shuckburgh, KCMG, CB (1877–1953) is hard to track. Even to as keen-eyed a researcher as Mark Cocker the onetime India Office spymaster was simply "a cautious, competent, India Office man" (in *Richard Meinertzhagen*, 148). Shuckburgh pretty much ran the political arm of British intelligence in Asia and Asia Minor for years, and evidently had a salty personality. In 1921–1923 he was to be RM's direct superior in the Middle East section of the Colonial Office. Shuckburgh had charge of efforts to bring Arabs and Jews together—a task in which he failed, and about which he remarked, "We are unfortunate in our clients." (Quoted by Tom Segev in *One Palestine, Complete*, 198.)
41. RM, *Army Diary*, 23.
42. RM, *Kenya Diary*, 9.
43. Mount Kenya, an extinct volcano, rises to an ice-capped 17,058 feet. North of the equator, it is the second-highest mountain in Africa (after Kilimanjaro, which lies approximately equidistant less than a hundred miles away on the other

side of the equator). For Europeans these heights were terra incognita. At the time of RM's arrival, reports of the existence of a second glacier-topped mountain in equatorial Africa were still being scoffed at and debated by members of geographical societies in London.

44. RM, *Kenya Diary*, 12–15.
45. PRO file FO 2/724, item tagged as number 70.
46. RM, *Kenya Diary*, 15–16.
47. "Annual Report Third K. A. Rifles," in PRO file WO 106/24, lists the KAR field companies and their commanders; see especially p. 353. RM held command only during a few brief intervals when he led small detachments from one post to another. On at least one such occasion he got lost, and turned up several days late for an ordered rendezvous. (Signal from Capt. F. A. Dickinson in PRO file WO 106/5992.)
48. RM, *Kenya Diary*, 51. To show the bloodthirsty savagery of British colonialists, the passage is quoted in Michael Chege's "Political Science as an Obstacle to Understanding the Problem of the State and Political Violence in Africa," *Codesria Bulletin*, October 2004, pp. 8–10. Such behavior as RM describes would have been justified and respected not only by his fellow soldiers but also by many Africans. The differences were more technological than moralistic—matters of respective ordnance and the sophistication of military skills.
49. RM, *Kenya Diary*, 60–64.
50. "Preface" by Elspeth Huxley, in RM, *Kenya Diary* (London: Eland Books, 1983), v. Huxley (1907–1997), celebrated author of *The Flame Trees of Thika* (1959), a 1935 biography of Lord Delamere, and several other books, grew up in Africa.
51. RM is described as "scourge of the Kikuyus in the early twentieth century" in some of Kenya's history courses; see "History: The Mau-Mau and the End of the Colony (1947–1963)," http://www.kenyalogy.com/eng/info/histo13.html.
52. RM, "Conquisitio Mea." (Pages are un-numbered.)
53. RM, *Kenya Diary*, 81.
54. "Inspector General Confirms Promotions," PRO file FO 566/1662 (year 1905). The War Office dates his captaincy from October 22, 1904 (*The Army List*, January 1925, 195), but the velocity of intercontinental communication being what it was in the age of steam, official written orders did not reach Nairobi until early the following year. Reports by the KAR's Inspector General, Brig. Gen. W. H. Manning, show that RM's captaincy did not take effect until it was recorded on February 3, 1905.
55. RM, *Kenya Diary*, 171–173.
56. RM, *Kenya Diary*, 181.
57. "East Africa Protectorate/King's African Rifles," in PRO file WO 106/5992. For published confirmation of the command structure at Nandi Fort in 1905 see Hubert Moyse-Bartlett, *The King's African Rifles: A Study in the Military History of East and Central Africa, 1890–1945* (Aldershot, UK: Gale & Polden, 1956), 204.
58. To the Nandi, the "Laibon" was known as Koitalel Arap Samoe. To the Maasai and to Europeans in the region the shaman was known by his Maasai designation, "Laibon" meaning roughly "medicine-man-in-chief." To simplify, we've called him the Laibon because that is how RM's diaries, official British records, and many publications refer to him.

59. The killings at Ket Parak Hill and the official inquiries that followed them occupy a major portion of RM's book *Kenya Diary*, 180–300.

60. Report from Captain Meinertzhagen to Major Pope-Hennessy, dated 19 October 1905, in PRO file CO 534/3. Some sources report that RM and his men sustained a few superficial injuries during the one-sided clash. His service record in the Army List indicates he was wounded in connection with the Ket Parak incident—an arrow cut on one finger, for which he was "mentioned in dispatches" belatedly in the September 18, 1906, issue of the *Gazette*, nearly a year after the event. No such wound is mentioned in his report or in *Kenya Diary*, in which he mentions only that one of his men suffered a superficial cut. In the typescript diaries he is more colorful—his sleeve is punctured by an arrow, he is nudged by a spear, and another arrow knocks off his helmet. He cannot have been seriously hurt, as he continued robustly about his duties in the ensuing weeks and months, scouting enemy locations and stealing Nandi livestock for the KAR.

    On November 9, 1905, RM's father in England cabled KAR headquarters to ask "present condition of wounds received in Nandi Expedition by Lt R Meinertzhagen." GPO logs show that the senior RM's inquiry was answered by cable from Mombasa on November 11, 1905, with a subsequent update sent on March 10, 1906. (KAR Register of Correspondence in PRO file CO 623/1, referring to Registered telegrams No. 39946 and GPO/145/06. The telegrams themselves have not survived the "weeding" process.) The references imply that Meinertzhagen Sr. had not followed his son's career with enough interest to know his current rank, but became concerned by what he read in the newspapers about injuries reported to have been sustained by his son. That is an indicator of the attention given to the Nandi ambush by the European press.

61. The controversy remains alive. In July 2002 a commission in Kenya took testimony that "[i]n 1905, Samoe [Laibon] Quoitalel [*sic*] was assassinated by Captain Menesagen [*sic*]." ("Verbatim Record of the Proceedings of the Constitution of Kenya Review Commission," Records of Public Hearing at Ainamoi Constituency, Kericho Teachers College, 16 July 2002.) In the same vein is the statement: "It was the October 1905 assassination of Nandi leader Koitalel that eventually landed Richard Meinertzhagen on the wrong side of the colonial establishment, and ultimately resulted in his expulsion from the colony in 1906." (Ahmad Irfan, "Land and Population: Colonial Interests in Kenya," in *Africa 2000* (London: News & Media, Ltd., 2000.) Articles about the Laibon's murder by RM continue to appear—see for instance pieces in the Kenya *Daily Nation* on October 20, 2005, and February 2, 2006.

62. Some records had been misfiled until recently. They include the report "Death of the Nandi Chief Laibon," PRO file CO 624/1; "Ket Parak," a fourteen-page typed report, plus attachments, dated 6 April 1906, at Nairobi and signed by Major Pope-Hennessy, PRO file CO 533/13 (and in the same file "Intelligence Diary, Nandi Field Force"); "Uganda Records, 1899–1904," PRO file FO 2/467 (the incident did not take place in Uganda, but administratively Uganda and Kenya were conjoined in the single KAR jurisdiction known as British East Africa); "Irregularities in Accounts of Nandi Station," PRO Document CO 533/2; Report from Captain Meinertzhagen to Major Pope-Hennessy dated 19 October 1905, KAR files, PRO document CO 534/3; letters from Walter Mayes and others in PRO file CO 534/3; numerous documents in PRO file 8007-31; Court of Enquiry Summary

Report, PRO file CO 534/3; Signal from Hayes Sadler to the Secretary of State, 25 May 1906, PRO file CO 533/14 (and in the same file "Commissioner's Exchanges," 25 May 1906). RM's own account of "Sammy" Butler's participation was published in *Kenya Diary*, 233. His additional remarks in that regard are in the unpublished typescript diaries, as cited in Mark Cocker's *Richard Meinertzhagen*, 58. See also Capt. James A. F. Cuffe's service record in Royal Marines (Admiralty) in PRO file ADM 196/63—Cuffe so strongly resented the cover-up of the massacre that he resigned from the KAR in 1906.

63. *The Army List*, January 1925.
64. Documents concerning the ambush and the inquiries can be found in PRO files 8007-31, CO 534/3, CO 533/14, CO 533/14 and (notably) "Death of the Nandi Chief Laibon" in PRO file CO 624/1. Other portions of the proceedings of the Courts of Inquiry, along with the Pope-Hennessy summary reports, are in PRO file ADM 196/63. ("CO" stands for Colonial Office; "ADM" stands for Admiralty. No wonder some records, particularly those recently found in the latter archive, were thought to have been lost.)
65. RM, *Kenya Diary*, 233.
66. The machine-gun ambush is also mentioned in RM's unpublished typescript diaries; it seems impossible to tell exactly when these were composed and/or revised. RM's decision to withhold it from public view for so many decades may have less to do with the Official Secrets Act than with his longstanding friendship with Sammy Butler—Maj. Gen. Stephen Seymour Butler, CMG, DSO—with whom RM kept in touch until Butler died at age eighty-four. With its murderous rate of fire of five hundred bullets per minute, the Maxim machine gun changed warfare. The model that Sammy Butler used against the Nandi had an effective range of one thousand yards (about a kilometer), so it would have been no great feat of marksmanship to mow down two dozen men who were clustered together only seventy-five yards away from him.

CHAPTER 4: SYCE

1. Members of the Meinertzhagen family have achieved great distinction. Sir Peter Meinertzhagen (1920–1999), a nephew of Richard, was one of three brothers, all of whom achieved prominence and success in finance. He served on the boards of the Bank of England, the Hoare Govett Group, and the Commonwealth Fund, of which he was a founder. Peter's brother Daniel became chairman of Lazard's and of Royal Insurance. Their brother Luke became senior partner in Cazenove & Co. Luke's son, Nicholas Meinertzhagen, is a distinguished antiquarian art expert, custodian of the Turner estate, and rare-book scholar.
    Richard's daughter Anne became a prominent research scientist and scholar, and his son Ran (Richard Randle Meinertzhagen) is a respected shipyard owner and the guardian of his father's estate.
2. In *Army Diary*, 30, RM recalls lunching at the Union Club and introducing himself to Generals Smuts and Botha. Is he again dropping names like breadcrumbs to mark his path through history? Perhaps not; it does no harm to concede that he may have met them.
3. RM, *Army Diary*, 33.

4. British Intelligence was run by skilled amateurs but was not altogether informal. It had structure, personnel, payrolls—and records for the period in question. RM does not appear in any of them. Information about the development of the early intelligence services may be found in several excellent and accessible sources including Alan Judd's *The Quest for C: Sir Mansfield Cumming and the Founding of the British Secret Service* (London: HarperCollins, 1999), and Stephen Dorril's huge and exhaustive *MI6: Inside the Covert World of Her Majesty's Secret Intelligence Service* (New York: The Free Press, 2000).

5. RM, *Middle East Diary*, 2–4.

6. RM, *Army Diary*, 11–12.

7. RM, *Army Diary*, 33–41.

8. RM, *Army Diary*, 42.

9. RM, *Army Diary*, 43.

10. The House of Lords Record Office contains letters exchanged between Le Roy-Lewis and Lloyd George. Some of Lloyd George's political cronies were suspicious. "Robertson and 'the soldiers' are jealous of Le Roy-Lewis's private correspondence with Lloyd George."—file description of a letter from Sir Alexander W. C. B. "Alick" Murray (in Paris) to David Lloyd George (in London), 19 November 1916, House of Lords Record Office, Palace of Westminster: The Parliamentary Archives, ref. LG/E/2/20/5. Until Lord Kitchener's death at sea in 1916, Le Roy-Lewis served him as his trusted personal translator in dealing with the French. (Lewis was half French.)

11. RMD, vol. 12, page number unclear; the entry appears under the date 17 December 1911.

12. RMD, vol. 21, 156.

13. RMD, vol. 12, 10.

14. RM, *Diary of a Black Sheep*, 331, and *Army Diary*, 4. RM may have been distantly related by blood to the Le Roy-Lewis clan. In one fit of RM's fury he wrote that Hermann Le Roy-Lewis was the illegitimate son of a French prostitute whose patron in Paris was a British Jew named Lewis (RMD, vol. 12, entry under the date 17 December 1911). This was written after Le Roy-Lewis's death and long after RM's bitter divorce from Armorel. It is sharply at variance with the entry in *Burke's Landed Gentry* showing Hermann Le Roy-Lewis as the (legitimate) son of Gen. Robert Le Roy and his wife Amelia Lewis, daughter of William D. Lewis, Collector of the Port of Philadelphia; Hermann had taken his mother's maiden name and appended it, by hyphenation, to his father's name, in the commonly accepted way of merging families and nationalities. See "Le Roy-Lewis of Westbury" in Sir Bernard Burke, *Landed Gentry of Great Britain*, 13th ed. ((London: The Burke Publishing Co., Ltd., 1921).

15. RM, "On the Birds of Mauritius," *The Ilbis*, 9th ser., 6, no. 21 (January 1912). (Interestingly, the article was published next to a paper by Walter Rothschild.) Robert Prys-Jones points out, "Almost no collecting by RM was involved in producing the paper, although he makes frequent references to specimens collected by others. It is the sort of paper one might expect from someone with a real interest in, but no deep knowledge of, ornithology." (Letter from R. Prys-Jones to the author, 28 June 2006.)

16. RM, *Army Diary*, 50.

17. The city of Quetta and its region are in what is now Pakistan.

18. RM, *Army Diary*, 58.

19. Anthony Cave Brown, *"C": The Secret Life of Sir Stewart Menzies, Spymaster to Winston Churchill* (New York: Macmillan, 1987), 167.
20. RM, *Army Diary*, 59.
21. RM, *Army Diary*, 63.
22. Brig. Gen. Sir Walter Pipon Braithwaite, GCB, KCB (1865–1945), served as Commandant, Staff College, Quetta, from 1911 to 1914. He was promoted to Major General in 1915, Lieutenant General in 1919, full General in 1926; he retired in 1931.
23. RM, *Army Diary*, 69.
24. RM, *Army Diary*, 69.
25. Our inquiries in India and Pakistan were directed by Pawanjit Singh Ahluwalia, Managing Director, Premier Investigations, New Delhi, in 1999 and 2000.
26. The line, "You didn't do it, and make sure it never happens again" didn't originate with RM. It appears in Mrs. [Elizabeth] Gaskell's Victorian novel *Wives and Daughters*, first published as a serial in 1864–1866. A bestseller for decades, it was reprinted frequently in hardcover. RM probably had read the story— it features a young scientist hero who ventures off to Africa to collect specimens.

CHAPTER 5: TANGA

1. RM's use of the pluperfect tense here is one of virtually countless textual clues that his "diaries" in fact were written years after the events. If he had written this passage when he claims to have written it, it would read more like, "I have received a note from the Commandant informing me I *have* been selected" or "I *am* selected."
2. RM, *Army Diary*, 77–81.
3. German East Africa was known to Germans by the ominous initials "D.O.A."— not "dead on arrival" but *Deutsche Ost-Afrika*. The colony in 1914 was larger than Germany and France combined. It included what would become the territory of three subsequent nations: Rwanda, Burundi, and Tanganyika (the mainland portion of today's Tanzania).
4. Gordon S. Johnson, *Tanga Diary*, Papers of Maj. G. S. Johnson, DSO, MBE, MC: Department of Documents, IWM, File 77/109/1. Entry for October 16, 1914. "GEA" refers to German East Africa.
5. Max Aitken, aka Lord Beaverbrook, was a back-room supporter of David Lloyd George in the latter's blossoming effort to unseat Asquith as Prime Minister. Beaverbrook was to remain very powerful in England right through World War II, by way of his close friendship with Winston Churchill.
6. RMD, vol. 15, 92–93.
7. L. H. Gann and Peter Duignan, *The Rulers of German East Africa, 1884–1914* (Palo Alto, CA: Stanford University Press, 1977), 271.
8. Byron Farwell, *The Great War in Africa, 1914–1918* (New York: W. W. Norton, 1986), 109.
9. Helmuth Stoecker, "The German Empire in Africa before 1914," in his *German Imperialism in Africa: From the Beginnings to the Second World War* (London: C. Hurst & Co., 1986), 185.
10. "Proceedings of Sub-Committee of the Committee of Imperial Defence," document dated 5 August 1914, PRO file CAB21/3.

11. Ada Schnee, *Bibi Mkuba: My Experiences in German East Africa During World War I* (San Bernardino, CA: The Borgo Press, 1995), 7. The initial British incursion led to four years' spirited and often ludicrous warfare over control of Africa's great lakes. See Peter Shankland, *The Phantom Flotilla: The Story of the Naval Africa Expedition, 1915–1916* (London: Collins, 1968), and Giles Foden, *Mimi and Toutou's Big Adventure: The Bizarre Battle of Lake Tanganyika* (New York: Alfred A. Knopf, 2005).

12. German raiding cruiser *Königsberg* daunted Allied shipping in the western Indian Ocean early in the war. Partly in retaliation for the British invasion from Uganda, and partly to replenish her stocks of coal, the *Königsberg* sacked and sank British collier-supply ship *City of Winchester* in the Gulf of Aden on August 6, 1914. That was the first British loss of a merchant ship in the war. The Royal Navy was incensed, and converged upon Dar es Salaam, which had been the *Königsberg*'s home port. When the *Königsberg* had first arrived in June the locals at first had been stunned by her low, sinister 378-foot length and big batteries of serious-looking guns. But they had come to accept her silhouette as a familiar sight against the morning sky in Dar's harbor. Her commander, *Fregattenkapitan* Max Looff, was to become one of the legendary heroes of the East African Campaign. During the next ten months the British kept constant watch on the harbor but *Königsberg* never reappeared at Dar es Salaam. An invisible ghost, she tied up the attention and costs of a twenty-ship British fleet complete with two squadrons of rickety aircraft, many tons of coal, and several thousand sailors.

    The *Königsberg* eventually was boxed in and pounded to death in the delta of the Rufiji River, but she yielded up her ten big guns: Lettow mounted them on wheeled carriages and dragged them all over East Africa as the *schutztruppe*'s artillery. See Kevin Patience, *Königsberg: An East African Raider* (Poole, Dorset, UK: Zanzibar Publications, 1997).

13. Commandant von Lettow-Vorbeck and Duty officers of Ostafrika: *Schutztruppe War Diary, 1914–1918*, English translation by M. S. J. C. Vantijen, entry dated 15 August 1914. This remarkable document was bound at Pretoria on April 9, 1920, by its translator. The typescript is an unabridged translation of the quasi-official war diary written daily by officers under Lettow's command, surrendered by the *schutztruppe* to the British in 1918. It is in four volumes, approx. 1,800 pages; IWM # 49538.

14. Lettow-Vorbeck, *Mein Leben*. To date Lettow's autobiography has not been published in English. An unpublished English translation, from which information is derived herein, is by my late good friend James P. Pierce, completed in 2000. More popular with armchair enthusiasts, but less personally revealing, is Lettow's *Meine Erinnerrungen aus Ostafrika* (My Memories of East Africa), which was published in 1919 and has appeared in several English-language versions.

15. "Committee of Imperial Defence: Expedition against German East Africa." CID Paper #112 C, providing retrospective information concerning events of September 9 and following dates; the document is dated 28 September 1914, PRO file CAB 5/3. If it is still required, this date adds a nail to the coffin of RM's claim that he knew his destination in August. It also puts the lie to his diary entries stating that he collected his (subsequently notorious) Forest Owlet specimen in India on October 9, 1914.

16. RM, *Army Diary*, 83. In mid-January 1915, after a change of commanders in East Africa, Mackay would be made commandant of the occupation garrison on Mafia Island. Despite RM's diary claims to the contrary it was not until 1915 that he himself for the first time became chief intelligence staff officer for the East Africa Force.

17. A carefully documented account is Ross Anderson's "The Battle of Tanga, 2–5 November 1914," *War in History* 8, no.3 (2001): 294–322. Another is Frank A. Contey's "British Debacle in German East Africa," *Military History* 13, no. 5 (December 1996): 58ff. Still another is David Rooney's "A German Guerrilla Chief in Africa," *History Today* 49, no. 11 (November 1999). Personal eyewitness accounts are found in Maj. A. Russell's articles "The Landing at Tanga, 1914" and "War Comes to Tanganyika," both published in Dar es Salaam's *Tanganyika Notes and Records* (n.d.). Interesting and useful chapters about the battle can be found in numerous books, including the various general histories of the campaign and quite a few specialized studies like S. D. Pradhan's *The Indian Army in East Africa, 1914–1918* (New Delhi: National Book Organisation/ South Asia Books, 1991); see also G. W. Hatchell's "The East African Campaign—1914 to 1919," *Tanganyika Notes and Records*, no. 21 (June 1946).

18. RM often tended to preserve the evidence of his misstatements; whether this was caused by compulsion or carelessness is not clear. In this instance he helpfully pasted the printed "Standing Orders" of Force "B" into his typed diaries at Oxford, vol.15, between pages 88 and 90. Comparison with the PRO's files shows that this paste-in is genuine. The Order of Battle (a military table of organization) destroys his claim to have been chief intelligence officer to the Indian Expeditionary Force at Tanga. It shows that the office was held by Mackay. Several other Intelligence staffers out-ranked RM as well, including Maj. Norman King (the former British consul to German East Africa) and Maj. Andrew Russell, a planter lately returned from German East Africa. Russell later wrote, "Lieutenant Colonel Mackay, Chief Intelligence Officer, and Maj. Norman King, late British Consul at Dar es Salaam [told me] that with my knowledge of German East Africa I had been earmarked for the Intelligence Department." (Maj. A. Russell, OBE, MC, "The Landing at Tanga, 1914," in *Tanganyika Notes and Records*, n.d.) Russell, a farmer who until the war had lived in German East Africa's Kilimanjaro district, was able to get out of enemy territory at the outbreak of war because he happened to be in Dar es Salaam at the time and stepped aboard one of the last ships to leave for Mombasa. Russell served out the entire war in the theater. After the Tanga landings in November 1914, he wrote, "I was given a job in intelligence and went with Colonel Mackay to Mombasa, but that is another story." (Andrew Russell, "War Comes to Tanganyika," *Tanganyika Notes and Records*, n.d., probably 1962, p. 195.) He makes no mention of Captain Meinertzhagen, even though Russell served in East Africa Intelligence twice as long as RM did. Like many chroniclers who were on the scene, Russell seems hardly to have noticed RM.

Former British Consul Norman King was a personable and competent mid-level Foreign Service official. His interesting life gives off a whiff of Mad-Dogs-And-Englishmen obliviousness, but he was observant and seems to have been competent in his postings. Born in 1881, he entered the Consular Service in 1907, served as Consul-General in Dar es Salaam from 1913 until August 1914, served in various military-intelligence and diplomatic posts in British East

Africa and the Middle East through the Great War, became Consul-General to Mexico City, 1920–26, Consul-General to Barcelona, 1926–38, and Consul-General to Marseilles, 1938–40. He was knighted in 1937 (KCMG). He died in 1963, aged eighty-two.

RM does not mention his old friend Mackay again, although others would notice Mackay in the thick of the upcoming battle for Tanga. On November 5, 1914, at a most discouraging point in the battle, Norman King wrote in his diary: "Waked by Mackay about 5:30 or 6 with the cheerful remark 'We're for it. The enemy are advancing on both flanks'" . . . followed later the same day by: "Mackay and I had charge of the case with the cyphers and secret papers. We went along behind the trenches. . . ." (*Diary of Sir Norman King, KCMG*, Microfilm of typescript, Documents Section, IWM file FF/MCP/150.)

19. See Gordon S. Johnson, "Tanga Diary," IWM file 77/109/1, entry for 16 October 1914. Within a few months, Johnson would become aide to RM.
20. For the officers' point of view, see for example the "Diary of Lt. Gen. Richard Wapshare," IWM file No. 88/61/1.
21. "Despatch on Tanga Operations" from G.O.C. IEF "B" (Major General Aitken) to War Office, dated 1 December 1914. PRO file WO 95/5289.
22. RM, *Army Diary*, 85.
23. The entire series of exchanges is held in PRO file ADM 137/9.
24. Telegram from the Admiralty to Senior Naval Officer Mombasa, 30 August 1914, in PRO file ADM 137/9; see also copies of relevant messages in PRO file ADM 137/10.
25. RM, *Army Diary*, 85. By shifting blame to Brig. Gen. James M. Stewart in this part of his account, RM distracts our attention away from his own failure to meet those responsibilities. He had not interviewed locals or spoken with Maj. Andrew Russell, who had numerous contacts in German East Africa. Russell was not hard to find; he went aboard ship with RM later the same day, and was to be among the first troops landed at Tanga. RM claims he told the generals Tanga probably had very little by way of defenses—but also told them that the German army could be brought there by rail in thirty-six hours. The delay caused by the truce—the notification in advance of the invasion—would give the Germans time to bring their reinforcements down from the hills. That's what actually happened, but the claim that he foresaw this and warned the generals about it appears only in his later writings.

Reports of the British Indian East Africa Expeditionary Force "B" are held in the PRO; many of them, including quite a few of RM's reports from 1915 and 1916, previously were thought to have been lost. The loss was neither actual nor sinister. The files were misplaced because, it appears, someone misfiled them in WO 95/2590 instead of WO 95/5290 where they belong. There are about 5,500 boxes of files in the WO 95 collection, so it is not surprising when a misfiled one proves elusive. Our friend and research-collaborator Robert W. O'Hara found these misplaced files.
26. James Chambers, "Colonies Answer the Call to Arms," *Daily Telegraph*, May 26, 1997.
27. RM, *Army Diary*, 116.
28. RM, *Army Diary*, 89. Contrary to such claims as these two, RM did not begin to file intelligence reports until 1915. These show an emphatic uncertainty about the enemy's dispositions.

29. Lt. Col. Charles Hordern, *History of the Great War: Military Operations, East Africa, Volume I: 1914–Sept. 1916* (London: H. M. Stationery Office, 1941), 78.

30. RM, *Army Diary*, 86.

31. *Diary of Sir Norman King*, entry for November 1, 1914, IWM file FF/MCP/150 (microfilm). King expresses with remarkable insouciance his astonishment at seeing General Aitken lying back in a deck chair, reading a novel.

32. Tanga faces north—it lies inside the open-ended circle of a natural harbor enclosed by the Ras Kasone peninsula. The town's shoreline runs east and west. Aitken's choice of landing beach was outside that circle, on an east-facing slope of the peninsula. It wasn't visible from anywhere in Tanga. It was, however, visible to any observer on the high ground of Ras Kasone.

33. Ross Anderson, "The Battle of Tanga, 2–5 November 1914," *War in History* 8, no. 3 (2001): 305.

34. Gordon S. Johnson, "Notes on the Official History of the Campaign in East Africa," letter dated 19 December 1934 to the editor (Lt. Col. Charles Hordern) of the forthcoming *History of the Great War: Military Operations, East Africa*; Johnson's letters and other documents are in PRO file CAB 45/35.

35. Log of HMS *Fox*, entry for 2 November 1914, in PRO file ADM 53/42071.

36. RM, *Army Diary*, 86.

37. Diary of Lt. Gen. Richard Wapshare, IWM file No. 88/61/1.

38. Brig. Gen. Michael Tighe, "Report on Action at Tanga," dated 5 November 1914 (document appended to the War Diary of Expeditionary Force "B"), PRO file WO 95/5289.

39. Handwritten diary of Lt. Col. Charles E. A. Jourdain, DSO, in PRO file WO 95/5339. At Tanga, aged forty-five, the veteran Jourdain commanded the Second Battalion of the Loyal North Lancashire Regiment, which acquitted itself with unusual military distinction. Two days later he would be left to hold the line and cover the retreat of the rest of the Force when it withdrew to its ships. A year later Jourdain was promoted and, perhaps as a result, RM behind his back began to blister him with unfounded accusations of cowardice and callousness.

40. Diary of Lt. Gen. Richard Wapshare, IWM file No. 88/61/1.

41. Gordon S. Johnson, *Tanga Diary*, entry for November 4, 1914.

42. Handwritten diary of Lt. Col. Charles E. A. Jourdain, PRO file WO 95/5339.

43. RM, *Army Diary*, 87–88. No hint of such an idea seems to appear in the "local German press," the daily newspaper *Die Zeitung* (which continued publication into 1916); even if it had, how would RM have known about it while the battle was going on?

Lieutenant Ishmael in fact had died much earlier—he was in the first boat that came ashore, and was shot to death soon after—a fact RM seems to have forgotten by the time he wrote this section. The passage seems to imply that British officers right and left were being shot down by their own troops. No such instance was recorded. The casualty rate among officers was high at Tanga (one in every three), but from accounts of survivors other than RM, clearly they were shot by enemy fire.

Like everyone else, RM can have had no idea there were as few as 250 German troops in the engagement. Probably because of his personal animus against Commander Caulfield, RM is wrong once again about the *Fox*, which in fact lobbed shells at the Germans whenever it received sufficient target information. That didn't occur very often, but the infrequency was due not to a reluctance to support the ground troops but to a fear of hitting them with "friendly fire."

RM was on shipboard or on the ground. Cut off from communication with other sectors, he had no way to judge the enemy's strength in machine guns; his statements were thrown in months or years later in order to impress us with his perspicacity. We know he read Lettow's memoir of the war at the time of its publication in 1919; this appears to have been a source for much of the "intelligence" about the Germans that he reports in his diaries and claims to have developed on his own during the early months of the war, but somehow failed to insert into the reports he filed at the time.

44. RM, *Army Diary*, 88–89, 91–92.
45. Lettow, *Mein Leben*, 127. The *Schutztruppe War Diary* (entry for 20 September 1914) notes, "Our Askari rifle 71 is much inferior to the English magazine rifle." The antiquated Krag model-1871 *Jägerbüchse* 11mm single-shot rifle put Lettow's troops at a severe disadvantage because each shot threw a spear of flame and a puff of muzzle smoke, immediately revealing the rifleman's location night or day. The enemy's smokeless-powder rifles provided fewer such give-away clues; his riflemen could remain invisible by day and hard to spot by night.
46. Lettow, *East African Campaigns*, 38, 95.
47. RM, *Army Diary*, 91–92. The "tall man with a fine face," as we'll see, is supposed to be Lettow.
48. The Second Battalion, Loyal North Lancashire Regiment would continue to serve honorably in East Africa under Colonel Jourdain until January 1917 when it would be sent to Cairo, whence as part of the Seventy-fifth Division it would participate in several actions including the Third Battle of Gaza where RM made his reputation with his self-advertised "haversack ruse."
49. Chambers, "Colonies Answer the Call to Arms."
50. Lettow, *East African Campaigns*, 37, 38.
51. Diary of Lt. Gen. Richard Wapshare, IWM file No. 88/61/1. The size of a company could vary from about 150 to about 225 men; a battalion consisted of two or more companies.
52. Lettow, *Mein Leben*, 129.
53. Lettow, *Mein Leben*, 125.
54. Gordon S. Johnson, "Notes on the Official History of the Campaign in East Africa," in PRO file CAB 45/35.
55. *Diary of Sir Norman King*, entry for 4 November 1914, IWM file FF/MCP/150 (microfilm).
56. Lettow, *East African Campaigns*, 40.
57. Some works of alleged nonfiction assert that as many as 120,000 British colonial troops were defeated by 4,000 German soldiers and huge swarms of furious bees in the swamps of Tanga. See for example Erik Durschmied's *The Hinge Factor: How Chance and Stupidity Have Changed History* (London: Arcade Publishing, 1999). Such assertions illustrate how the East African Campaign seems determined to perpetuate its myths.
58. The claim appears in the unpublished memoir that RM wrote in 1942–43 entitled *Me*. I have not had access to it. RM's allegation about the near-mutiny is retold in secondary sources, the best of which is Mark Cocker's perceptive biography *Richard Meinertzhagen*, 81.

59. Diary of Lt. Gen. Richard Wapshare, IWM file No. 88/61/1.
60. Lettow, *East African Campaigns*, 40.
61. One sepoy battalion—just a few hundred men—caused much of the chaos that would inspire derogatory comment. Lettow credited some of his own success to that unit, the Thirteenth Rajputs, whose troops bolted on two different days of the battle. They were untrained, unmotivated, and unwell. During the second rout the troops rushed out into the sea up to their necks, firing indiscriminately at other English troops who, thinking the Germans were attacking them from the rear, also broke and ran.

    Other than that unit, however, the troops behaved well. The failure of soldiers to act like soldiers has been greatly exaggerated. A few dozen men bursting out of the underbrush in a hysterical frenzy can look like an entire battalion in flight, if you watch them from a safe and distant perch. Wapshare describes collapse and panic in the Sixty-first Pioneers, but that's hearsay. He wasn't with them. Tighe often had no idea what was really going on. Aitken, often as not, didn't even bother to watch. Norman King saw most of it from shipboard or from the headland above the beach. And RM witnessed it from the worm's-eye view of a man in isolation whose range of vision was curtailed by jungle and self-absorption.

    Lt. Gordon S. Johnson, the only one of the commentators who actually spent most of his time in the thick of the fighting but was able to see quite a bit of it as well because he spent part of his time defending the high ground at Ras Kasone, wrote: "From personal observation I know [of only one] incident of misconduct on the Part of the Sixty-first Pioneers on 4 November 1914. The rest of the action was comparatively uneventful for that unit. . . . The statement [RM's, in one of his letters to historian Charles Hordern] that the 'bulk of the Sixty-first Pioneers had dispersed in panic' etc., was manifestly untrue. . . . From where I stood . . . I had a fair view of the beaches and saw nothing of the panic described. . . . There was no thought of retirement. . . . Most of the Battalion had been shot at from 1.30 PM to 6.30 PM without being able to retaliate effectively and the general feeling was one of impatience at being denied the opportunity." [Gordon S. Johnson, "Notes on the Official History of the Campaign in East Africa" in PRO file CAB 45/35.]
62. RM, *Army Diary*, 101.
63. This expression of former confidence in Force "B" makes sense only if the passage is one of the few surviving fragments from original, or very early, diary notes before RM began to revise both his history and his derisive predictions. In a later entry he writes, "The fight at Tanga was possibly the finest example of how an operation should not be conducted. . . . Our 8,000 men, with 16 machine guns, a mountain battery and the 6 inch guns of the *Fox*, were beaten by 1,000 of the enemy with only four machine guns and no artillery." (*Army Diary*, 97–104.) It may seem odd that we've returned to four German machine guns, when a day or two ago they were bristling from every window in Tanga.
64. News was not withheld from Whitehall, of course. On November 8, 1914, Caulfield sent a "Telegram from Senior Naval Officer, Mombasa, to Admiralty, on failure of attack on Tanga, German East Africa." (CHAR file 13/38/74-75). First Lord of the Admiralty Winston Churchill retorted by asking why *Fox* and

Goliath had not bombarded Tanga in support of the infantry attack (CHAR 13/38/72.)

65. The cited documents are in PRO file # WO 32/5810, "CLOSED UNTIL 1966—Gen. A. E. Aitken on the Operations at Tanga." (Lord Crewe, author of the dresing-down of Aitken, was Secretary of State for India in February 1915. A few months later he became Lord President of the Army Council.) The *London Daily Mail*, on January 4, 1924, reported, "After the British reverse at Tanga, of which owing to the censorship the public heard little at the time, he [Aitken] was removed from his command. [In 1921] it was announced in Parliament that General Aitken was not responsible for the reverse and that compensation would be made. [The Government] stated that he was permitted to retire with effect from 1918—the date on which he attained the age of fifty-seven—on the maximum pension of his rank." This generous postwar gesture was made by a Parliament of which Aitken's brother Lord Beaverbrook was a prominent Member. On January 3, 1924 Brig. Gen. Arthur E. Aitken, sixty-three, died of a sudden heart attack in a taxi while touring between Rome and Capri. At time of death he was District Commissioner at Bath, England, and described himself as an unreformed "red-hot Imperialist."

66. PRO file # WO 32/5810, "CLOSED UNTIL 1966—Gen. A. E. Aitken on the Operations at Tanga."

67. Lettow, *East African Campaigns*, 40.

CHAPTER 6: NAIROBI

1. RM, *Army Diary*, 172.
2. Gordon S. Johnson, "Notes on the Official History of the Campaign in East Africa," PRO file CAB 45/35.
3. Wapshare diary (microfilm), IWM file 88/61/1. By "Tommy" he does not mean a British soldier; he means a Thompson's Gazelle.
4. RM, *Pirates and Predators*, 199.
5. RMD, vol. 18, 108.
6. RM, *Army Diary*, 115–116. This statement can be taken with the customary grain of salt, as several of his photographs from Kenya—snapshots of fellow officers, various generals, and the like—later appear in his published books (notably *Kenya Diary*); are we to assume he lost his photos selectively?
7. Moyse-Bartlett, *The King's African Rifles*, 267. The saga of the man-eating lions and the construction of the Tsavo bridge has been retold in many books and several movies (e.g., *The Ghost and The Darkness*).
8. Lettow, *East African Campaigns*, 204. See also W. E. F. Ward and L.W. Ward, *East Africa: A Century of Change, 1870–1970* (New York: Africana Publishing Corp., 1971), 79. Lettow liked to describe himself as "ultraconservative" (*Mein Leben*, 14) but in the decades that followed the Great War—both during and after his parliamentary career in Weimar politics—he stood consistently against the Nazis, expressed openly his contempt for the Hitler gang, and refused to play a part in the fascist regime. After the war he continued to write, and in the 1950s he returned to Africa to help East Africans gain their peaceful independence (an effort in which RM claims to have participated as well). Today it probably would be accurate to describe Lettow not as an ultraconservative but as a libertarian. He honored traditions in which he had been brought up, but he

was a compassionate and brilliant man who did not adhere to doctrines unless they made sense to him.

9. In one capacity or another, nearly four hundred thousand Allied soldiers, sailors, naval, merchant-marine crews, builders, bureaucrats, and support personnel participated in the East Africa campaign. They were assisted in the field by an additional six hundred thousand African bearers. So the Allies employed nearly a million people in their fruitless pursuit of Lettow and his handful of merry warriors. See Geoffrey Hodges, ed. *The Carrier Corps: The Story of the Military Labor Forces in the Conquest of German East Africa, 1914–1019*, 2nd rev. ed. (Nairobi: Nairobi University Press, 2000), 20–206.

10. RM, *Army Diary*, 107.

11. RM, *Army Diary*, 195–196.

12. "GEA" was German East Africa.

13. Letter from Gordon S. Johnson, in IWM file 77/109/1. The letter evidently was addressed to Leonard Mosley's publisher. Undated, it must have been written in the early 1960s. Johnson writes that Mosley, in his 1963 book, "cannot . . . be blamed for swallowing everything he was told by von Lettow-Vorbeck and Meinertzhagen. . . . Meinertzhagen was eighty and gaga by the time this book was written and, in any case, wrote a fictional account of his adventures in GEA to suit his own prejudices and hatreds."

   By the accounts of those who knew RM in the 1960s, he was not "gaga"; nor was Lettow. Johnson hadn't seen either of them in years. (Lettow died in 1964, at age ninety-three.) Johnson is more reliable when he discusses RM's personal behavior in East Africa, because he was there. For two years in Nairobi he directly observed RM in action.

14. RM's official intelligence reports are scattered among PRO folders CAB 45/12, CAB 45/48, CAB 56/7, WO 32/5324, WO 95/5289, WO 95/5290 (misfiled as 2590), WO 95/5291, WO 95/5292, WO 95/5360, WO 95/5364, WO 106/346, WO 106/347, WO 106/348, WO 106/573, WO 106/576, WO 106/577, WO 106/578, WO 106/638, WO 161/21, WO 275/1120, WO 374/20803. See also Sheppard's diary in PRO file CAB 45/42.

15. *A Handbook of German East Africa*, published by the Admiralty War Staff Intelligence Division, various editions through January 1916.

16. Hugh Cholmondeley [pronounced "Chumley"], third baron of Delamere (1870–1931) presided over the association of British East African settlers from 1904 on. A social leader and ardent booster, he introduced quite a few agricultural innovations and did everything he could to make British East Africa into an African version of New Zealand by encouraging immigration from Europe. He and RM were not close, but they were acquainted and sometimes hunted together.

17. Wapshare diary for 1914–1915, IWM file No. 88/61/1, entry for 20 February 1915. By the date of this writing Colonel Mackay was still titular head of intelligence but had moved to his new post on Mafia Island and RM was de facto chief of intelligence at Nairobi. This was formalized in the spring.

18. Norman King's diary shows that during 1915, when not interviewing German prisoners of war and turning in his reports to RM, he went on safari, wrote a report on a leper settlement, and participated in planning a British take over of the German colonial government because evidently he expected to be appointed postwar governor of German East Africa. This was not destined to happen.

(The post would be awarded to Maj.-Gen. Sir Alfred H. M. Edwards, Comman-
dant-General of Rhodesian Forces, who signed the cease-fire with Lettow in
November 1918.)

19. F. B. Adler, A. E. Lorch, and H. H. Curson, *The South African Field Artillery in
German East Africa and Palestine, 1915–1919* (Pretoria: The South African National War Museum, 1958), 71.

20. In *The Army List*, 1917 ed., RM is shown as promoted from Captain to Major on
September 1, 1915. He served as Special Appointment "graded Gen. Staff Off.,
3rd grade" from February 15, 1916.

21. See RM's reports in PRO file WO 95/5291 and in PRO file CAB 45/12—"Intelligence notes on East Africa." Some officers who have served in such positions
have pointed out to me that if a hot item came into the Intelligence office, the
Duty Officer wouldn't necessarily wait to insert it in his daily or weekly report
(which had to be sent to the printer and set in type and then distributed within
the command). If urgent news came in, RM would have hurried to the telephone or run personally down the hall to deliver the news verbally. Of course
there must have been such occasions. But if he did go rushing to headquarters
with urgent intelligence, one would expect to find a report of it later in the
weekly Intelligence summaries and/or the headquarters war diaries. Occasionally such updates do appear. Often they are contributed by officers other than
RM. For example there are handwritten notes, scribbled by Col. S. H. Sheppard,
Tighe's Chief-of-Staff, on the margin of RM's printed report of 25 December
1915; it is in PRO file WO 95/5291, and displays the writer's frustration after
inserting the latest report on the day's German attack on the railway, which
Sheppard complains "must surely be THE most vulnerable 'war' railway in the
world!"

22. Wapshare diary for 1914–1915, IWM file No. 88/61/1. "Nairobi 4 Feb. [1915]
Thursday. Went out in car in the evening with Meinertzhagen. I unfortunately
hit a doe Tommy by mistake. He got a buck."; "Nairobi Monday 22 [March
1915]. Went out in car with Meinertzhagen. Got nothing." So forth.

23. Lt. Col. R. E. Murray writes, on 23 January 1916, "Intelligence unreliable."
One can sense the frustration in the abrupt scrawl of his handwriting. For
months the only intelligence he receives about the enemy comes from his own
scout patrols. (Murray's handwritten war diary in Hopkins' papers, IWM file
94/28/1.) Colonel Sheppard, on December 27, 1915, wired a pointed complaint
to HQ about the intelligence he wasn't receiving. (PRO file WO 95/2590; also in
WO 95/2593.)

24. RM, *Army Diary*, 164. The printing press belonged to the Nairobi *Standard*,
which had been well established for some years prior to the war, and is still
published today as *The East African Standard*.

25. Collectors' price information was provided to me in a letter of 24 February
2000 from historian-publisher, collector, East Africa expert, and good friend
Gerald Rilling. The use of paper currency in the colonies tended to be restricted
by custom to Europeans and Asians; native Africans didn't trust it and usually
insisted on being paid in coin or copper wire.

26. RM, *Army Diary*, 126–127, citing Hordern *History of the Great War: Military
Operations East Africa*, 119, 134, and 265.

27. Hordern, *History of the Great War: Military Operations East Africa*, 265.

28. RM, *Army Diary*, 193–194.

29. Arthur Weinholt, *The Story of a Lion Hunt* (London: Melrose Ltd., 1922), 102. When RM published his heroic memoirs, Wienholt was not around to dispute him. Wienholt disappeared while on a reconnaissance mission in Ethiopia during World War II.

30. See for example Christopher J. Thornhill, *Taking Tanganyika: Experiences of an Intelligence Officer, 1914–1918* (London: Stanley Paul & Co., 1937).

31. Lewis J. Greenstein, "The Nandi Experience in the First World War," in *Africa and the First World War,* Melvin E. Page (ed.) (London: Macmillan, 1987), 85.

32. RM, *Army Diary*, 162–163. The event is supposed to have taken place in 1915; in his typescripts RM mistypes the year as "1931." That may be the year when he actually wrote this nonsense.

33. RMD, vol. 17, 44–46.

34. PRO files CAB 45/31 (80614) and CAB 45/31B. The second folder contains a handwritten letter from J. J. Drought to F. S. Joelson, dated 17 November 1938, describing how, after a gruelingly fast march, he and his 'Skin Corps' reached Mwanza on Lake Victoria, ahead of a South African force—at Christmas 1915, when RM claims Drought was with him. See also PRO file WO 374/20803.

35. See RM's reports in PRO file WO 45/2540. On days when he was absent from his office, daily reports would be signed by the staff officer on duty—i.e., physically in the office. On occasion in 1914–1916 the reports are signed by Lt. Gordon Saffery Johnson, Capt. G. F. C. Shakespear, and Capt. Freddie Guest, among others. But the reports at Nairobi dated 24, 25, 26, and 27 December 1915 are all signed "R. Meinertzhagen, Major, General Staff." They all can be found in the PRO folder WO 95/5290 (which as aforesaid has been mislabeled 95/2590).

   All in all there is no chance that RM and James Drought were behind enemy lines way out west in the bush wiping out an enemy camp, killing the existential Graf, and eating the German's Christmas dinner on December 25.

   The German war diaries include no officer named Wecklenburg (or anything remotely similar), and neither the incident nor the Graf—*any* Graf—appears on the roster of German headquarters and subsidiaries. Yet in *Army Diary* (p. 163) RM appends this remark: "Many years later when I was in Amsterdam I was introduced to the Duke's brother who, on hearing I had been in East Africa during the war, asked if I could tell him the circumstances under which his brother was killed. I felt an utter brute and was unable to tell him the truth; it revealed the revolting and cruel nature of war." It seems difficult for a nonexistent person to have had a brother. The only known name-match in African history is Graf Adolf Friedrich Herzog, Grand Duke of Mecklenburg (born 1873), author of *From the Congo to the Niger and Nile* (1913)—was that book lying near RM's desk when he dreamed up the story? The real Mecklenburg had been Governor of Togoland before the War, but he was not within a thousand miles of East Africa at any time in 1915 or 1916, and he lived until 1969. (*Das Deutsche Biographische Adelsrepertorium*. Berlin: Institut Deutsche Adelsforschung, 1999.)

36. Twenty-sixth Squadron (RFC) Diary for March 1916, PRO file AIR 1/1250/204/7/21. See also Twenty-sixth Squadron extracts in PRO file CAB 45/65. The Twenty-sixth had arrived at Mombasa early in 1916 and for the rest of the year was almost constantly on the move. Its pilots flew photo/reconnaissance, dropped grenades and little bombs, and kept up intercommunications among isolated Allied detachments in the thick bush and mountains. The climate

ravaged aircraft and pilots; Twenty-sixth Squadron, or what was left of it, returned to England at the end of 1916 and was disbanded.

37. RM, *Army Diary*, 169.

38. The squadron's BE2C reconnaissance biplanes were of a 1912 Bleriot design (French). Only four of these were still flying in March 1916 when the squadron was re-supplied with a handful of Voisin reconnaissance "bombers" from South Africa. The Voisin was a French-designed craft that was manufactured mainly in Russia and used mainly on the Eastern front. At the time of RM's flight the Voisins had just arrived and the BE2C's were still on hand. He may have gone up in either model, as both were two-seaters with the typical fore-and-aft open cockpits of the period. But when he says the "engines were cut" he betrays an ignorance sublime. None of the powers had any multi-engine aircraft in East Africa; the phrase "cut engines" didn't come in until near the end of the war. Of course the plural may have been a simple slip of the tongue, but it's the sort of slip one might have made in the age of the Tri-motor or the twin-engine Dakota (when the "'diaries'" probably were actually written) rather than in 1916, when nobody thought of an airplane's engine in the plural.

    Both models of aircraft were slow and clumsy of maneuver. They had been retired quickly from active air-combat regions and served out the remainder of their service in exile, in theaters like RM's where there was little chance of a dogfight.

    The BE2C had a single 70hp Renault V8 engine, a maximum speed of 72 mph, and under ideal conditions a maximum ceiling of 10,560 feet. (RM claims, let's remember, that he and his pilot climbed nearly twice that high.) The Voisin, a heavier craft, was a steel-framed pusher biplane with a 120hp Salmson engine, a maximum speed of 65 to 80 mph depending on configuration and armament, and an effective maximum ceiling of the very same 10,560 feet. (The number is arrived at because of conversion from the metric—3,500 meters.) It was an exceedingly sluggish plane due to its weight, and had a very slow rate-of-climb. And the equator's abnormal barometric pressures, combined with sudden updrafts and downdrafts above the flanks of Kilimanjaro, made the region a very difficult place for flying.

39. Lettow, *Mein Leben*, 144–145.

40. Letter ("Ref. G/S/16") attached to Twenty-sixth Squadron (RFC) Diary for March 1916, PRO file AIR 1/1250/204/7/21.

41. The popular Smuts had proven himself a tough guerrilla leader when he had led Boer forces against the British a dozen years earlier. Most recently he had been South Africa's Defense Minister. His appointment to command East Africa was political—it was meant to rally South African opinion behind the British cause. Smuts arrived in early 1916 expecting a quick victory over Lettow and his little black army, and was not interested in listening to advice from East African veteran generals, like Tighe, who tried to tell him it wouldn't be so easy. RM says he was among those who tried to warn Smuts, but no one else supports him in this contention; from the respect and even camaraderie with which Smuts treated RM later in London and again after the war, it seems more likely that RM ingratiated himself, perhaps by agreeing with Smuts' prejudices. Smuts was a full-bore racist when it came to Africans; he believed they were not ready for war.

42. Lettow, *East African Campaigns*, 122.

43. The Right Honorable Frederick Edward Guest (1875–1937), third son of Ivor Guest (Baron Wimborne) and Cornelia Henrietta Spencer-Churchill Guest (Winston Churchill's aunt), came up from Winchester and initially set out to pursue an Army career, but after working as Churchill's private secretary for a few years went into politics on his own and served as a Liberal MP from 1910 forward. He was re-elected to Parliament in every contest between 1910 and 1929, from three successive districts. He named his son Winston in honor of his cousin Churchill. Frequently Freddie Guest signed documents guaranteeing loans that were taken out by Churchill, who was chronically broke. (See CHAR files 28/143/79, 28/143/81, 28/144A/62.) Guest's biographer, Donald Cregier, wrote to me that Churchill's wife Clementine "believed he was a bad influence on Winston. (More likely the opposite!)" [Don Cregier, letter to author, 30 October 2001.]
44. See daily Intel Reports in PRO file WO 95/5292.
45. Private diary (typed copy) of Brig. Gen. C. P. Fendall in British East Africa for 1916, PRO file CAB 45/44, p. 66.
46. Diary of Brig. Gen. C. P. Fendall, PRO file CAB 45/44, p. 65.
47. RM, *Army Diary*, 198.
48. RM betrays himself yet again. Lettow was a "light" Colonel. He did not become any sort of General until a year after RM's departure from the theater. Like so many others this passage cannot have been written when it purports to have been written.
49. RM, *Army Diary*, 205. Simla was the headquarters of the Indian Army.
50. RM, *Army Diary*, 200.
51. Early in the New Year, Smuts selected Freddie Guest to serve as his aide in the Imperial War Conference in London. After that, Guest moved wholly back into politics and became Chief Whip for Lloyd George's coalition government. He and RM got together at intervals—for example on March 2, 1917, RM dined with him in the Commons an hour or two after Guest had delivered a speech in the House. Not long thereafter when Guest was asked to draw up a plan for peace terms to be dictated to Lettow as soon as the latter was defeated [sic] in East Africa, RM confides in his diaries that he felt obliged to compose a lengthy critique of Guest's draft proposals (RMD, vol. 19, 106).
52. RMD, vol. 18, 96–98.

CHAPTER 7: ZION

1. RM's work with the Zionist leadership did not really begin until after his return to England at the beginning of 1918.
2. After he had completed academic studies in France in 1895, Aaron Aaronsohn (1876–1919) had been employed in Palestine as an agronomist by Baron Edmond de Rothschild. In 1906 Aaronson discovered wild wheat (*Triticum dicocoides*) at Rosh Pinah, a discovery that made his name in world botany and enabled him to build an agricultural research center near Haifa. In 1915, with his sister Sarah and several friends, Aaronsohn had established the underground NILI group to gather intelligence and inflict sabotage on the Ottoman Turks and the Arabs who dominated Palestine. In mid-1917 Aaronsohn moved to Cairo in order to coordinate the NILI network with the Intelligence apparatus of Allenby's Allied command; that was when he first met RM.

In 1919, with the Zionist delegation to the Paris Peace Conference, Aaron Aaronsohn reunited with RM as the two of them pressed for a definition of Palestine's boundaries. But Aaronsohn's contribution to the negotiations was cut short on May 15, 1919, when his plane crashed into the English Channel and he was killed.

3. The acronym NILI derives from the initials of a Hebrew saying from the Book of Samuel: Netzach Israel Lo Yeshaqer (The Glory of Israel shall not lie down). The four leaders of NILI were Aaron Aaronsohn, his sister Sarah, swashbuckling poet Absalom Feinberg, and the Aaronsohns' younger brother Alex.

   American-Israeli scientist and historian Dr. Shmuel Katz writes: "The price paid by Aaronsohn's group was high. In an attempt to reach Egypt overland by way of the Sinai Desert, Aaronsohn's chief collaborator, Avshalom Feinberg, was killed by Bedouins. In September 1917, the Turks exposed the NILI network. Two of its leaders, Naaman Belkind and Yosef Lishansky, were hanged in Damascus; many of the others were imprisoned and tortured. Among these was Aaronson's sister, Sarah, who had served as his deputy. During a respite from torture, she succeeded in shooting herself." (Samuel [Shmuel] Katz, *Battleground: Fact & Fantasy in Palestine* (New York: Bantam Books, 1977; reprint, New York: Taylor Productions, 2002. See Chapter 5.)

   The most spectacular overt accomplishment of the NILI group took place on September 6, 1917, when they blew up Yildrim's huge depot of munitions at Haidar Pasha. But it was outraged reaction to this crippling dose of sabotage that the Turks wiped out most of NILI's members, along with innocent Jews who'd had nothing to do with the spy-guerrilla organization.

   It seems odd, but is true (because it preceded his alliance with Zionism), that RM had no connection at all with the first Jewish element of the British Army, which was formed in August 1917 at the urging of Vladimir Jabotinsky and was commanded by British Lt. Col. J. H. Patterson, an East African veteran whom RM knew. Officially the 38th–42nd Royal Fusiliers, the regiment (actually only a battalion at first) became known as "The Jewish Legion." It fought in Allenby's army to great effect during the Palestine Campaign. One of its soliders was David Ben-Gurion. [J. H. Patterson, *With the Judeans in the Palestine Campaign* (New York: Macmillan, 1922)].

4. Anthony Verrier, *Agents of Empire: Anglo-Zionist Intelligence Operations, 1915– 1919: Brigadier Walter Gribbon, Aaron Aaronsohn, and the NILI Ring* (London: Brassey's, 1995), 320.

   Col., later Brig. Gen. Walter H. Gribbon, CMG, CBE (1881–1944), had organized the polo team at the Quetta Staff College while RM was allegedly beating his polo-pony groom to death there, but Gribbon's diaries mention neither the death of the syce nor the existence of RM. In Cairo, Gribbon was an Operations Staff Officer who became Allenby's de facto clearing-house for intelligence that helped form an appraisal of Turkish strength in the Levant. Under DMI Macdonough's orders, Gribbon worked closely with Aaron Aaronsohn and the NILI spy ring in 1916–1917.

5. Anthony Verrier, *Agents of Empire*, 320.

6. Quoted in Katz, *Battleground*, Chapter 5.

7. Aaron Aaronsohn, full-length unpublished diary in the Aaronsohn Archive at Zichron Ya'aqov, Israel; entry for 25 June 1917, in Cairo.

8. RM, *Middle East Diary*, 211.

9. Brig. Gen. Sir Wyndham Henry Deedes, CMG, DSO (1883–1956), served in 1917 as second-in-command to Brig. Gen. Sir C. Gilbert Clayton, head of the Military Intelligence Department (Cairo). Deedes was devoted to the Zionist cause and RM refers to him as eminently decent, but the overall flavor of the writings suggests that RM disliked him, presumably because of his socialist leanings. (After his Palestine office Deedes returned to the UK where he pursued social work in London's East End.)

Weizmann felt Deedes and RM were Zionism's only two friends at Court. The rest, he said, were all jackals and wolves. (Tom Segev, *One Palestine, Complete*, 142.)

In 1938 Deedes went to Vienna to try and help Jews get out. His effort was unsuccessful but it was meticulously reported, unlike RM's fanciful ones. (See "The Situation of the Jews in Austria," Report submitted to the Executive of the Zionist Organization by Dr. Leo Lauterbach, 29 April 1938. Tel Aviv: Zionist Archives, File S5/653.)

By the late 1940s Deedes was still doing good deeds—social work in Bethnal Green. He founded the Anglo-Israel Association in 1949.

Photocopies of some of Deedes's correspondence are housed in the Private Papers Collection, Middle East Centre, St. Antony's College, Oxford, File GB 165–0079. These, like the papers in the archives of the Anglo-Israel Association that he founded in 1949, contain virtually no references to RM. Deedes shows up in connection with RM mainly in one-way conversations—the information comes from RM, as when RM claims Deedes and Wavell were his co-conspirators in pulling off opium-cigarette drops over Turkish lines (*Army Diary*, 223). Geoffrey D. Paul, director of the Anglo-Israel Association, told me: "Given that Wyndham Deedes was a man of almost studied modesty, and Meinertzhagen apparently the exact opposite, they probably kept their distance from each other." (Geoffrey Paul, letter to the author, 8 August 2001.)

Deedes participated in 1945 in a controversial debate on Palestine with Dr. Maude Royden Shaw, who argued for the Arab position. The debate, broadcast by the BBC, was hosted by Ronald Storrs. RM makes no mention of it, although he probably felt snubbed by not having been included. (The radio debate, called "The Future of Palestine," aired on the BBC Home Service on October 26, 1945, and was transcribed and printed in *The Listener* 34, no. 877 (1 November 1945): 479–95.)

10. Quoted with permission from Ronald Florence, letters to author, 26 July 2005 and 31 July 2005.

11. RM, *Army Diary*, 257. Elsewhere, to make sure we don't miss the point, he adds: "The Jew means progress and perhaps the upsetting of modern governments, the Arab is stagnation and stands for immorality, rotten Government, corrupt and dishonest society." (RM, *Middle East Diary*, 12.) One might be a trifle more impressed with his sincerity were it not for the strident anti-Jewish rhetoric nearby in his writings.

12. An example of the sort of promise that was flogged so cavalierly is His Majesty's Government's dispatch of a special message that was carried personally by Cdr. David George Hogarth to Sherif Hussein. Dated 4 January 1918—two months after the Balfour Declaration had guaranteed British support for Zionist statehood in Palestine—it stated: "The Entente Powers are determined that the Arab race shall be given full opportunity of once again forming a nation in the world. . . . So far as Palestine is concerned, we are determined that no

people shall be subject to another." ("Report of a Committee on Correspondence between Sir Henry McMahon and the Sherif of Mecca," London, 1939: *Parliamentary Papers*, Cmd. 5974, His Majesty's Stationers, p. 48.

13. RM's network of agents appears in no record other than his diaries. British Intelligence had no organization of behind-the-lines agents. It relied on freelance sources, principally NILI. Not until the very end of 1917 was the Intelligence Staff expanded. At that time it became officially the Intelligence Corps (Cairo)— it recruited a large number of agents who spoke Turkish and/or Arabic and it began to achieve results toward the end of the war. All this occurred, however, after RM's departure from the theater.

14. Copies of Turko-German wireless intercepts, preserved in the files of the Public Records Office, include quite a few "SECRET" signals that are deciphered and transcribed into plain English; many of these are dated as early as January 1917—months prior to RM's arrival. See Egyptian Expeditionary Force documents, PRO file WO 106/1511.

15. RMD, vol. 27, 118.

16. RM's account of the episode is found in his typescript diary typescripts at Oxford. The date of the entry is 1 June 1926; there is no corresponding entry in the 1917 volumes, nor did he ever publish the story. One may entertain the opinion that it is all but emblazoned with neon letters spelling out "afterthought" and "fantasy."

   The context of this entry is one of his postwar meetings with Lettow in Germany. RM claims to have told Lettow about the Zeppelin caper, much to Lettow's amazement because—RM writes—Lettow had never known anything about the Fatherland's valiant attempt to re-supply him by air. That's ridiculous. Lettow knew all about it when it was going on. *Deutsche Ost-Afrika* had to be alerted in order to prepare a landing site for the huge craft, and everyone in Lettow's camp had been awaiting her eagerly and was deeply disappointed by the failure of her mission. Yes, communications were difficult, but for something this important, by 1917 Germany and the *schutztruppe* usually managed to make contact one way or another, creating impromptu radio-relay systems on temporary patchwork networks through neutral territories. The fact that Lettow didn't mention this fact to RM is but one among many indications that he didn't trust RM with any more information than he needed to impart in order to keep RM talking. Lettow learned a great deal from RM; RM seems to have learned very little from Lettow.

   What's more telling about this passage is that it appears in RM's 1926 diary and not in the 1917 one—and that he didn't publish it. This probably is why many previous historians and biographers either missed this whopper or failed to attach any importance to it. It did not, however, escape the attention of author Michael Occleshaw, who seems to have swallowed it whole and replicated it in his book *Armour Against Fate*. Mr. Occleshaw clearly did a great deal of deep digging and difficult research for that book and I don't mean to denigrate it; its main fault is one we all have shared—a willingness to believe stories that are told by someone who "was there."

   Occleshaw stated in 2005 that he still has not seen reason to change his mind about RM. (Michael Occleshaw, letter to author, 10 February 2005.)

17. Dirigible L-59 traveled about 4,200 miles in ninety-seven hours—a world record. It seemed to suggest the Germans could have bombed Chicago if they had chosen to. (For a variety of reasons, involving ballast and balance and prevail-

ing winds, that would have been an impracticable if not impossible one-way journey, but it did make for useful propaganda.)

A previous attempt to re-supply the *schutztruppe* by airship had failed when the moored dirigible was struck by lightning and exploded. *Marinezeppelin* L-59—last and greatest of the wartime dirigibles to be built under the personal direction of Graf von Zeppelin—was as long as an ocean liner. The fifty tons of military, medical, and food supplies she carried (including her structure and skin, which were to be dismantled and used as fabric, etc.) would have more than doubled Lettow's resources. The fact that the *schutztruppe* managed to struggle on without this vital shipment is testimony to the grit and valor of Lettow's band.

I'm obliged to Frank Contey (letter to the author, 26 October 2000) not only for information about L-59 but also for his patience in correcting several misconceptions I had formed about the flight. Historian Contey—who at the time was preparing a detailed article about L-59—provided this emphatic statement: "I can assure you that Meinertzhagen had nothing, repeat NOTHING, whatsoever to do with the L-59."

18. The name in various accounts is spelled Frank, Franke, Franck, Francke, or other variations thereof; and the first name is not always Fritz. (Incidentally, and unrelated, everyone in the family referred to RM's brother Frederick by his nickname Fritz.)

19. The date under which Murray's permission was granted, according to RM's typescript diaries at Rhodes House Oxford (vol. 20, pp. 16ff), was July 13, 1917. By that date, as keen-eyed clue-hunters will have noticed, Murray had been replaced by Allenby and had been gone from the Middle East more than a month. RM too seems to have noticed the discrepancy in his typescripts in time to head off their replication in his published books. Instead of re-typing whole pages yet again, however, he simply added a last-minute explanatory fillip for the published version, tipping in a casual mention (for the first time) claiming that he had approached Murray earlier—"When I first arrived out here"—to get the general's approval for the scheme. (*Army Diary*, 216.) The implication is that he wrote the entry in July, when the scheme was already up and running, but had obtained the permission two months earlier.

Nearly all the Fritz Frank entries in the typescript diaries are additional pages or replacement pages that look to have been typed later than the pages around them. In the typescript diaries, vol. 20, p. 16, near the bottom starts a section headed "5-7-17. Deir el Belah." The two paragraphs under the heading describe the regular pattern of shifts in wind direction. The top paragraph of p. 18 is another paragraph on the same topic, but between the two we shift from blue to black typewriter ink, and the left-hand margin abruptly becomes much wider. Here, near the bottom of the page under the date July 13, 1917 (Cairo), he begins to relate the tale of the "certain bogey agent whom nobody knew but of whom all had heard, called Frank."

20. RMD, vol. 20, 16ff.

21. Bulletin issued 8 November 1917 by EMSIB—Eastern Mediterranean Special Intelligence Bureau (Cairo), in PRO file FO 882/14.

22. The unidentified officer's diary entry, datelined Gafa, 7 October 1917, is quoted in R. E. C. Adams' book *The Modern Crusaders* (London: Routledge Ltd., 1920), 9–10. My thanks to Yigal Sheffy for discovering this item.

23. RM was a seasoned hunter, and he'd been under fire, but here he seems to have been influenced by the conventions of pulp fiction. Anyone who has been proximate to a moving bullet is aware that a near-miss doesn't whistle. It cracks, not only because it creates a mini-sonic boom but also because that sound blends into the boom of the gunshot itself unless the listener's ear is so distant from the gun that the sound of the discharge is delayed. In other words if someone shoots at you from nearby, what you hear mainly is the bang of the gunpowder exploding inside the gun, amplified by the crack of the speeding bullet as it breaks through the sound barrier. And if someone shoots at you from far away, you'll notice the sharp crack of the bullet as it goes by your ear, followed an instant later by the boom of the distant gunshot. (Techno-freaks will point out that there's no sonic boom if a bullet is half-spent with distance, or if it is a huge slow-moving bullet designed to stop a gorilla, or if it is a normal sort of bullet that's been fired by an old-fashioned black-powder weapon. Such projectiles do travel at subsonic speeds, but in the absence of any suggestion to the contrary we must assume that these bad guys took potshots at RM at fairly close range and with reasonably contemporary ammunition.)

24. RM, *Army Diary*, 217–219

25. The contents of one or two of these letters are typed into RM's diaries. None of the originals seems to have survived.

26. RMD, vol. 20, an update note typed on the reverse of p. 24 (opposite entries for July 1917). In vol. 21, p. 112, under an entry datelined Aleppo, 12 September 1919, is typed a line directing the reader to the entry for 13 July 1917 regarding that particular postwar encounter with Frank. This line, directing us to the earlier volume, is typed as a continuing portion of the text and not as a later insertion.

27. RMD, vol. 24, unnumbered page dated 10 August 1924.

28. Most of the entries concerning Frank/Franke appear in one isolated section, in vol. 20 starting at p. 16. The interviews with "the Greek" and the rest of the Frank story extend through to the bottom of p. 26. The next page is numbered 28. The topic is completely different, the typewriter ink is considerably fainter, and the left-hand margin considerably narrower than on the pages containing the Frank story.

29. Maj. Gen. Sir George Grey Aston, KCB (1861–1938) had been Colonel Commandant of the Royal Marines Barracks, Eastney, Portsmouth, when the Great War broke out. Then he was assigned to "Special Service, Admiralty War Staff," a capacity in which he led exploratory Royal Marine commando raids on Zeebrugge, Dunkirk, and Ostend—missions of great danger, requiring great skills and stamina of a man then in his mid-fifties.

After his official "retirement" from active service in 1917, Aston became a member of the Secretariat of the War Cabinet. Upon war's end he was tapped to help reorganize the Naval Intelligence Department at the Admiralty. Then he spent the last two decades of his life writing books that seem to reflect flights of fancy at varying altitudes. Some loyal admirers continued to take him seriously, however, and by the time his *Secret Service* was published it had become an open secret that the heroic "Mannering" in his allegedly true tales was in fact RM. Sir George Aston thus became one of the "reliable" sources upon whom later generations relied in re-telling many great stories of derring-do. He is inaccurately called "the real director of the Secret Service in the Middle East in World War I" by Richard Deacon in *A History of the British Secret Service* (London: Frederick Muller Ltd., 1969), 271.

30. Aston, *Secret Service*, 179ff. The book was first published in 1930, in New York, by the Cosmopolitan Book Corp. of J. J. Little & Ives Co.; in the American edition the same passage begins on p. 194. I've found no textual differences between the two editions, but their typesetting and pagination are different. The three-year delay in British publication may have been imposed by H. M. Government under provisions of the Official Secrets Act. The quoted sentence about "Fritz" is from p. 183 in the British edition; p. 199 in the American.

31. There was, in fact, a real Fritz Frank. A mild sort of archaeologist and surveyor of German descent but Turkish birth and citizenship, he was forty-one when the war broke out, and was not a figure to strike alarm into anyone. But he was dogged by the dragon's-breath of the "Fritz Frank" mythos for the rest of his long life. He happened to live in Palestine and he did a bit of topographical surveying work for the Turks early in the war, in Sinai—trying to find sources of water. This was no unimportant endeavor in that desert, and it did have military value, but the work could hardly be classified as covert espionage, as it was conducted openly on then-Turkish soil. He didn't speak English (with or without an Australian accent). He never infiltrated Allied lines or spied on Allied activities or masqueraded as a British officer or perpetrated dirty tricks, nor does he seem ever to have met—let alone threatened—RM. After the war he sometimes claimed he had been one of a group of saboteurs who had floated a mine in the Suez Canal; the mine sank the steamer *Teiresias* in 1915, partially obstructing the canal until it was removed. That incident took place but Frank probably was not involved in it—he may have trotted it forth defensively as a postwar dinner-party boast when confronted with blustering burghers who belittled him.

    The real Fritz Frank lived until 1969 (thus outliving his putative rival RM), alternately in Germany and Palestine and then Germany again. He never was able altogether to shake the mumbo-jumbo about his espionage adventures, but he did not argue that the nonsense was true, nor has anyone else shown a scrap of independent evidence to confirm any of it.

    I'm indebted for leads, and for information about the real Fritz Frank, to the real Yigal Sheffy, who has made a thorough study of both the real man and the fanciful agent. Sheffy's analysis is published in his article "The Spy Who Never Was: An Intelligence Myth in Palestine, 1914–1918," *Intelligence and National Security* 4, no. 3 (Autumn 1999): 123–142. The piece is well documented, good-humored, and directed mainly toward the ways by which nearly all of us sometimes choose "not to be confused by facts." Sheffy adds dryly: "The Frank segment, in fact, demonstrates the need for a critical approach to [RM's] diary. . . . Despite these discrepancies and questionable accounts, three biographies written about RM . . . all used his diary almost uncritically, treating the accounts of the disguised German spy as unshakeable fact."

    The fact that Fritz Frank actually existed is bad luck for RM. A real person can be traced; a fictitious one can't be.

32. RM, *Army Diary*, 227.

33. RM purportedly led an expedition into Siberia in an effort to rescue the Czar and his family by air in the summer of 1918. The full-length story (extrapolated from a few paragraphs in RM's diaries—see his *Army Diary*, 233–234) is related in Michael Occleshaw's *Armour Against Fate*. Never mind the fact that no airplane of 1918 was physically capable of such a rescue flight in terms of

either range or passenger capacity. The plane postulated—a single-engine De Havilland DH-4 biplane—could have gone a few hundred miles at most, at its cruising speed of 90 mph. It had only two open cockpits (one for the pilot) so it could have carried no more than one Romanov away from Ekaterinberg. Is one to picture the Czar and his family drawing straws?

Occleshaw weaves into his tale a co-conspirator who, disguised as a masseuse named Marguerite, safeguards the Grand Duchess Tatiana's epic journey across Canada. (Why Tatiana was picked, rather than another Romanov, is not clear.) According to Occleshaw the mysterious masseuse was in fact RM's estranged wife Armorel. When we consider the rancor and mistrust of that relationship, which would culminate in an angry divorce just a few months later, it is a bit difficult to believe RM would have entrusted Armorel with any sort of secret assignment.

The concoction in his diary may have grown out of his boredom with office work during the slow months in London that preceded his transfer to the Western Front. On March 17, 1918, he claims (*Army Diary*, 233–234) to have met at length with King George V; he says Queen Mary joined them and asked a number of questions about Lettow and the war in East Africa. She impressed RM with her interest and her knowledge, both of which he found more acute than the King's. After this, RM claims he met on further occasions with the King to receive orders for the Romanov caper, and that he concocted the scheme in concert with Maj. Gen. Hugh Trenchard, who was already famous as Chief of the Air Staff on the Western Front and soon was to become the father of modern air power and the creator of the Royal Air Force.

Trenchard and RM had met at the Other Club. Other than the actuality of that friendship, however, I believe the entire high adventure is purely a figment of RM's impish imagination. Trenchard was dead by the time RM published his hints about the caper. Meanwhile, interestingly, Trenchard had served in the 1930s as London Metropolitan Police Commissioner (i.e., Head of Scotland Yard) when investigations of RM's thefts were quashed at the British Museum around the same time—1934–35—when Trenchard and RM were co-founding the Anglo-German Fellowship Society (a Nazi front organization in London). For further information about Trenchard see Andrew Boyle, *Trenchard* (London: Collins, 1962).

Palace secretaries keep records of all visitors to members of the Royal Family, and in response to an inquiry whether any records support RM's claim that he met with the King at any time in 1917 or 1918, the Deputy Registrar of the Royal Archives, Windsor Castle, replied politely and patiently in a letter to my colleague Robert W. O'Hara, January 28, 2001, "'I regret that I cannot find any reference to a Maj. or Lt. Col. Richard Meinertzhagen, either in King George V's diary or in our other documentary sources." (If any meetings had taken place in confidence, they still would have been recorded. Their topics would have been marked "Secret" or "Confidential." In such a case, by the requirements of protocol, we would have received a polite answer to our inquiry informing us that the Registrar was not at liberty to answer our question.)

34. On October 3, 1918, the *Daily Telegraph* reported ". . . news of the fall of Damascus. . . . On the last night of September a force of cavalry rode into the city and took possession of it . . . and the fact that its captors were all of the Australian division is not the least fantastic detail." Chauvel's Light Horse had done its work again. Lawrence's own version and other subsequent romantic propaganda to the contrary, Lawrence and the Arabs did not reach Damascus until the following day.

35. Letters from Frederick E. Guest, House of Lords Record Office: The Lloyd George Papers, files LG/F/21/2/24 and LG/F/21/2/26. Additional information supplied in a letter to the author from Dr. Don Cregier, 26 May 2001. Cregier is Freddie Guest's biographer. Curiously in his diaries RM himself does not mention his Other Club membership (or many of his VIP connections). It is not clear how long he remained a member of the club.

     In his diaries RM tends to distance himself from Freddie Guest, whose forename he sometimes spells "Freddy," and who was an honored part of RM's wedding to Annie Jackson in 1921 just before Guest took office as Air Minister. In his diaries RM only infrequently mentions Guest, who was disliked by quite a few in the corridors of power who regarded him as a back room political serpent and bag-man. Guest undoubtedly was a sharp character who sometimes played close to the line, often while endeavoring to extricate his cousin Winston from the perils that followed one Churchillian gaffe or another.

36. 23 October 1918 is the date of the "Memorandum by Col. R. Meinertzhagen for Brigadier General, General Staff, GHQ, I: The Security Section," in PRO file AIR 1/1155.

37. RM, *Army Diary*, 234, 237. A few times in his heroic fantasies he fortifies himself with alcohol—during the sinking of the *Transylvania*, for example, and just after the fictitious crash-landing of Macintosh's biplane—but these pretended recollections do not seem to fit his pattern. He was not much of a drinker, according to those who knew him, and in times of stress he was not known to turn to alcohol. (Did he fear losing control?)

     These sections about the surrender documents and the explosion that blew him out of his car appear out of chronological order, both in the typescripts and in the book.

38. RM may have elaborated his role, or in memory may have confused it with his presence at the signing of the formal Treaty of Versailles several months later. (The official list of those who attended the latter signing can be found in PRO file FO 1011/118. RM is one of the sixty invited guests.)

     Several weeks after the November 11 armistice, he underwent surgery in a Red Cross hospital near Dieppe to correct the injury to his abdomen. Whether he had been blown out of a car by an explosion is open to question. It is not a matter of anyone's record other than RM's own. The surgery may have been due to the earlier injury from a horse-kick in the Mediterranean—if indeed *that* one actually occurred. The surgery evidently was dicey, for an infection set in and he suffered through an extremely high fever. He was hospitalized for a full month and was still on crutches weeks after that. In *Army Diary* (p. 246) he blames the injury and the resultant hospitalization for costing him command of British Military Intelligence in postwar Germany.

CHAPTER 8: ADRIFT

1. RM's recollection of the details appears in RMD, vol. 21, 38–40. The filing for desertion, and the granting of the divorce (pronounced decree absolute on 8 December 1919), are found in London Metropolitan Records file J77/1424. Armorel remarried in early 1922. The groom was Laurence Rivers Dunne, who was to become Chief Metropolitan Magistrate and would be knighted. Sir Laurence and Lady Dunne, as Armorel then became known, had a son and a

daughter, both of whom died in 1970 as did Sir Laurence himself. Armorel had died three years previously, "suddenly" according to the *Times* (London) of January 11, 1967. (Curiously, she expired in the same year as RM.)

2. M. R. D. Foot, "Richard Meinertzhagen," in *The Dictionary of National Biography: Missing Persons*, C. S. Nichols, ed., (Oxford: University of Oxford Press, 1993), 458–459.

3. Sir William Thwaites, the Director of Military Intelligence, wrote in his report to the War Office that the British Military Delegation to the Congress of Paris, January to August 1919, included six officers from the Directorate of Military Intelligence. None of the six names is RM. (Thwaites, "Summary Report of 6 May 1921," PRO file WO 32/10776.) There was nothing clandestine about RM's work at the Congress. He was there politically, on behalf of Zionism. Sir Charles Webster wrote: "At the [Paris Peace] conference I was Secretary of the Military Section of the British Delegation, a post I invented for myself, and had no special responsibility for Zionism which, so far as the General Staff was concerned, was in the capable hands of Colonel Gribbon and Colonel Meinertzhagen." (Sir Charles Webster, *The Art and Practice of Diplomacy* (New York: Barnes & Noble, 1962), 128.) But they were bypassed, for the most part. Foreign Office delegate Harold Nicolson wrote: "The Foreign Office section were [sic] from the outset given perhaps undue prominence, and perhaps too great a share of labor. The Military Section which included men of such marked ability as General Thwaites, Colonel Cornwall, Colonel Meinertzhagen, Colonel Heywood, Colonel Kisch, and Professor Webster, were in the early stages practically excluded from our deliberations. It must be confessed also that a certain element of departmental and professional jealousy entered into this discrimination." (Harold Nicolson, *Peacemaking, 1919: Being Reminiscences of the Paris Peace Conference* (Boston: Houghton Mifflin Company, 1933), 109–110.) In the book's index Nicolson refers precisely to the ranks of the officers listed. RM is shown as "Meinertzhagen, Lieut. Colonel R." (p. 376).

4. RM reports on an alleged intimate luncheon that included Churchill, Freddie Guest, John Shuckburgh, and T. E. Lawrence. RM's tirade begins with an outraged bleat about the millions it was costing Britain to finance Lawrence's support of an idiotic Arab policy. Then he noticed how Winston (in the diaries RM often refers to Churchill as "Winston") attended Lawrence's every word, idolizing him, captivated by Lawrence's "eulogistic" praise for Faisal and other Arab chieftains. RM wails in disgust about Winston's hero-worshipful childishness. (RM, *Middle East Diary*, 33.)

5. Debate about T. E. Lawrence persists among historians and biographers, especially those who, like me, may seem to have nothing better to do than parse other people's lives. The line is drawn between purists who seem to regard Lawrence's every statement as sacrosanct, and critics who recognize that in *Seven Pillars of Wisdom* Lawrence was expressing an emotional reconstruction of events seen through a mist of war and years. The book, in their view, is a splendid work of literature and only secondarily a history; it is gorgeously composed—its words and sentences and paragraphs are laid together with splendid grace. It contains distillations and interpretations and imprecise recollections, and at times can be an unreliable source of "facts," although it would easily withstand the sort of challenge we've put to RM's writings. (Lawrence may have erred but he seldom lied.) Lawrence himself was at considerable

pains to make the book's factual limitations clear in his 1926 Preface: "It [*Seven Pillars*] does not pretend to be impartial. . . . Please take it as a personal narrative pieced out of memory. I could not make proper notes." Lawrence was thoroughly traumatized by the war and by the duplicity of its political leaders, and in some ways never recovered from the madness of that experience. One thing that seems so sad about RM is that—traumatized or not—he went out of his way to insist his diaries and books were absolutely true.

6. In later years at social gatherings RM liked to tell a story about how, around this time, he "allowed himself to be captured by the Turks in World War I" for purposes of being interrogated so that he could break down and reveal phony secrets, after which he effected a miraculous escape back to his own lines. The capture and torture by Turks is virtually identical to the December 1917 experience related by T. E. Lawrence—not about RM but about himself. (The clause is quoted verbatim from a manuscript letter to the author dated 3 March 2002 from a correspondent who knew RM in the 1930s and who wishes to remain unidentified.) This unconfirmed personal recollection of RM's dinner-party tale suggests he may have adapted the story from an early version of the "Deraa" section in Lawrence's manuscript.

7. See for example RM's *Middle East Diary*, 40–41.

8. Months later, in the ultimate auctorial nightmare, Lawrence managed somehow to lose the only copy of his original manuscript on a railway platform at Reading Station. It was never recovered. He rewrote the entire book from memory.

9. Lawrence confirmed this in a letter to historian-biographer Basil Liddell-Hart, who reports it in his book *T. E. Lawrence to his Biographer Liddell-Hart* (London: Faber & Faber, 1938), 146. See also Basil Liddell-Hart, *Colonel Lawrence, the Man behind the Legend* (New York: Dodd, Mead & Co., 1934), 325. Jeremy Wilson, author of *Lawrence of Arabia: The Authorised Biography of T. E. Lawrence* (London: Heinemann, 1989), reported similarly in 1998 when discussing the publication of Michael Asher's book *Lawrence, The Uncrowned King of Arabia* (London: Viking, 1998).

   With regard to RM's two co-readers of Lawrence's original and subsequently lost manuscript, these notes: Maj.-Gen. Guy Payan Dawnay (1878–1952) had been Allenby's Chief-of-Staff in Egypt in 1917 and Haig's chief-of-staff in France in 1918. Gertrude Bell liked him enormously. (See letter to her mother dated 10 January 1916, in the Gertrude Bell papers at the Robinson Library, University of Newcastle upon Tyne.) Dawnay was a great friend of Wavell; he also was a friend of the Asquiths, the Churchills, and the Royal Family. Dawnay had been Lawrence's commanding officer in 1917. He was not universally liked or admired; he was generally regarded as being a sly fellow of conspiratorial bent, and while serving as Ian Hamilton's Chief-of-Staff at Gallipoli he had been instrumental in getting Hamilton relieved of his command. RM seems to have disliked but respected him; twenty years later he wrote that he had just dined with Guy Dawnay, and recalled, "I first met Guy in Palestine in 1917. He was BGGS [Brigadier General, General Staff] at GHQ. He was difficult and often gave me orders which Allenby would never have sanctioned, so I usedto [*sic*] go over his head, direct to Allenby. I told him so this evening and it rather shocked him." (RMD, vol. 42, 18; the entry is from 1937—RM was visiting Maud and Gilbert Russell at Mottisfont Abbey, and went bird shooting with Dawnay and others.)

Cdr. David George Hogarth, RNVR (1862–1927) was an academic who had volunteered for military service in the war but left the Navy immediately after the Peace Congress; he was not a career military man. An Arabist and scholar with an aptitude for the alleyways of intelligence, Hogarth had been appointed Director of the Arab Bureau in Cairo in 1916. He had been the pre-war curator of Oxford's Ashmolean Museum at Oxford, and had been Lawrence's mentor there, and in part it had been Hogarth's influence that had propelled Lawrence into the desert on his expeditions that had preceded the Great War.

10. RM—inevitably?—seems to have been unable to leave well enough alone. In his version, Lawrence occupied the hotel room directly above RM's. For reasons unexplained, Lawrence tied individual chapters in string and lowered them from his window so that RM could pull them in and read them in his own room. (RM, *Middle East Diary*, 51.) Various skeptics, including Lawrence's biographer Jeremy Wilson, have pointed out the absurdity of this alleged—and unnecessary—bit of melodrama.

J. N. Lockman (aka Jon Loken) published a monograph with the self-explanatory title *Meinertzhagen's Diary Ruse: False Entries on T.E. Lawrence* (Whitmore Lake, MI: Falcon Books, 1995), in which he examines RM's writings about Lawrence and seeks to demonstrate that virtually everything RM wrote about Lawrence was false. His analysis is valuable and much of it is on point. It does seem a trifle excessive in its zeal; Lockman seems to want us to believe the two men barely knew each other. That idea is not supported by the facts. It is worth noting, however, that at the time when the touted haversack ruse took place, Lawrence was hundreds of miles away from it all. Clearly he later accepted the RM version without questioning it; he does not seem ever to have encountered Lt. Col. Belgrave who, with Chetwode, had cooked up Allenby's wartime deceptions. Lawrence wrote: "After the Meinertzhagen success, deceptions, which for the ordinary general were just witty hors d'oeuvres before battle, became for Allenby a main point of strategy." (Lawrence, *Seven Pillars of Wisdom*, 537.)

The 1998 publication of *Seven Pillars*, annotated by Jeremy Wilson, contains for the first time in an open-market edition the full 1922 text of Lawrence's prodigious re-creation of his 1919 draft. Aside from a longer and oft-quoted passage about RM that can be found in the abridged editions (it is quoted earlier in this book), the single sentence about "the Meinertzhagen success" (meaning the Beersheba haversack ploy) is the only additional reference to RM in the unabridged *Seven Pillars*.

11. Chaim Weizmann, *Trial and Error*, 258. The "pogrom" was an Arab riot in Jerusalem at Passover. It was abortive—it was quelled by British soldiers—but its intent had been murderous.

12. Letter from Shuckburgh to Lord Ormsby-Gore, 15 September 1937, PRO file CO 733/352/75718/21. (See also pertinent index entries in Rabbi Dr. Chaim Simons's *International Proposals to Transfer Arabs from Palestine 1895–1947: A Historical Survey* (Hoboken, NJ: Ktav Press, 1988). It is clear from the text that RM must have allowed Shuckburgh to read selected portions of his diaries before this letter was written (the diaries were not published until more than twenty years later). RM may have typed out a few "diary" pages with appropriate emendations and changes, in order to impress Shuckburgh and in order to strengthen the Zionist position in Shuckburgh's mind and perhaps, by extension,

in Ormsby-Gore's. Of course this is a surmise, but it has ample precedent—see for example the diary pages he typed up in the late 1920s and provided to Cyril Falls, about the haversack story, for inclusion in the aforementioned official history of the war in Palestine.

Additional testimony regarding RM's significance in the peace talks can be found in numerous records. For example the docket of Peace Congress Minutes for 21 October 1919 offers this summary: "Palestine & Zionism. Transmits communication from Colonel Meinertzhagen in which he advances his pro-Zionist views & enumerates the difficulties to be encountered by Zionists in Palestine." (PRO file FO 608/98, pp. 479 and 480.)

13. The "Meinertzhagen Line" began to appear after the war in writings about the proposed partitioning. In time the designation generally came to be accepted by historians. In fact, however, the only primary source for this item of faux history is RM himself. No Meinertzhagen Line was drawn on any map or document created during the Paris conferences. We hunted through many records, but the only interesting discovery was a "Map showing boundaries of Palestine in the French proposals of March and June 1920 , the Sykes-Picot line and the Meinertzhagen line." This is Map no. 10 in vol. 4 of the massive *Palestine Boundaries 1833–1947*, a compendium of official and semi-official documents assembled and completed in 1994 and published by the Archive Editions Company (London). The map in question is based on a War Office map dated July 1915—that's the same one RM used as the basis for his 1917 battle-front maps—and, in the Archive Editions publication, the "proposed boundaries" of the alleged Meinertzhagen Line are drawn in simple pencil lines superimposed on that map. The maps with these superimpositions were not presented anywhere until a long time after the end of the Paris Congress. The pencil notes may have been drawn in at any time in or after 1919. Obviously they were inserted after the fact—otherwise why are they in pencil? It should be noted, also, that a section of the Minutes of the 1919 Paris Peace Congress describes the history of proposals for postwar Middle Eastern frontier boundaries. "The possible alternatives have been discussed"—and none include the term "Meinertzhagen Line."

The entire tedious progression of boundary proposals and rejections can be found in mind-numbing detail in a document compiled by Dr. Henry Churchill King and the Inter-allied Commission on Mandates in Turkey: "The King-Crane Commission Report on the Near East, August 28, 1919, vol. 55, no. 27, 2nd section (December 2)." Every conceivable set of Palestine boundaries is included in the myriad jigsaw-puzzle outlines that are shown as having been proposed over the years for partitioning the region. In all, these boundaries have hundreds of names. None of them is Meinertzhagen.

14. London's fear of possible French incursions was in part real but it also was in part obsolete. The secret Sykes-Picot agreement of 1916 had laid down "spheres of influence" for the two countries in a postwar Middle East, but the final years of the war had ruined any strength France might have wanted to commit to her imperial ambitions. France's efforts to spread her sway beyond Syria never came to much, and she eventually was pushed out of Syria as well, not by the British but by Arabs.

15. Letter from Dr. Chaim Weizmann to Lord Balfour, 17 August 1919, in the Weizmann Archive, Rehovot, Israel.

16. RM himself does not seem to have realized the intensity with which Lord Rothschild and the Zionists lobbied for his being selected for the job. It was Weizmann who insisted that the Foreign Office select RM to be chief political officer for Palestine. In meetings with Lord Curzon, Weizmann asserted emphatically that RM, while clearly loyal to the Crown, nevertheless "would have the full confidence of the Zionist Organization." (E. L. Woodward and R. Butler, eds., *Documents on British Foreign Policy, 1919–1939*, First series, vol. 4 (London: H. M. Stationery Office, 1952), 265.)

17. It is true that RM sported a code name, which a few aficionados have taken as proof that he was a secret agent. In school, when fellow students had found his name all but impossible to spell, some of them took to calling him "Montezuma." RM adopted the nickname as his cable address (Montezuma London). He used it in signing communications to members of his family, including his children as they grew up. In telegrams and letters, his daughter Anne often addressed him by the Aztec nickname. We have prowled the files of the secret services in search of it. The result: RM never used "Montezuma" in anything other than an innocent friends-and-family context.

18. RM's official posting as Political Officer is recorded in an archive titled "Peace Congress," PRO file FO 608/106, pp. 269–270.

19. Entries for 29 and 30 September 1919, typescript unabridged Diaries of Gertrude Bell in the Robinson Library, University of Newcastle upon Tyne. As Miss Bell later learned, General Clayton's belief was misplaced.

    Adventuresome Oriental scholar and archaeologist Gertrude Margaret Lowthian Bell (1868–1926) took a First at Oxford in history at the age of twenty—a remarkable feat for anyone, and especially for a woman in that time. She mountaineered in the Alps and explored the Middle East in depth, 1890–1914, writing books and monographs about what she learned; she also found time between 1897 and 1903 to go all the way around the world—twice. In 1915 her fluency in Arabic gained her a position in British intelligence during World War I, in the Arab Intelligence Bureau in Cairo and afterward in the colonial office as a political officer. She served various high commissioners in the Middle East and in 1923 she created the National Museum in Baghdad. For further information see, for example, Janet Wallach's *Desert Queen: The Extraordinary Life of Gertrude Bell; Adventurer, Adviser to Kings, Ally of Lawrence of Arabia* (New York: Doubleday, 1996).

20. RMD, vol. 23, 48–49. Entry for 17 November 1922 (datelined Baghdad).

21. Diaries of Gertrude Bell, entry for 2 October 1919. Miss Bell met with RM on quite a few occasions during his Middle East appointments in 1919–1923. She had trouble spelling his name, and often referred to him simply as "Col. M." She tended to be accepting and tolerant toward nearly everyone, but made an exception in his case. As for RM, he seldom mentioned Miss Bell other than in the brief entry mentioned above, in which he waxed vitriolic about her but then in the same paragraph backed off and admitted he was finding her less unreasonable than he had previously thought.

22. In the colonial mentality it was assumed by most Europeans of rank that they were destined to rule the Middle East. This assumption ran across the entire spectrum of European political thought from liberal to conservative and from those who favored Zionism to those who favored kicking the Jews out or exterminating them. The assumption continues into the twenty-first century. In

Gertrude Bell's day the rationale was that Europeans were more sophisticated and "civilized" than the locals, and/or that Europeans had built the Suez Canal and had a right to protect it in their own commercial and military interests. Later the rationale was broadened to include economic theory, particularly the notion that since the West was the primary consumer of Middle East oil, and since money from the West was what supported the political regimes of the Middle East, therefore the West had every right to impose its will on the region and its inhabitants. One may fairly argue the moral and practical foundations and consequences of such a rationale, and people do so—endlessly—but in the meantime insoluble conflicts have arisen from these assumptions.

23. Sahar Huneidi, "Was The Balfour Policy Reversible? The Colonial Office and Palestine, 1921–23," *Journal of Palestine Studies* 27, no. 2 (Winter 1998): 38, note 6. (Source of interior quotations: "Enquiry into Rioting in Jerusalem in April 1920," *The Palin Report*, Port Said, August 1920, PRO file FO 371/5121/E/9373, pp. 44–46.)

24. Generally RM's "diaries" were accepted as genuine. See for example the review of *Middle East Diary* in the *Times* (London) *Literary Supplement*, January 22, 1960.

25. RM, *Middle East Diary*, 45. He does not mention how or where the chauffeurs were supposed to sleep during such overnight roadside stays. There is no serious reason to disbelieve his claim about the cars. From 1915 on, the British army had obtained increasing numbers of armored cars based on the Rolls Royce Silver Ghost chassis; there was a surplus of them kicking around Cairo when the war ended.

26. RMD, vol. 21, 101, 106, 110, 116, 118, 130–140, 114, 118, 120. He also mentions dryly, on p. 120, "I nearly shoot Col. Waters-Taylor's wife"—Mrs. Waters-Taylor was an unabashed pro-Arab anti-Semite, and RM felt she exerted a profound and evil influence upon the actions of her husband, the British military's financial Chief-of-Staff in Palestine.

   Michael Nicoll earned his living as Assistant Director of the Zoological Gardens at Giza. RM's completion of the older ornithologist's monumental study of the ornithology of the lower Nile was prepared in cooperation with Nicoll's widow. It became the first of several major Meinertzhagen bird books; it was published under his name ("by Col. R. Meinertzhagen") but was entitled *Nicoll's Birds of Egypt* (two volumes; London: Hugh Rees Ltd., 1930).

27. See for example a politely petulant letter dated 4 September 1919 to Colonel Meinertzhagen, CPO, from the Executive of the Zionist Organisation, in PRO file FO 371/5283.

28. Memo from Watson to Allenby, dated 16 August 1919, in PRO file FO 371/1051/124482.

29. Louis Bols, who was Allenby's Chief-of-Staff until 1919, became Chief Administrator in Palestine and military governor of Jerusalem from June 1919 until July 1920. His term of office coincided more or less with RM's; the two men worked closely together. (The dates of RM's official appointment as Chief Political Officer, Palestine and EEF, were 21 August 1919 to 30 May 1920. "Meinertzhagen, Richard, D.S.O., p.s.c.," *The Army List*, January 1925 edition, p. 195.) The extent to which Bols interceded with Allenby on behalf of RM and the Zionists is not altogether clear, partly because Wavell, who was not terribly fond of Bols, was the keeper of records and the writer of the Allenby biography, and partly

because if Bols himself made or kept any notes about such matters, they did not survive World War II. According to his family and the Liddell-Hart archivists at King's College London, all Bols's papers were destroyed in the Luftwaffe's London Blitz. RM himself sometimes regarded Bols as an anti-Semite, but Bols's influence with Allenby was considerable, and he allied himself with RM more often than not.

30. Chaim Weizmann, *Trial and Error*, 251. The incident is also reported in RM's *Middle East Diary*, 47. RM regarded Congreve as one of the army's most dangerous "hebraphobes"—a word he adopted early and used liberally.

31. The Balfour Declaration is a 67-word typewritten letter from Lord Balfour, the Foreign Secretary (and thus a representative of the Government of His Majesty King George V) to Lord Walter Rothschild. It is dated 2 November 1917. Its text:

Dear Lord Rothschild,

I have much pleasure in conveying to you on behalf of His Majesty's Government the following declaration of sympathy with Jewish Zionist aspirations, which has been submitted to and approved by the Cabinet:

"His Majesty's Government view with favour the establishment in Palestine of a national home for the Jewish people, and will use their best endeavours to facilitate the achievement of this object, it being clearly understood that nothing shall be done which may prejudice the civil and religious rights of existing non-Jewish communities in Palestine or the rights and political status enjoyed by Jews in any other country."

I should be grateful if you would bring this Declaration to the knowledge of the Zionist Federation.

Yours sincerely,

Arthur James Balfour.

32. See for example "Lt. Col. Meinertzhagen, Cairo, to FO, 18 September 1919," PRO file FO 608/106, pp. 269 and 270. In this cipher he objects to French meddling, and makes clear that he had the power to censor the news—a previously unemphasized fact that will come to possess significance in examining his career at the beginning of World War II.

33. RM, *Middle East Diary*, 84. Sir Herbert Louis Samuel (1870–1963), 1st Viscount Samuel, was MP for Cleveland, Yorkshire, 1902–1918, served in the cabinets of both Asquith and Lloyd George, and was Home Secretary from 1916 to 1919. He was a leading figure in the fights for children's welfare, the eight-hour work day for miners, workers' accident compensation, and similar humanitarian legislation. It was at the urging of Lord Balfour, and upon the recommendation of Chaim Weizmann, that he was appointed to the new post of civilian High Commissioner of the Palestine Mandate, a post in which he served from 1920 to 1925.

Later, after his Middle East tenure, Sir Herbert became Labor MP for Darwen, Lancashire, and served again as Home Secretary (1931–1932). His tireless record of support for Labor and liberal causes cannot have endeared him to the rigidly conservative RM, and it must be stressed that the selection of Herbert Samuel as civilian administrator for Palestine was made not by RM but by Curzon, Balfour, and Lloyd George at the urging of Chaim Weizmann. Nevertheless RM supported Weizmann's choice—right up to the lynching.

For further details about RM's tenure on Allenby's staff and the in-house conflicts regarding the British Mandate, see (among other studies) J. J. McTague Jr., "The British Military Administration in Palestine, 1917–1920," *Journal of Palestine Studies* 7, no. 3 (Spring 1978): 55–76; John Marlowe, *The Seat of Pilate: An Account of the Palestine Mandate* (London: Cresset Press, 1959), 72; Christina E. Zacharia, *Palestine and the Palestinians* (Boulder, CO: Westview Press, 1997), 70ff; and for an overview, Tom Segev, *One Palestine, Complete*.

34. RM wrote: "I first met Jabotinsky in Jerusalem in early 1920. . . . Jabotinsky was arrested, tried by court martial and sentenced to six years imprisonment. After a most painful interview with his wife, I agreed to intercede. I took the matter up with General Congreve, Commander-in-Chief, who said he could not interfere with justice. I told him he could interfere with injustice and that Jabotinsky's sentence was spiteful and was evidence of discrimination against Jews. Congreve agreed to reduce the sentence to six weeks and deportation for twelve months." (RM, *Middle East Diary*, 178.) See also letter from Jabotinsky to RM, 27 December 1939, at the Jabotinsky Institute in Tel Aviv.

35. Tom Segev, *One Palestine, Complete*, 98 and 140ff. See also Samuel Landman, "Weizmann's French Impersonator," *The Jewish Chronicle* 11, no. 30 (1962): 53. (Landman was a colleague of Weizmann's and served as General Secretary of the World Zionist Organisation from 1917 to 1922.)

36. Martin Gilbert, *The Stricken World 1918–22* (Boston: Houghton Mifflin, 1975), 583; and also RM, *Middle East Diary, 1917–1956*, 97. Amin al-Husseini, who later became a prominent Nazi, was a forebear of the late Yasser Arafat and an alleged influence on Saddam Hussein.

37. Katz, *Battleground*, 63–65. Similarly, Martin Sicker describes how Allenby disregarded official policy by allowing anti-Zionist elements to dominate the day, in *Pangs of the Messiah: The Troubled Birth of the Jewish State* (New York: Praeger Publishers, 2000), 16–17.

38. "Colonel Meinertzhagen to Foreign Office, 14 April 1920," Woodward and Butler, *Documents on British Foreign Policy, 1919–1939*, 241. See also Meinertzhagen's cable as quoted in Marlowe, *The Seat of Pilate*, 80–81.

39. Details of the sacking of RM, and its fallout, are lengthy and complicated. They can be followed in PRO files FO 371/5117; FO 371/5118; FO 371/5119; FO 371/5227; E 3142/85/44; WO 0152/5139 (M.I.2); FO 371/5357–77556; FO 371/5203 (document tag 77556 2). See also Herbert Louis Samuel, *Grooves of Change* (New York: Bobbs-Merrill, 1946), 183–184.

40. Archibald J. B. Wavell, *Allenby: Soldier and Statesman*, vol. 3 (London: George G. Harrap & Co., Ltd., 1946), 261–262.

41. RM, *Middle East Diary*, 84.

42. Victor Wellesley, Under Secretary of State, Foreign Office, to Secretary of State Lord Curzon, 30 November 1920, Papers of George Nathaniel Curzon, 1st Marquess Curzon of Kedleston, in the IOL.

43. RMD, vol. 22, 94.

44. Letter of 11 April 1947 from Kinnear to the Museum Director, in the Meinertzhagen papers in the BMNH, file DF 1004/225, document number 2203/19. RM's dealings with the British Museum from 1919 through the 1950s, and the disciplines attempted or leveled against him for offences he committed there, are covered in an extensive file of reports and correspondence held in the museum under the umbrella file designation DF/1004/CP/225/1.

45. See RMD, vol. 22, various pages, and the extant biographies—notably Mark Cocker's *Richard Meinertzhagen*, 143–146.
46. The wedding photograph is pasted into the RMD in vol. 22 on the back of p. 42.
47. Letter from Churchill to Curzon, n.d., probably January 1921, in the Papers of George Nathaniel Curzon in the IOL. See also "Churchill invites me to work in the Colonial Office," RMD, vol. 22, 6.
48. Letter from Lord Curzon quoted in Gilbert, *The Stricken World 1918–22*, 528. (Sir Martin Gilbert is Winston S. Churchill's official biographer.)
49. Gilbert, *The Stricken World 1918–22*, 553–555. According to historian D. L. Hurwitz, "Winston Spencer Churchill came out to Cairo and Jerusalem in March 1921 to rearrange the Middle East," and supported Gertrude Bell, who had "schemed in Mesopotamia and meant Faisal to be chosen for the throne during the Conference." After the three quick days of the conference, "Winston and Clementine went off with Lawrence and Miss Bell to see the Pyramids and were photographed on camels in front of the Sphinx. Churchill set up his easel and painted." [David Lyon Hurwitz, "Churchill and Palestine," *Judaism: A Quarterly Journal of Jewish Life and Thought* 44, no. 1 (Winter 1995): 3–30. See also a letter expressing RM's recollection of the events—"Meinertzhagen, Col. Richard. (1878–1967). Copy of letter 12 January 1964 to Landman suggesting that Balfour and Lloyd George had a policy for Transjordan that was reversed by the Cairo Conference of 1921," Middle East Centre, Private Papers Collection, St. Antony's College, Oxford, file GB 165–0202.]

    The Cairo Conference was attended as well by Air Marshal Sir Hugh Trenchard, by Palestine's High Commissioner Sir Herbert Samuel, by Cairo's Lt. Gen. Sir Walter Congreve and by an assortment of lesser officials.
50. Against T. E. Lawrence's vehement objections, the same conferees laid out the formal boundaries of Mesopotamia, to be "given" to Faisal ibn Hussein. No one listened when Lawrence repeated his prescient warning that the only way for republican governments to survive in Mesopotamia (later Iraq) was to divide the territory into three separate countries—one each for the Kurds, the Sunni Muslims, and the Shi'a Muslims. Lawrence made this recommendation, mind you, in 1920. (Memo from Sir George Macdonough, and Memo from T. E. Lawrence to the Eastern Committee of the Cabinet, November 1918, quoted in Wilson, *Lawrence of Arabia*, 574–575 and 579.]
51. Disproportionate weight has been apportioned to RM by numerous histories of events in the Middle East during the 1920s. This is not surprising, since RM was used as a "primary" basic source for innumerable works, including *A Survey of Palestine: Prepared in December 1945 and January 1946 for the information of the Anglo-American Commission of Inquiry*, (1946–47; rev. ed., 2 vols., supp., Washington, D.C.: Institute for Palestine Studies, 1991).
52. RMD, vol. 22, 46–48.
53. Robert Graves and Basil Liddell-Hart, *T. E. Lawrence to His Biographers Robert Graves and Liddell-Hart* (Garden City, NY: Doubleday, 1963), 143.
54. The Liddell-Hart/Meinertzhagen correspondence file in the LHC contains a large number of letters about the African campaigns 1914–1916 and the Palestine campaign 1917, as well as larger issues of military and political history. In his letters, RM carefully and patiently led Liddell-Hart down the track of his version of events while he also tried to impose upon Liddell-Hart his salty opinions about the commanders under whom he had served.

55. *Colonial Office List 1922*, 1923, xiv–xv, xviii–xix. As with most official publications of this sort, a copy can be found in the Public Records Office.

56. The friendship between RM and Harry St. John Philby did not receive much ink in RM's diaries or books, but it is manifest in their correspondence and in their later collaborative work on the book *Birds of Arabia*. See letters in the Harry St. John Philby Papers, St. Antony's College, Oxford, Box 17, File 7, "Meinertzhagen Correspondence."

57. Anthony Cave Brown, *Treason in the Blood: H. St. John Philby, Kim Philby, and the Spy Case of the Century* (New York: Houghton Mifflin Co., 1994), 19ff. There are several general sources concerning St. John Philby. None individually can be regarded as always trustworthy, but in aggregate they provide a good portrait of the rogue Englishman. See the unpublished diaries of Gertrude Bell; the Harry St. John Philby Papers, St. Antony's College, Oxford—especially Box 17, File 7, Meinertzhagen Correspondence; RM's unpublished typescript diaries and *Middle East Diary, 1917–1956*; H. St. John Philby, *Arabian Days: An Autobiography* (London: Robert Hale, Ltd., 1948); H. St. John Philby, *A Pilgrim in Arabia* (Robert Hale Publishers, 1943); Elizabeth Monroe, *Philby of Arabia* (London: Pitman, 1973); and most recently (and most reliably on the early life of Philby Sr.) the dual biography by Brown, *Treason in the Blood*.

    Philby's memoir of his public life was published as *Arabian Days: An Autobiography*. He also wrote the books *Arabia of the Wahhabis* (1928), *Forty Years in the Wilderness* (1957), and *Sa'udi Arabia* (1955), but as a writer he probably was best known for the haunting *The Empty Quarter* (1933).

58. RM's account of the trip in Jordan and Syria appears in *Ibis* (1924): 87–100.

59. RM's lengthy memo to Shuckburgh is part of PRO file CO 733/38; its signature page is numbered 861.

60. Lt. Col. F. H. Kisch, "Palestine Zionist Executive—Palestine Diary," entry dated 18 March 1923.

61. PRO file CO 733/38.

62. Churchill's quip has been quoted many times. It appears, for instance, in David Lyon Hurwitz, "Churchill and Palestine," *Judaism: A Quarterly Journal of Jewish Life and Thought* 44, no. 1 (Winter 1995): 17.

63. RMD, vol. 23, 48–49 and 152–158. On the back of p. 156 is typed a long list of birds seen in the Fayoum.

    RM's friend Maj. Gen. Sir Percy Zachariah Cox (1864–1937) was a Harrovian who had joined the army in 1884. In the 1920s and early 1930s Sir Percy—an ornithologist of considerable repute, as well as a noted British minister—worked frequently with RM, Gertrude Bell, and T. E. Lawrence. (PRO file FO 371 16924, p. 123A; see also Frederick "Hatter" Bailey's letters in the IOL.) A member of the Royal Geographic Society, Sir Percy was a sometime guest at RM's parties in the 1930s. RM wrote admiringly of him in his book *Birds of Arabia* (p. 580).

64. RM, *Middle East Diary*, 124.

65. RMD, Vol. 22, 88.

66. See PRO files CO 733/15.

67. Reports of RM's work during 1921–1922, mainly to do with military bases, are included in such documents as those in PRO file CO 733/38. RM discusses this period in his typescript diaries, vol. 22, 58–154. See also his *Middle East Diary*, 100.

68. RM, *Middle East Diary*, 118
69. RM, *Middle East Diary*, 117; slightly but not materially different in RMD, vol. 22, 130. After p. 128, which deals primarily with the baby's growth and diet and other domestic matters, we find a sudden change of paper-color, a slight carbon-ish blurring of the italic typeface, and pages numbered "130" and "130a." Page "130b" is quite clearly the page that originally followed directly after 128. Pages 130 and 130a, equally clearly, are pages added later. The first of these two pages deals with the leakage of top-secret Middle East Department dispatches and telegrams to Chaim Weizmann, Shuckburgh's presumed suspicion that RM is behind the leakage, Shuckburgh's dismissal by RM as a frothing-at-the-mouth anti-Semite, Churchill's blunt questioning of RM, RM's offer to resign forthwith, Churchill's refusal to accept that offer, and RM's offer of his own alleged suspicion about the identity of the source of the leaks.
70. For years thereafter, RM continues to refer to Churchill in his diaries as if they remained in contact. But no documents that mention RM can be found in Churchill's files after the early 1920s. This is significant because Churchill was a notorious packrat. He never threw away a scrap of paper once it came into his possession. He never knew when he might need it as material to refresh his memory for a book.

    Some of Churchill's files (mainly personal and family documents) are housed and archived in the Churchills' house at Chartwell Manor in Westerham (Kent), which is in any case a lovely place to visit. None of these documents concerns RM. A number of letters, memos, and other documents from (or perused by) Churchill can be found in the LHC. Those too are mum on the subject of RM.

    The outstanding (and massive) collection of Churchill papers is held in CHAR. Some of the collections are searchable online at website http://www-archives.chu.cam.ac.uk/perl/search/. A global search of that website for "Meinertzhagen" will turn up nothing, at least at the date of this writing. The only references to RM are in the thus far unscanned pre-1923 documents, mainly those from Churchill's tenure with the Colonial Office. Richard Langworth, editor of the Churchill Society's semi-annual *Finest Hour*, confirmed in a letter to the author, 26 May 2001, that he knows of no documentation connecting Churchill with RM post-1922. Nor has Dr. Don Cregier, Freddie Guest's biographer, reported anything of that sort.

    Churchill's authorized biographer, the eminent historian Sir Martin Gilbert, who probably has made his way through more of Churchill's documents than anyone else alive today, was kind enough to take the time to examine his records and to assure me that we haven't missed anything—there are no references to RM in the vast tonnage of Churchill papers with which Sir Martin is familiar (not even in the private personal papers—letters, etc.) after 1924.

    It therefore pays to tread carefully through any RM diary entries about "Winston" that suggest any contacts between them after 1924.
71. RM, *Army Diary*, 271.
72. RMD, vol. 22, 136.
73. Lucknow is a bit east of north-central India, on the way to Nepal.
74. RM's final appearance in *The Army List* is in the January 1925 edition. Here is his complete record, as reported there, under GRADUATION LIST OF OFFICERS OF THE BRITISH ARMY, p. 195:

MEINERTZHAGEN, Richard, D.S.O., p.s.c. Born 3/3/78 (from Mil[iti]a.) R[oyal] Fus[iliers]. 2-Lt 18/1/99. Lt. 8/2/00. Capt. 22/10/04. Maj. 1/9/15. D[uke of] C[ornwall's] L[ight] I[nfantry] Maj. 17/2/23. Lt.-Col. (Brev.) 3/6/18.

Empld. with K.A.R. 13/4/02 to 26/7/06. Spec. Appt. (G.S.O.3) British E. Afr. and Uganda and E. Afr. Force 15/8/14 to 14/2/16. G.S.O.2 E. Afr. Force 15/2/16 to 26/11/16. Spec. empld. War Office 29/1/17 to 14/4/17. G.S.O.2 E.E.F. 24/4/17 to 18/1/18. G.S.O.1 War Office (temp.) (temp. Lt.-Col.) 1/2/18 to 29/9/18. G.S.O.1 France (temp.) 30/9/18 to –/–/19. Spec. Appt. (Class S) (Chf. Political Off.) Palestine and E.E.F. 21/8/19 to 30/5/20.

E. Afr. 1904. M. and Cl.

Nandi 1905–6. Wounded. Despatches L.G. 18/9/06. Cl. 1914–21.

Despatches L.G. 1/2/17 and 8/2/17. Brev. of Lt.-Col. D.S.O.

[*Notes by author*: "p.s.c." means graduate of staff college at Quetta or Camberley, but not Sandhurst, which is a notch or two higher. "Despatches LG" means "mentioned in despatches" to the *London Gazette*—a military honor that is in some ways equivalent to being awarded a medal.]

75. In those days the sum of one pound sterling—equal to twenty shillings, or 240 pence—was a large sum to carry around in one's pocketbook; comparisons with currency values a century later are misleading because some commodities change in value more than others do—clothing, for example, was relatively more expensive then than it is now (and therefore most men and women owned only three or four outfits that they wore and washed at frequent intervals) but the British pound until the 1950s fetched five or more American dollars, and perhaps the idea can be clarified this way: in the early 1920s an ordinary British family could easily afford to eat quite well for a week on £5 or less. A brand-new Ford car could be purchased for about £65. "The poor" were people who had to subsist on less than £4 a month—and it could be done. (The late novelist Ross Thomas once explained to me that the only way for our generation to understand money when we look at prices—in terms of what we think money ought to buy—is to move the decimal point another digit to the right every fifteen or twenty years.)

CHAPTER 9: FAMILY

1. RMD, vol. 24, 26. He implies that he should have had a decent income from his own inheritance but that his brother Louis, in complacent incompetence, had mismanaged the business.

2. "Decree granting authority to Richard Meinertzhagen to sell heritage (Mrs. Annie Constance Meinertzhagen's estate)," Warrants of Register of Acts and Decrees, 5th Series (1830–1994): date of decree 6 May 1937. Edinburgh: The National Archives of Scotland, RepCode 234, Ref No CS46/1937/5/40.

3. RM, *Diary of a Black Sheep*, 216; see also p. 115 for his remarks about his mother in this context.

4. *Mallophaga* (bird lice) are wingless chewing ectoparasitic insects that live and feed on the feather fragments, skin, or hair of the victim or "host"—usually a bird, but sometimes a rodent or farm animal. These lice have a low, flat silhouette, with short legs designed to cling to the host. Unlike the blood-sucking lice of the order *Anoplura* (which includes human body and head lice), *Mallophaga*

rarely infest humans and do not actually puncture the skin; they scavenge a living off the surfaces of their hosts.

Lice are classified in the phylum *Arthropoda*, class *Insecta*, orders *Anoplura* and *Mallophaga*. There are about three thousand known species of *Mallophaga*— the order of biting lice in the *Insecta* class of the phylum.

For these and other key details I am deeply indebted to Dr. Robert Dalgleish, whose patience with my ignorance has been endless, and who at the time of this writing was completing a digitized catalogue of the Theresa Clay–RM *mallophaga* collection. His amiability is all the more laudable because he remained indulgent toward me even after I boorishly began our acquaintance by saying, "I have two modest questions about that collection of '587,610 lice, mites and flies'—One: Who counted them? And Two: Did RM acquire them in the manner I suspect? i.e., were most of them mashed flat?"

5. RM wrote an extended account of the expedition—one of the longest of his life, both in time and in distance—in RMD, vols. 25 and 26. He covered the trip more briefly in his unpublished ornithological memoir "Conquisitio Mea," a copy of which is in the Smithsonian Institution (Washington, DC). He published shorter recollections of the birds of the trek in various journals of the late 1920s, including *Ibis*, and later in his book *Pirates and Predators*, pp. 85ff. For his cliff-hanging description of a vulture-hunt during the expedition, see his "In the Mountains of the Lammergeier," in *Discovery: Great Moments in the Lives of Outstanding Naturalists*, John K. Terres, ed., (Philadelphia: Lippincott, 1951).

"Hatter" Bailey (1879–1967), famed as both a spy and a collector of moths and butterflies, is one of the few intelligence agents mentioned by name in the India Office's Calendar of Political Department files and "secret" papers. Bailey saw service as Political Officer in Mesopotamia and Persia during the period when RM was on Allenby's staff. After the Soviet coup of 1917, the British became extremely anxious about a perceived Russian threat to India. That was when Bailey embarked on his celebrated intrigue in Tashkent. Bailey's "control," who directed him from afar, was Sir John Shuckburgh. (The assignment, and Bailey's imprisonment there, provided the title for his subsequent bestselling book *Mission to Tashkent*, (London: Jonathan Cape, 1946)—publication of which was delayed twenty years by government order. The book became a bestseller.) Bailey in 1918 was sent into Tashkent, an established hub of dark doings, to evaluate the Russian threat and pave a way for British Forces, should their deployment be deemed necessary, by using his butterfly nets and his "Political Officer" title as diplomatic cover for intelligence-gathering. Unfortunately the Reds assumed the worst. Under a "shoot on sight" death warrant, Bailey hid from the dreaded Cheka secret police in the shadows of Tashkent's narrow streets for an entire year, living on his wits and sometimes concealed by Muslim families who had no love of the Reds. His book about these adventures is the stuff of classic "boys' own" espionage, complete with risky dispatches of coded secret messages in invisible ink.

In the 1930s, whenever the Hatter and his wife Irma were in England they attended RM's parties. RM mentions Bailey infrequently in his diaries—not at all in proportion to the length or closeness of the relationship, which is revealed in the archive of Bailey's letters in the IOL.

Bailey sometimes signed himself, and was addressed as, "Eric." (His given name, Frederick, contains the word "eric.") Under that name, Eric Bailey, he is mentioned in William Stevenson's *A Man Called Intrepid* (London: Macmillan, 1976), as working for Sir William Stephenson as King's Messenger in the 1940s. RM apparently took part in Bailey's getting that job. (Intrepid and the Bensons had close contacts. And so the web of connections continued.)

Hatter Bailey retired to a quiet country life in Norfolk where he died just a few months before RM in 1967. His widow Irma attended RM's memorial service.

6. Sálim Ali, *The Fall of a Sparrow*, (Oxford: The Oxford University Press, 1986), 158.

7. Ali, *The Fall of a Sparrow*, 249.

8. Ali, *The Fall of a Sparrow*, 93–97.

9. Ali, *The Fall of a Sparrow*, 100.

10. Cocker, *Richard Meinertzhagen*, Chapter 10, endnote 9.

11. For the same period of time he writes in "Conquisitio Mea" that he was in Nanyuki, Kenya; and in his typescript diaries, vol. 27, 92, he claims extraordinarily to be traveling with "Theodore and Kermit Roosevelt"—a particularly odd bit of fantasy, as Theodore Roosevelt had been dead seven years by then.

12. A small fact leads to pure speculation, but it just seems impossible to ignore. In 1922–23, as the Weimar Depression settled on Germany and starvation became pandemic, even Lettow—Germany's greatest war hero—found himself near starvation, and was preparing to leave his Bremen home and move his family by wagon to Hamburg where there was the prospect of a menial job. In *Mein Leben* he says he believes the citizens of Bremen heard about his plight and felt his departure would be an injury to the city's pride. Next thing he knew, he had a job in the Bank Association of Bremen. At first it amounted to little more than a clerical apprenticeship in the billing department, but he was happy to have the job. There may be pathos in the thought that a country's greatest living general should be reduced to such demeaning work—he was only fifty-four at the time—but we also can find a quiet sort of triumph in the willingness and the lack of arrogance with which he performed it.

Lettow was a very fast learner. Within six months, even though he had started with a total ignorance of banking, and retained a substantial lack of interest in the subject for the rest of his life, he was promoted and given command of the Foreign Exchange Department. (A few years later he took up a life of farming, punctuated by frequent lecture tours; he also continued to publish monographs. That life suited him far better than banking.)

That much is fact. So is this: RM's family owned the large foreign-exchange merchant bank in Bremen. RM had apprenticed there in 1898. He had written to, and received letters from, Lettow since the war. It is not unreasonable to see a possibility that he became aware of Lettow's plight.

Lettow, at least in his writings, never saw any connection between RM's regard and his own sudden rise to prominence in a field for which he claimed to have had no aptitude.

RM never mentions it either, but in 1930 he was the houseguest of Lettow's banking colleague Muller (rather than any of the Huth or Meinertzhagen households).

Was there a favor here that RM resolved not to mention?

If so, perhaps he deserves another niche of respect in the hearts of those who disbelieve his every second word.

13. Cocker, *Richard Meinertzhagen*, 172.

14. Rachel Hobhouse Clay (1883–1981) was a daughter of Henry Hobhouse (1854–1937) and Margaret Potter Hobhouse (1854–1921), a sister of Georgina (Richard's mother). Rachel therefore was Richard's first cousin. She had married Sir Felix Clay (1871–1941). Their daughters Janet and Theresa were not Richard's nieces as some (including RM himself) sometimes stated in order to avoid having to make complicated explanations. Nor were the two girls his second cousins. They were, technically, Richard's first cousins once-removed—i.e., they were the daughters of his first cousin. The distinction was to assume a certain importance within the family after Richard was widowed in 1928 and the two girls came to live with him, to look after him and his children.

15. RM presented his claim of an unconsummated marriage with Armorel in his typescript diaries, vol. 12, 62, under the date 24 February 1912, beside a musing topic-headline: "Should women be abolished?" His claim of chastity seems unlikely, as Richard and Armorel continued to live together in India for at least a year in what appeared to be a lively marriage punctuated not only by spirited quarrels but also by affectionate reconciliations. The quarrels were caused by Richard's jealous reactions to her ribald promiscuity—a pattern of behavior that, some insist, he would not have tolerated for so long if he himself hadn't been getting some of the benefit of it.

16. Nicholas Meinertzhagen, in tape-recorded interview with Mark Cocker and the author at NM's house in London, 27 June 2003.

17. "Suffrage" meant not only the vote. It addressed itself as well to laws that prevented many women from signing contracts, owning property, and enjoying other privileges that were enjoyed as divinely sanctioned rights exclusive to men.

18. RM, *Army Diary*, 165.

19. RMD, vol. 63, 124.

20. RM's aunt wrote a fascinating contemporaneous study of the Potter-Meinertzhagen women and their struggles: Beatrice Webb, *My Apprenticeship* (London: Longmans Green, 1926).

21. R. Meinertzhagen, "Systematic Results of Birds collected at high altitudes in Ladak and Sikkim," *Ibis* (March 1927): 602ff; and "Some Biological Problems Connected with the Himalayas," *Ibis* (January 1928): 480ff.

22. Letter to the author, 20 February 2000, from an ornithologist who prefers to remain unidentified. The letter concisely incorporates a significant amount of information that has subsequently, in bits and pieces, appeared in papers delivered before ornithological societies, and in publications, by numerous reporters and scientists including Nigel Collar, Rex Dalton, Alan Knox, Michael Lipske, Robert Prys-Jones, Pamela Rasmussen, and Gail Vines. These people and others are highly reputed in journalism and science—people who do serious homework seriously. Most of them are too young to have known RM personally. They launched their inquiries independently and without axes to grind.

23. RMD, vol. 28, contains most of RM's snapshot photos of Janet and Theresa. There is a sort of innocence about those pictures. The girls strike poses, but seem to be teasing the photographer; it's childlike and all in good fun and not at all smutty. What seems dubious is not the girls or their behavior—it's the fact that having taken the pictures, *he kept them in his diaries*.

24. RMD, vol. 11, 126.

25. RMD, vol. 28, 36ff. One of my fellow diggers muttered, "It gets so spooky you don't even want to *go* there."

26. RMD, vol. 28, 40–42 (entry for 16 August 1927).
27. The *Sunday Despatch*, October 28, 1928.
28. RMD, vol. 22, 152–158. Typed on the back of p. 156 is a long list of birds seen in the Fayoum.

    Michael Nicoll was two years younger than RM. He had done some work in the Zoological Society of London then began to travel; he recounted his expeditions in the book *Three Voyages of a Naturalist* (London: Witherby and Co, 1908). He had been given the post of Assistant Director at the Zoological Gardens in Egypt and had published "A Hand List of the Birds of Egypt" (Cairo Government Publication Office, 1919). He had completed quite a bit of his masterwork—a comprehensive book on the nation's bird life—when he died.

29. *Nicoll's Birds of Egypt* "by Colonel R. Meinertzhagen" is a huge work—more than seven hundred pages with copious illustrations and maps. It was published in two volumes in London by Hugh Rees (1930).
30. More on the subject can be found later in this book; see also Cowles, "George Latimer Bates 1863–1940: An Investigation into the History of His Unpublished 'Birds of Arabia' Manuscripts," *Archives of Natural History* 24, no. 2 (1997): 213–235.
31. These are direct observations about the contents of the typescripts, but it is impossible to tell when a particular section of the diaries was written. Perhaps "gush" (my word, not RM's) is too strong a description, but that is the feeling the passages convey to me. These materials seem to reflect what actually happened. As his onetime aide, Gordon Saffery Johnson, pointed out (cited elsewhere), RM sometimes told the truth if it didn't suit his needs to alter it (although he tended to exaggerate and romanticize even when there was no apparent reason for him to do so). To the extent that passages like these are unconfirmed by other sources, we may believe or disbelieve. What he really felt toward Theresa and her sister remains problematic.
32. RMD, vol. 29, 71–84.
33. "North Castle Tragedy," *Aberdeen Weekly Journal*, July 12, 1928, p. 5, col. 2—a report on the death of Annie Meinertzhagen on her estate at Swordale Castle, near Evanton, Scotland. Inevitable questions suggest themselves. Example: how would the reporter know what belief was in her head?
34. RMD, vol. 24, 84–86, 106. Facing the latter diary page are two photos of the third Clay sister, Margaret, in her bathing costume on the beach at West Runton, dated August 1928.
35. I'm deeply indebted to investigator Gordon Johnson (no relation to RM's onetime aide) of Scotland, who embarked on epic investigations to find and obtain certified copies of the death certificate, the statement of the medical examiners, and a probated copy of Annie's will. The Death Certificate is No. 1928 070 11—Annie Constance Meinertzhagen, 38—in the files of the Edinburgh Registrar General. It reports that death took place on 6 July 1928 "Abt 11 am In Policy Grounds, Swordale, Evanton, [Parish of] Kiltearn. . . . Cause: Injury to spinal cord & lower part of brain from a bullet wound at short range as certified by Dr J P Smith & Dr J Broadfoot, Dingwall. Registered by: R Meinertzhagen (widower) Swordale, Evanton 12.7.1928. Register of Corrected Entries, Vol. 1, Page 67: Procurator Fiscal's office 12.7.1928."
36. It was (and still is) believed by some members of the ornithological community that RM killed his wife. Perhaps understandably, sources for these kinds of

remarks tend to prefer to remain unidentified. There are quite a few of them, but in the end their number does not matter, since none of them witnessed the incident or has direct evidence to offer.

37. A well known science journalist told me, "It was widely believed amongst the ornithological community that he'd killed her." These suspicions have been a matter of widespread speculation for years. Another of his relations, who also had known him quite well during RM's lifetime, wrote to me, "Of course, the death of his second wife during pistol practice together was no accident." These statements, even when proffered as fact, really are only opinions.

38. Ralfe Whistler, letter to the author, 26 September 2000.

39. Yet another motive is offered by an ornithologist who wrote to me on 17 June 2006, about RM's refusal to re-examine his decision to publish the fraudulent paper, "Why did RM pretend . . . ? . . . I wonder if he did it as an act of defiance or of provocation to Annie herself. I can imagine their patience wearing thin with each other. Or him doing it as a dare that he shared with Annie, even though she might not have approved, just to show that he could do it."

40. The RM–Grogan yarn was related to me—separately—by RM's grand-nephew Nicholas, in an interview, and in correspondence by Gerald Rilling, East Africa specialist and acquaintance of Grogan's grandson. I believe RM and Grogan told the story, but I still don't believe the story itself.

41. RMD, vol. 29, 86.

42. RM, *Pirates and Predators*, 215.

43. RMD, vol. 29, 128–136.

44. The former hospital, at Ruthin in northeast Wales on the Clwyd, is today a luxury hotel. In the 1920s and 1930s it was a diagnostic clinic that catered to wealthy patients with neurological conditions. [Stanley A. Hawkins, "The History of Neurology in Belfast: The First Hundred Years," *Ulster Medical Journal* 75, no. 1 (2006): 15.] RM may have been introduced to the clinic by someone in the Churchill circle—in 1900 Churchill's widowed mother had been married there to George West—or the referral may have come from one of RM's own in-laws, Gerald Wollaston, who later also recommended the place as a heart-diagnostic center for his friend the economist John Maynard Keynes. Keynes recovered there, over several months in 1937, from a mysterious infection that followed a coronary. Politician and thriller-writer John Buchan (*The 39 Steps* and others) also turned up there later in the decade; Buchan would be connected to RM in various Anglo-German enterprises in the mid-1930s. [Papers of John Maynard Keynes, file JMK/67/PP, King's College, Cambridge.] The hospital sprawled at the upper end of the rugged vale and usually was called Ruthin Castle, although it was not located inside the actual castle (a thirteenth century ruin that stands on a tor within the 475-acre estate). According to Keynes, the weekly fee of thirty guineas included a large luxurious room with a huge bed and a balcony view and a private bathroom. [Robert Skidelsky, *John Maynard Keynes: Fighting for Freedom, 1937-1946* (New York: Viking, 1971), 1–2.]

CHAPTER 10: ESPIONAGE

1. They had got together in Kenya in 1916 according to RM's typescript diaries, vol. 17, 64.
2. According to one belief—strongly rejected both by Wollaston's son Nicholas and by RM's grand-nephew Nicholas Meinertzhagen—Sandy Wollaston was so convinced of the guilt of his brother-in-law in the 1928 death of RM's wife that he not only refused to allow RM into his house but stopped attending ornithology meetings because Colonel Meinertzhagen might be present there. Several individuals have reported in personal letters or interviews that Wollaston barred RM from his door and refused to have any communication with him during the two years between Annie's shooting death and his own. These informants include two who knew RM, one of whom also had known Wollaston quite well. They hasten to add that Wollaston's wife Mary ("Polly," RM's sister) did not share in her husband's suspicions.

   When suddenly Sandy Wollaston too died of a revolver bullet, less than twenty-four months after Annie's death, the coincidence led to an abundance of (unfounded) suspicion.

   Nicholas Wollaston, a good writer who has published the biography *My Father, Sandy: A Son's Memoir* (London: Short Books, 2003), has assured me that no estrangement took place, and he does not recall any accusations being leveled against Uncle Dick by his father, nor any ever uttered by his mother whether before or after Sandy Wollaston's death. RM and Mary remained on cordial terms for the rest of her life (she died in 1943).
3. The shooting deaths of Alexander Wollaston, Police Detective-Superintendent Willis, and the suicidal murderer Douglas Newton Potts became something of a mystery for a while; details emerged only gradually. The triple homicide was covered in "Shooting Tragedy at Cambridge," *Cambridge Daily News*, 3 June 1930, p. 5; in "University Shooting Sensation," *Cambridge Independent Press*, 6 June 1930, p. 11; in the *Cambridge Chronicle and University Journal*, 4 June 1930, back page; and more recently and with updated detail in the student publication *Red Dragon Pie* (King's College, Cambridge), no. 99, February 1997.
4. PRO file KV 2/982. Documents collected in the 12 May 1927 raid enabled the boffins in Room 40 to crack some key Russian diplomatic and espionage ciphers; these results were kept secret for a few decades. Some information was kept under wraps by British and American intelligence departments before being released to the public in 1999–2003. The raid was commanded by Guy Maynard Liddell, CB, CBE, MC (1892–1958), who later, in 1939–1945, was to serve as one of Britain's principal wartime spymasters; his letters and diaries recently were opened to researchers (PRO file KV 4/185–196). Sources of information about the 1927 raid are PRO files KV 3/15–17, 34–35, and PRO files in folder KV 5, plus KV 2/639–646, which contains personal files relating to individuals involved in the ARCOS affair. None of these sources mentions RM. He himself seems never to have mentioned the 1927 raid, so there seems no reason to believe he played any role in it.
5. Michael Occleshaw's account, in *The Romanov Conspiracies*, of a 1923 raid on a Russian trade office in London appears to be based largely on an interview with an officer named Nigel Watson, who told Occleshaw he had served as a subordinate officer to RM in the earlier secret raid. In fact Lieutenant Watson

at the time was a serving officer in a cavalry regiment (Lt. Col. F. R. Burnside, *A Short History of the 3rd King's Own Hussars* (monograph)—London: privately published, n.d.) and there seems to be no connection between Watson and the secret services. Most other histories do not mention any such raid in 1923. Recently opened PRO file KV 3/18–33 does describe a 1925 raid on Communist Party Headquarters in London, but not in 1923 and not on ARCOS, and it does not mention RM or Nigel Watson.

6. Lettow was conservative but anti-Hitler. Throughout World War II he was held virtually under house arrest by the Nazis; at one point, to support his family, he was reduced to making wooden shoes.

7. Example: "I visited Afghanistan on the usual double purpose—natural history and 'my other work.'" RM, *Middle East Diary*, 163.

8. The pocket gun-battle at Ronda is described in much greater detail in Cocker, *Richard Meinertzhagen*, 191–200, and RM's own account can be found in RMD, vol. 30, 10 and 20–30. Official confirmations of the event do not seem to exist.

9. Guy Benson's handwritten log of the Spanish birding expedition of 1930 was provided to another inquirer by Benson's son Nicholas; information herein is based on photocopies of that log-diary.

   One can always buy a medal in flea markets. If the Spanish government actually had awarded RM a King Charles Medal or any other decoration (as he claimed), one would expect to find a mention in Spanish records, or in the index to the UK's Foreign Office papers if not in the papers themselves, or in the *Gazette*, for in order to be permitted to wear a foreign decoration, permission would have had to be sought from the British government (and usually would be published in the official *Gazette*). In none of these sources is there any mention of RM's having been awarded such a medal.

10. Lettow, *Mein Leben*, 32–33. See also General J. C. Smuts, *Africa and Some World Problems* (Oxford: Clarendon Press, 1930).

11. Diaries of Beatrice Webb, entry for 3 May 1934.

12. Diaries of Beatrice Webb, entry for 27 August 1934.

13. E. B. Morgan sent two letters to Ian Hamilton, dated 13 and 26 November 1929 (Papers of Gen. Sir Ian Hamilton, LHC file 14/2/1.) In the second letter, Morgan writes, "Lettow-Vorbeck's engagements are in the hands of his English host Colonel Meinertzhagen. So I have written Colonel Meinertzhagen, who is at present in Scotland, and am awaiting his reply which I hope to receive tomorrow."

14. Papers of Gen. Sir Ian Hamilton, LHC file 14/2/1. Note that UBS Warburg, now a "Swiss" banking giant, still had its own skyscraper on Park Avenue in midtown Manhattan in 2006. Multinational banks tend to survive and thrive, no matter who wins the wars.

15. Ernest William Dalrymple Tennant was a merchant banker colleague of RM's father and brother. For more on his involvement with Nazism see the Lord Wilfred Mount Temple Papers—Notes on Hitler and His Policies by Tennant, 1935–9, HL, File BR 81/10.

   Hitler's crony Joachim von Ribbentrop served as German ambassador at large (1935–36), ambassador to Great Britain (1936–38), and German foreign minister (1938–45). Details of his role in the Anglo-German associations, like Tennant's, are documented in HL, File BR 81/1. Tennant was a friend of

Ribbentrop—in fact after the war he was subpoenaed to testify about Ribbentrop at the Nuremburg war-crimes trials.

16. RMD vol. 37, 138.
17. RM, *Army Diary*, 239
18. PRO file KV 5/2, 3.
19. During the mid-1930s British newspapers like the *Daily Mail* wrote regularly in praise of Hitler and the Nazi regime.
20. RMD, vol. 9, 112.
21. RM is listed among the organization's charter members on p. 13 of the "Annual Report 1935–36, The Anglo-German Fellowship, Incorporated October 1935," in PRO file KV 5/3. In PRO file FO 371/13639, RM's is the top name on the first page of a list headed "Document No. 1: Anglo-German Fellowship." He and Ernest Tennant were at the forefront of the organization of the new *bund*. He made a notation, "Inauguration of Anglo-German Fellowship, with Ernest Tennant," in RMD, vol. 37, 138. A bit later, in "Document No. 3" of the Fellow-ship lists, four men were assigned to RM for his personal recruitment efforts: Gen. Sir Ian Hamilton, Earl Jellicoe, Lord William Percy, and Lord Semphill (PRO file KV 5/3.) The founding of the Anglo-German Fellowship is reported in the Foreign Office's collection for 1935, PRO file FO 371/18878. See also "An-nual Report 1935–35, The Anglo-German Fellowship, Incorporated October 1935," in PRO file KV 5/3. The same PRO file contains the Minutes of the Anglo-German Fellowship meeting "held at 2:45 p.m. on Monday, 11 March 1935 at 9, Mincing Lane, EC3." The list of sixteen who attended includes Rich-ard Meinertzhagen, D'Arcy Cooper, Paul Rykens, and Ernest Tennant.

Paul Rykens, (Sr.) and [Francis] D'Arcy Cooper were directors of the Brit-ish-Dutch conglomerate Unilever Ltd. (By 2002 Paul Rykens Jr. was chairman of Unilever, which through its subsidiaries like Lever Bros. had become the largest consumer products company in the world, and controlled nearly half the world's commerce in food supplies.) In the 1930s, Rykens Sr. was a dedi-cated member, and committee chair, of the Anglo-German Fellowship. Accord-ing to one of RM's letters to Hatter Bailey, Rykens was an occasional dining guest of RM. Rykens joined Tennant's Trade Delegation to Germany on 9 May 1934, and led "the Rykens Mission" to Berlin to discuss the Bank of England's role in Anglo-German Negotiations. He also was a member of an industrial delegation that saw Hitler on 20 September 1934 (with Ernest Tennant, Robert Vansittart, and others). Both Rykens and D'Arcy Cooper were in the party that attended the Nuremburg Rally of 1935, and were the subjects of a subsequent Foreign Office enquiry. Before they made the two trips to Germany, Cooper and Rykens had been advised by the Foreign Office in no uncertain terms that in any conversations with Nazi officials they were representing themselves and not the British Government. Their visit to Germany in 1935 was referred to in Foreign Office papers as "The Rykens Mission." Tennant and Vansittart were in the delegation; RM was not.

Tennant—connected to the Anglo-Palestine Bank—was a frequent visitor to Germany in the 1930s and was a member of the party that attended the Nuremburg Rally of 1935. (HL, file BR 81 1.) He headed a trade delegation to Germany with Paul Rykens and Montagu Norman (governor of the Bank of England); he had meetings with Rudolf Hess and Hitler, and he features in several published books on Ribbentrop. There is no question Tennant was of some importance to the Nazis. Riding to the Nuremburg Rally of 1935, Tennant sat in Ribbentrop's car directly behind Hitler. (HL, the Lord Wilfred Mount Temple Papers 1935–1939, file BR 81/10.)

Other sources include: PRO files FO 371 17734, pp. 94 and 393, and FO 371 20734, p. 190, and FO 371 17734, p. 94; HL file BR 81/1; and the Meinertz-hagen–Bailey correspondence in the IOL. See also PRO file CO 732 57 11.

It has been suggested, not too convincingly, that RM was working as an infiltrator, reporting back on the inner workings of the Anglo-German Fellow-ship to Weizmann's World Zionist Organization. ("Dick, like it or not, was plunged into political intrigue, but the Zionist cause always stayed anchored in his mind."—Capstick, *Warrior*, 255–258.) Zionist records do not confirm this.

22. *Directory of Directors, 1941,* 1942.

23. PRO file FO 371/20749, p. 133. See also HL, the Lord Wilfred Mount Temple Papers—Anglo-German Fellowship Correspondence 1936–38, files BR 81/161 and BR 81/1; and "Persecution of the Jews in Germany, correspondence 1933–38," file BR 81/15. In the HL's Special Collections, the Lord Mountbatten Papers, see also file BR 70/99, political correspondence of William Wilfrid Ashley, Baron Mount Temple, from the Broadlands estate papers. Note that one must gain access to the Hartley Library's files by permission of: The Archivist, Hartley Library, University of Southampton, Highfield, Southampton SO17 1BJ, UK.

24. For example, RM was present at a Fellowship dinner "in honour of Prince Bismarck" held at the Dorchester on November 28, 1935. (HL file BR 81/1; RM's presence at the dinner is confirmed in one of his letters of December 1935, in the Hatter Bailey correspondence, IOL, and in a letter dated 16 September 1936). On another occasion, in December 1935, Joaquim von Ribbentrop, then German Ambassador in London and soon to become Reich Foreign Minis-ter, and Frau von Ribbentrop, were among guests of Lord and Lady Mount Temple at their home at Broadlands, Romsey, for two days' bird-shooting. In attendance were RM and other "friendly" guests. (PRO file KV 5/3; and RMD, vol. 38, 62 and 76, and vol. 40, 90. See also PRO file FO 371/20749, p. 133; and HL file BR 81/9.)

RM hosted the annual dinner of the Anglo-German Fellowship in 1937. They dined well—luncheons, dinners, and banquets every few weeks, nearly always in the Dorchester. (Victor Cazalet, a director of the Dorchester, was a member.) (HL file BR 81/1.) Objectively considered, the organization seems to have been toothless despite efforts by some members to militarize its attitude. See RMD, vol. 42, 14. See also PRO files BT 31/33916/305554—Anglo-Ger-man Fellowship 1935: Board of Trade; and CO 847/12/16, Anglo-German Fel-lowship: Proposed conference at Hamburg in 1938: Colonial Office.

See also a letter from Kirkpatrick dated 25 May 1939, in PRO file FO 371 23027, p. 318. On the Anglo-German Group's German Propaganda in England, see PRO file FO 371 18868, p. 224. See also "Anglo-German Fellowship 1935," a Board of Trade document providing details of how the Fellowship was set up as a company, in PRO file BT 31/33916/305554, as well as PRO file CO 847/12/16, a Colonial Office file tracking proposals by the Anglo-German Fellow-ship to organize a conference at Hamburg in 1938, including notes on a search for a speaker on administration of law in British African colonies. See also the covering summary in PRO file KV 5/3.

25. "The Focus was a conspiracy, and Churchill remained conspiratorial about it until the end of his life—imploring Spiers not to publish a memoir of the group as late as 1963. It never held public meetings in its own name, always using the cover of the 'New Commonwealth Society' or 'League of Nations Union.' Indeed in letters Churchill himself described it as 'private and secret.' . . . Although superficially contradictory, it was not unbelievable for a thoroughgoing anti-Semite to find the idea of an independent Jewish state attractive, especially as pre-War Zionism's main opponents were to be found on the ultra-left, led by anarchists and the followers of Trotsky." (Mike Hughes, *Spies at Work* (Bradford, UK: 1 in 12 Publications, 1994). See also Mike Hughes, "Churchill and the Focus," *Lobster*, no. 25, June 1993.) The Focus has come into better focus since Churchill's death; it is discussed in Gilbert Martin's *Winston S. Churchill: The Prophet of Truth, 1917–1922*, vol. 5 of Sir Martin's authorized biography of Churchill (Boston: Houghton Mifflin, 1977); in Stevenson, *A Man Called Intrepid*; and in Lycett, *Ian Fleming*, among other works.

26. Lycett, *Ian Fleming*, 89ff.

27. In *Pirates and Predators*, RM wrote about the place as if it still belonged to him. Mottisfont Abbey, complete with its twelfth-century original portions and its aviary where the young brothers kept owls and eagles, is now open to the public under the auspices of the National Trust.

28. RMD, vol. 38, 134.

29. Lycett, *Ian Fleming*, 2, 5, and 60–61.

30. Maj. Sir (George) Joseph P. Ball, KBE, OBE (1885–1961) in 1940 became Churchill's Deputy Chair of the cabinet's Security Executive, a seat from which Ball supervised the entire intelligence apparatus of the British government, both civilian and military. The cynical pragmatist Ball was not altogether unlike Churchill's other behind-the-scenes players John Bevan and Maj. Sir Desmond Morton. Joseph Ball believed in stealing documents and covertly bugging "our own" politicians when he felt such practices might be useful. His agents—such thieves were not yet called "plumbers"—cheerfully pilfered minutes and memoranda from Labor Party offices. In addition, he served simultaneously as both director of the Government's Films Division and as a director of the Conservative Central Office.

      Until 1942 Ball was the official director of MI-5. Then from 1942–1945 he served officially as deputy chair of the secret spy-hunting Home Defence Executive. His position remained powerful although his precise role in events remains a bit shadowy, like that of quite a few performers in the secret intelligence circus. He is said to have burned all his notes and (if they existed at all) diaries. (HL file BR 81 / 1, and David Turner, "The Secret History that Lies Behind the Zinoviev Letter," *The Guardian*, February 5, 1999.)

31. Lycett, *Ian Fleming*, 438. Fleming made the remark in 1964 not long after he completed his final James Bond novel, *The Man with the Golden Gun*.

32. PRO file KV 2/668.

33. RM's father had known just what to think about every person around him. Like his son, he did not always like what he knew. As RM later recalled, "On one occasion, when Sidney and Beatrice Webb accompanied by a red-bearded Bernard Shaw arrived at Mottisfont on a bicycling tour, he [Dee] fled from the house." RM, *Diary of a Black Sheep*, 46.

34. RM, *Middle East Diary*, 143–144.

35. Nicholas Meinertzhagen, tape-recorded interview with the author and Mark Cocker at NM's house in London, 27 June 2003.

36. John Lord, *Duty, Honour, Empire: The Life and Times of Colonel Richard Meinertzhagen* (London: Hutchinson & Co., Ltd., 1971; New York: Random House, 1972), 386; and Rodney Legg, *Lawrence of Arabia in Dorset* (Somerset, England: Dorset Publishing/Wincanton Press, 1988). Oddly, RM seems to have received more attention for this nonexistent office than he did for his role in the actual preservation of Heligoland as a permanent bird sanctuary. Heligoland is an island in the open North Sea, sometimes called the German Bight. RM seems to have felt he was solely responsible for its being designated a bird sanctuary. In fact he was one among many, but his efforts were significant. He was hardly the first to recognize the importance of Heligoland as a gathering point for migratory birds [see H. Gätke, *Heligoland as an Ornithological Observatory: The Result of Fifty Years' Experience* (Edinburgh: David Douglas, 1985), 423–24], nor was he the main voice for preserving its nesting grounds in the British delegation to the Paris Peace Conference of 1919. The diaries of bird-watcher politician Sir Edward Grey indicate that his chief contribution to the Paris peace negotiations was the request that Heligoland be set aside as a bird sanctuary. (Matthew Parris, "If Mr. Blair Wants a Subject for a Hinterland, I Suggest Politics," *Spectator*, February 22, 1997.) The naval installations on Heligoland were bombed into ruin by the Allies in World War II. Thereafter, RM resumed the quest. See his letter of 12 May 1946 to Alex Wetmore (Smithsonian Institution, record unit 7006: collection division 1: Alexander Wetmore Papers, Meinertzhagen correspondence, box 40, folder 5). Five years later, on May 14, 1951, RM was still pursuing the goal; he wrote to Hatter Bailey expressing his ongoing concern about the Bird Observatory at Heligoland. (Meinertzhagen-Bailey correspondence, Foreign Office documents section, IOL.) In this RM was backed up by a petition signed by Lord Alanbrooke and others. Apparently the petition didn't go down well in the Foreign Office, and it took continuing struggle by RM and several dedicated partisans to achieve bird-sanctuary status for the island (R. Böttger-Schnack, "Jurgen Lenz," *Monoculus* 36 (October 1998): 22. Published by the University of Oldenburg, Germany.) Today Heligoland is a tourist resort as well as a nature and bird sanctuary. An ornithological research institute runs and organizes guided tours; information is available from the Heligoland Biology Institute (Inselstation Helgoland) and in *Ornithologische Jahresberichte Helgoland*, published by Ornithologische Arbitsgemeinschaft Helgoland, Postfach 869, 27498 Helgoland, Germany.

37. RMD, vol. 35, 94–100; and vol. 36, 32.

38. PRO files CO 732/57/11 and FO 371/16924, p. 153. See also RMD, vol. 36, 34 and 44—these actually are only five pages apart, as he usually typed on only the even-numbered side of each sheet, reserving the reverse for paste-ins of photos, documents, dried specimens, and the like.

39. Binyamin Netanyahu, *A Durable Peace: Israel and Its Place Among the Nations* (New York: Warner Books, 2000), 60. See also Karen Armstrong, *Holy War: The Crusades and Their Impact on Today's World* (New York: Anchor Books, 2001), 23; Benny Morris, *Righteous Victims: A History of the Zionist-Arab Conflict, 1881–2001*, (New York: Alfred A. Knopf, 2001), 97; and innumerable other books and articles on the topics of Zionism and the history of Palestine since 1900. Selections from RM's diaries and the official government documents that he wrote in

1917–1923 are seized upon frequently by both Israeli and Islamic writers, as well as Western historians, to support their histories, opinions, and positions.

40. Several of RM's letters-to-the-editor are recalled in the *Wall Street Journal*, July 26, 1979.
41. RM, *Middle East Diary*, 151–152
42. RM, *Middle East Diary*, 152–160.
43. PRO file FO 371/17734, 393.
44. HL file BR 81/9, the Lord Wilfred Mount Temple Papers, Anglo-German Fellowship Relations with Germany 1936–38.
45. "Jews Are Beaten by Berlin Rioters; Cafes Are Raided," "wireless to *New York Times*," July 16, 1935, and follow-up story, "Nazi Turmoil," *New York Times*, July 21, 1935.
46. "Hitler Visits a Shrine," *New York Times*, July 18, 1935.
47. Prof. Ernst Mayr, letter to the author, 18 August 2003. Prof. Mayr did not know Berlin very well and cannot have known there was no hotel or other residential building that gave an overview of Hitler's living quarters. RM apparently didn't know it either, until sometime later when he composed the story in his diaries and chose to substitute the pocketed revolver for the sniper's windowsill.

During the same June 1939 Berlin visit, RM claims some furtive Jews sneaked into his hotel room to beg him to carry word back to Whitehall that Nazis were slaughtering large numbers of Jews in gas chambers. In fact, no significant gas chambers existed in Germany at the time. The Nazis had begun to murder Jews, sometimes systematically and on a fairly large scale, but mainly with bullets until after 1940. The first of the large, genocidal gas chambers did not go into operation until August 1941, when Zyklon gas (produced by a Frankfurt subsidiary of IG Farben) was first introduced at Auschwitz. So once again RM is dealing in pre-facts.
48. RM, *Middle East Diary*, 159.

CHAPTER 11: BIRDS

1. Letter from RM to Frederick "Hatter" Bailey dated 26 June 1931, in Foreign Office documents section, IOL, file 157. Theresa Clay spent parts of 1933 at Edinburgh and finished her studies there in June 1934, but did not receive her doctorate until more than twenty years later (DSc 1955). In the 1930s much of her time was devoted to the care of RM and his household and children and chores, and her own scientific inquiries. A correspondent who knew her and who, for the moment, prefers anonymity, writes to me that Theresa Clay's "doctorate at Edinburgh almost certainly [was] 'facilitated' by the ole boy. Her first appointment at the British Museum, following the demotion of Gordon Thompson at the hands of RM, again places her where he wants her." This correspondent adds that she could be charming, "but the 'ice lady' when she disliked or disagreed with someone." She was a first-rate natural scientist (as was confirmed by her book-writing collaborator, Dame Miriam Rothschild) but clearly she had a more mysterious side. The same anonymous correspondent, in a different letter, writes to me, "Thompson wrote [in a letter to] Gordon Ferris (Stanford) ca. 1938, that RM was behind his firing [from the BMNH]. This is one area where Tess is not so innocent. Thompson was fired for having a

personal collection of specimens within his area. Clay was doing the same, except it was called the RM collection."

2. Nicholas Meinertzhagen, tape-recorded interview with the author and Mark Cocker at NM's house in London, 27 June 2003. The same was reported by Dame Miriam Rothschild at her home during a personal interview with ornithologists Nigel Collar and Robert Prys-Jones, 15 January 2002 (related in Drs. Collar and Prys-Jones, letter to the author, 19 February 2002), and she repeated it in a telephone interview with the author, 17 April 2003.

   See an article about RM in *TIME*, July 2, 1951, with photo, describing the two at work on *mallophaga*. "The colonel and Theresa" is a phrase repeated so that it becomes a sort of wink-wink, nudge-nudge innuendo. Tess is identified thus: "He teamed up with his young cousin, zoologist Theresa Clay."

3. Nicholas Meinertzhagen, interview with Mark Cocker and the author tape-recorded on 27 June 2003.

4. Hermione Hobhouse, letter to the author, 14 February 2004.

5. These accounts of his movements are cobbled together from his contemporaneous letters to Hatter Bailey, Jack Philby, and others, from his bird publications, and from portions of his diaries. They may not be entirely accurate, but they probably make their point whether or not the dates are precisely correct.

6. RMD, vol. 57, 198. We've made every effort to ensure that events and dates are correct, but these sometimes give no clue to what went on or did not go on behind closed doors—or inside people's heads.

7. The late Maj. W. H. "Billy" Payn was one source for this description of RM's alleged habit of getting duded up to visit nightspots. As taxonomist on several of RM's safaris, Payn had ample opportunity to observe his friend's behavior. (Payn's handwritten diary notebooks are in possession of Derek Moore, of West Wales.)

   Another source for another (but similar) version of the story is the late Philip A. Clancey, who traveled with RM on safari in 1948–49, and later reported RM's nocturnal sprees to several fellow ornithologists, apparently including Storrs Olson. Clancey recalled that in camp RM would return from bird-shooting about four in the afternoon, set about skinning birds, then on occasion give up in impatience and leave the rest of the work to Clancey while RM would "make himself up" and leave camp to go off to the nearest resort night-spots. The story gains credibility because P. A. Clancey had a photographic memory and was widely respected for his honesty. He was not easily intimidated by bluster, and his reputation for reliability remains extremely high.

8. Nicholas Meinertzhagen, interview with the author and Mark Cocker, 27 June 2003.

9. Dame Miriam Rothschild, telephone interview with the author, 17 April 2003. Dame Miriam co-authored numerous scientific articles and books with Theresa Clay and was probably her best friend from the late 1930s forward, but on these sorts of topics she too was guessing; Theresa Clay did not invite her to share intimate confidences.

10. Robert Dalgleish, several letters to the author, 24 January 2006 and thereafter into 2006. Robert C. Dalgleish, Ph.D., FRES, is Research Associate, Department of Entomology, Smithsonian (Natural Museum Natural History) and San Diego Natural History Museum. He is completing a digitized catalogue of the Theresa Clay–RM Mallophaga collection for publication in the near future. The

inescapable conclusion from evidence (specimen tags written in her own hand-writing, etc.) examined by Prof. Dalgleish is that Theresa Clay knowingly collaborated in RM's falsifications.

   If that is the case, it is ironic that in 1950 Theresa Clay complained, in print, about "authors who were ignorant of, or careless about, the rules of nomenclature [in the study of] Mallophaga." [Hopkins, G. H. E. and Theresa Clay, *A Checklist of the Genera and Species of Mallophaga* (London: British Museum (Natural History), 1952), 223.]

11. RMD, vol. 45, 18. Other creatures named after Tess are *Sylvia nana theresae, Melierax metabates theresae, Erythrospiza githaginea theresae, Alectoris barbata theresae, Scotocerca inquieta theresae, Galerida theklae theresae, Coccothraustes coccothraustes theresae, Riparia rupestris theresae, Oenanthe moesta theresae, Turdus viscivorus theresae, Garrulus glandarius theresae, Emberiza striolata theresae.* Few other scientists would have sought, or got, their way in imposing such nomenclatures; it was a mark of Meinertzhagen's prominence that the ornithological community let him get away with these wholesale namings.

12. RM, "Autumn in Central Morocco," *Ibis*, Fourteenth series, 4, no.1 (January 1940): 106–136, and concluding in the next issue, no. 2 (April 1940): 187–234. RM's statement in the text of the article that the trip to North Africa took place in 1939 is an error (typographical or otherwise).

   Interestingly, the latter issue also contains an obituary notice for George Latimer Bates, who died on January 31, 1940. It was Bates whose unpublished handbook RM and Jack Philby later used as a partial basis for RM's large book *Birds of Arabia*.

13. *Ibis* 4, no. 3 (July 1940). The announcement about Whistler and RM appears on p. 1. RM's article "How Do Larger Raptorial Birds Hunt Their Prey" appears on pp. 530–535.

14. RM had his guest list for the first party (1934) neatly printed up on a large card. Beatrice Webb's copy—among her diary papers—includes RM's explanatory notations, indicated here by italics. [Items in square brackets are the author's additions.]

   From year to year the guest-lists continued to include most of those listed below, plus Theresa Clay, as well as such occasional additions as Ian Fleming, Mr. and Mrs. Harry St. John "Jack" Philby, Theresa Mayor Rothschild, RM's brother Fritz, Alexander Wetmore of the Smithsonian, the Earl of Dudley, several of RM's sisters, the Webbs and Hobhouses and various other aunts and uncles and cousins, Gen. Sir John and Lady Kennedy, Malcolm and Kitty Muggeridge, Dr. Irwin Stresemann (leading German ornithologist and, according to some, the world's leading bird scientist), the various Bensons, Sir Felix Clay, and Dr. and Mrs. Ernst Mayr (curator of the Museum of Natural History in New York).

"Who's Who at the Epsom Derby Day 1934"

* Colonel And Mrs. F.M. Bailey. *Explorer, Naturalist. Late Resident in Kashmir. Was Lost in Russia during the War.*

* Mrs. & Mrs. David Bannerman. *Ornithologist—Speciality African Birds.*

* Capt. C. E. [Con] Benson and Lady Morvyth Benson. *Capitalist and Banker.*

* Mr. & Mrs. George Booth [George MacCaulay Booth]. *Shipowner.* [RM's aunt and uncle.]

* Miss Janet Clay. *My Cousin, Domestic Economist, and Runs My House and Children, Or Rather They Run Her.*
* Lady Eleanor Cole. *Landowner on Mount Kenya.*
* Sir Percy and Lady Cox. *Distinguished Diplomat and Administrator. President of the Royal Geographic Society.*
* Mr. & Mrs. Geoffrey Dawson. *Editor of the "Times."*
* Sir Edward Headlam. *Royal Indian Marine. Served with Distinction Throughout the East African Campaign.*
* Mrs. Alan Johnson. *Wife of Colonel Johnson. Royal Fusiliers of Trowle House, Wiltshire.*
* Miss Cecilia Kenna. *Daughter of Mrs. Johnson.*
* Mr. & Mrs. Louis Meinertzhagen and Their Daughter Gwynne. *Banker and Brother. She is a Pig-Breeder and Keeps Kinkajous.*
* Mary Montgomery. *Acts and Dances.*
* Mrs. Neale (Betty Potter). *Sister. Produces, Acts, Sings and Generally Entertains.*
* Mr. & Mrs. Newall. *Stockbroker and Ex Rn. Is Said to have Injured a Pedal Cyclist When He Ran His Ship Ashore. Commander. She is Sister of Captain Pollen.*
* Lord and Lady Wm. Percy. *Farmer in Norfolk. Expert in the Ducks of the World and a Superb Bird-Photographer.*
* Capt. & Mrs. [Walter "Ben" and Lindy] Pollen. *Mallophagologist. She is Sister of Captain Benson.*
* Mr. & Mrs. Margaret Praed. *Stock Exchange. Ornithologist.* [Printer's error. There was no "Margaret." The couple was Edith and Cyril MacKworth-Praed.]
* Mr. & Mrs. W. L. Sclater. *Distinguished Scientist. She Has Walked across Africa and Hails from the Usa* [sic].
* Sir Hereward and Lady Wake. *Distinguished Soldier (General). She is Sister of Mrs. Pollen and Captain Benson with Daughter Diane.*
* Dr. & Mrs. [Chaim] Weizmann. *Mainspring of Zionist Movement; Distinguished Scientist.*
* Lady Young. *Wife of Sir Hubert Young Governor of North Rhodesia.*
* Russian Ambassador and Mrs. [Ivan] Maisky.
* Miss Cecilia Kenna. *Daughter of Mrs. Johnson.*

15. Letter from Nicholas Wollaston to the author, 20 May 2003. Ian Fleming's widow also remembered the ruthlessness of RM's "Mau Mau" cocktails.
16. Ali, *The Fall of a Sparrow*, 160.
17. Entries for 20 and 27 December 1935, Diaries of Beatrice Webb. In RM's own diaries he claims he cultivated Maisky because it amused him to scandalize his Tory friends. That may be true. RM remained close to the Maiskys for years after he got his first Soviet visa. He introduced them to the Chaim Weizmanns and perpetrated other similar pairings that seem to have been motivated as much by his wicked sense of mischief as by anything overtly political.
18. Dame Miriam Rothschild, telephone interview with the author, 17 April 2003. The chapter about "Cunningham" is in the book by Miriam Rothschild, *Dear Lord Rothschild: Birds, Butterflies & History* (London: Balaban International Science Services, 1983).
19. Alan Knox, "Richard Meinertzhagen—A Case of Fraud Examined," *Ibis* 135 (1993): 320–35.
20. Author unidentified, "Bird Fraud," in *Animal People* 3, no. 5 (June 1994). There are several small inaccuracies in this brief piece—RM did not "leave" his collection; he gave it, during his lifetime, in segments, not to the British

Ornithologists' Union but to the Museum of Natural History, and most of the gifts were made formal in the 1950s rather than in 1967. The gifts, extraordinarily, included specimens that had been stolen from the very same museum.

RM probably is not "best remembered" for having killed his syce at Quetta (a "murder" that probably did not take place); in most quarters he is best remembered for the haversack ruse at Gaza in 1917, and in Africa he is notorious for having perpetrated the ambush-murders at Ket Parak Hill. But the thrust of the paragraph from the magazine *Animal People* accurately suggests the extent to which the community of naturalists was shocked by revelations of his bird thefts and frauds.

From the same season see also the longer and more narrowly focused piece by Gail Vines, "Bird world in a flap about species fraud," *New Scientist* 142, no. 1924 (7 May 1994): 10. Its abstract reads: "Reports on the validity of the 20,000 stuffed bird collection of Richard Meinertzhagen. Collection of Meinertzhagen in the Natural History Museum; Allegation of fraud by the British Ornithologists' Union; Inconsistencies of the data; Question on the subspecies of merlin, common snipe, and horned lark; Manipulation of data; Character of Meinertzhagen; Implication to the validity of the other collections."

21. An excellent summation of Pamela Rasmussen's work on the Meinertzhagen birds is John Seabrook's "Ruffled Feathers: Uncovering the Biggest Scandal in the Bird World," *New Yorker*, May 29, 2006, 50–61.

22. Dr. Robert Prys-Jones, "The bird collection of Richard Meinertzhagen: Fraud, its Detection and some Happy Endings"—an address before the conference "Lost, Stolen or Strayed" organized by the Society for the History of Natural History at the Naturalis Museum, Leiden, the Netherlands, May 10 and 11, 2001. I am grateful for advice and contributions and corrections of my unscientific gaffes generously provided by Drs. Prys-Jones, Rasmussen, and Collar.

See also at greater length and detail Pamela C. Rasmussen and Robert P. Prys-Jones, "History vs. Mystery: The Reliability of Museum Specimen Data," *Bulletin of the British Ornithology Club*, February 3, 2003, 66–94; and the article by Pamela C. Rasmussen and Nigel J. Collar, "Major Specimen Fraud in the Forest Owlet Heteroglaux (Athene Auct.) Blewiiti," *Ibis* 141 (January 1999): 11–21. In this latter study, the authors conclude that in the instance of the very rare Forest Owlet, RM's theft and forgery "has compromised the geographic and temporal record of this critically endangered bird."

23. Letter from Charles Vaurie to E. F. ["Effie"] Warr, 16 December 1974, in the Library of the British Museum of Natural Science at Tring.

The "Macdonald" to whom Vaurie referred was J. D. Macdonald, Curator of Birds, British Museum of Natural History, and clearly not a fan of RM; Macdonald published his own accusations in a letter to the *Daily Telegraph* (June 20, 1994). Vaurie, a scientist of high repute, wrote several books and articles, including *The Birds of the Palearctic Fauna* (2 vols.; London: H. F. & G. Witherby Ltd., 1959 and 1965) and the definitive *Tibet and Its Birds* (London: H. F. & G. Witherby Ltd., 1972.) In chapter 2 of the latter, Vaurie suggested icily that problems could be encountered by anyone who tried to make use of RM's specimens. Vaurie's 1974 letter caused a flap. It was not the first time Vaurie had cast suspicion on RM's honesty; in his book on Tibet, he had expressed reservations about RM's work, and he had long since earned RM's raging scorn by trashing RM's book *Birds of Arabia* in a review. (After that, it seems no happenstance that the front of the hardcover edition of RM's final bird book, *Pirates and Predators*, is adorned with a skull-and-crossbones emblem.)

For the historian or biographer, RM's bird books can be frustrating. He is meticulous in his source notes, making certain each quote is identified by author, publication, date, and (where possible) page number. He is well read in bird science and usually is quite responsible in apportioning credit for quoted material. But his books and articles rely less on those references than they do on personal anecdotal data, and in these instances the author hardly ever assigns a year, let alone a date, to each report. Perhaps his vagueness is deliberate. In quite a few of the scattered instances where he did attach a traceable date, it has turned out he could not have been in the place he claims to have been in at the time when he claims to have been there.

Scientists must work from the same premises as historians. One such premise is that when a reporter has been caught repeatedly telling lies, nothing said by that reporter can be trusted until and unless it has been verified by independent evidence. On the basis of what now can be known about RM, without confirmation from other sources one cannot even accept his statements that kites, plovers, buzzards, and/or tawny eagles can be found in the Sudan at all. (In fact they can be found there, sometimes in abundance, but unhappily one cannot simply take RM's word for it.)

24. Nigel Collar, letter to the author, 19 February 2002. See also such statements as "Records attributed to R. Meinertzhagen are justifiably treated with caution," in Richard Grimmett, Carol Inskipp, and Tim Inskipp, *A Guide to the Birds of India, Pakistan, Nepal, Bangladesh, Bhutan, Sri Lanka, and the Maldives* (Princeton, NJ: Princeton University Press, 1999).

As early as 1984, noted ornithologist Philip Clancey had discussed the RM collection in print; unfortunately his notes appeared in the relatively obscure South African bird journal *Bokmakierie*, vol. 36 (1984): 32–35: "The most recent findings that many specimens in it bear labels with questionable localities and dates makes its use in research projects far from easy. . . . [This is] material questionably acquired and provided with fictitious data. . . . What a tragedy that such a magnificent gift as the Meinertzhagen collection should be so flawed as to impair its worth as a research tool to the scientific community. It seems that ornithological gods, like some of the Old Testament ones, can have feet of clay."

See also Philip A. Clancey, "Miscellaneous taxonomic notes on African birds LXIV—On the validity of *Halcyon senegaloides ranivorus Meinertzhagen*, 1924," 13:172–174. Durban, South Africa: Museum Novit, 1984. [ROL data: Dowsett].

Clancey had produced a considerable number of publications on African as well as European birds, including *The Birds of Natal and Zululand* (London: Oliver & Boyd, 1964), and the definitive *Gamebirds of South Africa* (Cape Town: Purnell & Sons, Ltd). He also continued to create illustrations for books by other well-known wildlife authors, like David A. Bannerman's *History of the Birds of the Cape Verde Islands* (Edinburgh: Oliver & Boyd, 1969).

Clancey died in 2002 at the age of eighty-five, leaving his considerable fortune to several ornithological societies in the United Kingdom and Africa.

25. "The R. Meinertzhagen Collections, 1919–1950," in the British Museum of Natural History, Cromwell Road, London, BMNH file DF 1004/225, parts 1 and 2.

26. Letter from RM to Lord Rothschild dated 20 June 1931, in the Meinertzhagen papers, BMNH, file DF 1004/225.

27. The documents remain available for inspection in the Museum's files, including such notes as: "Since his readmission special arrangements had had to be made for his surveillance." (BMNH documents C.25 Oct. 19:3672; C.26 Jan. 36:4; C.23 Feb. 36:15; C.25 Jan. 36:3.]

    Amusingly, the name of the officer who investigated the case for the BMNH was Detective Sergeant McBain; the superior to whom he reported was Detective Inspector Law.

28. Memorandum dated 28 March 1947 from Kinnear (Keeper of Zoology) to the Director—in the Meinertzhagen papers, BMNH, file DF 1004/225.

29. Letter from C. B. Ticehurst to Hugh Whistler in BMNH File DF/1004/CP/225.

30. Hugh Whistler was the author of *Popular Handbook of Indian Birds* (London: Gurney and Jackson, 1928). The massive illustrated "handbook," which Whistler updated in 1941, was the first comprehensive book about the birds of India. It has since been supplanted by later contributions by Sálim Ali and others. (Whistler was also co-author, with Sálim Ali and Norman Boyd Kinnear, of a paper, "The Vernay Scientific Survey of the Eastern Ghat; Ornithological Section-Together with The Hyderabad State Ornithological Survey 1930--38".)

    Information from Ralfe Whistler is contained in his letter to the author, 26 September 2000.

    The bird rooms of the British Museum of Natural History in Cromwell Road, London, house the file of RM-related documents—BMNH File DF/1004/CP/225.

31. Ralfe Whistler, letter to the author, 26 September 2000.

32. These exchanges are to be found in the Meinertzhagen papers of the BMNH, file DF 1004/225.

33. Memorandum of 24 February 1947 from J. D. Macdonald (staff) to Norman Boyd Kinnear (Keeper of Zoology) in the Meinertzhagen papers, BMNH, file DF 1004/225.

34. Letter dated 22 April 1947 from C. Foster Cooper to Lord Macmillan, BMNH file DF/1004/CP/225/l.

35. Letter dated 22 April 1947 from C. Foster Cooper to Lord Macmillan, BMNH file DF/1004/CP/225/l.

36. BMNH Memo of 26 June 1954, item 284 in the RM papers. See also letter dated 27 April 1947 from Lord Macmillan to C. Foster Cooper, in BMNH file DF/1004/CP/225/l. Sir Gavin De Beer's Memo of 26 June 1954, confirming the honors to RM, is in the same file, tagged as item 284.

37. Any discussion of the isolation, identification, and attribution of *mallophaga* quickly becomes a complicated topic. Birds taken in the field often are carried back to camp in sacks containing other birds from the same day's collections. As a result, lice may "jump" from one bird to another, so that later, when the skins are shaken out, it can be difficult or impossible to be sure whether a particular bird was the actual host to a particular louse. Knowledgeable analysts routinely discard such questionable finds, but in some instances it can be all too easy to throw out the baby with the bathwater by making subjective judgments: "I don't think this louse belongs on this bird."

38. The investigation of Theresa Clay's involvement in RM's bird-lice frauds continues, by Prof. Robert Dalgliesh and Mary Meiners. At last report it was no longer a question of whether she had collaborated in his fakes; it was a question of how extensive her collaboration had been, and how greatly it has affected scientific cataloguing.
39. In RMD, vol. 28, 36–37, RM wrote that he had first met Theresa and Janet—the granddaughters of his Uncle Henry—when they were respectively sixteen and seventeen—i.e., in 1927. That is patently untrue.
40. Robert Dalgliesh, letter to the author, 24 January 2004.
41. Information about the Bates-Philby-Meinertzhagen work comes from various sources including Graham S. Cowles' "George Latimer Bates 1863–1940: An Investigation into the History of His Unpublished 'Birds of Arabia' Manuscripts," *Archives of Natural History* 24, no. 2 (1997): 213–35.
42. RM confirms it was Philby who got him interested in working on the *Birds of Arabia* project: "H. StJ. Philby wants me to write on Birds of Arabia," RMD, vol. 57, 78.
43. Handwritten letters between RM and Harry St. John Philby from 1947 to 1952 in the Harry St. John Philby Papers, St. Antony's College, Oxford, Box 17, File 7, Meinertzhagen Correspondence.
44. Letter from Harry St. John Philby to RM at Riyadh dated 17 July 1949, in The Harry St. John Philby Papers, St. Antony's College, Oxford—Box 17 File 7, Meinertzhagen Correspondence, 1945–1952; the letter is catalogued as Item 23.
45. Jack Philby, at the time when he ensnared RM in the *Birds of Arabia* project, was just publishing his own memoir of a life in the Middle East [*Arabian Days: An Autobiography* (London: R. Hale, 1948)].
46. Graham S. Cowles, "George Latimer Bates 1863–1940: an investigation into the history of his unpublished 'Birds of Arabia' manuscripts." *Archives of Natural History* 24, no. 2 (1997): 213–235.

CHAPTER 12: WARFARE

1. The handwritten (blue ink) wire is pasted into RMD, vol. 45, facing p. 46. A similar letter from Warburton on the letterhead of MI-6, Room 171, The War Office, Whitehall, dated 1 September 1939, is addressed to RM at Lunna House, Lerwick, Shetland; this document is pasted into the same diary volume facing p. 50.
   "Warburton" was Lt. Col. Warburton Davies, who had been in charge of RM's section of Military Intelligence during part of World War I. ("Military Press Control: A History of the Work of M.I.-7, 1914–1919—Section III," PRO file KV 4/183.)
2. Letter from RM dated 7 September 1939, in the Col. Frederick Marshman "Hatter" Bailey Correspondence with Col. R. Meinertzhagen, in Foreign Office documents section, IOL file 157.
3. RMD, vol. 45, 58.
4. Letter from RM dated 7 September 1939, in the Col. Frederick Marshman "Hatter" Bailey Correspondence with Col. R. Meinertzhagen, in Foreign Office documents section, IOL file 157.
5. Entry for 11 January 1940, RMD, vol. 46, 16.

6. RMD, vol. 45, 60 and 66. Cynics may note that none of the enterprises shut down on the basis of RM's information seems to have belonged to any of his banking friends.

7. Sir Robert Gilbert Vansittart (1881–1957) was a second cousin to Anthony Eden, Bertrand Russell, and T. E. Lawrence. Vansittart's writings (books, radio and theatrical plays, articles, speeches, poems, letters) revealed his cagey wariness toward what he regarded as the equally menacing dangers of fascism and communism. For more on these relationships and the life of the brilliant Vansittart, see B. McKercher, "The Last Old Diplomat: Sir Robert Vansittart and the Verities of British Foreign Policy, 1903–30," *Diplomacy & Statecraft*, no. 6.1 (London: Frank Cass Publishers, 1995). See also Donald S. Birn, *Middle East Politics and Diplomacy, 1904–1950: The Papers of Sir Ronald Storrs (1881–1955)* (London: Adam Matthews Publications, 1999).

8. Report from Ambassador Ivan Maisky to Soviet Commissar for Foreign Affairs at Narkomindel, 14 March 1939, PRO file FO DVP XXII, 1, pp. 183–84; and signal from Soviet Foreign Minister Maxim Litvinov to Maisky, 13 April 1939, PRO file FO DVP XXII, 1, p. 263.

9. RMD, vol. 45, 80 and 82. Entry for 26 September 1939.

10. Robert Vansittart, *The Mist Procession* (London: Hutchinson, 1958).

11. RMD, vol. 72. Entry dated 28 March 1962.

12. RM letter to Hatter Bailey, 17 February 1957.

13. RMD, vol. 45, 90. Entry dated 6 October 1939.

14. RMD, vol. 45, 140. Entry dated 7 December 1939.

15. Document on propaganda to Belgium, 27 January 1941, in SOE Papers 1940–1941, in the British Library of Political and Economic Science. See also "Secretary of State" memo from Robert Vansittart, 15 March 1939, PRO file FO C3202/15/18, 371 22966.

16. RMD, vol. 45, 98. Entry for 6 October 1939, continuing. It can be easy to identify documents typed by RM because, even though he was an expert and nearly errorless typist, he had certain eccentric traits. He never separated the word "at" from the word that followed it in compound modifiers like "at last" or "at least" or "at once."

   Leslie Hore-Belisha (1893–1957)—known after 1954 as Baron Hore-Belisha of Devonport—was Secretary of State for War when World War II began. He looked very much like Alfred Hitchcock and was ill-placed in the position he held. He was removed from office at the very end of 1939, when he expressed the belief that his downfall had been engineered by an anti-Semitic conspiracy (which either did or did not include RM—since the conspiracy itself existed mainly in Hore-Belisha's imagination, he was free to identify anyone he liked as a co-conspirator). He was returned briefly to office in 1945, and later granted a peerage. A Jew of Spanish ancestry, he had devoted his entire adult life to public service. He served bravely as an up-from-the-ranks officer through the Great War in France and Greece before he was invalided home with malaria as a Major in 1917. After he left the army in 1919 he resumed studies at Oxford where he made the acquaintance of people as diverse as Anthony Eden, Dorothy L. Sayers, T. E. Lawrence, and John Buchan. He became a Liberal MP in 1923, was appointed Minister of Transport from 1934 until 1937, then replaced

Duff Cooper in the top chair of the War Office, where at the time he was regarded as an alternative, infinitely preferred by Neville Chamberlain, to Winston Churchill. In all he served about two and a half years in the War Office.
Hore-Belisha was widely disliked. Churchill's private secretary, John Colville,
wrote in his diary for 13 October 1940: "Diana Sandys and I walked to the
Happy Valley where we sat and talked politics. I defended David Margesson
and Halifax; we both expressed our loathing of Hore-Belisha." (John Colville,
The Fringes of Power: 10 Downing Street Diaries, 1939–1955 (London: Hodder &
Stoughton, 1985), 264.) He was in fact an excellent get-things-done administrator but a woefully unimaginative warrior. Whether in or out of the Cabinet
he continued to serve the electorate. In 1957, while visiting France as leader of
a Parliamentary delegation, Baron Hore-Belisha died of a sudden heart attack.
His life and correspondence are illuminated in R. J. Minney, *The Private Papers
of Hore-Belisha* (London: Collins, 1960).

17. James Roger Brown, *The Organization of Intelligence* (Little Rock, AR: The Sociology Center, 2000). In the same connection it is worth noting that the Bevan
and Churchill banks were merged in 1920 (PRO file BT 31/25575/163955)—a
fact that is indicative of the social connections if not the finances of the men in
question; Winston Churchill had not inherited assets from the family bank, and
during most of his life was chronically short of money. He was infamous for
failure to pay his bills (as I learned repeatedly from the bemused complaints of
my good former father-in-law, the late Jack Botley, who had been the Churchills'
greengrocer and nurseryman at Chartwell Manor in Westerham, Kent). Churchill
kept trying to make money by writing books. He was quite successful in his
literary enterprises, but the income from his publications seldom kept pace
with the extravagance of his expenditures.

18. References for the listed appointments are as follows:
    * RM's official FO assignment: Entry for 1 March 1940, Diaries of Beatrice
    Webb, 1873–1943, microfiche of typed transcripts, in the British Library of
    Political and Economic Science, London.
    * Wavell: RMD, vol. 52, 112.
    * Kennedy: Nicholas Meinertzhagen, tape-recorded interview with the au-
    thor and Mark Cocker at NM's house in London, 27 June 2003: "Kennedy
    was the DMI during this period, plus Alanbrooke, plus Trenchard, and
    they all used to carouse down at Uncle Dick's." Actually, during 1940–
    1943 Maj. Gen. Kennedy was Director of Military Operations, not of Intel-
    ligence, but he became Assistant DMI in 1943 and that probably is a con-
    tributing cause of Nick's petite inaccuracy. Kennedy (RM's longtime friend
    Sir John Noble Kennedy, 1893–1970) had served as an artillery officer on
    the Western Front, 1916–1918, was wounded there, then transferred into
    Intelligence in 1918. He first met RM when both worked in Haig's head-
    quarters; Kennedy had been a captain—he was fifteen years younger than
    RM. In 1921 he was "specially employed, War Office" (as RM was simi-
    larly assigned by the Colonial Office). Working in Military Intelligence,
    Kennedy climbed the ladder of rank steadily from Captain to Brigadier
    General, becoming Deputy Director of Military Operations in 1938 and
    Director of Plans in 1939. He served as the War Office's Director of Mili-
    tary Operations and Plans, 1940–1943, then as Assistant Chief of the Im-
    perial General Staff for Operations and Intelligence, 1943–1945. After the

war Maj. Gen. Sir John Kennedy became Governor of Southern Rhodesia (1946–1954). A widely respected soldier, he wrote a memoir, *The Business of War* (London: Hutchinson, 1957).

* Cadogan: *The Diaries of Sir Alexander Cadogan O.M., 1938–1945*, ed. David Dilks (London: Cassell, 1971). Cadogan, who had replaced Robert Vansittart as Permanent Under-Secretary of State in the Foreign Office, refers to "Colonel Meinertzhagen of the War Office," so there is some confusion as to RM's precise assignment of record, but that is not uncommon amongst intelligence officers whose duties overlapped the boundaries of the War Office, the Foreign Office, and sometimes the Home Office. See also Philip Ziegler *London at War, 1939–1945* (London: Pimlico Press, 2002), 103.

* Chamberlain: RMD, vol. 46, 46—a meeting between Chamberlain and RM in St. James's Park, 1940.

* Maisky: RMD, vol. 46, 70.

* Bailey: RMD, vol. 47, 22.

* Wingate: RMD, vol. 47, 72. Orde Wingate and RM often are compared, as both were militant supporters of Zionism in Palestine, and Wingate's exploits in World War II (particularly in the jungles of Burma) were very similar to those of RM's record in the previous war, even down to a "dropped haversack" sort of deception perpetrated by Wingate on the Japanese with the aid of RM's acquaintance and Wingate's chief intelligence officer Peter Fleming (brother of Ian Fleming). Wingate was killed during World War II in an air crash in Southeast Asia.

* Knox: RMD, vol. 47, 192.

* DeGaulle: RMD, vol. 48, 68.

* Trenchard: RMD, vol. 50, 118, and vol. 52, 198.

* Dawnay: RMD, vol. 51, 22–26.

* Smuts: RMD, vol. 51, 46.

* Deedes: RMD, vol. 51, 178.

* Storrs: RMD, vol. 51, 178, and vol. 52, 38.

* Montgomery: RMD, vol. 54, 46.

19. RMD, vol. 45, 118. Entry dated 11 November 1939.

20. RMD, vol. 45, 138. Entry dated 6 December 1939.

21. RMD, vol. 45, 127–128. Entry dated 22 November 1939. Field Marshal Sir William Edmund Ironside (Baron Ironside of Archangel and Ironside, 1880–1959) was in command of the Home Forces until July 1940 when he was retired. Gen. Alan Brooke (later Lord Alanbrooke) took his place.

22. Fleming's service to the Crown and the US is described in Donald McLachlan, *Room 39* (London: Weidenfeld & Nicolson, 1968), and in Patrick Beesly, *Very Special Intelligence: The Story of the Admiralty's Operational Intelligence Centre, 1939–1945* (London: Hamish Hamilton, 1977).

The intelligence services achieved notable successes but they also inspired misgivings. MI-6, also known as the Secret Intelligence Service ("SIS") or as Foreign Office Intelligence, and known informally and internally as "The Firm," has as its official motto the ludicrous *Semper Occultus*. It is safe to say that much of the product of all intelligence services is inaccurate, worthless, or misused.

23. RMD, vol. 45, 150–152. Entry dated 20 December 1939. These pages replicate the contents of papers he claims to have submitted in favor of helping the Finnish resistance.
24. RMD, vol. 46, 12. Entry dated 11 January 1940.
25. Diaries of Beatrice Webb, entry for 1 March 1940, British Library of Political and Economic Science.
    Kermit Roosevelt, son of Theodore Roosevelt, had raised his volunteers informally. RM says he had lunch with Kermit Roosevelt during this period. Roosevelt went on to serve briefly as a volunteer in North Africa and, after the United States entered the war in 1941, joined the American forces fighting the Japanese in the Aleutian Islands until he died there in 1943.
26. Letter of 12 February 1941 from RM to Alexander Wetmore of the Smithsonian in Washington; Smithsonian collection.
27. Letter of 29 March 1942 from RM to Alexander Wetmore of the Smithsonian in Washington; Smithsonian collection.
28. SECRET Memo to J. Peck Esq., at 10 Downing Street, signed by Lord [Victor] Rothschild, dated 29 July 1942, in PRO file CAB 127/196.
29. Blunt was the first to be found out but he was not exposed publicly until 1979; for nearly three decades prior to that, he was "turned" and "managed" by British Intelligence. But by the time he came clean, his co-conspirators among the "Apostles" of the Cambridge espionage network had been identified and had fled to Russia—Guy Burgess and Donald Maclean in 1951, and Kim Philby in 1963. Burgess died in 1963; Donald Maclean and Anthony Blunt both died in 1983. Philby—whose mother (Jack's widow) lived to see him disgraced—died in 1988.
    Those who have studied the Cambridge Apostles suggest that the hypocrisy inherent in concealing their schoolboy homosexuality—and perhaps a twisted desire for revenge against those they blamed—made of Marxism a welcome refuge as well as an intellectual ideal to the youthful university intellectuals of the late 1920s and early 1930s. Its pursuit absolved them of their inbred class guilt. It made them feel cleansed, purified, virtuous: it made them feel they were better than those who had "corrupted" them (in a society that regarded homosexuality as a corruption).
30. RM's dinner with Jack Philby in April 1941 was recorded in his typescript diaries, vol. 48, 130. Records of Philby's detention from mid-1940 and his release in the spring of 1941 are in PRO files KV 2/1118-1119, released in 2002–2003. His principal act of betrayal appears to have been his having stood unsuccessfully for a seat in Parliament on the ticket of Oswald Mosley's openly fascist British People's Party. Curiously, although Philby was detained as a suspected Nazi sympathizer, the cover description on the file includes reference to such reports as an allegation of "correspondence from August 1929 with William Norman Ewer (see KV 2/1016–1017), a Soviet intelligence agent based in London and editor of the Daily Herald." It adds an allegation that Philby, who regularly sent his appraisals of developments in the Middle East to Colonial Secretary Lord Passfield and other London officials, had been in the habit of sending to Ewer copies of such reports. No evidence is provided to support this allegation, but it has long been taken for granted that Philby harbored what RM described as unorthodox views and seemed to have no trouble rationalizing his support for some ideas that were Far Right and others that were

Far Left. The only political sin of which he appears not to have been guilty was moderation.

31. Author's telephone conversation with Dame Miriam Rothschild, 17 April 2003. There is a typed letter tipped in (loose) in vol. 45 of RM's typescript diaries, dated 9 October 1939 (when RM had been working round-the-clock in the War Office for the past six weeks) from the Director of Mobilization to RM. It states: "It is regretted that you are ineligible for enrolment [sic] in any Reserve of Officers owing to your age. If, however, you desire that the offer of your services be recorded . . . [please] complete the enclosed envelope-card and return it to the Under-Secretary of State, The War Office (A.G. 12), Thames House." It is signed by Capt. D. Wallace "for the General." The document number typed on the letter is B.M.520. J.3. (A.G.12c) 7729.

    It probably was 11 December 1939 when RM let Miriam Rothschild in on his prank. RM wrote: "Miriam Rothschild dined here tonight . . . a great talker and kept us all amused." (RMD, vol. 45, 142.)

32. The formerly SECRET file "Military Press Control: A History of the Work of M.I. 7, 1914–1919" is a subhead under "History of Military Intelligence Directorate, including History of M.I.5. and other M.I. Services, 1914–1918." It is now accessible in PRO file KV 4/183.

33. Major (Brevet Lt. Col.) P. G. E. Warburton Davies was Director, MI-7, according to the entry for 26 October 1939 in the Guy Liddell Diaries (PRO file KV 4/185), with specific duties as to censorship and propaganda. Warburton previously had been in charge of RM's section of Military Intelligence during part of World War I: "Military Press Control: A History of the Work of M.I.-7, 1914–1919—Section III," PRO file KV 4/183.

    Regarding RM's claim that he was plucked from the Shetlands by seaplane and rushed to London in September 1939 because of his vital importance to the war effort, one may note a weakness or two in the story. Nothing other than RM's own publications ever mentioned a seaplane, nor does the Royal Navy have any record of such a passenger pickup and delivery. Nor does he appear to have hitched any rides on Navy ships. As it took five days for him to get from the Shetland islands to London, he almost certainly took a ferryboat, a bus, and a train—i.e., ordinary public transport. Also there is a serious inconsistency in the diaries where on one page he is in Scotland with Tess and his two sons, and on the next he leaves them all at Shetland while he rushes to London only to stop off at 17 Kensington Park Gardens where Tess makes him a nice hot breakfast. Either Tess was highly skilled in teleportation or he forgot she had traveled down with him, or he was entirely mistaken in one or the other (or both) of his entries. See RMD, vol. 45, 44–48.

34. RM's descriptions of his office, its work, and his mates are scattered through vols. 44 and 45 of the typescript diaries. Some of his entries from 1939–1940—the ones he apparently never bothered to remove or revise later on—leave little room for any dispute of the fact that his work was a bit more mundane than the James Bond mythology he created for himself. "It has been said of our room that we turn out more good material than any other room in the War Office." And: "M.I. 7 is engaged in trying to establish the kind of public opinion in this country for the information of the General Staff. It also has a close liaison with the Dept. of Propaganda Abroad, i.e., Campbell Stewart's Dept. Warburton has some scheme for using civilian internees as laboratory material

for certain experiments M.I.7 wish to carry out in order to estimate the effect of their own and allied depts.' Propaganda." And: "I have also written a paper on methods of propaganda which we might employ in Germany which is much appreciated, [as well as] a paper on our propaganda in Italy."

35. "Reorganization of the M.O. and M.I. Directorates," PRO file WO 208/4696. See also RMD, vol. 46, 12 and 18, "M.I.7 useles [sic] in 1940 Reorganisation."

36. In the 1940 *Army List* he is shown as having joined the CIGS Staff on 5 September 1939 as a low-ranking GSO3. The position lasted only a few months. By mid-1940 he has disappeared from the *Army List*. (Source for information about propaganda and the Political Warfare Executive is "Propaganda—A Weapon of War" in Manuscript Collections, Second World War Propaganda, Official Publications Unit, National Library of Scotland, Edinburgh.)

37. In 1940–1941 some of his letters were handwritten or typed on paper with the letterhead "Home Guard 'A' Zone" HQ—No. 3 Company, 1st Battalion, Westminster City School, 55 Palace Street, SW1." See for example several of RM's letters of that period to Hatter Bailey in the Col. Frederick Marshman Bailey Correspondence with Col. R. Meinertzhagen, in Foreign Office documents section, IOL, file 157.

38. See for example "Security Service Fortnightly Summaries 1940–1943" in PRO file KV 4/122–123. RM's name does not appear anywhere in them.

39. One RM aficionado whom I interviewed in 2003 said that in the 1940s RM had given him sheaves of documents from his files so that the aficionado could use their blank backsides as scratch-paper. (Paper was in great shortage.) The documents, the aficionado insisted, would show me that Dick was kept closely informed by highest Intelligence authorities throughout the length of the War. But then the aficionado found the documents. They proved to be minor intelligence documents, all dated 1939 or early 1940, concerned almost entirely with superficial analyses of events in Finland and with speculation about Germany's possible intentions to invade other countries in North Europe. Unquestionably the documents were genuine. Equally unquestionably, they were the sort of reports that MI-7 routinely used in performing its monotonous propaganda work during the few months of its existence. There was nothing of a secret nature in them.

With regard to official files in official archives, we believe we have examined virtually all relevant documents that are currently available. Many, of course, have been "Destroyed Under Statute"—the phrase refers to a law that allows routine weeding of documents. Prior to the era in which images of documents could be stored electronically, the basements of government bureaucracies periodically reached bursting point and executive decisions had to be made in order to keep the masses of paper from crowding everyone out into the streets. Documents were selected for disposal by mandarins, some of whom interpreted their vague guidelines along ideological lines while others, less partisan, felt they had an unlimited right to destroy the clutter so long as they kept a few token documents—perhaps 1 percent or 5 percent of the original archive—in case historians should care to "sample" them.

Document Keepers would consult with one another about "places of deposit"—the snooty name for out-of-town warehouses some of which may have existed only in the imaginations of supervisors. In the opinion of most research professionals the consultation process was a sham and a sop—a public-relations exercise designed to reassure scholars that the records being "moved to the country" were those least in demand. Sometimes the nature of missing documents may cause a raised eyebrow or two. For years researchers have been advised that only a fraction of SOE (Special Operations Executive) records exist, that many of these were damaged by fire and water, and that losses have been estimated at 85 percent.

The recently opened Guy Liddell diaries, giving daily accounts of the secret intelligence service at its most intense operating level, are a vast source. Additionally, for our present purposes, there is a heap of RM references in PRO file FO 371/4183. These were not indexed. This seems to have happened all too often with the older archives and it can frustrating for those who do not have the resources to pick through everything in order to rectify the archivists' inability to complete indices. Still, this book has been years in preparation and we are reasonably confident we have missed few, if any, available sources of true significance.

40. In the RM typescript diaries, many entries—some of which are carried over into the published books—appear out of sequence. One suspects the typist found it easy to include one- or two-paragraph additions onto half-page entries where earlier rewrites had left sufficient white space. In fact it is difficult not to believe that the entire mass of meticulously typed pages is not a mountain of afterthoughts that has buried such slender primary material as may lie hidden underneath it.

41. From the official history: Michael Howard, *Strategic Deception in the Second World War* (London and New York: W.W. Norton & Co., 1995), 203–204.

42. Col. John H[enry]. Bevan (1894–1978), a banker crony of Rex Benson and RM, had served in Intelligence in the First World War. (Brown, *"C": The Secret Life of Sir Stewart Menzies, Spymaster to Winston Churchill*, 513.) In banking circles the Bevan family was at least as prominent as the Bensons, the Churchills, the Flemings, and the Huth-Meinertzhagen clans. (Jehanne Wake, *Kleinwort, Benson: A History of Two Families in Banking* (Oxford: Oxford University Press, 1997), 52ff.) There were relationships-by-marriage connecting John Bevan with Hereward Wake, the Potter family, and the Meinertzhagens.

In World War II John Bevan, who made something akin to a fetish out of being as colorless and invisible as possible, was highly placed in British Intelligence, with unimpeded access to Churchill after the latter became Prime Minister. Bevan was instrumental in John Masterman's creation of the Double-Cross System. In 1940 Bevan was given the highest Intelligence job in Britain when Churchill appointed him Director of the extremely secret if benignly named London Controlling Section—"LCS." This office, working at the very top level of Allied war planning, was seated in the center of London's War Cabinet and coordinated its plans and operations with both the British and the American high commands. Bevan's power during World War II was literally worldwide: he coordinated Allied deception schemes in every theater. He had the power to call up the services of the OSS, MI-5, MI-6, the Special Operations Executive, and any other agencies he needed—military or civil. (William B. Breuer, *Hoodwinking Hitler: The Normandy Deception* (Westport, CT: Praeger Publishers, 1993), 50, and 60–61; and Martin Gilbert, *Road to Victory, 1941–1945*, vol. 7 of the authorized biography *Winston S. Churchill* (Boston: Houghton Mifflin, 1986), 228.)

Bevan's *über*-department was in charge of everything from large-scale cover deceptions for forthcoming invasions to the direction of wireless disinformation and the management of double agents. (It referred to the latter as "special means.") For more about John Bevan and the LCS see Roger Hesketh, *Fortitude: The D-Day Deception Campaign* (New York: Overlook Press, 2000); Charles Cruickshank, *Deception* (New York: Oxford University Press, 1979); Stephen Dorril, *MI6: Inside the Covert World of Her Majesty's Secret Intelligence Service* (New York: The Free Press, 2000); Howard, *Strategic Deception in the Second World War*; Ronald Lewin, *Ultra Goes to War:The First Account of World War II's Greatest Secret Based on Official Documents* (New York: McGraw Hill, 1978); J. C. Masterman, *The Double-Cross System in the War of 1939–1945* (New Haven, CT, and London: Yale University Press, 1972); J. S. Craig, *Conspiracies of World War II* (New York: Golden Bison Press, 1994); and two books by LCS veteran "spook" and well-known novelist Dennis Wheatley: *Stranger than Fiction* (London: Hutchinson, 1959), and *The Deception Planners: My Secret War* (London: Hutchinson, 1980).

43. Gilbert, *Road to Victory, 1941–1945*, 405–406.

John Bevan wrote in detail about the haversack ruse in "Appendix Five: Allenby in Palestine," *Historical Record of Deception in the War against Germany and Italy*, an unpublished book-length typescript in PRO files CAN 154/100 and CAB 154/101. His appendix about the haversack ploy is in the second of those files on pp. 251–252. Like the accounts of other RM acquaintances it follows the Meinertzhagen line.

44. Maj. Gen. Stephen Seymour Butler, "France 1916–1918" and "The Second World War, 1939–1945"; both documents are in IWM microfilm file PP/MCR/107. Near the end of the Great War in 1918 RM saw quite a bit of Butler at Haig's GHQ in France—see RM's *Kenya Diary*, 226–227.

45. RMD, vol. 46, 151–153.

46. Letter of 23 May 1941 from RM to Alexander Wetmore of the Smithsonian in Washington; Smithsonian collection.

47. Letter from RM dated 15 March 1941, in the Col. Frederick Marshman "Hatter" Bailey Correspondence with Col. R. Meinertzhagen, Foreign Office documents section, IOL, file 157. The second quote is from the previously noted "direct hit" letter of 23 May 1941 from RM to Wetmore.

48. RM himself states that in 1942 he began "to reconstruct my early life" (RMD, vol. 50, 126) and destroyed an earlier diary (RMD, vol. 50, 198).

CHAPTER 13: KENSINGTON

1. As we have seen, RM felt he had become the eldest son after the death of his brother Dan in 1898, and therefore it should be his right to name his firstborn son Daniel. RM's brother Louis was carrying on the family business as if he were the scion, so he had named his own first son (born in 1915) "Daniel Meinertzhagen." That unfortunate lad had to weather the ferocity of Uncle Dick, who forever regarded him as "Daniel the Pretender" and behaved virtually as if Louis's son didn't exist.

2. RM, *The Life of a Boy: Daniel Meinertzhagen, 1925–1944* (London and Edinburgh: Oliver & Boyd, 1947).

3. RM, *The Life of a Boy*.

4. Jean-François Porchez, *Une certaine vision de l'histoire des caractéres typographiques* (Malakoff, France: Gazette Porchez Typofonderie, 1997).

5. The *Transylvania* was a Cunard liner converted to use as a troop ship. RM asserts in his diaries that he was a passenger, on his way to Egypt "to take charge of General Allenby's Intelligence Section," when she was torpedoed off the coast of Italy. (RM, *Middle East Diary*, 5ff.) For a concisely detailed description of the ship and the sinking, see David Williams, *Wartime Disasters at Sea* (London: Patrick Stephens Ltd., 1997; New York: Haynes Publishing, 1997), 52.) If one chooses to be utterly skeptical, one may ponder whether RM was aboard *Transylvania* at all. Did he simply hear about the torpedoing and decide to incorporate it into his legend? The ship's complete passenger manifest did not survive the sinking, but no known facts appear to disprove RM's claim to have been aboard her. Some of his details about it are wildly wrong, but others are persuasive, such as his awareness of the horses that we know were tethered on deck; he claims to have been kicked in the stomach by one of them in the water, and he did suffer a stomach injury that required surgery a year later.

   His explanation for the typewriter's survival is that his luggage had been sent to Egypt on a different liner. This insertion in the typescript diaries seems to have been an obvious afterthought, like a number of other entries where the ink-ribbon and paper stock are different from the pages before and after.

6. Lt. Col. Sir John Alexander Dunnington-Jefferson (1884–1979) came from a line of Yorkshire aristocrats whose estates dated back to Elizabethan times. He was educated at Eton and Sandhurst and joined the Royal Fusiliers in 1904. Later, in 1936, he became Deputy Lieutenant of the East Riding of Yorkshire. RM's first meetings with him in 1907–1908 are recorded in the typescript diaries, vol. 7, 98–99, and vol. 8, 128. The Dunnington-Jefferson collection of letters and memorabilia was presented to the IWM by his widow not long after his death in April 1979; it is boxed under the file designation IWM 66/155/1. The listed dinners and visits are mentioned in RMD, vol. 21, 55; vol. 40, 110; vol. 52, 156; vol. 54, 154; vol. 56, 100 and 156; vol. 64, 122; and vol. 65, 38.

   In mentioning his social engagements in the diaries RM sometimes got the dates wrong, often left out as many meetings as he included, and wrote of some meetings that turn out to have been fictitious. However, the pattern of entries seems more reliable when they regard his get-togethers with lifelong friends who did not have droppable names. Dunnington-Jefferson was a respectable gentleman but not a celebrity, he had neither political nor financial clout, and one doubts it would have suited any purpose for RM to have concocted or imagined dinners with Dunnington-Jefferson that had not occurred.

7. We obtained photocopies of the letters from the IWM. The fact that it was Dunnington-Jefferson's widow who gave the three letters to the IWM is confirmed by archivist Anthony Richards of the IWM Department of Documents, letter to the author, 16 May 2003.

8. This expedition can be tracked partially by examining the visa applications for RM, Theresa Clay, and Lord William Percy in PRO file FO 371/62106.

9. RMD, vol. 57, 106, "I call at Haifa in 1948 and fight on the beaches."

10. Letter from RM to F. M. Bailey in the Meinertzhagen-Bailey correspondence in Foreign Office documents section, IOL, file 157.

11. PRO file FO 371/68418—see especially the document tagged 14175.

12. Philip Alexander Clancey (1917–2002), later head of the Durban Museum, was a world-class avian taxonomist who began the trip as an admirer of RM's and ended up loathing him. Evidently Clancey did not have anything like Sálim Ali's level of patience with RM's arrogant behavior. Years later Clancey recalled that in camp RM would return from bird-shooting about four in the afternoon, set about skinning birds, then on occasion give up in impatience and leave the rest of the work to Clancey while RM would "make himself up" and leave camp around seven to go off to the nearest fleshpot resorts. The story of RM's nighttime carousing in primitive lands is related third-hand by various sources, but it gains credibility simply because it originated with P. A. Clancey, a man with a photographic memory who was widely respected for his honesty. Clancey was not easily dissuaded, or intimidated by bluster, and his reputation for reliability remains extremely high.

13. David Snow, letter to author, 4 July 2006.

14. At the beginning of 1951 Theresa Clay wrote to Gavin De Beer at the BMNH:

Dear Dr. De Beer,
Colonel Meinertzhagen is abroad and I am dealing with his correspondence. He left instructions that the attached letter should be sent to you if there was no satisfactory letter from the American Museum by today. No such letter has arrived and I have therefore considerable pleasure in being able to forward this letter to you.

Yours sincerely, Theresa Clay.

The letter to which she refers is the one in which RM offered BMNH the gift of his enormous bird and *mallophaga* collections. He had discussed giving the collection to both the BMNH and the American Museum of Natural History in New York, where his friend Ernst Mayr was curator. Probably in an effort to cool things down and allow time to pass, Tess wrote to Ernst Mayr on RM's italic typewriter:

Dear Dr. Mayr,

Your letter of 19.12.1950 to Colonel Meinertzhagen—he has recently left for Arabia and will not be back for some months. I am keeping it here until his return unless you would like me to take any other action. With best wishes for the New Year.

Yours sincerely, [signature:] Theresa Clay

(Letter in the Papers of Ernst Mayr, Pusey Library, Harvard University, Cambridge, Massachusetts, USA, in file HUGFP 14–7, box 8, folder 399.)

15. The ostrich eggs—probably from an extinct race of Syrian ostriches, rather than a species—are described in a letter from A. C. Trott to Foreign Secretary Ernest Bevin, dated 1 March 1951 and datelined Jeddah, in PRO file FO 371/91761.

16. Brown, *Treason in the Blood*, 126.

17. Paradoxically, among the peoples native to the Middle East, the Arabs as well as the Jews are Semitic. But through a complicated process the term "anti-Semite" has come specifically to mean one who hates Jews.

18. Memorandum of 1 March 1951 from A. C. Trott to Foreign Secretary Ernest Bevin, in PRO file FO 371/91761.

19. RM, *Pirates and Predators*.

20. The C.B.E. (Commander of the British Empire) ranks lower than a life peerage; it is not a knighthood but it is by no means trivial. The Crown bestowed the award on Meinertzhagen in 1957, at the urging of the trustees of the British Museum.

21. "I have . . . consulted staff in 10 Downing Street to see whether they have any record of a knighthood having been offered to Colonel Meinertzhagen at any time, and declined by him. They have confirmed that they hold no such record." (John Green, Prime Minister's Office Records, Corporate Service Group, Infrastructure Division, Historical and Records Section, Cabinet Office, letter to the author, 4 February 2002.)

22. J. G. Mavrogordato, *A Hawk for the Bush: A Treatise on the Training of the Sparrow-Hawk and Other Short-Winged Hawks* (London: H. F. & G. Witherby, 1960).

23. For a few representative samples of RM's letters to the editor, see *Times* (London), February 7, 1938; *Times* (London), September 8, 1939; *Ibis* 3, no.4 (October 1939): 797–798; *Time and Tide*, October 5, 1956; *Times* (London), October 6, 1967.

24. Nicholas Wollaston, letter to the author, 20 May 2003. In the fall of 1960 RM was involved in a court case involving a neighbor and the neighbor's dog, whom RM held responsible for his bone-breaking fall on the pavement of Kensington Park Gardens; on 16 October 1960 RM wrote to an acquaintance, "I have been overwhelmed by a six-day law suit with two hours in the witness box which has been most exhausting." (Letter from RM to Mr. Morrison-Scott, in BMNH file DF 1004/225, Part 2.)

25. Letter dated 27 February 1958 from Ernst Mayr to RM ("Dear Richard") in the Papers of Ernst Mayr, Pusey Library, Harvard University, Cambridge, Massachusetts, USA, file HUGFP 74–7, box 5, folder 688.

26. Letter dated 12 September 1951 to Dr. R. C. Murphy, "the Museum," from Ernst Mayr in the Papers of Ernst Mayr, Pusey Library, Harvard University, Cambridge, Massachusetts, USA, file HUGFP 14–7, box 8, folder 366. At the time when we corresponded, Professor Mayr—who was most generous and helpful in the preparation of this book—was one hundred years old and emeritus on the faculty of Harvard University, where he was still teaching and writing. Without exaggeration one of the most influential scientists of the twentieth century, he was largely responsible for shaping modern genetic-evolutionary theory. He had earned both his graduate degrees by the time he was twenty-two years old, in 1926. At age ninety-seven he had published a new book, *What Evolution Is* (New York: Basic Books, 2001). Before he moved to Harvard in 1953 he had spent twenty years as curator of the American Museum of Natural History in New York. He died on February 3, 2005. It is a privilege to have known him.

27. The BMNH bird rooms are now at Tring; all RM's specimens are there today, housed in standard NHM bird cabinets. A decade after he gave away his birds, RM gave his typescript diaries to Rhodes House (the Bodleian Library, Oxford)—that was on February 17, 1965. Access to the latter papers is subject to the permission of the Meinertzhagen family trustees until June 18, 2037, but a complete Index to the diaries has been compiled and published at San Diego.

28. Letter of 2 May 2001 to Mark Cocker from Dr. William P. Bourne.
29. Letter from RM to Mr. Morrison-Scott, dated 16 October 1960, in BMNH file DF1004/225, Part 2.
30. David Snow, letter to author, 4 July 2006.
31. Letter from J. D. Macdonald, Curator of Birds, to RM, dated 20 October 1961, in BMNH zoology library file DF 230/52.
32. Letter from RM to Derek Goodwin at the museum, postmarked November 1962, in BMNH zoology library file DF 230/52.
33. I am grateful to Colin Rickards for having shared his memories of RM's last interview. The article, incorporating RM's information, was published as "The Cranks Go into Battle: An Untold Story of World War I," in *Tidbits*, April 13, 1967. Rickards sent a copy to RM, who thanked him for it.
34. The long list of those who attended RM's memorial service, according to the *Times* (London) of June 30, 1967, included his children Anne Meinertzhagen Payn and [Richard] Randle Meinertzhagen, and such relations, in-laws, and friends as Theresa Clay, B. Mayor (RM's sister), Teresa Mayor Rothschild, Luke Meinertzhagen, Peter Meinertzhagen, Nicholas Meinertzhagen, P. Warre-Cornish, Rachel Lady Clay (Theresa's mother), J. Hobhouse, Lord Parmoor, W. H. "Billy" Payn, Irma (the Hon. Mrs. F. M. "Hatter") Bailey, the Hon. Mrs. Claud Philimore, Gen. Sir John Kennedy, Rex Benson, Lady Huxley, Sir James Marshall-Cornwall, Capt. C. Pitman, John ["Jack"] Mavrogordato, Cdr. N. Whitestone, Barnaby Benson, J. C. Lister, Cyril W. Mackworth-Praed, P. J. Mackworth-Praed, L. Stein, Rodney G. "Bill" Searight, and Eric Simms.
35. Theresa Rachael Clay, diplomate of St. Paul's Girls' School, London, was awarded a D.Sc. in 1955 by the University of Edinburgh. At the BMNH she had worked independently, under the tutelage of RM, until 1938 when she became an Unofficial Worker. In 1949, she was officially appointed Temporary Staff Member responsible for the *Mallophaga*, *Anoplura*, and *Apterygota*. She was promoted to Senior Scientific Officer in 1952. In 1970 she was appointed Deputy Keeper. She retired from active museum work in 1975 but continued informally to assist BMNH until shortly before her death.
36. Searight's collection of watercolors is now at the Victoria and Albert Museum in London. It toured the United States in 1995 by arrangement with the Smithsonian. (There seems to be something odd, if admittedly insignificant, in the fact that watercolors would attract the devotion of a man who was otherwise devoted to oil.)
37. [Members of] American Psychiatric Association, *Diagnostic and Statistical Manual of Mental Disorders*, 4th ed. (DSM-IV) (Arlington, VA: American Psychiatric Press, 1994, revised 2000).
38. Malcolm Muggeridge, "Richard the Lion-Heart," *The Observer* (London), March 28, 1971, p. 49. Reprinted virtually in its entirety, by kind permission of the David Higham Company.

SELECTED BIBLIOGRAPHY

NOTE: Unpublished works are marked with an asterisk (*).

*Aaronsohn, Aaron. Full-length unpublished diary. The Aaronsohn Archive at Zichron Ya'aqov, Israel.

Adams, R. E. C. *The Modern Crusaders*. London: Routledge Ltd., 1920.

Adler, F. B., A. E. Lorch, and H. H. Curson. *The South African Field Artillery in German East Africa and Palestine, 1915–1919*. Pretoria: The South African National War Museum, 1958.

Aldington, Richard. *Lawrence of Arabia: A Biographical Enquiry*. London: Collins, 1955.

Allenby, Edmund H. H. *A Brief Record of the Advance of the Egyptian Expeditionary Force, July 1917 to Oct 1918, Compiled From Official Sources*. Cairo: The Palestine News, 1918. Reprint, London: His Majesty's Stationery Office, 1919.

Ali, Sálim. *The Fall of a Sparrow*. Oxford: The Oxford University Press, 1986.

American Psychiatric Society, [Members of]. *Diagnostic and Statistical Manual of Mental Disorders*. 4th ed. (DSM-IV). Arlington, VA: American Psychiatric Press, 1994. (Rev. ed. 2000.)

Anderson, Ross. "The Battle of Tanga, 2–5 November 1914." *War in History*, vol. 8, Number 3 (2001): 294–322.

Armstrong, Karen. *Holy War: The Crusades and Their Impact on Today's World*. New York: Anchor Books, 2001.

The Army List. London: H. M. Stationery Office, various years.

Aston, Sir George. *Secret Service*. London: Faber & Faber, 1933.

Bannerman, David A. *History of the Birds of the Cape Verde Islands*. Edinburgh: Oliver & Boyd, 1969.

Bayur, Yusuf Hikmet. *Turk Inkilabi Tarihi*. Vol. 3, *1915–1917*. Ankara: TTK (The Turkish History Foundation), 1957.

Beesly, Patrick. *Very Special Intelligence: The Story of the Admiralty's Operational Intelligence Centre, 1939–1945*. London: Hamish Hamilton, 1977.

Belen, Fahri. *The Ottoman Empire in the Twentieth Century*. Istanbul: Remzi Kitabevi, 1973.

*Bell, Gertude. Diaries of Gertrude Bell. Typescript, unabridged. Robinson Library, University of Newcastle upon Tyne.

*Benson, Guy. Handwritten log of the Spanish birding expedition of 1930. Provided to Mark Cocker by Nicholas Benson (son).

Breuer, William B. *Hoodwinking Hitler: The Normandy Deception*. Westport, CT: Praeger Publishers, 1993.

Brown, Anthony Cave. *Bodyguard of Lies*. New York: Harper & Row, 1975.

———. *"C": The Secret Life of Sir Stewart Menzies, Spymaster to Winston Churchill*. New York: Macmillan, 1987.

———. *Treason in the Blood: H. St. John Philby, Kim Philby, and the Spy Case of the Century*. New York: Houghton Mifflin Co., 1994.

Brown, James Roger. *The Organization of Intelligence*. Little Rock, AR: The Sociology Center, 2000.

Bullock, David L. *Allenby's War: The Palestine-Arabian Campaigns, 1916–1918*. Poole, Dorset (UK): Blandford Press, 1988.

Burke, Sir Bernard. *Landed gentry of Great Britain*. Edited by A. Winton Thorpe. 13th ed. London: The Burke Publishing Company, Ltd., 1921.

Burnside, Lt.-Col. F. R. *A Short History of the 3rd King's Own Hussars* (monograph). London: privately published, n.d.

Cadogan, Alexander. *The Diaries of Alexander Cadogan, O.M., 1938–1945*. Edited by David Dilks. London: Cassell, 1971.

Caine, Barbara. *Destined to be Wives: The Sisters of Beatrice Webb*. Oxford: Clarendon Press, 1986.

Capstick, Peter Hathaway. *Warrior: The Legend of Colonel Richard Meinertzhagen (1878–1967)*. New York: St. Martin's Press, 1997.

Chambers, James. "Colonies Answer the Call to Arms." *Daily Telegraph*, May 26, 1997.

*Chauvel, Sir H. G. Unpublished autobiography, ADFA Special Collection, no. 254613. Australian War Memorial, Canberra.

Chege, Michael. "Political Science as an Obstacle to Understanding the Problem of the State of Political Violence in Africa." *Codesria Bulletin*, October 2004.

Clancey, Philip A. *The Birds of Natal and Zululand*. London: Oliver & Boyd, 1964.

———. "Miscellaneous taxonomic notes on African birds LXIV—On the validity of *Halcyon senegaloides ranivorus Meinertzhagen*, 1924." 13: 172–174. Durban, South Africa: Museum Novit, 1984. [ROL data: Dowsett.]

Clancey, Philip A, and R. Meinertzhagen. "The Genus Rhynchostruthus." *Ibis* 92 (1950): 147.

Clarke, Peter. *The Cripps Version: The Life of Sir Stafford Cripps*. London: Allen Lane, 2002.

Clay, Theresa. "A Key to the Species of Actornithophilus Ferris, with Notes and Descriptions of New Species." *Bulletin of the British Museum (Natural History), Entomology* 11 (1962): 191–244.

Clay, Theresa, and Miriam Rothschild. *Fleas, Flukes & Cuckoos: A Study of Bird Ectoparasites*. London: Collinson and Co. Ltd, 1952.

Clay, Theresa, and R. Meinertzhagen. "The Relationship between Mallophaga and Hippoboscid Flies." *Parasitology* 35 (1943): 11–16.

Clifford, Sir Hugh. *The Gold Coast Regiment in the East African Campaigns*. London: John Murray, 1920. A facsimile of the first edition with an introduction by Thomas P. Ofcansky. Nashville: The Battery Press, 1995. (Published jointly by the Imperial War Museum, London, and by Gerald Rilling, Rockford, Illinois.)

Cocker, Mark. *Richard Meinertzhagen: Soldier, Scientist, Spy*. London: Secker & Warburg, 1989.

Colville, John. *The Fringes of Power: 10 Downing Street Diaries, 1939–1955*. London: Hodder & Stoughton, 1985.

Contey, Frank A. "British Debacle In German East Africa." *Military History* 13, no. 5 (December 1996): 58.

Cowles, George C. "George Latimer Bates, 1863–1940: an investigation into the history of his unpublished 'Birds of Arabia' manuscripts." *Archives of Natural History* 24, no. 2 (1997).

Craig, J. S. *Conspiracies of World War II*. New York: Golden Bison Press, 1994.

Cruickshank, Charles. *Deception*. New York: Oxford University Press, 1979.

Dalton, Rex. "Ornithologists Stunned by Bird Collector's Deceit." *Nature*, vol. 437 (15 September 2005).

Deacon, Richard (pseudonym for Donald McCormick), *A History of the British Secret Service*. London: Frederick Muller Ltd., 1969.

Dorril, Stephen. *MI6: Inside the Covert World of Her Majesty's Secret Intelligence Service*. New York: The Free Press, 2000.

Dunya, Birinci. *Harbi'nde Turk Harbi Sina–Filistin Cephesi*. Ankara: Genelkurmay Basimevi, 1986.

Durscmied, Erik. *The Hinge Factor: How Chance and Stupidity Have Changed History*. London: Arcade Publishing, 1999.

Eddowes, Andrew W., USN. *The Haversack Ruse and British Deception Operations in Palestine during World War I*. Newport, RI: The Naval War College, 1994.

Emir, Hussein Husni. *Yildirim*. Istanbul: Remzi Kitabevi, 1920.

Falls, Capt. Cyril. *Military Operations—Egypt & Palestine—From June 1917 to the End of the War*. 2 vols. London: H. M. Stationery Office, 1930. A facsimile of the first edition. Nashville: The Battery Press, 1996. (Published jointly by the Imperial War Museum, London. Part of the official *History of the Great War* series.)

Farwell, Byron. *The Great War in Africa, 1914–1918*. New York: W.W. Norton, 1986.

Ferris, John, ed. *The British Army and Signals Intelligence during the First World War*. Avon (UK): The Bath Press/Alan Sutton Publishing Ltd., for the Army Records Society, 1991.

Flores, Graciela. "Impact on Bird Fraud Unclear." *The Scientist* (October 17, 2005).

Foden, Giles. *Mimi and Toutou's Big Adventure: The Bizarre Battle of Lake Tanganyika*. New York: Alfred A. Knopf, 2005.

Foot, M. R. D. "Richard Meinertzhagen," in *The Dictionary of National Biography: Missing Persons* (C. S. Nichols, ed.) Oxford: Oxford University Press, 1993.

Gann, L. H. and Peter Duignan. *The Rulers of German East Africa, 1884–1914*. Palo Alto, CA: Stanford University Press, 1977.

Gardner, Brian. *Allenby of Arabia: A Biography*. London: Cassell & Co., Ltd., 1965.

Gardner, Brian. *German East*. London: Cassell & Co., Ltd., 1963. (Published in the United States under the title *On To Kilimanjaro: The Bizarre Story of the First World War in East Africa*. Philadelphia: Macrae Smith Co., 1963.)

Gerard, Philip. *Secret Soldiers*. New York: Dutton (Penguin Putnam, Inc.), 2002.

Gilbert, Martin. *The First World War: A Complete History*. New York: Henry Holt & Co., 1994.

———. *Road to Victory, 1941–1945*. (Volume 7 of the authorized biography *Winston S. Churchill*) Boston: Houghton Mifflin, 1986.

———. *The Stricken World, 1918–22*. Boston: Houghton Mifflin, 1975.

———. *Winston S. Churchill: The Prophet of Truth, 1917–1922*. Boston: Houghton Mifflin, 1977.

Gimmett, Richard, Carol Inskipp, and Tim Inskipp. *A Guide to the Birds of India, Pakistan, Nepal, Bangledesh, Bhutan, Sri Lanka, and the Maldives*. Princeton, NJ: Princeton University Press, 1999.

Graves, Robert, and Basil Liddell Hart. *T. E. Lawrence to His Biographers Robert Graves and Liddell Hart*. Garden City, NY: Doubleday, 1963.

Gray, Randall. *Chronicle of the First World War*. Oxford: Facts on File, vol. 2, 1991.

Greenstein, Lewis J. "The Nandi Experience in the First World War," in *Africa and the First World* War, edited by Melvin E. Page. London: Macmillan, 1987, 81–94.

Gullett, Sir Henry. *The Official History of Australia in the War of 1914–1918*. Vol. 7, *The Australian Imperial Force in the Sinai and Palestine*. Sydney: Angus & Robertson, 1923.

Hancock, C. G., and A. C. B. Neate. "The Situation in the Balkans." 17 March 1930— RIIA /8/1–RIIA/8/569; Reference: RIIA/8/77. http://www.hmc.gov.uk/archon/searches/locresult.asp?LR=2132.

Handel, Michael I., ed. *Intelligence and Military Operations*. London: Frank Cass, 1990.

Hatchell, G. W., "The East African Campaign, 1914 to 1919," *Tanganyika Notes and Records*, no. 21 (June 1946).

———. "Maritime Relics of the 1914–18 War." *Tanganyika Notes and Records*, no. 32 (January 1954).

Hawkins, Stanley A. "The History of Neurology in Belfast: The First Hundred Years." *Ulster Medical Journal* 75, no. 1 (2006).

Hesketh, Roger. *Fortitude: The D-Day Deception Campaign*. New York: Overlook Press, 2000.

Hodges, Geoffrey, ed. *The Carrier Corps: The Story of the Military Labour Forces in the Conquest of German East Africa, 1914–1019*. 2nd rev. ed., Nairobi: Nairobi University Press, 2000.

Hordern, Lt. Col. Charles. *History of the Great War: Military Operations, East Africa, Volume I: 1914–Sept. 1916*. London: H. M. Stationery Office, 1941. Part of *The Official History of the Great War* series. (Note: there is no Volume 2; the project was not completed, although material for a rough draft is kept in the Public Records Office, with copies in the Imperial War Museum. Note 2: Colonel Hordern's name does not appear on the original volume, but he was its author.

Howard, Michael. *Strategic Deception in the Second World War*. London and New York: W. W. Norton & Co., 1995. (Previously published in 1990 by Her Majesty's Stationery Office as *Strategic Deception*, Vol. 5 of *British Intelligence in the Second World War*.)

Hughes, Matthew. *Allenbya and British Strategy in the Middle East, 1917–1919*. London and Portland, OR: Frank Cass Publishers, 1999.

Hughes, Mike. "Churchill and the Focus." *Lobster*, 25 (June 1993). (Published at 214 Westbourne Avenue, Hull, UK.)

———. *Spies at Work*. Bradford, UK: 1 in 12 Publications, 1994.

Huneidi, Sahar. "Was The Balfour Policy Reversible? The Colonial Office and Palestine, 1921–23." *Journal of Palestine Studies* 27, no. 2 (Winter 1998).

Hurwitz, David Lyon. "Churchill and Palestine." *Judaism: A Quarterly Journal of Jewish Life and Thought* 44, no. 1 (Winter 1995).

Husni, Lt. Col. Hussein [Hüseyin Hüsnü] Emir [Amir] Bey. *Yildirim*. Istanbul: Remzi Kitabevi Press, 1920.

Ingham, Kenneth. *A History of East Africa*. London: Longmans, 1963.

Irfan, Ahmad. "Land and Population: Colonial Interests in Kenya," in *Africa 2000*. London: News & Media, Ltd., 2000.

Judd, Alan. *The Quest for C: Sir Mansfield Cumming and the Founding of the British Secret Service*. London: HarperCollins, 1999.

Katz, Samuel [Shmuel]. *Battleground: Fact & Fantasy in Palestine*. New York: Bantam Books, 1977. Reprint, New York: Taylor Productions, 2002.

Kisch, Lt. Col. F. H. "Palestine Zionist Executive—Palestine Diary," 18 March 1923.

Knox, Alan. "Richard Meinertzhagen—A Case of Fraud Examined." *Ibis*, 135 (1993): 320–335.

Kressenstein, Freidrich Freiherr Kress von. *Die Kriegfuehrung in der Wueste*. Berlin: T. Wiegand, 1920.

———. *Mit den Tuerken zum Suezkanal*. Translated by James Pierce. Berlin: Otto Schlegel, 1938.

Landman, Samuel. "Weizmann's French Impersonator." *The Jewish Chronicle* 11, no. 30 (1962).

Langworth, Richard, ed. *Finest Hour: A Day By Day Account of the Life of Winston Churchill*. Washington, DC: *Journal* of the Churchill Center and Societies, 1996ff.

Lauterbach, Dr. Leo. "The Situation of the Jews in Austria." Report submitted to the Executive of the Zionist Organization, April 29, 1938. Tel Aviv: Zionist Archives File S5/653.

Lawrence, T. E. *Seven Pillars of Wisdom*. Annotated by Jeremy Wilson. London: Castle Hill Press, 1998. (First printing of the full unabridged text of Lawrence's 1922 manuscript.)

———. *Seven Pillars of Wisdom*. New York: Anchor Books, Random House, 1991. (Reprint of 1926 edition, London: Victoria University Library).

Legg, Rodney. *Lawrence in Dorset*. Somerset (England): Dorset Publishing/Wincanton Press, 1988.

Lettow-Vorbeck, [Generalmajor] Paul [Emil] von. *Afrika, Wie Ich es Wiedersab* [Africa, how I saw it again]. Munich: J. F. Lehmann, 1955.

———. *Die Weltkriegsspionage (Original-Spionage-Werk): Authentische Enthüllungen über Entstehung, Art, Arbeit, Technik, Schliche, Handlungen, Wirkungen und Geheimnisse der Spionage vor, während und nach dem Kriege auf Grund amtlichen Materials aus Kriegs- Militär-, Gerichts- und ReichsArchiven*. Munich: J. Moser Verlag, 1931.

———. *East African Campaigns*. Foreword by John Gunther. New York: Robert Speller & Sons, 1957. (U. S. English language translation of *Meine Erinnerrungen aus Ostafrika*, 1919.)

———. *Meine Erinnerrungen aus Ostafrika* [My Memories of East Africa]. Leipzig: K. F. Koehler, 1919.

———. *Mein Leben, herausgegeben von Ursula von Lettow-Vorbeck* [My Life, edited by Ursula von Lettow-Vorbeck]. Translated by James Pierce. Biberach an der Riss: Koehlers Verlagsgesellschaft, 1957.

———. *My Reminiscences of East Africa*. London: Hurst & Blackett, Ltd., 1919. (English translation of *Meine Erinnerrungen aus Ostafrika*).

———. *My Reminiscences of East Africa*. 1920. A facsimile of the first edition with an introduction by Thomas Ofcansky. Nashville: The Battery Press, 1995.

———. *Was Mir die Englaender ueber Ostafrika erzaehlten: Zwanglose Unterhaltungen mit ehemaligen Gegnern* [What the English Told Me About

East Africa: Informal Conversations with Previous Opponents]. Leipzig: K. F. Koehler, 1932.

*———, and duty officers of the *Ostafrika Schutztruppe*. *War Diary 1914–1918*. Translated by M. S. J. C. Vantijen. Pretoria, bound on April 9, 1920, by M. S. J. C. Vantijen. Unpublished typescript, English translation of the quasi-official war diary written daily by officers under Lettow's command, surrendered by Lettow to the British in 1918; in the archives of the Imperial War Museum, four volumes, approx. 1,800 pages; IWM #49538. (Note: This document was not available to Lettow when he wrote *Meine Erinnerrungen aus Ostafrika*; but his memory was impeccably accurate.)

Lewin, Ronald. *Ultra Goes to War: The First Account of World War II's Greatest Secret Based on Official Documents*. New York: McGraw Hill, 1978.

Liddell Hart, Basil H. *Colonel Lawrence, the Man behind the Legend*. New York: Dodd, Mead & Co, 1934.

———. *T. E. Lawrence to His Biographer Liddell Hart*. London, 1938: Faber & Faber.

Lloyd George, David. *War Memoirs*. Vol. 1. London: Odhams Press, Ltd., 1937.

Lockman, J. N. (aka Jon Loken). *Meinertzhagen's Diary Ruse: False Entries on T.E. Lawrence*. Whitmore Lake, MI, 1995: Falcon Books.

Lord, John. *Duty, Honour, Empire: The Life and Times of Colonel Richard Meinertzhagen*. London: Hutchinson & Co., Ltd., 1971; New York: Random House, 1970.

Lycett, Andrew. *Ian Fleming: The Man behind James Bond*. London: Orion Books, 1996.

MacMillan, Margaret. "Paris 1919: Lloyd George and the Colonies—A Seat at the Table and the Birth of Canadian Sovereignty." *Options Politiques* (April 2003).

Magee, Frank J. "Transporting a Navy through the Jungles of Africa in War Time." *National Geographic Magazine* 42, no. 4 (October 1922).

Marlowe, John. *The Seat of Pilate*. London: Cresset Press, 1959.

Masterman, J. C. *The Double-Cross System in the World War of 1939–1945*. New Haven, CT, and London: Yale University Press, 1972.

Mavrogordato, J. G. *A Hawk for the Bush: A Treatise on the Training of the Sparrow-Hawk and Other Short-Winged Hawks*. London: H. F. & G. Witherby, 1960.

McLachlan, Donald. *Room 39*. London: Weidenfeld & Nicolson, 1968.

McTague, J. J., Jr. "The British Military Administration in Palestine, 1917–1920." *Journal of Palestine Studies* 7, no. 3 (Spring 1978).

Meinertzhagen, D., and R. P. Hornby. *Bird Life in Arctic Spring: The Diaries of the Mottisfont Birds and Their Master*. Preface by Georgina Meinertzhagen. London: R. H. Porter, 1899.

Meinertzhagen, Col. Richard. *Army Diary, 1899–1926*. London and Edinburgh: Oliver & Boyd, 1960.

———. "Autumn in Central Morocco." *Ibis*, Fourteenth Series, 4, no. 1 (January 1940; concluding in the next issue, no. 2, April 1940).

———. *Birds of Arabia*. Edinburgh and London: Oliver & Boyd, 1954.

*———. "Conquisitio Mea: A Record of My Ornithological Activities and Collections." Unpublished typescript in the Smithsonian Institution, Washington, DC, 1942.

———. *Diary of a Black Sheep*. London: Oliver & Boyd, 1964.

———. "How Do Larger Raptorial Birds Hunt Their Prey?" *Ibis* (1940): 530–535.

———. "In the Mountains of the Lammergeier" in *Discovery: Great Moments in the Lives of Outstanding Naturalists*. Edited by John K. Terres. Philadelphia: J. B. Lippincott, 1951.

————. *Kenya Diary, 1902–1906*. Edinburgh: Oliver & Boyd, 1957. Reprinted with a new preface by Elspeth Huxley. London: Eland Books, 1983.

————. *The Life of a Boy: Daniel Meinertzhagen, 1925–1944*. London and Edinburgh: Oliver & Boyd, 1947.

————. *Middle East Diary, 1917–1956*. London: Cresset Press, 1959; New York: Thomas Yoseloff, 1960.

————. *Nicoll's Birds of Egypt*. 2 vols. London: Hugh Rees Ltd., 1930.

————. "Note on Afghan Birds." *Ibis* (April 1939).

————. "A Note on the Birds of Hoy, Orkney." *Ibis* (April 1939).

————. "On the Birds of Mauritius." *Ibis*, 9th ser. 6, no. 21 (January 1912).

————. *Pirates and Predators: The Piratical and Predatory Habits of Birds*. London and Edinburgh: Oliver & Boyd, 1959.

————. "The speed and altitude of bird flight (with notes on other animals)." *Ibis* (September 1955): 81–117.

————. "Some Biological Problems Connected with the Himalayas." *Ibis* (January 1928).

————. "Systematic Results of Birds collected at High Altitudes in Ladak and Sikkim." *Ibis* (March 1927): 602–603.

*————. Unpublished diaries—typescripts, looseleaf, 82 volumes including index, at Rhodes House Library, The Bodleian, Oxford, UK.

Merker, M. *Die Masai*. Berlin: Dietrich Reimer, 1904.

Michie, Helena. "Victorian Honeymoons: Sexual Reorientations and the 'Sights' of Europe." *Byline* 43, no. 2 (1 January 2001): 229.

Miller, Charles. *Battle for the Bundu: The First World War in East Africa*. New York: Macmillan & Co., Inc., 1974.

Minney, R. J. *The Private Papers of Hore-Belisha*. London: Collins, 1960.

Monroe, Elizabeth. *Britain's Moment in the Middle East, 1914–1956*. Baltimore, MD: Johns Hopkins Press, 1963.

————. *Philby in Arabia*. London: Pitman, 1973.

Morehouse, Dennis. "The Architect of Beersheba; Soldier and Spy." OCLC (Online Computer Library Center), November 1, 2000. http://www.suite101.com/article.cfm/944/50974.

Morris, Benny. *Righteous Victims: A History of the Zionist Arab Conflict 1881–2001*. New York: Alfred A. Knopf, 2001.

Morris, Pat. "From the Archives." *The Linnean* 17, no. 1 (January 2001).

Mosley, Leonard. "Affairs in East Africa during World War I." *Times Literary Supplement*, September 13, 1963.

————. *Duel for Kilimanjaro*. London: Weidenfeld & Nicolson, 1963; New York: Ballantine Books, 1963.

Moyse-Bartlett, Lt. Col. Hubert. *The King's African Rifles: A Study in the Military History of East and Central Africa, 1890–1945*. Aldershot, UK: Gale & Polden, 1956.

Muggeridge, Malcolm. "Richard the lionheart." *The Observer*, March 28, 1971.

Naval Staff, Geographical Section of the Naval Intelligence Division (The Admiralty). *A Handbook of German East Africa*. London: H. M. Stationery Office, 1921.

Netanyahu, Binyamin. *A Durable Peace: Israel and Its Place among the Nations*. New York: Warner Books, 2000.

Nicolson, Harold. *Peacemaking, 1919: Being Reminiscences of the Paris Peace Conference*. Boston: Houghton Mifflin Company, 1933.

Occleshaw, Michael. *Armour Against Fate: British Military Intelligence in the First World War and the Secret Rescue from Russia of the Grand Duchess Tatiana*. London: Columbus Books, 1989.

———. *The Romanov Conspiracies*. London: Orion Paperbacks, 1994.

Paasche, Hans. *The Journey of Lukanga Mukara*. Translated by Alan Nothnagle (1992, 1998). London: Chaos Productions Unlimited, 1998.

Patience, Kevin. *Königsberg: A German East African Raider*. Poole, Dorset (UK): Zanzibar Publications, 1997.

Patterson, Lt. Col. J. H. *The Man-Eaters of Tsavo*. London: Macmillan, 1919.

———. *With the Judeans in the Palestine Campaign*. New York: Macmillan, 1922.

Percy, Lord William. *Three Studies in Bird Character*. London: Country Life, 1951.

Philby, H. St. John. *Arabian Days: An Autobiography*. London: Robert Hale, 1948.

———. *A Pilgrim in Arabia*. London: Robert Hale Publishers, 1943.

Porchez, Jean-François. *Une certaine vision de l'histoire des caractéres typographiques* [A certain historical view of typographical fonts]. Malakoff, France, 1997: Gazette Porchez Typofonderie.

Pradhan, S. D. *The Indian Army in East Africa, 1914–1918*. New Delhi: National Book Organisation/South Asia Books, 1991.

Pretorius, Maj. P. J. *Jungle Man*. New York: E. P. Dutton, 1948.

Prys-Jones, Robert P. "The Bird Collection of Richard Meinertzhagen: Fraud, Its Detection and Some Happy Endings." An address before the conference "Lost, Stolen or Strayed" given by the Society of Natural History, Naturalis Museum, Leiden, The Netherlands, May 10 and 11, 2001.

Prys-Jones, Robert P., and Rasmussen, Pamela C. "Richard Meinertzhagen and fraud: Removing the mystery from a flawed collection," in *Proceedings of the 22nd International Ornithological Congress*, N. J. Adams and R. H. Slotow, eds. Durban: Oriental Bird Club, 1998.

Rasmussen, Pamela C. *A Guide to the Birds of South Asia: The Ripley Guide*. 2 vols. Washington, DC: Lynx Editions (Smithsonian Institution), 2006.

Rasmussen, Pamela C., and Nigel J. Collar. "Major specimen fraud in the Forest Owlet Heteroglaux." *Ibis* (January 1999): 11–21.

Rasmussen, Pamela C., and Robert P. Prys-Jones. "History vs. Mystery: The Reliability of Museum Specimen Data." *Bulletin of the British Ornithology Club* 3 February 2003, pp. 66-94.

Raugh, Harold E., Jr. *Wavell in the Middle East, 1939–1941: A Study in Generalship*. London: Brassey's, 1993.

———. "Intelligence: Meinertzhagen's haversack ruse helped break the stalemate at Gaza and led to the capture of Jerusalem." *Military Heritage* (April 2001): 18–23.

Recer, Paul. "Researchers Uncover Scientific Fraud." *Washington Post*, December 28, 1997.

Rickards, Colin. "The Cranks Go Into Battle: An Untold Story of World War I." *Tidbits*, April 13, 1967.

Rooney, David. "A German Guerrilla Chief in Africa." *History Today*, 49, no. 11 (November 1999).

Rothschild, Miriam. *Dear Lord Rothschild: Birds, Butterflies & History*. London: Balaban International Science Services, 1983.

Rothschild, Miriam, and Theresa Clay. *Fleas, Flukes & Cuckoos: A Study of Bird Ectoparasites*. London: Collins, 1952.

Russell, Maj. Andrew. "The Landing at Tanga, 1914." *Tanganyika Notes and Records*. (n.d.)

———. "War Comes To Tanganyika—1914." *Tanganyika Notes and Records*. (n.d.)

Samuel, Herbert Louis. *Grooves of Change*. New York: Bobbs-Merrill, 1946.

Schnee, Ada. *Bibi Mkuba: My Experiences in German East Africa During World War I*. Translated and edited by Sam E. Edelstein, Jr. San Bernardino, CA: The Borgo Press, 1995.

Seabrook, John. "Ruffled Feathers: Uncovering the Biggest Scandal in the Bird World." *New Yorker*, May 29, 2006, pp. 50–61.

Segev, Tom. *One Palestine, Complete: Jews and Arabs under the British Mandate*. Translated by Haim Watzman. New York: Metropolitan Books, 2000.

Shankland, Peter. *The Phantom Flotilla: The Story of the Naval Africa Expedition, 1915–1916*. London: Collins, 1968.

Shapiro, Jay M. *The Colonel's Team*. Ginot Shomron, Israel: Palphot Ltd., 2002.

Sheffy, Yigal. *British Intelligence in the Palestine Campaign, 1914–1918*. London: Frank Cass, 1997.

———. "The Spy Who Never Was: An Intelligence Myth in Palestine, 1914–1918." *Intelligence and National Security* 4, no. 3 (Autumn 1999). Portland, OR, and Ilford, Essex, England: Frank Cass Journals.

Sicker, Martin. *Pangs of the Messiah: The Troubled Birth of the Jewish State*. New York: Praeger Publishers, 2000.

Simons, Rabbi Dr. Chaim. *A Historical Survey of Proposals to Transfer Arabs from Palestine, 1895–1947*. Arba, Israel: Kiryat, 1999.

Skidelsky, Robert. *John Maynard Keynes: Fighting for Freedom, 1937–1946*. New York: Viking Press, 1971.

*Smith, Vincent S. *Avian Louse Phylogeny (Phthiraptera: Ischnocera): A Cladistic Study Based on Morphology*. Ph.D. diss., Division of Environmental and Evolutionary Biology, Institute of Biomedical and Life Sciences, University of Glasgow, 2000. Accessible online: http://Darwin.zoology.gla.ac.uk/~vsmith/phd/phd.pdf.

Smith-Dorrien, Gen. Sir Horace. *The Ypres Times* 5, no. 1 (January 1930).

Smuts, General J. C. *Africa and Some World Problems*. Oxford: Clarendon Press, 1930.

Spears, Tom. "The Phony Bird Collector" *Ottawa Citizen*, October 3, 2005.

Spock, Benjamin *The Common Sense Book of Baby and Child Care*. New York: Duell, Sloan & Pearce, 1946.

Stevenson, William. *A Man Called Intrepid*. London: Macmillan, 1976.

Stoecker, Helmuth, ed. *German Imperialism in Africa: From the Beginnings to the Second World War*. London: C. Hurst & Co, 1986.

Stuart, Campbell, Sir. *Secrets of Crewe House*. London: Hodder & Staughton, 1920.

A Survey of Palestine: Prepared in December 1945 and January 1946 for the information of the Anglo-American Commission of Inquiry. London: H. M. Stationery Office, 1946–1947. Reprinted in 2 volumes. Washington, D.C.: The Institute for Palestine Studies, 1991.

Taylor, A. J. P., ed. *Lloyd George: A Diary by Frances Stevenson*. New York: Harper & Row, 1971.

Thornhill, Christopher J. *Taking Tanganyika: Experiences of an Intelligence Officer, 1914–1918*. Foreword by Francis Brett Young; introduction by Capt. S. H. La Fontaine. London: Stanley Paul & Co., 1986.

Trzebinski, Errol. *The Kenya Pioneers*. New York: W. W. Norton & Co., 1986.

Tuohy, Ferdinand. *The Crater of Mars*. London: Heinemann, 1929.

———. *The Secret Corps: A Tale of "Intelligence" on All Fronts*. London: John Murray Ltd., 1920.

Turner, David. "The Secret History that Lies Behind the Zinoviev Letter." *The Guardian*, February 5, 1999.

The United States Central intelligence Agency. *The Meinertzhagen Haversack Ruse*. Washington, D.C.: Mathtech Inc. and Everest Consulting Associates Inc., 1981. (No author identified.)

Vaurie, Charles. *The Birds of the Palearctic Fauna*. 2 vols. London: H. F. & G. Witherby Ltd., 1959, 1965.

———. *Tibet and Its Birds*. London: H. F. & G. Witherby Ltd., 1972.

Verrier, Anthony. *Agents of Empire: Anglo-Zionist Intelligence Operations, 1915–1919: Brigadier Walter Gribbon, Aaron Aaronsohn, and the NILI Ring*. London: Brassey's, 1995.

Vines, Gail. "Bird World in a Flap about Species Fraud." *New Scientist* (May 7, 1994): 10.

Wake, Jehanne. *Kleinwort, Benson: A History of Two Families in Banking*. Oxford: Oxford University Press, 1997.

Wallach, Janet. *Desert Queen: The Extraordinary Life of Gertrude Bell; Adventurer, Adviser to Kings, Ally of Lawrence of Arabia*. New York: Doubleday, 1996.

The War Office, Admiralty: Geographical Section of the Naval Intelligence Division, Naval Staff. *A Handbook of German East Africa*. London: H. M. Stationery Office, 1921.

Ward, W. E. F., and L.W. Ward. *East Africa: A Century of Change, 1870–1970*. New York: Africana Publishing Corp., 1971.

Wavell, Field-Marshal Viscount Archibald J. B., *Allenby*. 3 vol. London: George G. Harrap & Co., Ltd., 1940, 1943, 1946, 1956.

———. *The Palestine Campaigns*. London: Constable & Co. Ltd., 1928.

———. *The Diary of Beatrice Webb*. Edited by Norman and Jeanne Mackenzie. 4 vols. London: Virago, 1982–1985.

Webb, Beatrice. "Diaries of Beatrice Webb, 1873–1943." Microfiche of typed transcripts in the British Library of Political and Economic Science, London.

———. *My Apprenticeship*. London: Longmans Green, 1926.

Webster, Sir Charles. *The Art and Practice of Diplomacy*. New York: Barnes & Noble, 1962.

Weidensaul, Scott. *The Ghost with Trembling Wings: Science, Wishful Thinking, and the Search for Lost Species*. New York: North Point Press, 2002.

Weinholt, Arthur. *The Story of a Lion Hunt*. London: Melrose Ltd., 1922.

Weizmann, Chaim. *Trial and Error: The Autobiography of Chaim Weizmann, First President of Israel*. New York: Harper & Brothers, 1949.

Wheatley, Dennis. *The Deception Planners: My Secret War*. London: Hutchinson, 1980.

———. *Stranger Than Fiction*. London: Hutchinson, 1959.

Whistler, Hugh. *Popular Handbook of Indian Birds*. London: Gurney and Jackson, 1928.

Williams, David. *Wartime Disasters at Sea*. London: Patrick Stephens Ltd., 1997; New York: Haynes Publishing, 1997.

Wilson, Jeremy. *Lawrence of Arabia: The Authorised Biography of T. E. Lawrence*. London: Heinemann, 1989.

Woodward, E. L., and R. Butler, eds. *Documents on British Foreign Policy, 1919–1939*. First series, vol. 4. London: H. M. Stationery Office, 1952.

Zacharia, Christina E. *Palestine and the Palestinians*. Boulder, CO: Westview Press, 1997.

Ziegler, Philip. *London at War, 1939–1945*. London: Pimlico Press, 2002.

INDEX

ABOUT THE AUTHOR

Brian Garfield is the author of the Pulitzer Prize finalist in history, *The Thousand-Mile War: Alaska and the Aleutians in World War II*. He is known for his bestselling novels that became Hollywood movies (including *Hopscotch*, *Death Wish*, *Wild Times*, and the forthcoming *Death Sentence*). A former president of both the Mystery Writers of America and the Western Writers of America, the Edgar Award–winning writer lives with his wife, Bina, in Studio City, California.